# A PEACE ·READER·

## ESSENTIAL READINGS ON WAR, JUSTICE, NON-VIOLENCE AND WORLD ORDER

Edited by Joseph J. Fahey and Richard Armstrong

PAULIST PRESS
New York/Mahwah

*To Ita Ford, M.M.*
*May her light end the darkness*

Library of Congress Cataloging-in-Publication Data

A Peace reader: essential readings on war, justice, non-violence, and world order/
    edited by Joseph J. Fahey and Richard Armstrong.—Rev. ed.
        p.  cm.
    Includes bibliographical references.
    ISBN 0-8091-3317-2
    1. Peace.  2. Conflict management.  3. International organization.  4. Non-violence.  5. Social justice.  I. Fahey, Joseph.  II. Armstrong, Richard, 1932–
JX1952.P345   1992
327.1'7—dc20                                                          92-15129
                                                                         CIP

Published by Paulist Press
997 Macarthur Boulevard
Mahwah, New Jersey 07430

Printed and bound in the
United States of America

# Contents

Introduction . . . . . . . . . . . . . . . . . . . . . . . . . . . . . . . . . . . . . . . . . . . 1

**SECTION ONE • War and the Arms Race**

1. The New Litany of "Innate
   Depravity," or Original Sin
   Revisited                              *Ashley Montagu* . . . . .5
2. The Causes of War                      *Michael Howard* . . . .20
3. Patriarchy, Peace and Women
   Warriors                               *Christine Sylvester* . .33
4. Planning for Economic Conversion       *Seymour Melman and*
                                          *Lloyd J. Dumas* . .51
5. Militarism in America                  *The Defense*
                                          *Monitor* . . . . . . . . .61
6. A Declining Empire Goes to War         *Paul Kennedy* . . . . . .76
7. Conscience and War                     *Joseph J. Fahey* . . . . .80
8. ROTC Today and Tomorrow                *Robert F. Collins* . . .86
9. War Is No Way To Start a Career        *Peter Passel* . . . . . . .91
10. War Preparers' Anonymous              *Kurt Vonnegut* . . . . .95
11. "All Quiet on the Western Front"      *Erich Maria*
                                          *Remarque* . . . . . . . .99

**SECTION TWO • Social Justice**

1. Pacem in Terris                        *Pope John XXIII* . . .107
2. Letter from a Birmingham Jail          *Martin Luther*
                                          *King, Jr.* . . . . . . . .113
3. Socialism Informs the Best of Our
   Politics                               *Michael*
                                          *Harrington* . . . . .129
4. The Wail of the Children               *Mother Jones* . . . . . .138

iii

5. The Case against Helping the Poor     *Garrett Hardin* . . . .141
6. Chief Seattle's Message     *Chief Seattle* . . . . . .152
7. First Letter to the Delaware Indians     *William Penn* . . . . .157
8. Amnesty International     *Amnesty International* . . . .159
9. Aims and Means of the Catholic Worker     *The Catholic Worker* . . . . . . . . .163

## SECTION THREE • Non-Violence

1. Ahimsa, or the Way of Nonviolence     *Mohandas K. Gandhi* . . . . . . . . .171
2. Letter to Anthony a Bergis     *Desiderius Erasmus* . . . . . . . .176
3. To Oliver Cromwell and The Time of My Commitment     *George Fox* . . . . . . .183
4. Address to the Congrès de la Paix     *Victor Hugo* . . . . . .187
5. Letter to a Non-Commissioned Officer     *Leo Tolstoy* . . . . . . .191
6. Why I Leave the F.O.R.     *Reinhold Niebuhr* . . . . . . . .198
7. The Individual Conscience     *A. J. Muste* . . . . . . .205
8. Are You a Conscientious Objector?     *CCCO* . . . . . . . . . . .213
9. The Challenge of Peace: God's Promise and Our Response     *National Conference of Catholic Bishops* . . . . . . . . .218
10. The Techniques of Nonviolent Action     *Gene Sharp* . . . . . . .223
11. The Holocaust as a Problem in Moral Choice     *Robert McAfee Brown* . . . . . . . . . .230
12. Those Who Said 'No' to the Holocaust     *David Kitterman* . .249

## SECTION FOUR • Conflict Resolution

1. A Nuclear Age Ethos: Ten Psychological-Ethical Principles     *Robert Jay Lifton* . .255
2. Communication and Conflict— Management Skills     *Neil H. Katz and John W. Lawyer* . . . . .258

3. Identifying Alternatives to Political
   Violence: An Educational
   Imperative                        *Christopher Kruegler*
                                     *and Patricia*
                                     *Parkman* ......267
4. You Be the Arbitrator            *American Arbitration*
                                     *Association* .....279
5. Conflict Resolution: Isn't There a
   Better Way?                       *Warren E.*
                                     *Burger* .........287
6. Arbitration vs. Mediation—
   Explaining the Differences        *John W. Cooley* ...296
7. Getting to "Yes" in a Nuclear Age  *Roger Fisher* ......315

## SECTION FIVE • World Order

1. Universal Declaration of Human
   Rights                            *United Nations* ....333
2. Redefining National Security      *Lester R. Brown* ...339
3. Foreign Aid and U.S. National
   Interests                         *George Shultz* .....345
4. Arbitration: An International
   Wallflower                        *Robert Coulson* ...356
5. The Lesser Evil over the Greater Evil  *Jeane Kirkpatrick* ..362
6. America's Liberal Tradition       *Charles William*
                                     *Maynes* .........370
7. Can Peace Be Imagined?            *Elise Boulding* ....377
8. Toward a Paradigm of Peace        *Betty A. Reardon* ..391
9. The Scandal of "Peace Education"  *André Ryerson* ....404
10. Scientists and the Peace Movement *Johan Galtung* ....421

## SECTION SIX • Imagination and Hope

1. September 1, 1939               *W. H. Auden* ......433
2. Dover Beach                     *Matthew Arnold* ...436
3. The Soldier                     *Rupert Brooke* ....438
4. The Coward                      *Eve Merriam* ......439
5. Conscientious Objector          *Edna St. Vincent*
                                   *Millay* ..........440
6. The March into Virginia         *Herman Melville* ..441

7. Independence · · · · · · · · · · · · · · · · · *Henry David Thoreau* . . . . . . . 443
8. War Is Kind · · · · · · · · · · · · · · · · · · · *Stephen Crane* . . . . 445
9. Counter-Attack · · · · · · · · · · · · · · · · *Siegfried Sassoon* . . 446
10. Strange Meeting · · · · · · · · · · · · · · · *Wilfred Owen* . . . . 448
11. The Battle of Blenheim · · · · · · · · · *Robert Southey* . . . . 450
12. The Canticle of Brother Sun · · · · · · *St. Francis of Assisi* . . . . . . . . . 452
13. The War Prayer · · · · · · · · · · · · · · · · *Mark Twain* . . . . . . 454
14. "A Theft from Those Who Hunger . . ." · · · · · · · · · · · · · *Dwight D. Eisenhower* . . . . . 455
15. Hero—Zero · · · · · · · · · · · · · · · · · · · *Anonymous G.I.* . . . 456
16. "A Debt of Generosity . . ." · · · · · · · *Thucydides* . . . . . . 457
17. Incident at Damascus, Arkansas · · · · *John Fandel* . . . . . . 458
18. The Hairy Man from the East · · · · · · *Chief Luther Standing Bear* . . . 459
19. My Religion · · · · · · · · · · · · · · · · · · · *Leo Tolstoy* . . . . . . 460
20. The Dhammadapada · · · · · · · · · · · · *Buddha* . . . . . . . . . 461
21. The Way of Life · · · · · · · · · · · · · · · · *Laotse* . . . . . . . . . . 462
22. "Break up Your Fallow Ground . . ." · *Hosea* . . . . . . . . . . 464
23. "Hear This . . ." · · · · · · · · · · · · · · · · *Micah* . . . . . . . . . . 465
24. "Swords into Plowshares . . ." · · · · · · *Micah* . . . . . . . . . . 466
25. "Seek Good and Not Evil . . ." · · · · · · *Amos* . . . . . . . . . . 467
26. "Let Justice Roll . . ." · · · · · · · · · · · · *Amos* . . . . . . . . . . 468
27. "He Has Put Down the Mighty . . ." · *Luke* . . . . . . . . . . 469
28. "The Spirit of the Lord . . ." · · · · · · · *Luke* . . . . . . . . . . 470
29. "Blessed Are the Poor . . ." · · · · · · · · *Matthew* . . . . . . . . . 471
30. "Put on the Armor that God Gives . . ." · · · · · · · · · · · · · · *Ephesians* . . . . . . . . 472
31. 198 Methods of Nonviolent Action · · *Gene Sharp* . . . . . . . 473
32. Peace Upon Earth · · · · · · · · · · · · · · *Thomas Hardy* . . . . 480
33. Neither Blame Nor Praise · · · · · · · · · *Dante Alighieri* . . . . 481
34. Easy Essay · · · · · · · · · · · · · · · · · · · · *Peter Maurin* . . . . . . 482

# Acknowledgments

The articles reprinted in *A Peace Reader* first appeared in the following publications and are reprinted with permission: "The New Litany of Innate Depravity of Original Sin Revisited" from *Man and Aggression*, ed. Ashley Montagu, Oxford University Press, 1975; *All Quiet on the Western Front* by Erich Maria Remarque, Little, Brown, Co., 1929, 1957; "The Causes of War" from the *Wilson Quarterly* by Michael Howard; "Patriarchy, Peace and Women Warriors" from *Peace, Meanings, Politics, Strategies*, Praeger, 1989; "Planning for Economic Conversion" by Seymour Melman and Lloyd J. Dumas is reprinted from *The Nation* magazine/The Nation Company, Inc., 1990; "Militarism in America" from *The Defense Monitor*, 1986 #3; "A Declining Empire Goes to War" from *The Wall Street Journal*, January 24, 1991; "ROTC Today and Tomorrow" from the *Military Review*, 1986 by Robert F. Collins; "War Is No Way to Start a Career" by Peter Passel, May 23, 1990 by the New York Times Company; "War Preparers' Anonymous" by Kurt Vonnegut from *The Nation* magazine/The Nation Company, Inc., 1983; *Pacem in Terris*, April 1963 by Pope John XXIII; "Letter from a Birmingham Jail" from *Why We Can't Wait*, Harper, 1963 pp. 76–95 by Martin Luther King, Jr; "Socialism Informs the Best of Our Politics" from *In These Times*, Feb., 1988; "The Wail of the Children" from *Mother Jones Speaks*, pp. 100–103, Pathfinder Press; "The Case Against Helping the Poor" in *Psychology Today*–Vol. 8, No. 4, 1974, pp. 38–43, 123–126 by Garrett Hardin; "Aims and Means of the Catholic Worker" from *The Catholic Worker*, May, 1987; "Gandhi's Non-Violence" from *Friends Journal*, November 1, 1983 by Haradis T. Muzumdar; "Why I Leave the F.O.R." by Reinhold Niebuhr from *The Christian Century*, January 3, 1934; "The Challenge of Peace: God's Promise and Our Response" from the *Pastoral Letter on War and Peace*, United States Catholic Conference, Washington, D.C., 1983; "The Techniques of Non-Violent Action" from *Exploring Nonviolent Alter-*

*natives*, 1970 by Gene Sharp; "The Holocaust as a Problem in Moral Choice" by Robert McAfee Brown, pp. 46–63 in *Dimensions of the Holocaust*, ed. Elie Wiesel, Northwestern University Press; "Those Who Said 'No' to the Holocaust" by David Kitterman, from *Nonviolent Sanctions*, Spring, 1991; "A Nuclear Age Ethos: Ten Psychological–Ethical Principles" by Robert Jay Lifton from the *Journal of Humanistic Psychology*, February, 1985, Sage Publications, Inc.; "Communication and Conflict—Management Skills" from *National Forum*, Fall, 1983 by Neil H. Katz and John W. Lawyer; "Identifying Alternatives to Political Violence: An Educational Imperative" from *Harvard Educational Review*, 55:1, 1985 by Christopher Kruegler and Patricia Parkman; "You Be the Arbitrator" from a pamphlet by the American Arbitration Association; "Conflict Resolution: Isn't There a Better Way?" from *National Forum*, Fall, 1983 by Warren E. Burger; "Arbitration vs. Mediation—Explaining the Differences" from *Judicature*, Feb. 1986 by John Cooley; "Getting to 'Yes' in a Nuclear Age" from *Getting to "Yes": Negotiating Agreement* by Roger Fisher; "Redefining National Security" from *Nuclear Times*, June, 1986 by Lester R. Brown; "Arbitration: An International Wallflower" from *National Forum*, 1983 by Robert Coulson; "The Lesser Evil Over the Greater Evil" from *Commentary*, Nov., 1981 by Jeane Kirkpatrick; "America's Liberal Tradition" from *Commentary*, Nov., 1981 by Charles William Maynes; "Can Peace Be Imagined" from *Peace, Meanings, Politics, Strategies*, Praeger, 1989; "Toward a Paradigm of Peace" from *Peace, Meanings, Politics, Strategies*, Praeger, 1989; "The Scandal of 'Peace Education'" by André Ryerson from *Commentary*, June, 1986; "Scientists and the Peace Movement" from the *Bulletin of Peace Proposals*, 1986 by Johan Galtung.

[Acknowledgments for selections in Section Six: Imagination and Hope appear at the beginning of each excerpt, if available.]

# Introduction

## Joseph J. Fahey and Richard Armstrong

At the first Peace Studies seminar held at Manhattan College in 1971, a survivor of Nazi and Soviet prison camps gave a first-hand account of the tragedy that befell millions in the midst of a world war. Avraham Yekel's message was one of reconciliation in international affairs. He told of his work among young people—both Arab and Israeli—to promote peace in the Middle East.

He was asked if there was one mistake he hoped his audience would never make. His reply: "You must never make the mistake of thinking that, because you are educated, you are also civilized." That, he said, was the error made by his generation of the 1920s and 1930s: that higher education meant higher levels of humanity. World War II, in which fifty million people were annihilated, shattered that myth forever. Heeding the advice of Avraham Yekel, the editors urge the reader to explore this book with an open heart and an open mind. Many of the contributions to this volume were available to the world in the 1920s and 1930s. That knowledge did not prevent war. Other selections are quite recent. But mere knowledge does not guarantee that its possessors will put it into action. Failure to act can be as great a stumbling block as ignorance.

We have included articles reflecting opposing viewpoints, employing various methodologies and offering competing visions of the future. Some selections are long; some are very brief. Such variety, we feel, provides an effective teaching tool. In their efforts to develop critical thinking, students must learn to detect flaws and omissions in otherwise sound arguments, to take into account the literary form (discursive, poetic, scientific, etc.) and to be alert to signs of special pleading. In Peace Studies, many approaches have their legitimate place.

Each selection is preceded by a brief introduction and is followed by five questions for class discussion or written assignment. This book was conceived by Paulist Press as a primary source reader in Peace

1

2 / *Joseph J. Fahey and Richard Armstrong*

Studies, but its use is not limited to one field. It can be used in a course on contemporary moral issues, on international affairs, or in political science or sociology, or even a course on reading skills in literature.

The editors wish to thank those who have helped us. In particular, we acknowledge our gratitude to Dr. Catherine Shanley of the Cardinal Hayes Library, Manhattan College, for her patience and cooperation in tracking down obscure sources. We also acknowledge the invaluable advice and contributions of Virginia Armstrong, Ken Brown, Louis M. Brown, Esq., Richard Deats, Martin Fergus, John Keber, Bruce Kent, John MacDougall, Betty Reardon, Tom Stonier and Gerard Vanderhaar. We are grateful for the assistance of colleagues at the Peace Studies Program, Manhattan College; the Consortium on Peace Research, Education and Development (COPRED); the Peace Studies Association; and the International Peace Research Association. Finally, we thank Kevin Lynch and Douglas Fisher of Paulist Press for encouraging us every step of the way.

Peace Studies has a noble task: not just the dissemination of knowledge, but the formation of a global civilization—one based on free inquiry and justice for all. Only then will the words of Avraham Yekel to the pioneering students in Peace Studies have any lasting effect.

August 15, 1991

# SECTION ONE

## War and the Arms Race

# 1

# The New Litany of "Innate Depravity," or Original Sin Revisited

## Ashley Montagu

This article originally appeared in *Man and Aggression* (second edition), Oxford, 1973.

*Recorded history is strewn with tales of wars, bloodshed and aggression. Is humanity genetically programmed to do violence, or is such deplorable behavior something that is learned—and can therefore be unlearned?*

*Ashley Montagu, the Princeton University anthropologist, takes issue with those who blame it all on "nature." His chief targets are Robert Ardrey, author of African Genesis, and Konrad Lorenz, who wrote On Aggression.*

*Ardrey is faulted for letting his preconceptions distort prehistoric evidence of primitive man's use of tools. Are these for use in building, hunting and agriculture, or are they primarily weapons—to be used to conquer one's foes? In the age-old debate of nature vs. nurture, Montagu opts for nurture. He accuses Ardrey of selectively interpreting scientific findings and extrapolating human behavior from the aggression he posits in animals.*

*As for Konrad Lorenz, the author states that reference to "innate aggression" is "lacking in any understanding of the uniqueness of man's evolutionary history." Montagu cites field studies of the lesser and great apes (human predecessors) to point out that most of them "are amiable and quite unaggressive."*

*The author explains the wide popular reception of his opponents' theories by stating that, if we can blame nature for our aggressive actions, then we are absolved of responsibility to do something about reversing this murderous trend. His conclusion: "It is not man's nature, but his nurture . . . that requires our attention."*

It is reported that when the Bishop of Worcester returned from the Oxford meeting of the British Association in 1860, he informed his wife, at tea, that the horrid Professor Huxley had declared that man was descended from the apes. Whereupon the gentle lady is said

5

to have exclaimed, "My dear, descended from the apes! Let us hope it is not true, but if it is, let us pray that it will not become generally known."

It would seem that the last forty years of anthropological research and discovery in the field and in the laboratory, taken together with the findings of the behavioral sciences, place us in much the same position as the Bishop's lady, for while the findings of these disciplines are wholly opposed to the deeply entrenched view that man is an innately aggressive creature, most people tend to dismiss these findings out of hand or ridicule them as a rather eccentric idealistic heterodoxy, which do not deserve to become generally known. In preference to examining the scientific findings they choose to cast their lot with such "authorities" as William Golding who, in his novel *Lord of the Flies*,[1] offers a colorful account of the allegedly innate nastiness of human nature, and Robert Ardrey who, in *African Genesis*[2] and in a second volume *The Territorial Imperative*,[3] similarly seeks to show that man is an innately aggressive creature.

The first part of *African Genesis* is devoted to a demonstration, which the author brings off quite convincingly and with éclat, of the validity of Professor Raymond Dart's claims for an osteodontokeratic culture among the australopithecines. It is in the second part that Mr. Ardrey makes one of the most remarkable extrapolations from the first part I have ever encountered in any work. Mr. Ardrey argues that since the australopithecines made use of tools, and employed some of them as implements with which to bash in the skulls of baboons, the australopithecines were therefore "killers," and that *therefore* human beings are "killers" by nature! Mr. Ardrey's book constitutes, perhaps, the most illuminating example of the manner in which a man's prejudices may get in the way of his reason and distort his view of the evidence. Mr. Ardrey refers to some of his early personal experiences of violence which convinced him of the murderousness of human nature. Hence, when through the distorting glass of his prejudgments he looks at a tool it becomes not simply a scraper but a weapon, a knife becomes a dagger, and even a large canine tooth becomes "the natural dagger that is the hallmark of all hunting mammals," while in "the armed hunting primate" it becomes "a redundant instrument." "With the advent of the lethal weapon natural selection turned from the armament of the jaw to the armament of the hand."

But the teeth are no more an armament than is the hand, and it is entirely to beg the question to call them so. Virtually all the members of the order of primates, other than man, have large canine teeth, and these animals, with the exception of the baboons, are predominantly vegetarians, and it is because they are vegetarians that they require large canine teeth; that such teeth may, on occasion, serve a protective purpose is entirely secondary to their main function, which is to rip and shred the hard outer coverings of plant foods. Primates are not usually belligerent unless provoked, and the more carefully they are observed the more remarkably revealing do their unquarrelsomeness and cooperativeness become. The myth of the ferocity of "wild animals" constitutes one of Western man's supreme rationalizations, for it not only has served to "explain" to him the origins of his own aggressiveness, but also to relieve him of the responsibility for it—for since it is "innate," derived from his early apelike ancestors, he can hardly, so he rationalizes, be blamed for it! And some have gone so far as to add that nothing can be done about it, and that therefore wars and juvenile delinquents, as Mr. Ardrey among others tells us, will always be with us! From one not-so-minor error to another Mr. Ardrey sweeps on to the grand fallacy.

At this point it needs to be said that Mr. Ardrey's views are firmly based on and derived from those of Professor Raymond Dart, who in an article entitled, "The Predatory Transition from Ape to Man,"[4] published in 1953, argued that man's animal ancestry was carnivorous, predatory, and cannibalistic in origin, and went on to add that "The blood-bespattered, slaughter-gutted archives of human history from the earliest Egyptian and Sumerian records to the most recent atrocities of the Second World War accord with early universal cannibalism, with animal and human sacrificial practices or their substitutes in formalized religions and with the world-wide scalping, headhunting, body-mutilating and necrophiliac practices of mankind in proclaiming this common bloodlust differentiator, this predaceous habit, this mark of Cain that separates man dietetically from his anthropoidal relatives and allies him rather with the deadliest of Carnivora."[5]

Mr. Ardrey puts this in the following words: "The human being in the most fundamental aspects of his soul and body is nature's last if temporary word on the subject of the armed predator. And human history must be read in these terms."

In furtherance of this argument "tools" for Mr. Ardrey are not only identified as "weapons," but, he goes on to imply, nay, indeed, he states, "that when any scientist writes the word, 'tool,' as a rule he refers to weapons. This is a euphemism" (p. 306).

Perhaps this opportunity should be taken to assure Mr. Ardrey that when scientists write the word "tool" they mean exactly what they say, and that euphemisms are not, as Mr. Ardrey says, "normal to all natural science" (p. 306). Some tools may be used as weapons and even manufactured as such, but most tools of prehistoric man, from his earliest days, were most certainly not designed primarily to serve as weapons. Knives were designed to cut, scrapers to scrape, choppers to chop, and hammers to hammer. That such tools could be used as weapons is true, but to serve as weapons was not their primary purpose nor the reason for which they were devised.

"Man," Mr. Ardrey tells us, "is a predator whose natural instinct is to kill with a weapon" (p. 316). But man has no instincts, and if he had, they could hardly include the use of weapons in their psychophysical structure.

Early man's hunting, according to Mr. Ardrey, was due to instinctive belligerence, not to the hunger for food. "When the necessities of the hunting life encountered the basic primate instincts, then all were intensified. Conflicts became lethal, territorial arguments minor wars. . . . The creature who had once killed only through circumstance now killed for a living" (p. 317). This was "the aggressive imperative."

The evidence does not support Mr. Ardrey's theories. Whatever "the basic primate instincts" may be, they are not what Mr. Ardrey implies. Indeed, when he forgets himself, he writes of "the nonaggressive, vegetarian primate," which is precisely what all primates tend to be. But Mr. Ardrey would have us believe the contrary: the basic primate instincts according to him are aggressive. And, of course, with the assumption of hunting as a way of life, these, according to him, would become intensified. But in previous pages, and at greater length elsewhere, I have given the evidence for the contrary view. This evidence renders Mr. Ardrey's interpretations quite unacceptable. Everything points to the non-violence of the greater part of early man's life, to the contribution made by the increasing development of cooperative activities, the very social process of hunting itself, the invention of speech, the development of food-getting and food-preparing tools, and the like. These facts are never once mentioned by Mr. Ardrey, except perhaps obliquely as a doctrine which scheming scientists have foisted upon an unsuspecting world. The truth is that Mr. Ardrey is arguing a thesis. It is the thesis of "innate depravity." It is an unsound thesis, and it is a dangerous one, because it perpetuates unsound views which justify, and even tend to sanction, the violence which man is capable of learning, but which Mr. Ardrey erroneously believes to be inherited from man's australopithecine ancestors.

When man hunts he is the predator and the hunted animal is the prey. But prehistoric man did not hunt for pleasure, in order to satisfy his "predatory instincts." He hunted for food, to satisfy his hunger, and the hunger of those who were dependent upon him. He did not hunt because he was a "killer," any more than contemporary men are "killers" who kill animals in abattoirs so that others may eat them. Prehistoric man was no more a "killer" than we are "killers" when we sit down at table to consume a chicken or a steak which, by proxy, someone else has "killed" for us. It would be interesting to know who are the "murderers," the men who are paid to slaughter the animals we eat, or we who pay the cashier at the supermarket? Or perhaps it is really the owner of the store in which we buy meat who is the "murderer," the "killer"? Prehistoric man hunted because he desired to live—*that* hardly makes him a killer, any more than our continuing in the habit of eating meat makes us killers.

When Mr. Ardrey admiringly presents us with *West Side Story* as a "vivid portrait of natural man," in which "we watch our animal legacy unfold its awful power," in the form of juvenile delinquents in their "timeless struggle over territory, as lunatic in the New York streets as it is logical in our animal heritage," we can only say, "in police parlance," that it is worthy of William Golding's *Lord of the Flies*, in which a similar view of the depravity of human nature is unfolded. In Golding's novel two groups of children, abandoned on an island, take to hunting each other to the death. This novel has enjoyed a wide readership on American college campuses, and it has been made into a film. Its appeal to young people is not strange, for in the world of violence in which they live Golding's novel supplies them with an easy "explanation." I understand that the novel is used in some sociology courses as a good exemplification of "innate depravity," of the alleged natural nastiness of man. It could hardly be expected to be otherwise.[6]

Mr. Ardrey has further elaborated his views in his book entitled *The Territorial Imperative*,[7] published in August 1966. In this work Mr. Ardrey endeavors to show that man's aggressiveness is based on his allegedly innate territorial nature. Man, he argues, has an innate compulsion to gain and defend exclusive territory, preserve or property. The territorial nature of man, he says, is genetic and ineradicable.

Mr. Ardrey devotes the greater part of his book to a discussion of territoriality in many different kinds of animals. He attempts to show that territoriality in animals is innately determined. The informed student of these matters would be interested in knowing why the evidence has not been considered which leads to the opposite conclusion. Mr. Ardrey writes that "The disposition to possess a territory is innate. . . . But its position and borders will be learned" (p. 25). Certainly it is biologically and socially valuable for many animals to possess their own special territory, and certainly there are strong drives in most animals to defend their territory against trespassers, but such drives are not necessarily innate. They may be learned in just the same way in which animals learn the position and borders of their territory. Territory is defined as an area defended by its occupant against competing members of the same species. But there are many animals that do not exhibit such behavior. The California ground squirrel, adult male long-tailed field mice, she-wolves, the red fox, the Iowan prairie spotted skunk, the northern plains red fox, and in the superfamily to which man belongs, the Hominoidea, the orang-utan, the chimpanzee, and the gorilla, as well as many other animals. As Bourlière has observed in his admirable book, *The Natural History of Animals*, "It would seem that territorial behavior is far from being as important in mammals as in birds."[8] Somehow, Ardrey manages to neglect to consider the significance of these many exceptional cases. And while he does mention the chimpanzee, he omits any reference to the orang-utan[9] and the gorilla.[10] On the naturally amiable chimpanzee's non-territoriality he comments, "The chimpanzee has demonstrated, I presume, that we must reckon on some degree of innate amity in the primate potential; but as I have indicated, it is a very small candle on a very dark night" (p. 222).

On the contrary, the non-territoriality of great apes constitutes, one would have thought, a very bright lodestar in a cloudless sky, for if, as is evident, man's nearest collateral relatives are wanting in anything resembling an inborn territorial drive, it is highly improbable that any form of man was ever characterized by such a drive. Arguments based on fish, birds, and other animals are strictly for them. They have no relevance for man. "The otherwise admirable animal," the chimpanzee, is for Mr. Ardrey, "an evolutionary failure" (p. 223), while the aggressive baboon is "an outrageous evolutionary success" (p. 222).

Apparently evolutionary failure or success is to be measured by the yardstick of population number. The baboons are many, the great apes are few and are threatened with extinction. There is little evidence that the great apes were ever numerous, but that they are today few in number and threatened with extinction is all too tragically true. The diminishing numbers of these animals is due not to their lack of territoriality, but to the encroachments upon both their habitats and their lives by men with weapons against which they are utterly defenseless. No matter how highly developed their territorial sense might have been, they could never have withstood these onslaughts.

What we are witnessing in Mr. Ardrey's "territorial imperative" is a revival in modern dress of the good old "Instinct of Property" which, together with such oddities as the "Instinct of Philoprogenitiveness" and other such curiosities were repudiated by scientists half a century ago.[11]

Mr. Ardrey deplores the rejection of "instinct" in man, and actually goes so far as to suggest that "a party line" has appeared in American science designed to perpetuate the "falsehood" that instincts do not exist in man. Mr. Ardrey needs the concept of "open instincts," of innate factors, to support his theorizing. But that requirement constitutes the fatal flaw in his theory, the rift in the playwright's lute, for man is man because he has no instincts, because everything he is and has become he has learned, acquired, from his culture, from the man-made part of the environment, from other human beings. Mr. Ardrey declines to accept that fact, being more enamored of his theories than he is of facts. This is rather a pity because he would serve himself and us all a great deal more worthily if he would only realize that a scientist is not interested in proving or in disproving theories, in believing or in disbelieving, but in discovering what *is*. Thomas Henry Huxley once remarked of Herbert Spencer that his idea of a tragedy was a beautiful theory killed by an ugly fact. In Mr. Ardrey's case the beautiful facts render his ugly theories otiose.

What is the explanation of the appeal such books have for so many people? Golding's novel is a rattling good story. Ardrey's books are excitingly written and hold the reader spellbound. But these qualities are not the secret of their appeal. What, then, is?

Such books are both congenial to the temper of the times and comforting to the reader who is seeking some sort of absolution for his sins. It is gratifying to find father confessors who will relieve one of the burdensome load of guilt we bear by shifting the responsibility for it to our "natural inheritance," our "innate aggressiveness."

If it is our "nature" to be what we are, if we are the lineal descendants of our "murderous" ancestors, we can hardly be blamed or blame ourselves for the sin of being little more than made-over apes. Our orneriness is explained, and so is the peccant behavior of children, juvenile delinquency, crime, rape, murder, arson, and war, not to mention every other form of violence. It is all simply explained: it is due to man's innate aggressiveness.

There is nothing new in all this. We have heard it before. During the latter half of the 19th century, and during the early part of the 20th century, this viewpoint formed the foundation for the doctrine of "Social Darwinism." It was implied in such ideas as "The Survival of the Fittest" and "The Struggle for Existence," and in such phrases as "The weakest go to the wall," "Competition is the life-blood of a nation," and the like.

Such ideas were not merely taken to explain, but were actually used to justify, violence and war. As General von Bernhardi put it in 1912, "War is a biological necessity . . . it is as necessary as the struggle of the elements in Nature . . . it gives a biologically just decision, since its decisions rest on the very nature of things."[12] One wonders what von Bernhardi would have said after the "biologically just" defeat of Germany in two World Wars? No doubt, the general would have had little difficulty in finding an "explanation."

The new liturgy of "innate aggression," as an explanation of man's proclivities to violent behavior, does not seek to justify that behavior, but by thus "explaining" it to point the direction in which we must proceed if we are to exercise some measure of control over it. Toward this end, Dr. Konrad Lorenz, one of the founders of the modern science of ethology—the study of behavior under natural conditions of life—has dedicated himself in his book, *On Aggression*, published in April 1966.[13]

In *On Aggression* Lorenz has set out his views at length. In many respects they parallel those of Ardrey.

Ardrey's and Lorenz's views suffer from the same fatal defect, namely, extrapolation from other animals to man.

Why do reasonable beings behave so unreasonably, asks Lorenz. And he answers, "Undeniably, there must be superlatively strong factors which are able to overcome the commands of individual reason so completely and which are so obviously impervious to experience and learning" (p. 237). "All these amazing paradoxes, however, find an unconstrained explanation, falling into place like the pieces of a jigsaw puzzle, if one assumes that human behavior, far from being determined by reason and cultural tradition alone, is still subject to all the laws prevailing in all phylogenetically adapted instinctive behavior. Of these laws we possess a fair amount of knowledge from studying the instincts of animals" (p. 237).

It is in these sentences that the flaws in Lorenz's argument are exhibited. First he assumes that man's frequent irrational behavior is phylogenetically based. Second, this enables him to conclude that the "laws" derived from the "study of the instincts of animals" are applicable to man.

There is, in fact, not the slightest evidence or ground for assuming that the alleged "phylogenetically adapted instinctive" behavior of other animals is in any way relevant to the discussion of the motive-forces of human behavior. The fact is, that with the exception of the instinctoid reactions in infants to sudden withdrawals of support and to sudden loud noises, the human being is entirely instinctless.

Those who speak of "innate aggression" in man appear to be lacking in any understanding of the uniqueness of man's evolutionary history. Unacquainted with the facts or else undeterred by them they insist on fitting whatever facts they are acquainted with into their theories. In so doing they commit the most awful excesses. But, as is well known, nothing succeeds like excess. Lorenz's assumptions and interpretations are typical.

"There is evidence" he writes, "that the first inventors of pebble tools—the African Australopithecines—promptly used their new weapon to kill not only game, but fellow members of their species as well" (p. 239). In fact there is not the slightest evidence for such a statement.

Lorenz continues, "Peking Man, the Prometheus who learned to preserve fire, used it to roast his brothers: beside the first traces of the regular use of fire lie the mutilated and roasted bones of Sinanthropus pekinesis himself" (p. 239).

Lorenz's interpretation of the "evidence" is one he shares with many others, but it is gravely doubted whether it is sound. The cracked bones of Peking man may represent the remains of individuals who died during a famine and who may well have been eaten by their surviving associates. This sort of thing has been known to occur among most peoples of whom we have any knowledge. There is, however, no record of any people, prehistoric, nonliterate, or anywhere in the annals of human history, who made a habit of killing their fellow men in order to dine off them. It is absurd to suggest that Peking man used fire "to roast his brothers." Does Lorenz seriously believe that Peking man made a practice of "roast brother"? As another possibility it does not appear to have occurred to Lorenz that, like some contemporary peoples, burning the corpse may have been Peking man's way of disposing of the dead.

Lorenz writes, "One shudders at the thought of a creature as irascible as all pre-human primates are, swinging a well-sharpened hand-ax" (pp. 241–42). For a serious student of animal behavior Dr. Lorenz appears to be singularly ill-informed on the temperaments of prehuman primates. It is not "irascibility" which is the term most frequently used to describe the temperaments of "pre-human primates" by those who know them best, but "amiability." The field studies of Schaller on the gorilla, of Goodall on the chimpanzee, of Harrisson on the orang-utan, as well as those of others,[14] show these creatures to be anything but irascible. All the field observers agree that these creatures are amiable and quite unaggressive, and there is not the least reason to suppose that man's pre-human primate ancestors were in any way different. Captured monkeys and apes in zoos and circuses are not the best examples from which to deduce the behavior of such creatures under natural conditions.

Lorenz writes of early man faced with "the counter-pressures of hostile and neighboring hordes" (p. 243). Again, there exists not the slightest evidence of hostility between neighboring hordes of early man. The populations of early man were very small, a few score or a few hundred individuals at most. "Neighboring hordes" would have been few and far between, and when they met it is extremely unlikely that they would have been any less friendly than food-gathering hunting peoples are today.

The hostile neighboring tribe," writes Lorenz, "once the target at which to discharge phylogenetically programmed aggression, has now withdrawn to an ideal distance, hidden behind a curtain, if possible of iron. Among the many phylogenetically adopted norms of human social behavior, there is hardly one that does not need to be controlled and kept on a leash by responsible morality" (p. 253).

And there we have it: man's aggressiveness is "phylogenetically programmed," and can be kept on a leash by "responsible morality." The reference to an "iron" curtain is presumably not undeliberate; the whole passage has an ominous political overtone. One wonders whether it is the State or the individual who is to hold the leash.

Lorenz knows a great deal about the behavior of animals, but with respect to man he apparently knows very little else that is not in the realm of nineteenth-century desk anthropology. Like Ardrey, he extrapolates his dubious interpretations of animal behavior to still more dubious conclusions concerning man.

Since all instincts, according to Lorenz, are characterized by "spontaneity," and it is this spontaneity which makes "the aggression drive" so dangerous, one would have thought that he would have provided the reader with some convincing examples of such spontaneous aggression in man. But all that Lorenz can do is to cite the "very exact psychoanalytical and psycho-sociological studies on Prairie Indians, particularly the Utes" of Sydney Margolin (p. 244). According to these "very exact" studies the Prairie Indians "led a wild life consisting almost entirely of war and raids," and that therefore, "there must have been an extreme selection pressure at work, breeding extreme aggressiveness." Since Dr. Omer Stewart has shown how utterly erroneous this account is of the Prairie Indians in general and of the Utes in particular, it only needs to be remarked that Lorenz's example of spontaneous aggression in man has not a leg to stand upon, and that the alleged "excess of aggression drive" "may have produced changes in the hereditary pattern" (p. 244) of the Utes are statements which derive no support whatever from the facts.

But Lorenz chooses to see aggression his way. Nowhere, for example, does he deign to consider how other scientists have looked at aggression. He neglects, for example, to discuss the possibility that a considerable proportion of aggressive behavior represents a reaction to frustration.[15] Nor does he pay the least attention to the view that in many instances aggressive behavior is situational, provoked by situations and conditions which have nothing whatever to do with anything "phylogenetically" or otherwise "programmed" in the individual. As a general and outstanding example of the spontaneity of instinctive aggression in man Lorenz cites "militant enthusiasm" which can be "elicited with the predictability of a reflex" when the proper environmental stimuli are available (p. 272). The possibility that "militant enthusiasm" may be learned behavior is not even considered by Lorenz. Lorenz's declarative statements are no substitute for the hard evidence that militant enthusiasm, like every other kind of enthusiasm, is learned.

The roles of learning and experience in influencing the development and expression of aggression are largely ignored by Lorenz. Yet the evidence is abundant and clear, both for animals and man, that learning and experience play substantive roles in the history of the individual or of the group in relation to the development of aggression. Where aggressive behavior is unrewarded and unrewarding, as among the Hopi and Zuñi Indians, it is minimally if at all evident.

"Let dogs delight to bark and bite, it is their nature to." Lorenz, who has written a charming book on dogs,[16] feels it is the nature too, of men. Is it? What is human nature?

What is most important to understand in relation to that question is man's unique evolutionary history, the manner in which an ape was gradually transformed into a man as he moved from a dimension of limited capacity for learning into an increasingly enlarging zone of adaptation in which he became entirely dependent upon learning from the man-made part of the environment, *culture*, for his development as a functioning human being; that his brain, far from containing any "phylogenetically programmed" determinants for behavior, is characterized by a supremely highly developed generalized capacity for learning; that this principally constitutes his innate *hominid* nature, and that he has to learn his *human* nature from the human environment, from the culture that humanizes him, and that therefore, given man's unique educability, human nature is what man learns to become as a human being.

This is not to say that man is born a *tabula rasa*. Clearly the reason why man is not an ape is that he possesses certain genetic capacities, the result of a long and unique evolutionary history, which, under the appropriate environmental stimulation enable him to function as a human being. The most important of these genetic capacities is that for learning, educability, literally the species trait of *Homo sapiens*. Man is capable of learning virtually anything.

As we trace the details of man's evolutionary history we see that it is with the development of culture that man's brain began to grow and develop in a simultaneous feedback interaction with culture as an organ of learning, retrieval, and intelligence. Under the selection pressures exerted by the necessity to function in the dimension of culture, instinctive behavior would have been worse than useless, and hence would have been negatively selected, assuming that any remnant of it remained in man's progenitors. In fact, I also think it very doubtful that any of the great apes have any instincts. On the contrary, it seems that as social animals they must learn from others everything they come to know and do. Their capacities for learning are simply more limited than those of *Homo sapiens*.

As Clifford Geertz has put it,

"Recent research in anthropology suggests that the prevailing view that the mental dispositions of man are genetically prior to culture and that his actual capabilities represent the amplification or extension of these pre-existent dispositions by cultural means is incorrect. The apparent fact that the final stages of the biological evolution of man occurred after the initial stages of the growth of culture implies that "basic," "pure," or "unconditioned," human nature, in the sense of the innate constitution of man, is so functionally incomplete as to be unworkable. Tools, hunting, family organization, and, later, art, religion, and "science" molded man somatically; and they are, therefore, necessary not merely to his survival but to his existential realization. It is true that without men there would be no cultural forms; but it is also true that without cultural forms there would be no men.[17]

Given the limits set by his genetic constitution, whatever man is he learns to be.

Throughout the five million or so years of man's evolution the highest premium has been placed on cooperation, not merely *intra*group cooperation, but also upon *inter*group cooperation, or else there would be no human beings today.[18] Intra- or intergroup hostilities, in small populations, would have endangered the very existence of such populations, for any serious reduction in numbers would have made the maintenance of such populations impossible. There is not the slightest evidence nor is there the least reason to suppose that such conflicts ever occurred in human populations before the development of agricultural-pastoral communities, not much more than 12,000 years ago.

The myth of early man's aggressiveness belongs in the same class as the myth of "the beast," that is, the belief that most if not all "wild" animals are ferocious killers. In the same class belongs the myth of "the jungle," "the wild," "the warfare of Nature," and, of course, the myth of "innate depravity" or "original sin." These myths represent the projection of our *acquired* deplorabilities upon the screen of "Nature." What we are unwilling to acknowledge as essentially of our own making, the consequence of our own disordering in the man-made environment, we saddle upon "Nature," upon "phylogenetically programmed" or "innate" factors. It is very comforting, and if, somehow, one can connect it all with findings on greylag goslings, studied for their "releaser mechanisms," and relate the findings on fish, birds, and other animals to man, it makes everything all the easier to understand and to accept.

What, in fact, such writers do, in addition to perpetrating their wholly erroneous interpretation of human nature, is to divert attention from the real sources of man's aggression and destructiveness, namely, the many false and contradictory values by which, in an over-crowded, highly competitive, dehumanized, threatening world, he so disoperatively attempts to live. It is not man's nature, but his nurture, in such a world, that requires our attention.

## References

1. William Golding, *Lord of the Flies*, New York: Harcourt, Brace & Co., 1954.

2. Robert Ardrey, *African Genesis*, New York: Atheneum, 1961.
3. Robert Ardrey, *The Territorial Imperative*, New York, Atheneum, 1966.
4. Raymond A. Dart, "The Predatory Transition from Ape to Man," *International Anthropological and Linguistic Review*, vol. 1, 1953, pp. 201–8.
5. Ibid. pp. 207–8.
6. For a critical examination by various authors of Golding's thesis, see William Nelson (ed.), *William Golding's Lord of the Flies: A Source Book*, New York: Odyssey, 1963.
7. Robert Ardrey, *The Territorial Imperative*.
8. Francois Bourlière, *The Natural History of Animals*, New York: A. A. Knopf, 1954, pp. 99–100.
9. Barbara Harrisson, *Orang-Utan*, New York: Doubleday, 1963.
10. George Schaller, *The Mountain Gorilla: Ecology and Behavior*, Chicago: University of Chicago Press, 1963, and the same author's *The Year of the Gorilla*, Chicago: University of Chicago Press, 1964.
11. L. L. Bernard, *Instinct*, New York: Holt, 1924; Otto Klineberg, *Social Psychology*, New York: Holt, 1954, pp. 63–75; David Krech and Richard S. Crutchfield, *Theory and Problems of Social Psychology*, New York: McGraw-Hill, 1948.
12. Friedrich von Bernhardi, *Germany and the Next War*, New York: Longmans, 1912.
13. Konrad Lorenz, *On Aggression*, New York: Harcourt, Brace & World, 1966.
14. Jane Goodall, "My Life among Wild Chimpanzees," *National Geographic*, vol. 124, 1963, pp. 272–308; George B. Schaller, *The Mountain Gorilla*; Barbara Harrisson, *Orang-Utan*; Charles H. Southwick (ed.), *Primate Social Behavior*, Princeton, N.J.: Van Nostrand, 1963; Irven DeVore (ed.), *Primate Behavior*, New York: Holt, Rinehart & Winston, 1965; Allan M. Schrier, Harry F. Harlow & Fred Stollnitz (eds.), *Behavior of Nonhuman Primates*, 2 vols., New York: Academic Press, 1965.
15. John Dollard *et al.*, *Frustration and Aggression*, New Haven, Yale University Press, 1935.
16. Konrad Lorenz, *Man Meets Dog*, Boston: Houghton Mifflin, 1955.
17. Clifford Geertz, "The Growth of Culture and the Evolution of Mind," in Jordan Scher (ed.), *Theories of the Mind*, New York: Free Press, 1962, p. 736.
18. Ashley Montagu, *Darwin, Competition and Cooperation*, New York: Schuman, 1952; Ashley Montagu, *The Human Revolution*, New York: Bantam Books, 1967.

*Questions*

1. What influence did Robert Ardrey's personal experience of violence have on his theory of aggression? How does this compare with the scientific goal of weighing evidence on its own merits? Give examples of this process in your own life.

2. Which of the two (Ardrey or Montagu) has the better of the argument on the primary use of tools by prehistoric man? Give your reasons.

3. What reason does the author give for the popularity of William Golding's novel, *Lord of the Flies?* Why or why not do you think Montagu's explanation is the better one?

4. Based on this article, does Lorenz assume or prove that human violence is innate and instinctive? How do you define "instinct"?

5. Which authorities does the author cite to rebut Lorenz' contention that pre-human primates (gorillas, orangutans, etc.) were prone to violence? What are some practical consequences of Lorenz' theories?

2
# The Causes of War

## Michael Howard

This article originally appeared in *Wilson Quarterly*, Summer 1984.

---

*As far back as ancient Greece, historians have sought to discover the causes of war. In this essay, Michael Howard of Oxford University finds human psychology not very different from what it was in the days of the Greek historian Thucydides (400 B.C.) when Sparta acted out of fear of Athenian power. Through the centuries, other explanations have been offered: ignorance and immaturity, survival of the fittest (Social Darwinism) and pathological aberration.*

*As a student of the Prussian strategist von Clausewitz, Howard holds that states go to war to achieve specific ends—that war is a product of human reason. He sees it as an action undertaken to preserve or enlarge the power of a particular state, with all its political and cultural overtones. This derives from a "superabundance of analytic rationality." With modern technology, the scope of war has changed, but not its goals. "Arms races," in Howard's view, are the modern equivalent to dynastic marriages of an earlier day. England and Germany, for example, in their eagerness to strengthen their navies before World War II, were the modern counterparts of Athens and Sparta. Today, Russia seeks to be treated as an equal by the United States.*

*At the same time, Howard argues that some things have changed. The stakes are higher and a revulsion to war, though not universal, is far more widespread. But war will continue to be an instrument of policy, says the author, so long as nations think that they can achieve more by fighting than by remaining at peace. The advent of nuclear weapons, he concludes, is perhaps the best deterrent to this willingness to go to war, since it would mean suicide for the parties involved.*

Since the mid-18th century, many European and American theorists have attempted to explain war as an aberration in human affairs or as an occurrence beyond rational control. Violent conflicts between nations have been depicted, variously, as collective outbursts of male aggression, as the inevitable outcome of ruling-class greed, or as necessary, even healthy, events in the evolutionary scheme. One exception to the general trend was the 19th-century Prussian strategist Karl von Clausewitz, who declared, in an oft-quoted dictum, that war was the extension of politics "by other means." Here, historian Michael Howard argues further that war is one of Reason's progeny—indeed, that war stems from nothing less than a "superabundance of analytic rationality."

No one can describe the topic that I have chosen to discuss as a neglected and understudied one. How much ink has been spilled about it, how many library shelves have been filled with works on the subject, since the days of Thucydides! How many scholars from how many specialties have applied their expertise to this intractable problem! Mathematicians, meteorologists, sociologists, anthropologists, geographers, physicists, political scientists, philosophers, theologians, and lawyers are only the most obvious of the categories that come to mind when one surveys the ranks of those who have sought some formula for perpetual peace, or who have at least hoped to reduce the complexities of international conflict to some orderly structure, to develop a theory that will enable us to explain, to understand, and to control a phenomenon which, if we fail to abolish it, might well abolish us.

Yet it is not a problem that has aroused a great deal of interest in the historical profession. The causes of specific wars, yes: These provide unending material for analysis and interpretation, usually fueled by plenty of documents and starkly conflicting prejudices on the part of the scholars themselves.

But the phenomenon of war as a continuing activity within human society is one that as a profession we take very much for granted. The alternation of war and peace has been the very stuff of the past. War has been throughout history a normal way of conducting disputes between political groups. Few of us, probably, would go along with those sociobiologists who claim that this has been so because man is "innately aggressive." The calculations of advantage and risk, sometimes careful, sometimes crude, that statesmen make before committing their countries to war are linked very remotely, if at all, to the displays of "machismo" that we witness today in football crowds. Since the use or threat of physical force is the most elementary way of asserting power and controlling one's environment, the fact that men have frequently had recourse to it does not cause the historian a great deal of surprise. Force, or the threat of it, may not settle arguments, but it does play a considerable part in determining the structure of the world in which we live.

I mentioned the multiplicity of books that have been written about the causes of war since the time of Thucydides. In fact, I think we would find that the vast majority of them have been written since 1914, and that the degree of intellectual concern about the causes of war to which we have become accustomed has existed only since the First World War. In view of the damage which that war did to the social and political structure of Europe, this is understandable enough. But there has been a tendency to argue that because that war caused such great and lasting damage, because it destroyed three great empires and nearly beggared a fourth, it must have arisen from causes of peculiar complexity and profundity, from the neuroses of nations, from the widening class struggle, from a crisis in industrial society. I have argued this myself, taking issue with Mr. A. J. P. Taylor, who maintained that because the war had such profound consequences, it did not necessarily have equally profound causes. But now I wonder whether on this, as on so many other matters, I was not wrong and he was not right.

It is true, and it is important to bear in mind in examining the problems of that period, that before 1914 war was almost universally considered an acceptable, perhaps an inevitable and for many people a desirable, way of settling international differences, and that the war generally foreseen was expected to be, if not exactly brisk and cheerful, then certainly brief; no longer, certainly, than the war of 1870 between France and Prussia that was consciously or unconsciously taken by that generation as a model. Had it not been so generally felt that war was an acceptable and tolerable way of solving international disputes, statesmen and soldiers would no doubt have approached the crisis of 1914 in a very different fashion.

But there was nothing new about this attitude to war. Statesmen had always been able to assume that war would be acceptable at least to those sections of their populations whose opinion mattered to them, and in this respect the decision to go to war in 1914—for continental statesmen at least—in no way differed from those taken by their predecessors of earlier generations. The causes of the Great War are thus in essence no more complex or profound than those of any previous European war, or indeed than those described by Thucydides as underlying the Peloponnesian War: "What made war inevitable was the growth of Athenian power and the fear this caused in Sparta." In Central Europe, there was the German fear that the disintegration of the Habsburg Empire would result in an enormous enhancement of Russian power—power already becoming formidable as French-financed industries and railways put Russian manpower at the service of her military machine. In Western Europe, there was the traditional British fear that Germany might establish a hegemony over Europe which, even more than that of Napoleon, would place at risk the security of Britain and her own possessions, a fear fueled by the knowledge that there was within Germany a widespread determination to achieve a world status comparable with her latent power. Considerations of this kind had caused wars in Europe often enough before. Was there really anything different about 1914?

Ever since the 18th century, war had been blamed by intellectuals upon the stupidity or the self-interest of governing elites (as it is now blamed upon "military-industrial complexes"), with the implicit or explicit assumption that if the control of state affairs were in the hands of sensible men—businessmen, as Richard Cobden thought, the workers, as Jean Jaurès thought—then wars would be no more.

By the 20th century, the growth of the social and biological sciences was producing alternative explanations. As Quincy Wright expressed it in his massive *A Study of War* (1942), "Scientific investigators . . . tended to attribute war to immaturities in social knowledge and control, as one might attribute epidemics to insufficient medical knowledge or to inadequate public health services." The Social Darwinian acceptance of the inevitability of struggle, indeed of its desirability if mankind was to progress, the view, expressed by the elder Moltke but very widely shared at the turn of the century, that perpetual peace was a dream and not even a beautiful dream, did not survive the Great War in those countries where the bourgeois-liberal culture was dominant, Britain and the United States. The failure of these nations to appreciate that such bellicist views, or variants of them, were still widespread in other areas of the world, those dominated by Fascism and by Marxism-Leninism, was to cause embarrassing misunderstandings, and possibly still does.

For liberal intellectuals, war was self-evidently a pathological aberration from the norm, at best a ghastly mistake, at worst a crime. Those who initiated wars must in their view have been criminal, or sick, or the victims of forces beyond their power to control. Those who were so accused disclaimed responsibility for the events of 1914, throwing it on others or saying the whole thing was a terrible mistake for which no one was to blame. None of them, with their societies in ruins around them and tens of millions dead, were prepared to say courageously: "We only acted as statesmen always have in the past. In the circumstances then prevailing, war seemed to us to be the best way of protecting or forwarding the national interests for which we were responsible. There was an element of risk, certainly, but the risk might have been greater had we postponed the issue. Our real guilt does not lie in the fact that we started the war. It lies in our mistaken belief that we could win it."

The trouble is that if we are to regard war as pathological and abnormal, then all conflict must be similarly regarded; for war is only a particular kind of conflict between a particular category of social groups: sovereign states. It is, as Clausewitz put it, "a clash between major interests that is resolved by bloodshed—that is the only way in which it differs from other conflicts." If one had no sovereign states, one would have no wars, as Rousseau rightly pointed out—but, as Hobbes equally rightly pointed out, we would probably have no peace either. As states acquire a monopoly of violence, war becomes the only remaining form of conflict that may legitimately be settled by physical force. The mechanism of legitimization of authority and of social control that makes it possible for a state to moderate or eliminate conflicts within its borders or at very least to ensure that these are not conducted by competitive violence—the mechanism to the study of which historians have quite properly devoted so much attention—makes possible the conduct of armed conflict with other states, and on occasion—if the state is to survive—makes it necessary.

These conflicts arise from conflicting claims, or interests, or ideologies, or perceptions; and these perceptions may indeed by fueled by social or psychological drives that we do not fully understand and that one day we may learn rather better how to control. But the problem is the control of social conflict as such, not simply of war. However inchoate or disreputable the motives for war may be, its initiation is almost by definition a deliberate and carefully considered act and its conduct, at least at the more advanced levels of social development, a matter of very precise central control. If history shows any record of "accidental" wars, I have yet to find them. Certainly statesmen have sometimes been surprised by the nature of the war they have unleashed, and it is reasonable to assume that in at least 50 percent of the cases they got a result they did not expect. But that is not the same as a war begun by mistake and continued with no political purpose.

Statesmen in fact go to war to achieve very specific ends, and the reasons for which states have fought one another have been categorized and recategorized innumerable times. Vattel, the Swiss lawyer, divided them into the necessary, the customary, the rational, and the capricious. Jomini, the Swiss strategist, identified ideological, economic, and popular wars, wars to defend the balance of power, wars to assist allies, wars to assert or to defend rights. Quincy Wright, the American political scientist, divided them into the idealistic, the psychological, the political, and the juridical. Bernard Brodie in our own times has refused to discriminate: "Any theory of the causes of war in general or any war in particular that is not inherently eclectic and comprehensive," he stated, " . . . is bound for that very reason to be wrong." Another contemporary analyst, Geoffrey Blainey, is on the contrary unashamedly reductionist. All war aims, he wrote, "are simply varieties of power. The vanity of nationalism, the will to spread an ideology, the protection of kinsmen in an adjacent land, the desire for more territory . . . all these represent power in different wrappings. The conflicting aims of rival nations are always conflicts of power."

In principle, I am sure that Bernard Brodie was right: No single explanation for conflict between states, any more than for conflict between any other social groups, is likely to stand up to critical examination. But Blainey is right as well. Quincy Wright provided us with a useful indicator when he suggested that "while animal war is a function of instinct and primitive war of the mores, civilized war is primarily a function of state politics."

Medievalists will perhaps bridle at the application of the term "primitive" to the sophisticated and subtle societies of the Middle Ages, for whom war was also a "function of the mores," a way of life that often demanded only the most banal of justifications. As a way of life, it persisted in Europe well into the 17th century, if no later. For Louis XIV and his court war was, in the early years at least, little more than a seasonal variation on hunting. But by the 18th century, the mood had changed. For Frederick the Great, war was to be pre-eminently a function of Staatspolitik, and so it has remained ever since. And although statesmen can be as emotional or as prejudiced in their judgments as any other group of human beings, it is very seldom that their attitudes, their perceptions, and their decisions are not related, however remotely, to the fundamental issues of power, that capacity to control their environment on which the independent existence of their states and often the cultural values of their societies depend.

And here perhaps we do find a factor that sets interstate conflict somewhat apart from other forms of social rivalry. States may fight—indeed as often as not they do fight—not over any specific issue such as might otherwise have been resolved by peaceful means, but in order to acquire, to enhance, or to preserve their capacity to function as independent actors in the international system at all. "The stakes of war," as Raymond Aron has reminded us, "are the existence, the creation, or the elimination of States." It is a somber analysis, but one which the historical record very amply bears out.

It is here that those analysts who come to the study of war from the disciplines of the natural sciences, particularly the biological sciences, tend, it seems to me, to go astray. The conflicts between states which have usually led to war have normally arisen, not from any irrational and emotive drives, but from almost a superabundance of *analytic rationality*. Sophisticated communities (one hesitates to apply to them Quincy Wright's word, "civilized") do not react simply to immediate threats. Their intelligence (and I use the term in its double sense) enables them to assess the implications that any event taking place anywhere in the world, however remote, may have for their own capacity, immediately to exert influence, ultimately perhaps to survive. In the later Middle Ages and the early Modern period, every child born to every prince anywhere in Europe was registered on the delicate seismographs that monitored the shifts in dynastic power. Every marriage was a diplomatic triumph or disaster. Every stillbirth, as Henry VIII knew, could presage political catastrophe.

Today, the key events may be different. The pattern remains the same. A malfunction in the political mechanism of some remote African community, a coup d'état in a minuscule Caribbean republic, an insurrection deep in the hinterland of Southeast Asia, an assassination in some emirate in the Middle East—all these will be subjected to the kind of anxious examination and calculation that was devoted a hundred years ago to the news of comparable events in the Balkans: an insurrection in Philippopoli, a coup d'état in Constantinople, an assassination in Belgrade. To whose advantage will this ultimately redound, asked the worried diplomats, ours or theirs? Little enough in itself, perhaps, but will it not precipitate or strengthen a trend, set in motion a tide whose melancholy withdrawing roar will strip us of our friends and influence and leave us isolated in a world dominated by adversaries deeply hostile to us and all that we stand for?

There have certainly been occasions when states have gone to war in a mood of ideological fervor like the French republican armies in 1792; or of swaggering aggression like the Americans against Spain in 1898 or the British against the Boers a year later; or to make more money, as did the British in the War of Jenkins' Ear in 1739; or in a generous desire to help peoples of similar creed or race, as perhaps the Russians did in helping the Bulgarians fight the Turks in 1877 and the British dominions certainly did in 1914 and 1939. But, in general, men have fought during the past two hundred years neither because they are aggressive nor because they are acquisitive animals, but because they are reasoning ones: because they discern, or believe that they can discern, dangers before they become immediate, the possibility of threats before they are made.

But be this as it may, in 1914 many of the German people, and in 1939 nearly all of the British, felt justified in going to war, not over any specific issue that could have been settled by negotiation, but to maintain their power; and to do so while it was still possible, before they found themselves so isolated, so impotent, that they had no power left to maintain and had to accept a subordinate position within an international system dominated by their adversaries. "What made war inevitable was the growth of Athenian power and the fear this caused in Sparta." Or, to quote another grimly apt passage from Thucydides:

> The Athenians made their Empire more and more strong . . . [until] finally the point was reached when Athenian strength attained a peak plain for all to see and the Athenians began to encroach upon Sparta's allies. It was at this point that Sparta felt the position to be no longer tolerable and decided by starting the present war to employ all her energies in attacking and if possible destroying the power of Athens.

You can vary the names of the actors, but the model remains a valid one for the purposes of our analysis. I am rather afraid that it still does.

Something that has changed since the time of Thucydides, however, is the nature of the power that appears so threatening. From the time of Thucydides until that of Louis XIV, there was basically only one source of political and military power—*control of territory*, with all the resources in wealth and manpower that this provided. This control might come through conquest, or through alliance, or through marriage, or through purchase, but the power of princes could be very exactly computed in terms of the extent of their territories and the number of men they could put under arms.

In 17th-century Europe, this began to change. Extent of territory remained important, but no less important was the effectiveness with which the resources of that territory could be exploited. Initially there were the bureaucratic and fiscal mechanisms that transformed loose bonds of territorial authority into highly structured centralized states whose armed forces, though not necessarily large, were permanent, disciplined, and paid.

Then came the political transformations of the revolutionary era that made available to these state systems the entire manpower of their country, or at least as much of it as the administrators were able to handle. And finally came the revolution in transport, the railways of the 19th century that turned the revolutionary ideal of the "Nation in Arms" into a reality. By the early 20th century, military power—on the continent of Europe, at least—was seen as a simple combination of military manpower and railways. The quality of armaments was of secondary importance, and political intentions were virtually excluded from account. The growth of power was measured in terms of the growth of populations and of communications; of the number of men who could be put under arms and transported to the battlefield to make their weight felt in the initial and presumably decisive battles. It was the mutual perception of threat in those terms that turned Europe before 1914 into an armed camp, and it was their calculations within this framework that reduced German staff officers increasingly to despair and launched their leaders on their catastrophic gamble in 1914, which started the First World War.

But already the development of weapons technology had introduced yet another element into the international power calculus, one that has in our own age become dominant. It was only in the course of the 19th century that technology began to produce weapons systems—initially in the form of naval vessels—that could be seen as likely in themselves to prove decisive, through their qualitative and quantitative superiority, in the event of conflict. But as war became increasingly a matter of competing technologies rather than competing armies, so there developed that escalatory process known as the "arms race." As a title, the phrase, like so many coined by journalists to catch the eye, is misleading.

"*Arms races*" are in fact continuing and open-ended attempts to match power for power. They are as much means of achieving stable or, if possible, favorable power balances as were the *dynastic marriage policies* of Valois and Habsburg. To suggest that they in themselves are causes of war implies a naive if not totally mistaken view of the relationship between the two phenomena. The causes of war remain rooted, as much as they were in the preindustrial age, in perceptions by statesmen of the growth of hostile power and the fears for the restriction, if not the extinction, of their own. The threat, or rather the fear, has not changed, whether it comes from aggregations of territory or from dreadnoughts, from the numbers of men under arms or from missile systems. The means that states employ to sustain or to extend their power may have been transformed, but their objectives and preoccupations remain the same.

"Arms races" can no more be isolated than wars themselves from the *political circumstances* that give rise to them, and like wars they will take as many different forms as political circumstances dictate. They may be no more than a process of competitive modernization, of maintaining a status quo that commands general support but in which no participant wishes, whether from reasons of pride or of prudence, to fall behind in keeping his armory up to date. If there are no political causes for fear or rivalry, this process need not in itself be a destabilizing factor in international relations. But arms races may, on the other hand, be the result of a quite deliberate assertion of an intention to change the status quo, as was, for example, the German naval challenge to Britain at the beginning of this century.

This challenge was an explicit attempt by Admiral Alfred von Tirpitz and his associates to destroy the hegemonic position at sea which Britain saw as essential to her security, and, not inconceivably, to replace it with one of their own. As British and indeed German diplomats repeatedly explained to the German government, it was not the German naval program in itself that gave rise to so much alarm in Britain. It was the intention that lay behind it. If the status quo was to be maintained, the German challenge had to be met.

The naval race could quite easily have been ended on one of two conditions. Either the Germans could have abandoned their challenge, as had the French in the previous century, and acquiesced in British naval supremacy; or the British could have yielded as gracefully as they did, a decade or so later, to the United States and abandoned a status they no longer had the capacity, or the will, to maintain. As it was, they saw the German challenge as one to which they could and should respond, and their power position as one which they were prepared, if necessary, to use force to preserve. The British naval program was thus, like that of the Germans, a signal of political intent; and that intent, that refusal to acquiesce in a fundamental transformation of the power balance, was indeed a major element among the causes of the war. The naval competition provided a very accurate indication and measurement of political rivalries and tensions, but it did not cause them; nor could it have been abated unless the rivalries themselves had been abandoned.

It was the general perception of the growth of German power that was awakened by the naval challenge, and the fear that a German hegemony on the Continent would be the first step to a challenge to her own hegemony on the oceans, that led Britain to involve herself in the continental conflict in 1914 on the side of France and Russia. "What made war inevitable was the growth of Spartan power," to reword Thucydides, "and the fear which this caused in Athens." In the Great War that followed, Germany was defeated, but survived with none of her latent power destroyed. A "false hegemony" of Britain and France was established in Europe that could last only so long as Germany did not again mobilize her resources to challenge it. German rearmament in the 1930s did not of itself mean that Hitler wanted war (though one has to ignore his entire philosophy if one is to believe that he did not); but it did mean that he was determined, with a great deal of popular support, to obtain a free hand on the international scene.

With that free hand, he intended to establish German power on an irreversible basis; this was the message conveyed by his armament program. The armament program that the British reluctantly adopted in reply was intended to show that, rather than submit to the hegemonic aspirations they feared from such a revival of German power, they would fight to preserve their own freedom of action. Once again to recast Thucydides:

> Finally the point was reached when German strength attained a peak plain for all to see, and the Germans began to encroach upon Britain's allies. It was at this point that Britain felt the position to be no longer tolerable and decided by starting this present war to employ all her energies in attacking and if possible destroying the power of Germany.

What the Second World War established was not a new British hegemony, but a Soviet hegemony over the Euro-Asian land mass from the Elbe to Vladivostok; and that was seen, at least from Moscow, as an American hegemony over the rest of the world; one freely accepted in Western Europe as a preferable alternative to being absorbed by the rival hegemony. Rival armaments were developed to define and preserve the new territorial boundaries, and the present arms competition began. But in considering the present situation, historical experience suggests that we must ask the fundamental question: What kind of competition is it? Is it one between powers that accept the status quo, are satisfied with the existing power relationship, and are concerned simply to modernize their armaments in order to preserve it? Or does it reflect an *underlying instability* in the system?

My own perception, I am afraid, is that it is the latter. There was a period for a decade after the war when the Soviet Union was probably a status quo power but the West was not; that is, the Russians were not seriously concerned to challenge the American global hegemony, but the West did not accept that of the Russians in Eastern Europe. Then there was a decade of relative mutual acceptance between 1955 and 1965; and it was no accident that this was the heyday of disarmament/arms-control negotiations. But thereafter, the Soviet Union has shown itself increasingly unwilling to accept the Western global hegemony, if only because many other people in the world have been unwilling to do so either. Reaction against Western dominance brought the Soviet Union some allies and many opportunities in the Third World, and she has developed naval power to be able to assist the former and exploit the latter. She has aspired in fact to global power status, as did Germany before 1914; and if the West complains, as did Britain about Germany, that the Russians do not need a navy for defense purposes, the Soviet Union can retort, as did Germany, that she needs it to make clear to the world the status to which she aspires; that is, so that she can operate on the world scene by virtue of her own power and not by permission of anyone else. Like Germany, she is determined to be treated as an equal, and armed strength has appeared the only way to achieve that status.

The trouble is that what is seen by one party as the breaking of an alien hegemony and the establishment of equal status will be seen by the incumbent powers as a striving for the establishment of an alternate hegemony, and they are not necessarily wrong. In international politics, the appetite often comes with eating; and there really may be no way to check an aspiring rival except by the mobilization of stronger military power. An arms race then becomes almost a necessary surrogate for war, a test of national will and strength; and arms control becomes possible only when the underlying power balance has been mutually agreed.

We would be blind, therefore, if we did not recognize that the causes which have produced war in the past are operating in our own day as powerfully as at any time in history. It is by no means impossible that a thousand years hence a historian will write—if any historians survive, and there are any records for them to write history from—"What made war inevitable was the growth of Soviet power and the fear which this caused in the United States."

But times have changed since Thucydides. They have changed even since 1914. These were, as we have seen, bellicist societies in which war was a normal, acceptable, even a desirable way of settling differences. The question that arises today is, how widely and evenly spread is that intense revulsion against war that at present characterizes our own society? For if war is indeed now universally seen as being unacceptable as an instrument of policy, then all analogies drawn from the past are misleading, and although power struggles may continue, they will be diverted into other channels. But if that revulsion is not evenly spread, societies which continue to see armed force as an acceptable means for attaining their political ends are likely to establish a dominance over those which do not. Indeed, they will not necessarily have to fight for it.

My second and concluding point is this: Whatever may be the underlying causes of international conflict, even if we accept the role of atavistic militarism or of military-industrial complexes or of sociobiological drives or of domestic tensions in fueling it, wars begin with conscious and reasoned decisions based on the calculation, made by both parties, that they can achieve more by going to war than by remaining at peace.

Even in the most bellicist of societies this kind of calculation has to be made and it has never even for them been an easy one. When the decision to go to war involves the likelihood, if not the certainty, that the conflict will take the form of an exchange of nuclear weapons from which one's own territory cannot be immune, then even for the most bellicist of leaders, even for those most insulated from the pressures of public opinion, the calculation that they have more to gain from going to war than by remaining at peace and pursuing their policies by other means will, to put it mildly, not be self-evident. The odds against such a course benefiting their state or themselves or their cause will be greater, and more evidently greater, than in any situation that history has ever had to record. Society may have accepted killing as a legitimate instrument of state policy, but not, as yet, suicide. For that reason I find it hard to believe that the abolition of nuclear weapons, even if it were possible, would be an unmixed blessing. Nothing that makes it easier for statesmen to regard war as a feasible instrument of state policy, one from which they stand to gain rather than lose, is likely to contribute to a lasting peace.

## Questions

1. What was the general European attitude toward war before 1914?

2. What occurred to change it?

3. Do you think wars result from pathological or "superrational" causes? Give your reasons.

4. What causes does Howard give for the underlying instability of U.S.–Soviet relations?

5. Do you agree with his contention that the elimination of nuclear weapons would make it easier to go to war? Identify other factors that may be taken into consideration.

# 3
# Patriarchy, Peace and Women Warriors

## Christine Sylvester

This article originally appeared in *Peace, Meanings, Politics, Strategies*, Praeger, 1989.

*The author, an associate professor of political science at North-
ern Arizona University, challenges the assumption that women are
necessarily pro-peace. She cites the Woman of the Year designations
of the female leads of "Cagney and Lacey," cops in the police TV
series, as women who molded their characters in conformity to a
man's world. Nor would she consider Margaret Thatcher, England's
first female prime minister, as peace-loving.*

*Sylvester is not against all war—only wars that support the pa-
triarchal establishment. To clarify her position, she evaluates four
forms of feminist politics as proposed by Alison Jaggar: (1) liberal, as
exemplified by the National Organization for Women (NOW), (2)
Marxist, which sees women's oppression as secondary to the
overthrow of capitalism, (3) radical, which strives above all to liberate
women from patriarchy, and (4) socialist, which mixes Marxist analysis with the same struggle.*

*The author clearly prefers the radical and socialist forms of
women-warriorism, with their emphasis on "disorderly" and "irrational" (from the establishment viewpoint) strategies. She sees value in
confrontation over persuasion, movement toward woman-culture
free of male interference, and a situation in which "women and men
disappear as socially constituted categories." Her own experience as
the child of a woman who was forced into an unhappy marriage and
abandoned by an alcoholic husband undoubtedly shaped her views.*

*Sylvester feels it is too early to draw sharp conclusions. But she is
comfortable with the present situation as "healthfully incoherent."
She places great hope in "women warriors" who expose "patriarchal
wars and peaces as bankrupt pieces of order."*

It is common to think of women as being pro-peace. Women are
highly visible in such peace activist groups as the Greens, Women's
Pentagon Action, Greenham Common, The Women for Peace Move-

ment and the Peace People. Polls show that Western women oppose increases in military expenditures and deployment of new weapons more frequently than men.[1] Some feminist literature even suggests women may not be prone to warlike abstractions, or soldierly expressions of power, as dominance.[2] Yet, among the Women of the Year for 1986, designated by *Ms.* magazine, are Sharon Gless and Tyne Daly, who play sometimes-armed cops on the television series "Cagney and Lacey." Lauded for building characters who are good female buddies, these actresses also have molded those characters either to like fighting in a man's world (Gless), or, to have a closer relationship with a man than with her children (Daly).[3] Winnie Mandela, another *Ms.* Woman of the Year, says calmly: ". . . we are at war with white South Africa." [4] She speaks as much for African women of that country as she does for her famous husband and other male nationalists. She is unarmed in a region where many of her sisters are, or were, combatants in national liberation struggles. In addition to these "outstanding" women, there are other "nonpeacefuls," like Margaret Thatcher, "the iron lady," who broke the sex barrier of high public office and also directed the Falklands/Malvinas war; and women who volunteer to train for war.

The purpose of this chapter is to consider some seemingly nonpeaceful women—women warriors. These women create and follow more antiestablishment, or establishment-skeptical, politics than woman serving in the police, armed forces, or high public offices of state. The latter are an integral part of dominant society and, through their careers, officially defend a public realm which "has always been defined in opposition to dangerous, disorderly, and irrational forces . . . consistently conceptualized as female." [5] Women who hold such positions may do so out of feminist convictions; that is, they may fight for power within an establishment that has heretofore excluded women and, in the process, actually strike a blow against that establishment. Women warriors are less well-adjusted to dominant society and, in fact, fight to make creative spaces for "irrational" and "disorderly" feminist projects which defy the rules and practices of social order. Their strategies are multiple, yet contain a common element of power through energy, capacity, competence, and effectiveness.[6]

This chapter will consider features of establishments which oppress women in war and in peace, and arguments that women would set societies on more peace-loving courses if they held power. In sympathy with the women-peace link, one wonders, nevertheless, if it is somewhat stereotypical and power-limiting in the sense of fitting too neatly into establishment-supporting gender expectations. To think/labor creatively about war and peace, women may have to labor as warriors (against male-dominated order, and for healthier pieces of disorder). Clues to women-warrior strategies emerge in branches of feminism, that reveal, delegitimate, and challenge, in unthinkable ways, the wars and peaces of patriarchal societies.

## WOMEN: MORE PEACE-LOVING THAN MEN?

Birgit Brock-Utne thinks it noteworthy that "women have never institutionalized violence." [7] Would they do so if they held power? She thinks many might, unless they were to involve themselves in a different education to counter "the training in patriarchal thinking in formal school systems and political life [which] generally guarantees that women will think like men, will compete the way they do, and hold the same value systems." [8] Components of this education include "developing our 'women's logic,' continuing to care for others, feel compassion, share power, and become more assertive." [9] Brock-Utne is suggesting that women's experiences impart a privileged understanding of oppression, injustice, and that which passes for power in patriarchal society. If women could act on their special understandings in unity, and with an alternative power to that propagated by men's logic, they would not lead societies into war, tolerate rape and abuse, withhold resources, pollute, and injure through discrimination. But since women live in patriarchal societies, where all of the above practices dominate, it is difficult to find favor for peace-loving inclinations, let alone forge a social movement which advances "a morally and scientifically preferable grounding for our interpretations and explanations of nature and social life." [10]

Patriarchy is a system of power relations which creates and bolsters male supremacy, and "denotes the historical depth of women's exploitation and oppression." [11] Its emergence at different times in different societies may be linked to "man-the-hunter's" use of tools as weapons to assault and conquer others, acquire economic resources and control politics.[12] Understood this way, patriarchy is a form of colonialism that advances one group at the expense of others; in this case, at the expense of women who now systematically occupy less lucrative, less prestigious and influential statuses—the occasional woman politician or millionaire notwithstanding.

The power relations of male supremacy seem timeless and in the order of things when, in fact, they were socially created like other forms of colonialism. As with most accepted ideologies and practices, once in place, patriarchy is self-sustaining: If a majority of politicians, scientists, priests, ministers, popes, professors, chairs of corporate boards, physicians, job supervisors, judges, and peacemakers are always men, then challenges to that group's monopoly can actually seem unnatural, silly, or even harmful to social order. Those who push for changes in the structures and practices of power soon find that powerful men are the ones who decide how challenges to people like themselves will be handled. Such nonneutral decision makers have historically tried to ignore women's demands (women could not vote in this country until the 1920s, and just recently gained that right in Switzerland), or to accommodate them in incremental ways, so change will not seriously disrupt the existing hierarchy of power (American women got the vote, but it took decades for them to get equal access to credit).

Arguably, then, patriarchy is a system in which there is constant, covert, low-intensity, structural warfare against women—in "war" and in "peace." During shooting wars between states, the war-within-the-war often features male-dictated changes in the "normal" gender division of labor. Protecting national interests requires that male laborers leave for the battlefront and women "man" the factories at the homefront. Since women rarely hold positions in the public realms, where decisions of war and peace originate, those national interests, that shooting war to safeguard them, and the accompanying redivision of labor, are imposed. So, also, is the peace which comes when men who declare (or as often as not these days, nondeclare) the shooting war decide to stop fighting. With the cessation of "hostilities," women have been abruptly dismissed from the homefront jobs that pay and sent back to their "natural" nonpaying jobs in the private household. Both the shooting wars and subsequent peaces contain hidden wars of dominance over women.

As a second example of patriarchal war-peace, consider the landmark U.S. Supreme Court decision in *Roe versus Wade*. The issue was abortion—whether women could decide to maintain or terminate their pregnancies. The Supreme Court handed down a decision lauded by prochoice women around the country—their abortion rights had been "established." That some very powerful men had deigned to allow women to have some control over procreation was lost in the celebrations. Moreover, it can be argued that an exchange was implied in this decision: Women, with abortion rights, would put money in the pockets of mostly male physicians and halt self-gynecological practices that endangered, in the sense of undermining, accepted medical practices for example, giving each other pelvic exams and seeking mind-to-body abortions.[13] Under this interpretation, *Roe versus Wade* is not so much a victory for women as a war strategy designed to lull them into a false sense of power and security under conditions of patriarchal peace.

In each case, patriarchy wins because male "rights" to decide everything have become one of the mainstays of civilization. As well, there are rewards for women who accept patriarchy, play by its rules, and defend it from harm. These rewards include male protection from other marauding males, "freedom" to specialize in the labor of reproduction and caretaking or in public sector careers, approval for efforts to improve physical appearance (under patriarchy, "letting yourself go" has a negative connotation), and appreciation for handing over sons to the public realms which define war and peace. Under patriarchy, women may value something called "peace," and be peace-abiding. To paraphrase Brock-Utne, they need that different education to open their eyes to complicity in a violent, exploitative, and oppressive peace. The object-relations school of psychoanalytic theory suggests that even without a different education, women are more peaceable than men, more fundamentally disinclined to institutionalize violence. This difference has to do with preconscious responses boys and girls develop to the challenge of individuating from the women who mother them.[14]

For boys, there is an early and quite jarring realization that she who nurtures (with whom they feel symbiotic attachment), is a physical other, a not-I. This preconscious dawning sets up the structural personality conditions for male efforts to individuate from mothers in ways which repress and deny all associations with mother-world. To be male is to be not female. It is to be so defensive about the feminine sides of one's personality as to embrace opposing traits: "Real men," as the saying goes, are rugged individuals, competitive, independent, above cleaning dirty diapers, and, above all, rational. The appropriate model of masculine behavior is father, having himself been properly socialized to embody many of these "ideal" characteristics. This model, however, is often absent from the household, which means that boys learn to identify with an abstract figure who leaves home to work "out there."

Preconscious struggles and subsequent training to be properly masculine, prepare adult males to think in either/or terms and to feel most comfortable when distance is maintained from other people through mental comfort-zones of high abstraction. Customary social interactions reveal this: *Robert's Rules of Parliamentary Procedure* prevent meetings from becoming usefully disorderly by establishing intricate barriers to communication; men try not to cry or appear too emotional in public; they "hang tough" and never let another guy, or especially a woman, "get the better of them;" their friendships often center on "shop talk," competitive sports, and denigration of women and "wimps"—characteristics the 1987 hit movie, *Beverly Hills Cop II,* showcase.

In maintaining distance from anything "of women" and mother-world, men can unconsciously glorify war as the ultimate means of individuation. For the "good" battle (a just war against those who would take away what "we" have gained) men willingly undergo painful and humiliating training that, as shown in *Full Metal Jacket,* openly celebrates the fact that "here there are men and no women" (except for the few recruits who "don't make it").[15] The terror of battle temporarily breaks down rigid barriers to closeness and facili-tates intense male bonding, about which men wax nostalgic once the war ends. Death in war is honorable and gains the soldier immortality as a "man"; he has faced the enemy. Yet, where intimacy and con-tempt are thesis and antithesis, and where fear of losing hard-fought identities as "not females" is omnipresent, those "just wars" con-tinue into peacetime—consciously or unconsciously, patriarchal peace maintains the defenses against women.

For girls, the challenge of becoming individuals centers on resist-ing a mesmerizing and seductive sameness with "mother." [16] This individuating struggle, however, has fewer defensive components, because girls do not have to reject the first relation and adopt behav-iors different from those of their mothers in order to be acceptably feminine. As well, their basic role model is concrete rather than ab-stract, self rather than other, and connected rather than distant. Ac-cordingly, "girls emerge from this period with a basis for 'empathy' built into their primary definition of self in a way that boys do not." [17] Sara Ruddick maintains that daughters go on to learn special lessons in their mothers' houses, which norms of masculinity prevent sons from learning:

> Women are daughters who learn from their mothers the activity of preservative love and the maternal thinking that arises from it. These 'lessons' from 'her mother's house' can shape a daughter's intellectual and emotional life even if she rejects the activity, its thinking, or, for that matter, the mother herself. Preservative love is opposed in its fundamental values to military strategy. Maternal theories of conflict are more pacifist than militaristic. A daughter, one might say, has been trained to be unsoldierly.[18]

As adults, women carry out their unsoldierly training by seeking more to preserve and enhance life than to jeopardize it. They look to the community as the realm of effective action, and learn from material experiences of childrearing that power is not a fixed, hierarchical, either/or thing; for example, they watch infallible parent power ebb as their children mature.[19] Of course, the world of "her" is not all laudatory. Although women might have less defensive and more connected postures toward the world, their gender lessons can freeze this potential around roles which sustain patriarchy. We can connect, for example, to the point of losing ourselves and our power in mesmerizing mergers with men or children. We can become a community of self-sacrificers that lacks the ability to challenge the "order" effectively.

The theories of men-women differences developed in object-relations scholarship and built upon by Brock-Utne, constitute a brilliant and useful case for linking women with peace and men with war. Yet, it seems that we might be digging our own graves within patriarchy when we think in the either/or terms of that dominant society. Is it not possible that war and peace are of a single piece, instead of being negations of each other, and that at this moment in time that piece is patriarchal? If so, one type of different education for women would consist of undertaking wars against the established patriarchal monopoly of war and peace, for the disorderly and irrational reorderings which feminize that piece, and change it fundamentally.

To state the problematique this way is not to say that women must become war- rather than peace-oriented in any patriarchal sense of those terms. It is not an argument that women secretly welcome rape or are impatient to institutionalize violence. Nor does it necessarily negate the idea that women may be more peace-loving than men. Rather, it recognizes that patriarchy may damage and distort women's perspectives as well as those of men: women may be embracing (and calling our own) peacemaker images that reflect and serve the prevailing gender order.[20] If so, this will limit the types of strategies women find acceptable for fighting patriarchal monopolies, and lead us to think, perhaps too righteously, that "real women" are totally opposed to destructive acts. In this respect, we often hear that women's liberation will liberate everyone, men and women, in non-violent ways. Yet to say this is to deny that liberation brings pain, confusion, and loss—that it destroys as it generates new options. Also, an argument of this nature can deny the many women who take up arms in anti-colonial struggles.

The question we are led to is this: What constitutes patriarchy-alternative war-peace-lovingnesses, and what strategies will bring them into focus? The following section considers the different educations which feminist theories of social change represent, and highlights those which seem most conducive to educating women warriors.

## FEMINIST STRATEGIES

Feminism is a diverse philosophical, political, and cultural movement to analyze women's oppression and to end it through the effective use of power. Some argue that feminism provides the framework for developing both the power of women and the power of peace, because feminists speak to issues of powersharing, egalitarian structures and freedom from direct as well as indirect or structural violence.[21] There is no such thing as *a* feminist perspective any more than there is consensus on what constitutes war and peace.[22] Lessons on war-peace-lovingness from feminism, therefore, vary widely within a set of parameters which focus attention on women's potential and the social changes needed to realize it.

Alison Jaggar enumerates four distinct types of feminist politics: Liberal, Marxist, radical, and socialist.[23] Of these, radical and socialist feminisms are women-warrior philosophies and politics. This does not mean there are no women warriors within the liberal or Marxist traditions, or that some feminists are misguided—all feminisms are so far from realizing their goals that should any come to prevail, the foundations of patriarchy would at least shake.[24] Women-warrior feminisms stand out for revealing the depths of the male-dominant order and for proposing strategies to combat it which differ from those used to sustain it. The warrior feminisms highlighted in this chapter simply suggest the possibilities.

Liberal feminism poses the challenge of women's power and goals as gaining equal rights with men within a marginally changed social system. To advance, women should have opportunities to participate fully in the heretofore male-dominated spheres of science, government, industry, commerce and education, without suffering pay and status discrimination, or sexual harassment on the job. As well, women who work within the household should be remunerated, or at least, their work should be highly respected. To accomplish what is essentially a goal of integrating women into mainstream society, liberal feminism uses two nonviolent strategies: Organizations such as NOW (National Organization for Women) and magazines such as *Ms.* work to raise women's consciousness by providing evidence both of women's accomplishments and of discriminations they suffer by virtue of being erroneously perceived as less rational and orderly than men. They also lobby male powerholders to recognize and rectify inconsistencies and injustices in the law and its implementation, proposing corrective measures, like the Equal Rights Amendment, when appropriate. Both efforts rely on reasoned argumentation and objective evidence of discrimination, as well as on shows of support through rallies and protests.

There are always disorderly or irrational elements in efforts to bring women into the system. The goals and methods of liberal feminism, however, are not especially disordering or irrationalizing—the aim, women's "achievement in a competitive society," [25] is based on a view of the West as a "fair meritocracy";[26] the methods, "demand articulation and aggregation," are accepted within liberal patriarchal societies. Accordingly, liberal feminism can seem naive or bourgeois to Third World women, who tend to think our system is always against "people like them." As well, liberal feminists can work diligently for a demilitarized foreign policy and a nuclear freeze, but since their perspective does not locate obstacles in deep structures of patriarchal power relations (among other sources), they may underestimate the challenge and become bitter, frustrated, or politically ineffectual. Theirs is a nonviolent, system-reforming peace-lovingness which can inadvertently work hand in glove with patriarchal peaces.

Classical Marxism is a warrior philosophy, but not especially a woman-warrior philosophy. Its focus on the struggles of male and female workers for emancipation from exploitative structures, leads to deeply antiestablishment proposals and practices, so long as the establishment is defined as capitalism. There is little or no recognition within classical Marxism that capitalism may be the latest economic arm of patriarchy. Hence, men-women relationships emerge as secondary contradictions within the large problematique of class exploitation. The women question has to do with women's usual job assignment under capitalism—homemaking. Homemakers specialize in reproducing new workers and reproducing existing workers' daily needs. To many Marxists, these are nonproductive labors which put women at the margins of history—reproducers do not sell their labor power to the highest bidder and then experience their surplus value drained in profits; nor is their labor subject to the types of technological change which affect whole societies, as did for example, the invention of steam engines. Isolated from economic activity in societies which live by producing commodities for exchange in a market, homemakers are thereby isolated as well from the lessons in exploitation which such productive economic activity imparts, and from the revolutionary activities which propel societies towards increasingly progressive futures. The challenge for women is to join the lessons-imparting workforce as proletarians and fight alongside men for a new order.[27]

But what precisely will women thereby gain? Americans often think of Marxism as a monolithic, dangerous, disorderly and ever-so irrational "creed." Yet capitalists never caricature Marx as a woman, but as an anti-Christ—a turncoat male. This may be so because "Marxists have interpreted "labor" to mean primarily the production and exchange of objects—the kind of work that they associate with men." [28] Marxist feminism makes the important contribution of showing linkages between contemporary household structures that relegate women to subservient if not historically insignificant statuses, and the broader division of labor into haves and have-nots that fuels capitalist development. But, to the degree that classical Marxism does not usually acknowledge that one of its key concepts (production) is male-biased, Marxist women can naively believe that a socialist order will remedy women's exploitation by enlarging their opportunities beyond "backward" reproduction. In fact, socialism can be only a form of enlightened patriarchy in which women simply conform to economic activities which define socialist man, and men do not reciprocate by doing women's traditional work.[29] If so, the war-peace piece remains male-monopolized.

Radical and socialist feminisms are women-warrior philosophies and politics, although their proponents do not often label themselves as such. Each, in its own way and with permutations depending upon where one lives, fundamentally aims at disordering and irrationalizing the norms and practices which sustain patriarchal wars and peaces.

Radical feminists argue that women comprise an oppressed class in societies that they believe are characterized above all by patriarchy. Women's advancement in such systems is impossible, because the wars against them are omnipresent, multiple, and deep. Women must strive to emancipate from patriarchy by analyzing who they were before patriarchy descended on them, and how they should behave now to be true to themselves. The first step is to investigate and reclaim aspects of a buried, invalidated, and undervalued "her-story." Much, radical feminists argue, has been taken from women, and Mary Daly is brilliant in her search to "re-member" the lusty wanderers of the realms of pure lust and to separate them from the main demonic attackers of aggression and obsession.[30] Seeing no purpose in trying to persuade patriarchs to value the very qualities "the political community has been defined in opposition to . . . forces which threaten its very existence and which require a masculine retreat to the well-defended barracks," [31] and eschewing equality with men in a system of power through coercion, the second step for radical feminists is to separate or detach from dominant society and move wholeheartedly into woman-culture. This often entails creating women-centered communities where hierarchical power relations and the institutions they produce (war, rape, militarism and compulsive heterosexuality) intrude as little as possible. Basing the good life on women's revalorized experiences alone, makes radical feminism quintessentially disorderly, irrational and dangerous to legitimate patriarchal wars and peaces.

Socialist feminists infuse radical feminism with aspects of Marxist analysis. They claim that the problem facing women is not patriarchy or capitalism alone—although each system of unequal power relations is formidable enough. The problem is capitalist patriarchy, with its corollaries of racism and imperialism. Jaggar presents the issue in these terms:

> Socialist feminists claim that a full understanding of the capitalist system requires a recognition of the way in which it is structured by male dominance and, conversely, that a full understanding of contemporary male dominance requires a recognition of the way it is organized by the capitalist division of labor. [32]

The two concerns come together in an analysis of interlocking components of a sexual division of labor which keeps women and other groups economically exploited, socially oppressed or both. These divisions are as follows: Between procreation and production of commodities for exchange in a market (the latter valued as men's "real" economic toil); within procreation, such that only women are childbearers while men control their sexual, procreative and emotional labor; and within commodity production, such that women's paid labor is often for different jobs than men perform, and compensated at a lower rate. [33]

The explicitly antiestablishment goal of socialist feminism is to eliminate those sexual divisions of labor in *every* realm of life, which means "women (and men) should disappear as socially constituted categories." [34] Moreover, these feminists argue that it is completely possible to accomplish this. For example, Western societies have the technology to enable men to carry and bear children, but lack the interest and will to make this a social option. Typically, the Strategic

Defense Initiative (Star Wars) sounds more sane and desirable than men having babies.

To proceed to socialist feminist levels of disorder and irrationality, several strategies are useful. Organizations exclusively for women provide spaces for ideas, approaches to labor, and social agendas to percolate in semi-isolation from patriarchy. Becoming involved in complementary movements which chip away at the sexual division of labor (through fights for women's reproductive rights, childcare and comparable worth, and against rape, battering and abusive practices of animal vivisection which the strong impose on their subservients) also makes sense.[35] The key is self-education through struggles to "transform the social relations which define us." [36] This perspective inclines some socialist feminists to support women in armed combat against established states refusing to give up colonial conquests of a by-gone era, or those sponsoring particularly hideous policies like apartheid. In these cases, people's war is necessary labor, distinct from the unnecessary coercion imposed by colonialism. Moreover, it helps women build energy, competence, capability and effectiveness as shapers of new societies, and suggests that, against certain types of patriarchies, those which are fascist, genocidal, and racist, certain types of coercion become destructive-constructive.[37] Overall, socialist feminism draws attention to historical materialist structures of patriarchal culture, and the different and oppressive expectations which exist for males and females. It is a feminist politics of struggle on the terrain of patriarchal society, but against the very practices which make that society seem orderly and rational. It thus poses dangers to established roles, lifestyles and expectations.

Radical and socialist feminisms provide two different philosophies and politics to help women move beyond equality with men in societies created and led by men, and kept safe by patriarchal wars and peaces. We must realize that these are only rough guidelines for women-warrior thought, strategy, and labor, and may be inadequate to the challenges of diverse circumstances. In all forms, however, the woman warrior is actively skeptical of prospects for peace wherever and whenever order is a smokescreen for dominance.

## WOMEN WARRIORS WHO ARE NOT FEMINISTS?

Do you have to be a radical or socialist feminist to be a woman warrior? Were there no women warriors in earlier times, that is, before the advent of contemporary feminist theories and politics? The evidence, limited as it is, suggests that women may need to develop and embrace some woman-warrior feminism to be effective in re-shaping war and peace, and these are relatively new, as is some of the knowledge which underlies them.

There have always been women who actively or tacitly combatted aspects of patriarchal wars and peaces. Mies draws attention to slave women denying patriarchy its lifeblood by refusing to bear children.[38] Joan of Arc single-handedly threatened the established gender order by leading troops against the British in France. Pre-feminist "great women," however, became isolated within "his-stories." They acted irrationally by patriarchal standards, but lacked the "her-stories" and organized power bases necessary to formulate disorderly outcomes and fight patriarchal monopolies effectively. In the case of Joan of Arc, a man-god gave her the idea and a man-monarch accepted her help, and then allowed Joan to be sold to her enemies, tried instead of ransomed (the latter more the custom under such circumstances), and burned at the stake as a witch-heretic.[39] Similarly, for years preceding slave women's birth strikes, colonials discouraged slave childbearing, since this took time from productive labor in the fields. When antimotherhood became a form of resistance to slavery, one could argue that "the ideology of the ruling classes . . . became the accepted ideology of the oppressed." [40] These resistances, therefore, although momentous, contained double messages about who is rightfully in charge, and did not come out of powerful movements against patriarchy per se.

Even today there is evidence that women can enter into combat against some patriarchal pieces of war and peace, without challenging the entire monopoly. Such has been the experience of women in southern African people's wars.[41] There, women have power bases in the numerous women's organizations established to promote and support revolution, and often labor as combatants, which is irrational and role-altering. Yet, the press of events leads women to merge with "the" national liberation struggle without setting woman-centered conditions on their participation, such as equal numbers of command posts during the war and public authority after it. There is certainly strength in national unity. The problem, of course, is that the women sacrifice twice for the nation—they risk their lives, as do male combatants, and then refade into the background as the male warriors direct the newly liberated societies. Men like Robert Mugabe of Zimbabwe, or the late Samora Machel of Mozambique, are pro-women; indeed, they have ensured that the worst inequities in customary laws are rectified, such as the practice of treating adult women as minors. But it is clear that the education-labor involved in ousting foreign patriarchs provides only partial training for the task of dislodging accepted practices of local patriarchy, such as men running the public affairs of state.[42] Arguably, these pieces of patriarchal peace will ebb only when women with warrior inclinations become women warriors under terms of local warrior feminisms.

Along the way, women with warrior inclinations, who know nothing about or even reject warrior feminisms, can provide appropriate soldiering lessons for their daughters. Such was my upbringing. My mother had suffered war and peace at the hands of her alcoholic father who taunted her, killed her plans to attend college, and then forbade her to dissolve an unhappy marriage engagement with my father. In her mother's house, she was sheltered from all-out abuse by this patriarch, but was also taught to value, conform to, and defend male dominance. As an adult, mother was simultaneously warrior- and patriarchy-inclined—feisty in the company of patriarchs, she nonetheless worked to keep "fortress patriarchy" strong by training me, or trying to train me, to "act like a lady." Fighting patriarchal monopolies is not ladylike. I learned this through a war of survival brought on by the abrupt departure of father when I was twelve. Mother and I were reluctant draftees to this war because abandoned women often have few liquid assets, considerable guilty embarrassment, and a sense that "a woman who is not 'loved' by a man is a nobody." [43] Their households, however, often become the paragons of constructive irrationality and disorder, as mothers who may not have worked outside the household for more than ten years suddenly change their labor in order to hold off bill collectors, and daughters are stirred from innocence to clean houses, babysit, clerk, and sell magazines by phone as their war contribution.

My mother survived her war within patriarchal peace with considerable elan. She then, however, admonished the adolescent me to "let men do the driving." It did not work. Keeping the peace patriarchy-style was simply too dissonant with the other lessons I had learned about sacrificing oneself for a falsely secure order. Nonetheless, were it not for the new scholarship on women and my exposure to women warriors, I might not have nurtured the woman warrior part of me—to this day, mother sees herself as a warrior, not a feminist.[44]

## CONCLUSIONS

It is inappropriate to draw sharp conclusions about interrelationships of women, peace-lovingness, women warriors, and strategies for tipping patriarchal war-peace pieces in more feminist directions. This thinking and action is very much in process and is also healthfully incoherent. Suffice it to say we should carefully examine claims that war and peace are negations of each other, and that women are unified in a natural or conditioned opposition to war and embrace of peace. Looking around the world, we see examples of mothers teaching their daughters to think in warlike abstractions, and of some women killing so as not to prolong community pain. We see others frankly appalled at the thought of violence, and still others who struggle first and foremost as workers or as citizens, entitled to equal rights with men under the law. We are all women; we are all learning about women, war, and peace; and all of our experiences have validity. Within this kaleidoscope of experience, women warriors are "nonpeacefuls" who expose patriarchal wars and peaces as bankrupt pieces of order. Count on them to stand in the way of any new, just, 'world order' that is not sufficiently disordering and irrational to challenge longstanding monopolies of power.

## Notes

Thanks to Morny Joy, Katherine Young and Nancy Hirschmann for helping me think about women warriors; to Warren Wagar, Linda Forcey, and the SUNY-Binghamton Peace Studies program for inviting me to present first thoughts; and to Louis Kriesberg and the Program on the Analysis and Resolution of Conflicts at Syracuse University for an opportunity to refine them. Bradley Klein, John Agnew, Joan Bokaer, and Mark Rupert had useful comments; and Gettysburg College supported this and all my work for the nearly seven years I taught there.

1. Birgit Brock-Utne, *Educating for Peace: A Feminist Perspective* (New York: Pergamon, 1985), 33.

2. Sara Ruddick, "Pacifying the Forces: Drafting Women in the Interests of Peace," *Signs*, v. 8, no. 3 (1983).

3. M. Gordon, "Sharon Gless and Tyne Daly, Stars of 'Cagney and Lacey,' " *Ms.* (January, 1987).

4. Winnie Mandela, "Interview," *Ms.* (January, 1987): 83.

5. Nancy Hartsock, "The Barracks Community in Western Political Thought: Prolegomena to a Feminist Critique of War and Politics," *Women's Studies International Forum*, v. 5, no. 3/4: 283.

6. The four aspects of feminist power are discussed in Nancy Hartsock, *Money, Sex, and Power: Toward a Feminist Historical Materialism* (Boston: Northeastern University Press, 1985).

7. Brock-Utne, *Educating for Peace*, 33.

8. Ibid.

9. Ibid., 148.

10. Sandra Harding, *The Science Question in Feminism* (Ithaca, N.Y.: Cornell University Press, 1986), 26.

11. Maria Mies, *Patriarchy and Accumulation on a World Scale: Women in the International Division of Labour* (London: Zed, 1986), 38.

12. Ibid., chapters 2 and 3, "Social Origins of the Sexual Division of Labour" and "Colonization and Housewifization."

13. This interpretation of *Roe versus Wade* extends a point Sonia Johnson made at Gettysburg College, November 2, 1987.

14. Nancy Chodorow, *The Reproduction of Mothering: Psychoanalysis and the Sociology of Gender* (Berkeley: University of California Press, 1978); and Dorothy Dinnerstein, *The Mermaid and the Minotaur: Sexual Arrangements and Human Malaise* (New York: Harper and Row, 1976).

15. For a discussion of masculine images in war discourse, see Bradley Klein, "The Textual Strategies of Military Strategy: or Have You Read Any Good Defense Manuals Lately?" paper for the International Studies Association, Washington, D.C. (April, 1987).

16. Nancy Hirschmann suggested this wording.

17. Chodorow, *The Reproduction of Mothering*, 167.

18. Ruddick, "Pacifying the Forces," 479.

19. See discussions in Marilyn French, *Beyond Power: On Women, Men, and Morals* (New York: Summit Books, 1985); and Hartsock, *Money, Sex, and Power*.

20. A similar point is made by Jane Flax, "Postmodernism and Gender Relations in Feminist Theory," *Signs*, 12, no. 4 (1987). Contrast this with the approach of Jean Bethke Elshtain, *Women and War* (New York: Basic Books, 1987).

21. Brock-Utne, *Educating For Peace*, chap. 1, "What is Peace"?; and Betty Reardon, *Sexism and the War System* (New York: Teachers College Press, 1985).

22. See discussion on defining peace in Christine Sylvester, "UN Elites: Perspectives on Peace," *Journal of Peace Research*, v. 17, no. 4 (1980).

23. Alison Jaggar, *Feminist Politics and Human Nature* (Totowa, N.J.: Roman & Allenheld, 1983), 5. Not all feminists think it is useful to categorize feminisms. See also Mies, *Patriarchy and Accumulation*, 12.

24. This argument runs throughout Harding, *The Science Question in Feminism*.

25. Jaggar, *Feminist Politics*, 194.

26. Ibid., 193.

27. See discussion in Selma James and Mariarosa Dalla Costa, *The Power of Women and the Subversion of Community* (Bristol: Falling Wall, 1973); and work by Clara Zetkin in *Socialist Register 1976*, Hal Draper and Anne Lipow, trans., Ralph Miliband and John Saville, eds. (London: Merlin, 1976).

28. Jaggar, *Feminist Politics*, 79.

29. For a discussion of why reproduction should be considered socially productive labor subject to technological change and consciousness-raising

results, see Alison Jaggar and William McBride, "Reproduction as Male Ideology," *Women's International Forum*, v. 3, no. 8 (1985).

30. Mary Daly, *Pure Lust; Elemental Feminist Philosophy* (Boston: Beacon, 1984), ix.

31. Hartsock, "The Barracks Community," 283.

32. Jaggar, *Feminist Politics*, 124.

33. Ibid., 130–37.

34. Ibid., 132.

35. Mies, *Patriarchy and Accumulation*, chap. 7, "Towards a Feminist Perspective of a New Society."

36. Nancy Hartsock, "Feminist Theory and the Development of Revolutionary Strategy," in *Capitalist Patriarchy and the Case of Socialist Feminism*, Zillah Eisenstein, ed., (New York: Monthly Review, 1979), 62. In Mies, *Patriarchy and Accumulation*, chap. 7, "Towards a Feminist Perspective of a New Society," Mies argues it would be a sign of considerable self-education and power for men's groups to form around the issue of violence to women, and for women's groups to boycott industries which promote images of them needing constant beautification or romantic love to be happy and fulfilled.

37. See discussion in Mies, Ibid.; and in Christine Sylvester, "Some Dangers in Merging Feminist and Peace Projects," *Alternatives*, v. 4, no. 12 (October, 1987).

38. Ibid. chap. 3, "Colonization and Housewifization."

39. Marina Warner, *Joan of Arc: The Image of Female Heroism* (New York: Knopf, 1981).

40. Rhoda Reddock, *Women, Labour and Struggle in 20th Century Trinidad and Tobago 1898–1960* (The Hague: Institute of Social Studies, 1984), 17; cited in Mies, *Patriarchy and Accumulation*, 92.

41. See discussions in Stephanie Urdang, *Fighting Two Colonialism Women in Guinea Bissau* (New York: Monthly Review, 1979); and, "Women in Contemporary National Liberation Movements," in *African Women: South of the Sahara*, Jean Hay and Sharon Stichter, eds. (New York: Longman, 1984), Mies, Ibid.; and Sylvester, "Some Dangers in Merging Feminist and Peace Projects."

42. Olivia Muchena, "Are Women Integrated Into Development?" *African Report*, v. 12, no. 2 (1983); Stephanie Urdang, "The Last Transition? Women and Development" in *A Difficult Road: The Transition to Socialism in Mozambique*, John Saul, ed., (London: Monthly Review, 1985).

43. Mies, *Patriarchy and Accumulation*, 233.

44. For more discussion of this example, see Sylvester, "Some Dangers of Merging Feminist and Peace Projects."

*Questions*

1. Why is the author ambivalent about the stars of "Cagney and Lacey"? Do you agree or disagree—and why?

2. What is your reaction to the author's opinion that "the power

relations of male supremacy seem timeless [but] . . . were socially created like other forms of colonialism"? Give instances of ways in which male dominance has been chipped away in this century.

3. The Supreme Court decision on abortion (Roe vs. Wade, 1973) can be seen as giving women some control over procreation, or as a device giving more business to (mostly male) physicians. What other interpretations might be given to this landmark case? Which strikes you as best—and why?

4. Robert's Rules of Parliamentary Procedure is given as an instance of preventing meetings from becoming "usefully disorderly." Do you agree or disagree—and why?

5. Which, if any, of the feminist strategies (liberal, Marxist, radical, socialist) seems to hold the best prospect of liberating women from oppression? Briefly describe the strategy that you think is the most promising.

# 4
# Planning for Economic Conversion

## Seymour Melman and Lloyd J. Dumas

This article originally appeared in *The Nation*, April 16, 1990.

*This is the era that Messrs. Melman and Dumas have been waiting for all their professional lives. For years they have insisted on the essentially wasteful nature of military spending, in economic terms. At long last—thanks to the collapse of the communist empire in Europe—they see an opportunity to redirect countless billions from guns to butter. And they underscore the necessity for such conversion if the United States is to recover its competitiveness in world markets.*

*In almost numbing detail, Melman and Dumas document the vastness of the military economic machine, its immunity to market forces, its lack of concern for cost-cutting and the fact that weapons contribute nothing directly to real national wealth. They describe the descent of America from a creditor to a debtor nation in a few short years, and to the tripling of the national debt since 1980.*

*But they see positive forces at work. Budget-balancing, in their opinion, "is simply a matter of fiscal reality." Competitiveness, too, has become a popular rallying cry, but the authors declare that civilian employees of the military require special assistance to retool. A third positive force for change is the loosening of the command economy, especially in the U.S.S.R., which faces similar and graver problems than the West.*

*The authors identify certain institutional and ideological barriers to economic conversion, but remain hopeful that these can be overcome.*

*Melman and Dumas do not underestimate the difficulty of retraining many of the six and a half million civilian and military personnel employed in more than thirty-five thousand factories, laboratories and bases. But, they conclude, a "peace dividend" is possible if the federal government makes careful plans and carries them out in a serious way.*

It's time to start planning the conversion of America's defense economy to civilian work. By conversion we mean political, economic and technical measures for assuring the orderly transformation of labor, machinery and other economic resources now being used for military purposes to alternative civilian uses. The political impetus for conversion is gaining momentum as a result of the relaxation of cold war tensions. Another stimulus to action is America's deteriorating competitive position in the world economy.

A major factor in America's decline to the status of a second-class industrial power has been the voracious appetite of the military-industrial complex, which employs 6.5 million civilian and military personnel in more than 135,000 factories, laboratories and bases. From 1947 to 1989 this country diverted to military purposes resources whose value exceeded the fixed reproducible, tangible wealth of the entire civilian economy. Tens of thousands of factories became virtual wards of the Pentagon; sheltered from the discipline of the marketplace, they adopted inefficient and costly methods. An indirect consequence of the larger share of tax dollars funneled into the military establishment was a diminution of public investment in the infrastructure and its resulting decay. The debilitating effect of all those developments on American industrial strength is readily apparent.

Labor productivity, a key indicator of long-term efficiency, has significantly declined. Between 1968 and 1988 labor productivity (measured by the dollar value of output per hour of workers in the nonagricultural business sector) rose by 24 percent, approximately one-third of the gain between 1948 and 1968.

In every year between 1894 and 1970 the United States ran a trade surplus—exporting more goods than it imported. In 1971 these surpluses turned into deficits. By 1987 the foreign trade deficit hit a peak of $170 billion, more than 160 percent above the record level set only four years earlier. "Made in the U.S.A." once meant well-made, high-quality, reasonably priced goods produced by industrial workers earning the highest wages in the world. Now U.S. trade deficits reflect in part a decline in quality and productive efficiency.

In 1982 the American economy plunged into its worst economic downturn since the Great Depression. By the end of the 1980s, however, the unemployment rate fell to more tolerable levels. Inflation remained well below the double-digit rates of the late 1970s. And the real gross national product grew more than 25 percent between 1982 and the third quarter of 1988, when it passed the $4 trillion mark.

Supposedly, the country is in the midst of the strongest economic recovery since World War II.

But that is an illusion. We have merely pumped up the economy with a huge infusion of public and private debt. This facade of prosperity is not based on the efficient production that drove the economy's remarkable growth throughout much of America's industrial history—an expansion whose benefits were spread among the population rather than going to one small segment of it at the expense of all the rest.

Between fiscal 1980 and fiscal 1989 the national debt more than tripled, from $914 billion to $2.8 trillion. In less than three years after 1985, the federal government added nearly $780 billion in debt, an amount equal to more than 85 percent of the *total* national debt as of 1980. State and local government debt, and the private debt of households and nonfinancial institutions, soared from nearly $3 trillion in 1980 to more than $6 trillion by September 1988. Between 1980 and 1987 the United States went from being the world's largest creditor nation, to whom $106 billion was owed, to being the world's largest debtor nation, with a net international debt approaching $400 billion.

All that borrowing served temporarily to paper over deep-seated economic problems, giving us a fleeting reprieve. But it has also created a "bubble of debt" on top of a steadily eroding economic base, adding the possibility of a sudden collapse to the continuing long-term deterioration in American economic performance.

## THE FORCES OF REAL RECOVERY

Despite these very serious problems, the end of the 1980s has brought some cause for optimism. Three powerful political forces have begun to develop that may just push the United States in the direction it needs to go to turn this downbeat picture around: the growing pressure to balance the federal budget, the increasing prominence of the competitiveness issue and the extraordinary opportunities created by *perestroika* and *glasnost* in the Soviet Union and Eastern Europe.

*Balancing the Budget.* The enormous increase in the national debt between 1980 and 1989 was clearly the result of the Reagan Administration's tax cuts combined with a military spending binge. Had the borrowing been in support of a major program of public investment in infrastructure, education and the like, it would not have been a great problem. Productive investment would have eventually generated more than enough additional wealth to pay back the borrowed money with interest. But unproductive use of the money for military expansion means that it must now be paid back out of existing wealth—and that will be painful.

Annual military budgets more than doubled during that period, and this accelerated spending accounted for more than 50 percent of the increase in national debt. The military-driven debt, in turn, led to a near tripling of the annual net interest on that debt, from $53 billion to $152 billion. Looked at differently, without this explosive increase in the national debt, the interest savings alone would have taken us two-thirds of the way to balancing the federal budget.

In the 1987 fiscal year, spending on the military and interest on the national debt accounted for almost 90 percent of all the federal income tax revenues collected from both individuals and corporations. In the absence of draconian tax increases or slashes in social programs greater than the public was willing to accept from the previous administration, significant cuts in the military budget are highly likely. Without them it will be impossible to balance the federal budget in the foreseeable future. This is not a question of ideology or political preference. It is simply a matter of fiscal reality.

*Competitiveness.* The fiscal pressures for cutbacks in military spending reinforce demands for the changes that are needed to rebuild American industrial competitiveness. More than forty years of high military spending has diverted from civilian industry the resources that are critical to efficient, competitive production, including roughly 30 percent of the nation's engineers and scientists and a comparable portion of its capital. Engineers and scientists trained to design and produce for cost-minimizing in civilian industry are the key to developing technology for better product designs and more efficient methods of production; capital allows these innovations to be put into use on the factory floor. The long-term drain of these resources has undermined the ability of U.S.-based factories to maintain competitive position, especially relative to those nations (Japan and Germany, for example) whose commercial industries are only lightly burdened by that drain.

To revitalize the competitiveness of American industry we must attack the structural causes of inefficiency. This can be accomplished in a solid, long-term way only by an infusion of capital and technical talent. That means redirecting a significant fraction of these critical resources from military to civilian research and production.

*Perestroika and Glasnost.* The remarkable changes in the Soviet

Union and Eastern Europe offer great promise of substantial arms reduction. We have seen only a beginning, but it is a hopeful one. The prospect of a 50 percent reduction in strategic nuclear arsenals— even talk of the total elimination of nuclear weapons within a decade or two—has moved from the realm of an impossible dream to the real world of negotiations. Progress toward reduction of conventional forces has begun.

Each of the three forces we have been discussing has its counterpart in the Soviet Union, which has finally admitted that it too is plagued by out-of-control budget deficits. The military's diversion of critical resources from the country's civilian industrial base has played no small part in rendering those industries hopelessly inefficient. At the same time, the attention of the nations of Western Europe has turned increasingly to economic integration rather than military adventurism. As far as the Soviet Union is concerned, this surely diminishes the threat to their security.

The convergence of these three forces in both the United States and the Soviet Union has made large-scale demilitarization an increasingly practical, attainable goal. And large-scale demilitarization is just what is needed to free sufficient resources for building healthy, growing economies in both nations.


## OBSTACLES TO CONVERSION

Nevertheless, there are strong institutional and ideological barriers to implementation of economic conversion. The most prominent of these are the managements in central government offices and the private firms that are dependent on the military economy. Government departments are ordinarily viewed as "bureaucracies"; however, the central management in the Defense Department that controls the operations of 35,000 prime contracting establishments is, functionally, a central administrative office. This central administrative office is probably the largest such entity in the world and performs the same functions as similar offices in large corporations.

Furthermore, the management of the Pentagon's central office controls the largest block of finance capital in the hands of any single American management. Every year since 1951 the new capital made available to the Defense Department has exceeded the combined net profits of all U.S. corporations. The top managers in the Pentagon and their subordinates are endowed with the usual managerial imperative to maintain and enlarge their decision-making power. Accordingly, they have consistently opposed all proposals for economic conversion planning in the United States.

This managerial opposition to conversion planning is not specific to any particular social structure, political ideology or management technique. Thus the managers of the U.S. military economy perform their command function via allocation of money resources, while those of the Soviet Union perform the command function by direct physical resource pre-emption and allocation. The results in each case are similar: pre-emption of major resources from civilian production and powerful pressures for operating in an unproductive, cost-maximizing way.

The work force and surrounding communities of factories, bases and laboratories that serve the military are another institutional barrier to economic conversion. In the United States 3.5 million men and women work in the military industry. An additional 1 million are employees of the Pentagon, including civilian workers on bases, and there are 2 million in the armed forces. For these 6.5 million people and their families and surrounding communities, the military-serving facilities have been the principal sources of jobs for most of their lives. The skills they have developed and the relationships with which they are familiar are powerful incentives to continue working for the military. The people in such enterprises know that even the appearance of an interest in the idea of economic conversion would bring the disfavor of the Pentagon's top managers.

The nation's organized engineering societies include large numbers of engineers beholden to the military economy. This has a significant effect on the contents of society meetings, the subject matter of journals and learned papers, and the network of contacts available for employment opportunity. At this writing no single engineering society has ventured to propose contingent conversion planning for its members as a way of coping with the possible reversal of military budget growth. In its November 1989 issue *Spectrum*, a journal of the Institute of Electrical and Electronics Engineers, published a special report titled "Preparing for Peace," a serious, courageous attempt to survey the military engineers' prospects during a subsiding cold war.

Finally, there are the universities, particularly the larger ones, which have grown accustomed to receiving major R&D grants from the Defense Department and to administering major research institutions, like the Lawrence Livermore and Los Alamos nuclear weapons laboratories, for the Pentagon. At the same time the departments of universities that might be expected to have some connection with civilian production, the engineering and business schools, have become less production-oriented during the long cold war period. Some schools are beginning to make an effort to reestablish the importance of civilian production in their curriculums, but the emphasis is small compared with the military-oriented research activities. The universities also contain large departments and schools—such as political science and international relations—whose faculties and curriculums have focused on training cold war technicians, researchers and administrators.

For all the personnel of the military-serving institutions it is significant that the knowledge for performing their tasks comprises their intellectual capital and work skills. Therefore a change to a civilian economy entails the obsolescence of intellectual capital and the necessity for learning new skills.

Alongside these direct economic ties to the military at the universities there are a number of ideological commitments that play an important part in sustaining support for military institutions. Among economists, for example, it is generally accepted that money equals wealth, that the proper measure of economic product is in money terms, that the money value of an economic activity denotes its value independent of the usefulness of the product. Military goods and services are thus counted as additions to real wealth despite the fact that they do not contribute to the central purpose of the economy—to provide the material standard of living. They add neither to the present standard of living (as do ordinary consumer goods) nor to the future standard of living by increasing the economy's capacity to produce (as do industrial machinery, equipment and the like).

Since the Great Depression, economists, and indeed the larger society, have defined the central problem of the U.S. economy as the maintenance of proper levels of market demand, and thereby of income and employment. From this perspective, expenditures that generate market demand are critical, regardless of the nature of the product. A consensus formed that military spending is the best way to accomplish this effect. Thus, most economics textbooks do not differentiate between firms producing military goods and civilian enterprises.

From these assumptions it is a short step to the idea that the United States is uniquely capable of affording guns *and* butter for an indefinite period of time. This belief has facilitated the acceptance of sustained negative trade balances and spreading incompetence in U.S. manufacturing. Large subsidies to the American standard of living in the form of trade imbalances are therefore considered normal, while the role of the military economy in causing a collapse of production competence is ignored. Nevertheless, domestic economic problems and international political changes compel attention to the feasibility of economic conversion.

## THE PROCESS OF ECONOMIC CONVERSION

The ideology of the free-market economy argues that the labor and facilities no longer needed in the military-serving sector will flow smoothly and efficiently toward an expanding civilian sector once military spending is cut. The market will take care of the transition. There is no need for special attention and certainly no need for advance preparation.

But this isn't true. The world of military industry is very different from the world of commercial industry. For one thing, military-serving firms do not operate in anything like a free-market environment. In the military production system, the nature, quantity and price of output are not determined by impersonal market forces. They are set by the interaction of the Pentagon's central planners and the managers of the military-industrial firms. Military industry, unlike any civilian industry, has only one customer—the Defense Department. Even when military firms sell to other nations, they typically sell products initially designed and produced to satisfy the needs of the Defense Department and can sell abroad only with its permission. Furthermore, the vast majority of defense contracts are negotiated rather than awarded through true price-competitive bidding.

More important, competition in the civilian commercial marketplace provides a crucial element of cost discipline that is largely absent in military industry. In practice, most major military contractors operate on a cost-plus basis, being reimbursed for whatever they have spent plus a guaranteed profit. In such an environment, there are no real penalties for inefficient production. In fact, company revenues can be increased by jacking up costs. Such cost escalation would spell bankruptcy for firms operating in a free market.

The sales function of a typical civilian company involves dealing with large numbers of potential customers, ranging from perhaps a few dozen for firms purveying industrial products to millions for consumer goods producers. For military firms the sales function means knowing the Armed Services Procurement Regulations, developing contacts within the Defense Department and being adept at lobbying. The most crucial job of managers in civilian industries is keeping costs down while producing good quality products. Managers in defense firms need pay relatively little attention to cost, but they must try to manufacture products capable of operating under extreme conditions while delivering every possible increment of performance.

It is not a question of one kind of management being easier or harder than the other. The point is that they are very different. It is simply not reasonable to expect a manager used to operating in one of these worlds to perform efficiently in the other without undergoing substantial retraining and reorientation. That takes time and will not happen automatically. Civilian firms may well prefer to hire inexperienced civilian managers instead of facing the costs involved in retraining an experienced military manager for civilian work. The same consideration holds for engineers and scientists—the other main component of the military-serving labor force—who would require substantial retraining and reorientation.

The products of military industry are notorious for their poor reliability, despite requirements that only components meeting stringent military specifications be used. These components are not only remarkably costly but also certified to withstand extraordinary extremes of shock, temperature and so on. Poor reliability is an unavoidable consequence of the increasing complexity of military weaponry. Thus sophisticated military aircraft have been in repair a third or more of the time. That's bearable when the cost of maintenance is not a limiting factor. But city transportation systems cannot accept vehicles that are "not mission capable" a third of the time. Hence, the retraining of military-experienced engineers and managers is an essential aspect of economic conversion. Of course, the physical facilities and equipment of military industry will require modification as well.

## PLANNING FOR CONVERSION

Advanced contingency plans for moving into alternative civilian-oriented activity could help carry the nation smoothly through the transition to a demilitarized economy and protect militarily dependent communities against the considerable economic disruption they will otherwise experience. The transformation of a facility and its work force to civilian production must be planned locally, by those who know them best—not by distant "experts." Even at its best such a planning process will be lengthy. A great many details must be worked through to insure that the transition is smooth and that the resulting facility and work force are properly restructured to be an efficient civilian producer, able to operate profitably without continuing subsidies. It is long past time to get this process under way.

*Questions*

1. What are two major reasons the authors give for the timeliness of economic conversion from military to civilian uses? Can you think of any others?

2. Why has productivity in the U.S. declined in recent years? What has military production had to do with it? What other factors have contributed to the slide in productivity?

3. Name three factors that are driving government leaders to take the idea of economic conversion seriously.

4. Identify as many influential groups as you can which would be expected to oppose the dismantling of military research and production. Do you agree with them? If not, how would you counter their arguments?

5. To what uses could the so-called "peace dividend" be put? What magnitude could it reach over the next decade? Do you think it will really happen? Why or why not?

# 5
# Militarism in America

## Staff of The Defense Monitor, #3, 1986

---

*The following essay turns away from superpower confrontation and argues that a permanent war psychology may be threatening the very freedoms the United States seeks to defend. It was written by the staff of a newsletter published by the Center for Defense Information, a Washington-based "think tank" which has been a voice of moderation in military spending since 1972. In this article, the authors point to the growing influence of the military establishment on U.S. domestic and foreign policy since World War II. Under the label of "national security," policy-making has shifted from civilian agencies and has been entrusted to the military. Besides reordering domestic priorities from civilian needs and adding significantly to the national debt, the Pentagon budget, in this view, has damaged America's high-tech industry and scientific endeavor.*

*The authors view with alarm the glorification of the military in American society, citing popular films and toys, advertising campaigns for military recruitment and a general loss of sensitivity to the dangers of using force to achieve national goals.*

*The article cites with concern the pervasiveness of the "military-industrial complex," about which President Eisenhower warned in 1961. With so many companies doing business with the military establishment, the authors envision a nation on a permanent war economy. Congressional representatives, eager to preserve their local military installation or factory, appear unresponsive to the need to limit the defense budget. Besides making allies in Congress, the Pentagon is depicted as a major force in hiding legitimate scientific achievements under the label of secrecy. According to this article, the efforts of too many engineers, scientists and university researchers have been harnessed to the nation's war machine. The authors also take aim at Reserve Officer Training Programs (ROTC) on campus and even in high schools as other instances of the "militarization of America."*

*The increasing sales of war toys in the past few years are another con-*

cern of the authors, as is the tremendous growth of pistols and automatic weapons in the hands of civilians.

The authors decry the impoverishment of civilian programs as a result of a bloated military budget. They call for what they consider more constructive methods to promote national interests through diplomatic, scientific, economic and cultural means.

Most Americans do not think of the United States as being particularly militaristic. We are not at war. Gun-toting soldiers do not patrol our streets. Young men are no longer drafted. In many ways, however, militarism pervades America.

Since 1945 the role of the military in American government and society has changed dramatically. Military issues have been given high priority in shaping American foreign and domestic policies. The militarization of our domestic political economy and everyday American society is an increasingly dangerous phenomenon that demands careful examination if we are to keep it in check.

In his Farewell Address to the American People in 1961, President Dwight D. Eisenhower warned Americans of the far-reaching effects of militarism when he said: "[The] conjunction of an immense military establishment and a large arms industry is new in the American experience.

"The total influence—economic, political, even spiritual—is felt in every city, every State house, every office of the Federal government. We recognize the imperative need for this development. Yet we must not fail to comprehend its grave implications. Our toil, resources and livelihood are all involved; so is the very structure of our society."

The Pentagon greatly influences America's foreign policy, domestic priorities, economy, and the nature of our government. The long established tradition of civilian control over the military is eroding as an increasing number of military men fill government positions previously held by civilians and our civilian leaders permit the military to play a greater role in policy-making.

Military concerns affect economic priorities nationwide. Hundreds of Billions of tax dollars are spent to support the largest peacetime military buildup in American history while social programs are cut, the debt becomes unmanageable and the probability of nuclear war increases.

In the post-WWII period military priorities have shaped American law and contributed to sweeping reorganization of the government. Defined almost exclusively in military terms, the abstraction of *"national security"* has been used to justify a broadening of the military's authority. More recently, *executive orders* and directives have been passed down from the White House taking policy-making power away from civilian agencies and entrusting it to the military.

America's lead in *high-tech* industry and the international scientific community is fading because of the reordering of national priorities to accommodate military requirements and rising levels of secrecy. Scholars and scientists are discouraged by far-reaching restrictions imposed in the interest of national security that prevent them from discussing their research with other scientists. Civilian resources—both intellectual and monetary—are being redirected to support programs like the Strategic Defense Initiative (Star Wars) that will yield few civilian benefits and commit the U.S. to even greater military spending.

America's increasing emphasis on the military as a means of maintaining and determining our position within today's complex world has many consequences for American society. Films like Rambo, Rocky IV, and Invasion U.S.A. urge the U.S. to impose America's will and establish world order through force. From Rambo to G.I. Joe, we are presented with the idea that Americans have the right to pursue military solutions so long as their convictions are strong and their arsenals well-stocked. Similarly, on the home front, aggressiveness and violence in society are more easily accepted as a normal means by which to achieve individual goals.

As paramilitary weapons, dress, jargon, and values are assimilated into everyday American life, we become desensitized to the dangers of employing force as a means of achieving our goals. Instead of viewing the growing influence of the military with a cautious and critical eye, we myopically see it as simply a sign of rekindled strength.

In subtle and provocative ways modern advertising calls to America's youth, portraying the Armed Services as a sort of large vocational institute offering opportunity and excitement, while calls for military reform and a definition of how U.S. forces fit in with overall national objectives remain unanswered. With new-found enthusiasm, universities and high schools across the country teach military values through the Senior and Junior Reserve Officer Training Corps. War toys and television initiate junior high and elementary school age children to state-of-the-art weaponry and military jargon.

The glorification of the military within American society has become a general trend in the United States—a trend which distorts our view of both foreign and domestic policy and raises serious concerns for the future of the democratic process in a stable, productive society.

The effects of militarism on foreign policy will be examined in a future *Defense Monitor*. This *Defense Monitor* details the rising trend of militarism in American society today and warns of the potentially dangerous consequences facing America if this trend remains unchecked.

## NATIONAL SECURITY STATE

• Following World War II, the U.S. carved the world up into military regions for purposes of military planning, putting a four star general or admiral in charge of each. No other country has divided the world up in quite this way.

• The National Security Act of 1947 created the National Military Establishment (now the Department of Defense), the Central Intelligence Agency (CIA), and the main national security decision-making body, the National Security Council (NSC). The Act officially introduced the catchall abstraction "national security" that has since served to justify everything from the procurement of questionable weapons systems to the invasion of Grenada.

• NSC-68, a document drafted by the NSC in 1950, identified the "Soviet threat" as the foundation upon which to build U.S. foreign and domestic policy. NSC-68 assured Americans that, "The integrity of our system will not be jeopardized by any measures, covert or overt, violent or non-violent, which serve the purposes of frustrating the Kremlin design. . . . " Unfortunately, American society *is* being challenged and its integrity threatened. Preoccupation with military responses to the Soviet Union and rhetoric that conjures images of the "enemy" and an "evil empire" promote militarism by overstating the need for more military power. The frustration Americans feel with regard to combatting terrorism further aggravates growing militarism and promotes vigilantism within the United States.

• The military services, DoD, and the defense industries presently employ some 6.5 million people in the United States, generating well over $146 Billion in business between the Pentagon and private companies each year.

• The U.S. now has nearly half a million military personnel abroad at more than 333 military installations in 21 different countries. The U.S. also has plans to come to the defense of over 50 nations.

**National security concerns are firmly entrenched and articulated in our foreign and domestic policies. Strong emphasis on "national security" is used over and over to justify unnecessary growth of the defense establishment.**

## PERMANENT WAR ECONOMY

• Preparing for war in peacetime has become big business in the U.S. In the 1940's, U.S. military production was carried out in an estimated 1,600 federally-owned plants. After WW II, the government relinquished direct power over production by contracting out to private firms. The government now owns only 72 defense production plants, 14 of which are on standby status.

• Over 30,000 companies are engaged in military production. Each day military agencies sign 52,000 contracts—more than 15 million a year.

• In FY85, America spent over 27% of all federal government expenditures on the military: nearly $1100 for each of its 234 million inhabitants. In contrast, the European NATO countries combined spent less than 10% of their government expenditures on the military, about $250 per person in a population of over 332 million.

• Companies not normally associated with defense have redirected their production in order to get a share of defense contracting dollars. Singer, IBM, Goodyear Tire, Motorola, AT&T, and Westinghouse are just a few companies which have crossed the line from civilian to military contracting. Some 80% of the Singer Company's revenues came from the firm's aerospace electronics business in 1985, compared to 15% ten years ago. Singer's nuclear-related contracts have included work on Trident and Pershing missiles, and simulators for the B-52 bomber.

• Today, close to 70% of every federal dollar allotted for Research and Development (R&D) goes to the military establishment. Since 1981 overall military research spending has increased by 62% above inflation, while funding for civilian research has decreased by 10%. Military R&D will rise to over $44 Billion in FY87.

• According to President Reagan's Commission on Industrial Competitiveness, over the past twenty years the U.S. has been losing ground in seven out of ten technology-oriented industries.

**Ever-expanding military spending weakens the ability of the U.S. to compete in world markets by concentrating our resources on military production instead of the development of civilian technology.**

## UNWARRANTED INFLUENCE

"In the councils of government, we must guard against the acquisition of unwarranted influence, whether sought or unsought, by the military-industrial complex." Dwight D. Eisenhower, 1961

• Out of 3,041 counties in the U.S., only nine received less than $1,000 in DoD funds in 1984. Hundreds of military bases and facilities are spread across the U.S. Because people focus on short-term economic benefits resulting from weapons production, the military is often invited into communities without careful examination and questioning of the real costs involved.

• Political Action Committee (PAC) contributions from the twenty largest defense contractors have increased by 225% since the early eighties, totaling $3.6 million during the 1984 campaign. Some $440,000 went to members of the Senate Armed Services Committee, which authorizes funds for military spending.

• The Pentagon influences Congress through a process called legislative liaison which allows the Pentagon to maintain a permanent, active, and costly military lobby on Capitol Hill at the taxpayer's expense. The Pentagon circumvents direct lobbying restrictions by such questionable practices as offering to pay for entertainment and trips to the Paris Air Show.

• Representatives and Senators often vote in favor of weapons built within their districts regardless of whether or not those weapons fit in with national objectives. In FY83, Defense Secretary Weinberger accused Congress of tacking nearly $3 Billion worth of unnecessary items onto the Pentagon budget in deference to constituent demands for jobs.

**Members of Congress often support DoD spending on weapons systems and military bases that provide their constituents with short-term economic benefits—benefits which are often incongruent with long-term national interests. PAC monies and legislative liaison push members of Congress to vote in support of weapons more for the number of jobs they will provide than for their effectiveness in defending the nation.**

## RISING SECRECY

• The Reagan Administration has made many attempts to restrict the flow of information from both the executive branch and the Pentagon to the public. Executive orders have been introduced which take away oversight powers from Congress, authorize the collection of "foreign intelligence" in the U.S., and challenge the integrity of academic freedom within the international scientific community.

• The Pentagon spends massive amounts of money each year on secret or "black" projects. The Department of Defense's FY87 budget request includes more than $22 Billion in secret funds, constituting a 300% increase in black funding since 1981. Huge secret projects include the Advanced Technology Bomber, a program whose total cost will be between $50 and $75 Billion, and the Advanced Cruise Missile program estimated to cost some $7 Billion.

• To date, two space shuttle missions have been classified in order "to deny our adversaries" information about satellite launches. No information was publicly disclosed on payloads, mission objectives, exact launching times or flight duration. Networks and newspapers were personally asked by Secretary of Defense Caspar Weinberger to suppress stories on secret space shuttle missions in the interest of national security. The National Aeronautics and Space Administration (NASA) estimates that military missions will make up 25-30% of all shuttle flights over the next decade.

• The Reagan Administration is classifying more documents in a misguided attempt to improve U.S. security. The "Preliminary Joint Staff Study on the Protection of National Secrets" reveals that in FY84 "the government classified 19,607,736 documents, a 9% increase over the previous year and a 60% increase from 1973." Nearly 4 million military, civilian and contractor personnel have security clearances, 164,000 of whom have been required to sign life-long legal contracts forbidding them to publish their views or "any information" relating to "intelligence." Instead of redefining the classification system, the Administration is weakening it by classifying more documents, censoring the work of government employees, and overemphasizing the importance of polygraph tests.

• Increased secrecy has greatly affected the press' ability to inform the public. In October 1983, the press was barred from reporting on military operations in Grenada. "It seems as though the reporters are always against us," Secretary of State George Shultz has said. "They're always seeking to report something that's going to screw things up." When asked, Shultz defined "us" as "Our side militarily—in other words, all of America." New practices requiring senior officials to obtain top-level approval before giving interviews indicate broader efforts to limit press coverage. All too often the information which the Administration seeks to suppress is already known to the Soviets through their intelligence system and satellites. Muzzling the press only leaves U.S. citizens in the dark.

**To ensure that exorbitant amounts of money are not misspent it is crucial that the public and Congress be kept well informed about military projects and that security concerns be weighed thoughtfully against the values of an open and democratic society.**

## EVER-EXPANDING PENTAGON POWERS

• Administration officials have overstated national security concerns and emphasized the need for broader Pentagon powers.

• In March 1984, President Reagan signed a directive extending DoD's powers to matters previously handled by the Department of Commerce. The Pentagon gained new authority to block the export of high-tech products (microelectronics, computers, and sophisticated instruments that could have military application) to 15 non-communist countries. The Commerce Department and many U.S. companies fear that Pentagon interference may delay "harmless" or non-controversial trade and thus needlessly handicap U.S. exports.

• DoD Directive 5525.5 establishes new ties between DoD, civilian law enforcement agencies, and the U.S. Customs Service. The Directive sets a dangerous precedent by directing the use of military equipment and personnel for the gathering of intelligence, and the apprehension of drug transporters and illegal aliens. Not since 1878 when the militia was separated from the Armed Forces by law has the military been so closely involved with the enforcement of civilian law.

• A National Security Decision Directive (NSDD-145) signed in September 1984 allows a steering committee—composed mainly of military officers, with National Security Agency Director Lieutenant General William Odom as committee head—access to computer data banks in over 1,000 federal departments, agencies, boards, and commissions. The Directive orders a complete restructuring of government computer systems, giving NSA and DoD broad powers to classify information that is security "sensitive" and to "encourage, advise, and where appropriate, assist the private sector" in identifying "sensitive non-government information, the loss of which could adversely affect the national security."

• A recent report issued by the National Academy of Sciences reveals that the Pentagon is more frequently citing national security concerns to determine which papers will be presented at scientific conferences and the direction of studies to be pursued in American universities. "The Defense Department has embarked on a course that—as patriotic and well-intentioned as it may seem—may threaten the technological supremacy of the U.S.," says Richard J. Gowan, ex-President of the Institute of Electrical and Electronic Engineers. The unnecessarily broad application of security measures discourages scientific research.

• The Pentagon has now been given broad statutory powers to withhold unclassified technical data when responding to Freedom of Information Act requests. Seven new classification categories have been established, making it harder to obtain information on military tests and contractor performance.

**In an effort to control espionage and leaks to the press, the Administration is giving DoD the power to restrict information to a degree which limits informed public debate on important military policies and programs. The Pentagon is gaining new authority in matters previously handled by civilian agencies, allowing the military to play an increasingly important role in determining foreign and domestic policy.**

## DoD ON CAMPUS

• Since WW II, approximately 42% of the U.S. scientific workforce has been employed in military-related projects. Today almost one-third of America's scientists and engineers are employed by the defense establishment.

• The Pentagon is pushing hard to expand its presence on campuses by calling for improved laboratory facilities and graduate and professor training programs designed to encourage scientists and engineers to undertake DoD research. In FY84, over 4,000 graduate students received Pentagon funding through university research programs. DoD has also devised a wide variety of new programs to interest undergraduate and high school students in working for the military.

• Universities are becoming more dependent on DoD as a source of funding and a provider of laboratory equipment that is not easily adaptable to non-military research. In 1983, DoD established a five-year, $150 million program to supply equipment for research of primary concern to the military. Under this program, over 650 grants have been awarded to 152 institutions located in 47 states, DC, Guam, and Puerto Rico.

• Universities now do about half of the Pentagon's basic research. Pentagon spending for basic research has grown by 217% over the past ten years, with an estimated $987 million going for basic research in FY87.

• Contracts involving Strategic Defense Initiative (SDI) research will add substantially to the growing military presence on campus. Universities pulled in some $206 million for SDI contracts in 1985, for a total of $254 million since 1983.

• "We're shaping research at the nation's universities in a line directed by the military," asserts physicist Vera Kistiakowsky from the Massachusetts Institute of Technology.

**Military research conducted through universities saps available resources for more widely applicable civilian research and allows military funding and objectives to determine academic priorities. Imposed levels of secrecy reduce the efficiency of scientific development and threaten academic integrity.**

## STUDENT SOLDIERS

• Recruiters are targeting high school and college students with newfound zeal. Packaging the military as a leadership training program, DoD is pushing hard to increase the number of students recruited.

• In the Junior Reserve Officer Training Corps (JROTC) students as young as 14-years-old are instructed in military theory, the use of firearms, and military history. Students are taught to follow orders and unquestioningly accept a military curriculum which does not adequately prepare them for careers outside of the military. JROTC units may also participate in war simulations or undergo forms of basic training.

• At present 227,448 students participate in JROTC in over 1,375 high school units across the nation, up from 287 twenty years ago. In FY86 DoD's $52.1 million budget for JROTC bought texts, arms, and uniforms while schools were expected to provide a portion of the instructors' salaries, drill areas and classroom facilities with ample storage space for arms.

• With increasing college tuition and a decreasing number of non-DoD scholarships available, more students—especially women and minorities—are joining the Senior Reserve Officer Training Corps (ROTC). Senior ROTC is active in 530 college detachments and involves 110,872 students, up 50% from 1975.

• Skills learned in the Armed Services are difficult to market outside of the military due to differences between military and civilian applications. A study conducted at Ohio State University in 1985 concluded that only 12% of men and 6% of women in a sample study could easily transfer their skills from the military to the civilian work force.

• Although recruiting quotas have been met with great success since 1981, the Pentagon is waging an aggressive recruiting campaign which will cost the taxpayer $1.8 Billion in FY86, with advertising budgets alone totaling over $216 million. In 1985 the Army paid roughly $4,000 in recruiting costs for each new recruit.

• Recruiters promise students the opportunity to pick up valuable career skills but statistics compiled by the Defense Department's Manpower Data Center state otherwise. In 1983 only 17% of Army jobs required high-tech skills while less technical jobs, such as general infantry duties, accounted for close to 50%.

• Recruiters make use of referrals, phone books, and high school yearbooks to fill quotas. Schools are legally required to supply lists of graduates in 18 states. The distribution of literature and visits by recruiters are largely unregulated with over 15,000 military personnel working to recruit—roughly one for every 185 high school seniors in the public school system.

• The Armed Services Vocational Aptitude Battery Test (ASVAB) has been administered in at least 14,000 schools nationwide. The test provides recruiters with information on student qualifications and aptitude for military service. Students are frequently led to believe that the test is mandatory and are often uninformed as to how test results are used in the recruiting process.

• The services have gone to slick Madison Avenue-type advertising techniques to make the military an alluring and sexy career option. For example the Pentagon spent $60,000 to make a rock video featuring breakdancing to encourage registration for the Selective Service. The Army's Recruiting Support Command has another new gimmick in mobile units that have visited over 2,000 schools in 1984. Students are shown films about the Army and pressed to sign up for more information.

• Currently, 66 Civilian Aides to the Secretary of the Army act as recruiters and "good will ambassadors" for the military. Civilian Aides are influential members in communities who use their positions and contacts with the press to convince communities of the need for a larger military.

**After being presented with a glamorous picture of the military, high school students are persuaded to make the military a career before being made aware of other career options available to them. School officials and parents have little or no control over course content yet are expected to help fund ROTC and JROTC programs at a time when other extracurricular funding is being cut.**

## RAMBOMANIA

• A spate of violent, militaristic films are developing cult followings, bringing military language, gear, and dress into vogue. Anti-Soviet films, commercials, and advertisements contribute to the perception that the Russians are a dehumanized enemy and that we are superior to them in every way.

• In its first 23 days "Rambo: First Blood Part II" grossed $75.8 million at the box office—a success topped only by two other films in history.

• Rambo spin-offs have flooded the market with some 25 companies negotiating distribution rights to Rambo-related merchandise. Rambo trivia games are broadcast on the radio and Sylvester Stallone lookalikes have made a business of delivering "Rambograms." The U.S. Army displays Rambo posters outside recruitment stations to encourage young people to sign up. The President is even caught up in Rambomania. "Boy, I saw Rambo last night," he commented, "Now I know what to do the next time this [terrorist seizure of hostages] happens."

• The Coleco Company, best known for its Cabbage Patch dolls, is marketing a new Rambo doll, claiming that "the character is emerging as a new American hero, a hero that has a high degree of excitement and patriotism and a thirst for justice associated with him."

• Militaristic films like Red Dawn, Commando, Missing In Action, Iron Eagle, and Invasion U.S.A. fuse chauvinism with righteousness to promote vigilantism.

**American films and fads promote a sort of war hysteria that desen-**

sitizes Americans to the gravity of military action as a means of foreign policy. Such films trivialize the use of force and promote the false idea that American might is always right.

## TV AND TOYS-*ARE*-US

• Sales of war toys in the U.S. have increased 600% since 1982, making the war toys industry worth over $1 Billion in 1985. More than 218 million war toys and accessories were sold in 1985, roughly five for every child in the U.S.

• The major toy companies have joined forces with television producers to air cartoons featuring war toys. The number of cartoon series publicizing such toys jumped from zero in 1983 to ten in 1985.

• According to the National Coalition on Television Violence, the average American child is now exposed to 250 cartoons with war themes, and 800 television advertisements for war toys a year.

• While G.I. Joe and his team battle "jungle-dwelling guerrillas dedicated to totalitarian world takeover" on TV, Joe is muscling his way onto the breakfast table with his new cereal, G.I. Joe Action Stars.

• Other action figures like "HeMan" and "SheRa, the Princess of Power" promote victory through force. "Transformers," robots, and dolls with names like Ripsaw, Flashfists, Twinblade, Slice, and Clawgut come equipped with multiple machine guns, particle-beam cannons, and nuclear-powered laser guns.

• By the age of sixteen, the average child will have watched some 20,000 hours of TV, taking in 200,000 acts of violence and 50,000 attempted murders—33,000 of which will involve guns.

• A report from The Center for Media and Public Affairs, in which 500 television programs were monitored over the past thirty years, documents a noticeable shift towards the use of military-style assault weaponry. Popular television series like the "A-Team" and "Miami Vice" promote the use of guns as necessary for survival.

**Television programs and war toys introduce Americans to military jargon, tactics, and weaponry from a very early age, teaching war in the spirit of play.**

## UNDER THE GUN

• America is the largest producer of firearms in the world and has the weakest gun control laws of any western democracy. Americans now own 35–40 million pistols and revolvers and over 100,000 registered machine guns. The number of people licensed to sell machine guns has tripled since 1980.

• There are an estimated 500,000 unregistered military-style assault guns owned in the United States.

• The sale of semi-automatic machine guns, which require a separate trigger pull for each shot fired, remains completely unregulated by federal law despite an increasing number of criminal incidents involving this type of gun. Semi-automatics can be easily converted into automatic weapons capable of firing up to 1,200 rounds per minute. Such conversions are on the rise, making illegal, unregistered machine guns accessible to the public and more difficult for police to trace.

**Due to increased firepower, easier concealment, and greater availability, military-style assault weapons may soon replace the handgun as the weapon of choice on American streets. Gun control laws have not been revised to effectively regulate the flood of military weapons into the civilian market.**

## WAR GAMES PEOPLE PLAY

• In 1981, National Survival Inc. came out with a game that allows Americans to translate their fascination with guns into action. With approximately 600 playing fields, air gun games with names like Skirmish, Combat Zone, and the Ultimate Game are sweeping the United States. The game lasts approximately two hours, costs $20–$25, and provides the thrill of a man-hunt for over 50,000 Americans each week. Players capture the other team's flag then retreat to their camp, gunning down members of the opposing team with air guns that shoot paint pellets.

• Shooting galleries, once limited to penny arcades, are now in vogue in the U.S. But instead of using fake rifles to shoot plastic ducks, Americans today are using high-powered automatic machine guns to blast away at "commie pins" (bowling pins painted red) and posters of the Ayatollah Khomeini. These shooting galleries, largely unregulated by federal law, introduce people to the sense of power achieved by blazing away with Uzis, MAC-10s, and other paramilitary weapons.

• A new category of guns is capturing the market. Pistols, shotguns, and an impressive line of paramilitary guns can now be purchased in the form of "soft airguns." The guns look like the "real McCoy" but shoot plastic munitions and eject fake shells.

• According to the Federal Bureau of Investigation (FBI) 16 American survivalist camps now provide "differing types of programs to include firearms, martial arts, survivalist techniques and paramilitary training."

Paramilitary, survivalist and mercenary camps are presently operating in at least eleven states.

• Two schools in Michigan and Alabama have been described by the FBI as legal paramilitary schools. Known as the Mercenary Association, the schools train students in the use of firearms, guerrilla and counter-guerrilla operations, planning, tactics, logistics, armed and unarmed combat, land navigation, and other military instruction, and provide "information to their graduates regarding foreign employment in security and mercenary positions abroad."

• Frank Camper's Alabama mercenary school received a great deal of attention when a Sikh graduate of the course put his skills to test in a plan to assassinate Indian Prime Minister Rajiv Gandhi. Camper says his goal is "to train mercenary soldiers in international weapons and combat techniques and do it far better than the US Army Ranger School did. We lost the war in Vietnam. Maybe I keep fighting these wars because we lost our war there. Maybe if we had won, I could have stopped."

• Magazines like *Soldier of Fortune, SWAT, International Combat Arms*, and *Firepower* publicize mercenary camps as the place to learn or perfect survival skills before traveling to actual "hot spots" of armed conflict such as Central America or Angola. Over 500,000 people subscribe to magazines put out by the Omega Corporation, the company that publishes *Soldier of Fortune.*

• *Soldier of Fortune's* founder and current editor, Robert K. Brown, asserts: "We have been the innovators in private-sector aid to resistance groups. We were the initiators. It goes back to sending a training team to Afghanistan in the fall of 1980. Then we got involved down in Salvador in early 1983 . . . For the immediate future we'll focus on El Salvador and assisting the Nicaraguan insurgents."

**War simulations, machine gun ranges, and paramilitary magazines and camps introduce the average citizen to high-tech weapons and war tactics. War is associated with fun and sport, a connection which oversimplifies and desensitizes Americans to the grave consequences of using military force as a tool of diplomacy.**

## CONCLUSIONS

• Militarism is on the rise in the United States. While a strong military posture is essential, overemphasis on military power within the government and American society undermines our strength as a nation and jeopardizes the democratic process in the United States.

• Huge and increasing amounts of money support military programs while civilian programs are under-funded or eliminated altogether. This diversion of resources to the military threatens the American values our military is supposed to defend.

• Military concerns dominate America's foreign and domestic policies and its economy. Americans are persuaded to accept and support military actions instead of pursuing more constructive methods to promote U.S. interests through diplomatic, economic, scientific, and cultural means.

## Questions

1. Do you think that America is pervaded by militarism? Give your reasons. Can you think of any opposing facts or arguments?

2. Is the government's emphasis on "national security" a legitimate response to espionage or an excuse to keep vital information from the people? What relationship do you see between the military (defense) budget and the funding available for domestic needs? Do you think the government's present policies are justified? Why, or why not?

3. Is the Pentagon too deeply involved on college campuses, through research projects and ROTC programs? Is there anything inherently wrong with the military services using advertising techniques ("Madison Avenue") to spur recruitment?

4. How closely related are Pentagon policies to the increase in automatic weapons, war toys and the growth of paramilitary schools?

5. What can the average citizen or student do to make sure that the U.S. does not become a highly militarized society? Give examples.

6
# A Declining Empire Goes to War

## Paul Kennedy

This article originally appeared in *The Wall Street Journal*, January 24, 1991.

---

*Paul Kennedy, professor at Yale and author of* The Rise and Fall of the Great Powers, *takes vigorous issue with the belligerent editorial policy of* The Wall Street Journal.

*He holds up to ridicule the argument that the United States needed a victory to recover its self-esteem. Against this proposition, he proposes the reluctance of the Founding Fathers to engage in "entangling alliances." As an historian, he finds an apt example in seventeenth century Spain to press his argument.*

*With a declining economic base, dependence on foreign manufacture, an archaic tax structure and beggary and homelessness at home, King Philip IV seeks in war to restore his country's declining reputation—and with predictable results: after several decades of warmaking, the long, slow slide into backwardness begins.*

*Kennedy is quick to assert that the parallel is not exact. But, he reminds his editors, there are enough similarities to make a thoughtful observer think twice. Who can argue with the truism that a strong economic base, financial stability and a secure social fabric mean more to a nation's greatness than victories on the battlefield? In the euphoria following the "ten-day war" against Saddam Hussein's Iraq, a great number of Americans seem to have overlooked the lessons of history.*

*The author calls for the U.S. to seek a balance between its capacities and its obligations. Among those obligations, he places the rebuilding of the nation's inner cities, strengthening its public education and repairing its crumbling superstructure far ahead of "reported distant glories in war."*

Over the past five months this paper has offered many justifications for its strong support of America's decision to fight Saddam Hussein, and with the largest and most impressive display of force possible.

But perhaps the most remarkable new argument from the Journal came just a few days ago in its editorial of Jan. 18, "A Declining Power." The reported early successes against Iraqi forces, the wizardry of American military technology, the firmness and "moral courage" of the president in ordering the attack, would all help—so the editorialists hoped—to break the mood of self-doubt and defeatism that has existed among the country's elites since the 1960s. In proving that the U.S. was not a declining power suffering from "imperial overstretch," the easy battlefield victories in the Middle East might thus allow the nation to recover its self-esteem. Well, well.

We have come a long way since the Founding Fathers warned their countrymen against overseas entanglements, but whatever reasons were given for American interventions in earlier wars of this century—protecting freedom of the seas, responding to Pearl Harbor, stopping North Korean aggression—I do not think that the recovery of America's lost self-esteem was one of them.

To the historian of international politics, however, this reasoning has a very familiar and disturbing ring to it. For example, anyone dipping into the relevant chapters of John Elliott's masterly biography "The Count-Duke of Olivares" will discover Philip IV's great minister frequently justifying Spain's distant military interventions of the 1630s and 1640s on the grounds of "reputation."

## "THE GREATEST VICTORY OF OUR TIMES"

True, there were many other reasons—strategic, dynastic, support of faithful allies—and most of them could be advanced at the same time, as occurred in 1634 and 1635 when fresh armies of Spanish troops were sent across Europe to aid their beleaguered Austrian Habsburg cousins during the Thirty Years' War. But behind such deployments—which were just as impressive, with allowance made for time and technology, as the recent dispatch of U.S. forces to Saudi Arabia—there was also Olivares's firm belief that victories in the field would confound the domestic and foreign critics who spoke of Spain's decline.

When the news of the first battlefield success (at Noerdlingen, in September 1634) reached Madrid, therefore, Olivares declared it to be "the greatest victory of our times." Once again, Spain had proved its detractors wrong; because of its military prowess, it was still number one in international affairs.

Yet if one glanced at the non-military dimensions of power, a different picture emerged. Spain's industries had become less and less competitive, and it increasingly relied upon foreign manufacture. Vested interests fought, all too successfully, against any diminution of privilege and against all proposals to amend an inefficient and archaic tax structure. The social fabric was torn; beggars, unemployed laborers, the homeless, could be seen in city streets, while rural poverty was widespread. Above all, the country's debts were increasing from day to day, and Olivares was finding it ever more difficult to borrow from foreign bankers—or to get Spain's allies to share the burdens of war—so that the more the military operations continued, the more the country went into the red. Nevertheless, Madrid felt that the borrowings would have to continue, for without them the military endeavors would fade, and with it Spain's own reputation. And so, the show went on—for another few decades.

Before the critics rush in to declare that Bush's America is not Philip IV's Spain, let me hasten to agree with them; of course it is different, just as every nation and century are different. But the point of this historical analogy is to remind readers what the theory of "imperial overstretch" is really about. Essentially, it rests upon a truism, that a power that wants to remain number one for generation after generation requires not just military capability, not just national will, but also a flourishing and efficient economic base, strong finances and a healthy social fabric, for it is upon such foundations that the country's military strength rests in the long term. The latter phrase is a critical one, and not well understood by those who think only of the present.

In those controversial pages of "The Rise and Fall of the Great Powers" that discuss the American condition, I observed that if the country allows a gap to open up between its capacities and its many obligations, it "runs the risk . . . of what might roughly be called 'imperial overstretch.' " Logically, therefore, it can seek to avoid that risk.

## THE 'DECLINE DEBATE'

So much of the "decline" debate seems to be obsessed with where America is now; hence, no doubt, the rejoicings by this paper's editors at the way in which current military successes supposedly prove that the U.S. is not "a declining power." My own concern is much more with the future, a decade or more down the road, if the trends in national indebtedness, low productivity increases, mediocre educational performance and decaying social fabric are allowed to continue at the same time that massive American commitments of men, money and materials are made in different parts of the globe. Like the late Victorians, we seem to be discovering ever-newer "frontiers of insecurity" in the world that we, the number one power, feel impelled to guard.

I do not want the U.S. to follow the path of imperial Spain and Edwardian Britain; but it is no use claiming that America is completely different from those earlier great powers when we are imitating so many of their habits—possessing garrisons and bases and fleets in all parts of the globe and acting as the world's policeman on the one hand, running up debts and neglecting the country's internal needs on the other.

The dilemma that the U.S. faces during the next decade in achieving a proper balance between ends and means—thus avoiding "imperial overstretch"—is awkward enough. But the last thing that is needed is for its people to be encouraged to seek its self-esteem on the battlefield. If the U.S. wishes to recover its "reputation," it might begin by repairing its inner cities, public education, crumbling infrastructure and multiple social needs, at the same time resisting the temptation to follow the path of Spanish grandees. The "sense of self-confidence and self-esteem" that Americans desire to see restored would be more appropriately felt in a democracy like this one if it rested upon evidence of the nation's health and strength rather than upon reported distant glories in war.

*Questions*

1. Why were the editors of *The Wall Street Journal* so enthusiastic about "teaching Hussein a lesson"? What lessons do you draw from this editorial approach?

2. What ways other than foreign wars does a nation have to recover its self-esteem? Give several positive and negative examples.

3. Do you think the similarities between the U.S. and seventeenth century Spain outweigh the differences? State your reasons, pro or con.

4. The author cites in passing the example of Edwardian Britain. What cataclysm followed for England in the early twentieth century? And with what results for the Empire?

5. Does Professor Kennedy's call for internal reform strike you as isolationism or as a prudent balancing of capacities and obligations? Give your reasons.

7
# Conscience and War

*Joseph J. Fahey*

---

*The military draft habitually falls upon eighteen-year-olds who are poorly equipped to respond to it in an informed manner. The following considerations, by the director of the Peace Studies Program at Manhattan College, serve as an introduction to the range of options available to young people when conscription is imposed.*

*The formation of conscience is a complex process, involving some scientific knowledge of human nature and depending a great deal on the words and example of "educators" (almost anyone in a position to exert influence).*

*As conscience relates to whether one will serve in a particular war, the author outlines the three fundamental responses, which are as ancient as human history itself.*

*Although these responses are highly schematic, they provide a valuable outline for anyone striving to form a right conscience. Emphasis in most democratic countries centers on the just war vs. pacifist positions. But many modern wars involve totalitarian states, in which Total War is the unquestioned order of the day. Serious reflection on these three widely differing attitudes can be helpful to anyone who wishes to answer the questions: (1) What is my attitude toward war? and (2) If called upon to serve, could I conscientiously assist my country in the prosecution of this war?*

In the event of a national military draft, young people will have to examine their conscience to make a personal decision whether they will obey their government's order to serve in the military forces. Each man and woman must decide whether war is a moral or an immoral activity and whether his or her conscience will permit him or her to serve in this particular war.

## THE PATH TO CONSCIENCE

Conscience is the innate ability to distinguish between that which is morally good, bad, and indifferent. Since conscience is more an "ability" than a fact, a great deal of education is necessary before one can have what is called a "correct" or "authentic" conscience. One must examine, for example, the nature of morality itself along with the moral nature of a specific act or command.

Many hold that morality is synonymous with authentic human behavior so that it may be stated that an moral act is a human act while an immoral act is an inhuman one. Morality must, therefore, be based on the scientific examination of human nature. An authentic conscience must be founded on the arts and sciences of biology, anthropology, history, psychology, philosophy, sociology, religion, literature, and politics. Educators are our guides to conscience. Contemporary educators include parents, teachers, films, magazines, politicians, television news, music, advertisers, religious leaders, and, of course, our friends.

Consequently, the formation of an authentic conscience is a highly complex process which demands a great deal of study on the part of an individual before he or she can make a sound decision on such a serious matter as participation in war.

## THREE KINDS OF RESPONSE

How does one follow the dictates of conscience in regard to war? History can be our guide here since the question of participation in—and resistance to—war is at least six thousand years old. Historically, there have been three broad responses to the question of conscience and war: total war, just war, and pacifist. Each position will be discussed in turn.

**I. Total War.** There have always been individuals who believe that the purpose of war is the absolute annihilation of their enemies. Participation in war is a glorious activity, and the warrior holds a very high social status in a society which is in a permanent state of military preparedness. This type of response to war holds that:

(1) human society is in a perpetual state of war;

    (2)  war is a natural and morally praiseworthy human activity;

    (3)  war is the normal instrument of national policy and may be used as a first resort in a crisis;

    (4)  offensive wars are morally legitimate;

    (5)  total victory justifies the possession and use of atomic, biological, and chemical weapons of mass destruction;

    (6)  the killing of civilians is justified (and sometimes desired) as a means to victory;

    (7)  civilian and military commanders can expect unquestioning obedience of their soldiers;

    (8)  the war must end in absolute victory in which the losing party must surrender unconditionally;

    (9)  national security states must be formed which have a mandatory military draft and a permanent military/industrial/university complex for the research and development of new weapons systems.

Today, some nation states presume that their citizens follow most of the total war principles. Nations ask no "proof" for this kind of conscience and will demand that their soldiers strictly follow all orders to execute a war in which whole civilian populations are sometimes considered to be legitimate targets. Those who are asked to serve in the military can expect that killing—or being killed—without question and without limits will be strictly required of them.

*Military Service:* A person with a "total-war" conscience can serve in any branch of the military although he or she may prefer to serve in those forces which employ weapons of mass personal and ecological destruction—atomic, biological, and chemical weapons. There are no restrictions on the quality and quantity of weapons to be used in a war.

**II. Just War.** Throughout history some have held that war must be limited in its objectives and that strict rules must be followed both before going to war and after a war has started. The just war principles presume that war is not natural to human beings but war may be necessary due to the evil and perversity which exists in human nature. Hence, the burden of proof is on national leaders to demonstrate to their citizens that a given war is necessary.

The following are the widely regarded rules which must be followed:

(1) Just Cause. Citizens may engage in a war only to defend the innocent. Offensive wars are not permitted.

(2) Legitimate Authority. Only those duly constitutionally authorized may declare a war if it is to be legitimate. In the United States this power is exclusively reserved to the Congress.

(3) Right Intention. Total victory must not be the goal of the war but rather the restoration of injured rights.

(4) Last Resort. All nonviolent methods must be exhausted before a war can legitimately begin. This includes boycotts, mediation, arbitration, diplomacy, and the activity of international institutions such as the United Nations and the World Court.

(5) Probability of Success. There must be a reasonable and measured hope that injured rights will be restored without disproportionate damage to any resulting peace. A war may not be fought if it is probable that the evil results will outweigh the desired good.

(6) Just Conduct. Innocent civilians may not be objects of military action. The war is to be strictly limited to combat between opposing soldiers, and even then not all weapons are permitted (such as atomic, biological, and chemical weapons).

(7) Proportionality. A war ceases to be just when it becomes evident that the evil actually committed outweighs the expected good. Proportionality always demands that any surrender will recognize legitimate conditions for surrender proposed by the losing nation.

Many experts hold that all of these conditions must be met before a nation may engage in war. Hence, national leaders must carefully demonstrate to their citizens that the war has limited objectives and that its evil consequences will not outweigh the good to be achieved by war. A soldier may not be asked to kill civilians and her or his conscience must be respected if she or he refuses to follow an immoral command. Above all, there is a **prima facie** moral duty to demonstrate that all nonviolent methods have been used prior to going to war.

*Military Service:* A person with a "just war" conscience can serve in the military but he or she may use only those weapons which guarantee discrimination between soldiers and civilians. Hence, only traditional "small arms" weapons may be used, consequently restricting military service largely to a traditional infantry unit.

**III. Pacifism.** Pacifism and "nonviolence" are—in Gandhi's words—"as old as the hills." Pacifism is found in almost every culture and civilization and its proponents are even found in nations which are highly militaristic in nature. Pacifism (which originates in the Latin "peacemaker") has the following characteristics:

(1) war is an unnatural and immoral human social institution;
(2) evil must be resisted but only the methods of nonviolent resistance are morally legitimate;
(3) the 4,000 plus methods of nonviolence provide a more than adequate "arsenal" of defense to restore violated rights;
(4) nonviolence is a spiritual weapon which seeks the reconciliation—not the extinction—of enemies;
(5) nonviolent resistance and sanctions are based on the power of love to convert one's opponent;
(6) pacifism seeks a win/win solution to a conflict rather than the win/lose strategy of war;
(7) a world juridical community must be formed which will outlaw war and use nonviolent sanctions to prevent war.

Pacifism has largely been disregarded or ignored in our history books. Perhaps this is because many cultures and nation states make a close connection between virility and violence and because national leaders are no more schooled in the science of peacemaking than is the kindergarten child in basic arithmetic. Consequently, the pacifist can expect to be ridiculed and even persecuted for her or his beliefs.

*Military Service:* Under no circumstances may a pacifist serve in a military combat unit. Some pacifists choose to serve in the military but in a strictly non-combat capacity such as a medic or chaplain's assistant. Should a draft be reinstated, a pacifist—or conscientious objector (CO)—will have to document her or his beliefs in order to receive an exemption from military service. The CO will also be required to perform alternative national service in wartime.

It behooves parents, teachers, political leaders, and members of the press and media to explore with our young people the range of conscientious responses they have available to them regarding participation in war. Young people need to know how to form a conscience and what steps to take to insure that his or her conscience is followed.

And, in addition, it is incumbent on citizens of every age to examine the national conscience.

*Questions*

1. How does the author define "conscience"? From your own reflection, the dictionary or other sources, how would you modify this definition?

2. Summarize the steps you have gone through in the formation of your own conscience, especially in relation to the use of violence against another.

3. Which of the three attitudes toward war do you think is dominant in the United States today? Do you share that attitude? Why, or why not?

4. Ethical or moral action has been described as a process of "line drawing." Where would you draw the line if you were called on to fight for your country?

5. Describe the role of public opinion in the formation of a national conscience toward war. List various ways in which you could contribute to a national debate on the morality of a particular war.

8

# ROTC Today and Tomorrow

## Col. Robert F. Collins

This article originally appeared in *Military Review*, May 1986.

---

*A spirited defense of the Reserve Officer Training Corps (ROTC) is offered by an Army colonel involved in campus recruitment. He decries the low priority given to these programs by senior army leadership, especially in view of the fact that three-quarters of all officers enter the Army by this route.*

*Far from contributing to the "militarization of America," Collins regards ROTC programs as the best guarantee that the services will not be run by "a highly specialized, rigid, elitist group of mercenaries." He sees ROTC officers, drawn from a representative portion of American society, as a contribution to the ideal of "citizen soldiers."*

*The author argues for more funding for ROTC and for promotion of its graduates on an equal level with those who graduate from the military academies. His concluding argument draws on the experience of Vietnam, when the American people did not support what the military was doing. To ensure popular support for future conflicts, he feels that ROTC, as a civilian-based program, will play a critical role. The program, as Col. Collins pictures it, is "the presence of the university in the military," rather than vice versa.*

The Reserve Officers' Training Corps (ROTC) is the lifeblood of the Army officer corps. It is critical to the nation's security, but the senior Army leadership today does not appear to properly value the contribution ROTC makes to the Army's mission.

Currently, ROTC commissions approximately 75 percent of all officers entering the Army—an incredible statistic. Three out of every four new lieutenants entering the Army are products of this program. Last year, approximately 8,300 college graduates were commissioned from ROTC programs offered at more than 1,400 colleges and universities throughout the nation.

But, public support of ROTC is not a given, nor is continued high enrollment in the program guaranteed. ROTC has received increased in-

86

terest by the news media. Most of the articles are factual, objective and balanced, but there are also opinions questioning the presence of ROTC in civilian universities.

For various reasons, the authors challenge the need for a strong military, the "militarization" of American society, the military-industrial complex, the nuclear arms race, terrorism, Department of Defense contracting abuses, mounting deficits, and so forth. They somehow relate these issues to ROTC or, more generally, to the Army or the current administration. In my view, not only is the US military one of the brighter components of our democratic success story, but ROTC is one of the strengths of our democratic form of government.

Laying aside arguments on the size of the military, percentage of the gross national product for defense, minimalist versus maximalist theories of deterrence, and so forth, the bottom line is—whom do we want to lead our Army? Do we prefer a highly specialized, rigid, elitist group of mercenaries schooled only in military tactics who will react unquestioningly and unthinkingly to all orders no matter what they might be? Or do we prefer to entrust the leadership of our young men and women to well-educated, idealistic, questioning and responsible college graduates representative of all sectors of society?

Do we not prefer a citizen-soldier-led Army with a small professional career group of officers providing guidance and direction to those citizen-soldiers? Do we not want our military to be strengthened by the constant infusion of bright young men and women who serve a limited time on active duty and then return to the civilian community with a better understanding of this nation's security needs? Both common sense and history tell us that the larger interests of a free society are best served by military officers who are drawn from the society they serve, share its values, are broadly representative of the best that is in us, reflect the richness of our diverse origins and are committed to the great and common purposes of our nation.*

The vast majority of the people commissioned by ROTC will not make the Army a career, but they will serve their country honorably on active duty for a short period and then return to civilian life. They bring new ideas, new perspectives and a productive vitality to our Armed Forces. They return to civilian life, perhaps to continue to serve in the Reserve

---

*Dewitt C. Smith Jr., "To Protect a Free Society: Maintaining Excellence in the Military." *Educational Record*, Winter 1985. Lieutenant General Smith is rightly regarded as one of the nation's leading soldier-statesmen. He has been a most eloquent military spokesman on the importance of the Reserve Officers' Training Corps (ROTC). My views on ROTC have been strongly influenced by Smith's writings and conversations with him about ROTC.

components, having gained leadership experience, managerial skills, a sense of responsibility and service, and tremendous self-confidence. This pool of leadership will serve our country well in the event of a national emergency. Who else can better defend the country?

ROTC is vital to our security in another way. Effective military leaders, supported by both the troops and the public, are absolutely essential if the United States is to prevail in any future conflict. For a variety of reasons, the American public, historically and today, views the military with skepticism, mistrust and sometimes open hostility. Officers operating in this environment are called upon to understand and support the liberal values and traditions of society while nurturing and safeguarding the controls established in the US Constitution.

US officers undeniably must be different from those in other societies in outlook, commitment, perspective, responsibility, obligation and approach. Here is the main strength of ROTC—it prepares officers who are varied in perspective and representative of our entire society. No other system for selecting the majority of our military leaders can work as well as ROTC. Actions associated with the Total Army concept—Active Army, Army National Guard and US Army Reserve—strengthen the importance of ROTC's role in promoting our national security. ROTC is providing the officers to fill the previously unmanned spaces in the total force structure.

In spite of its importance to national security, the contributions of ROTC are largely unappreciated by the senior Army leadership and, consequently, the Army at large. Admittedly, my perceptions may be biased because of my close association with ROTC as a professor of military science. However, I spent 23 years in the Army listening to disparaging remarks about ROTC before becoming involved in the program. The senior Army leadership provides neither requisite funding for the contributions provided by the program nor the necessary leadership emphasis to the program to attract qualified officers to seek ROTC assignments. Regardless, the Army has received excellent returns from the ROTC program, and it seems that it will try to obtain these returns "on the cheap" in the future. What job in the Army in peacetime is more important than training its future leaders?

The prevailing perception in the Army today is that an ROTC assignment is a necessary evil that is to be avoided if one wants to advance one's career. This perception is not going to change until two events occur—the senior Army leadership provides more support to the program through increased funding and active promotion of the importance of ROTC, and promotions, assignments, schooling, and so forth show that ROTC assignments make those officers competitive with their peers.

Indications are that ROTC assignments are not highly regarded by promotion boards, nor are the Army's best officers encouraged to seek ROTC jobs. Current policies that do not portray these assignments in a positive manner are extremely shortsighted. The relative "good times" that the program now enjoys will not last as both public opinion and demographics will work against sustaining ROTC enrollments in the future. Unfortunately, the wide appeal of the glitz and glitter of technology has obscured once again the basic truth that the real strength of the US Army is its people. We have to put forth our best efforts to identify, motivate and mold the future leaders of the Army—that is what ROTC does.

ROTC has been a successful program, and it represents something uniquely American. We should encourage our bright, dedicated young men and women to participate in the program. We bear the responsibility of providing the best possible preparation for our future leaders. The strength of our nation and our democratic system is due, in large measure, to our differing origins and perspectives that promote individual worth and dignity ahead of subservience to the government. ROTC serves as a guarantor that our form of government will endure.

We should have learned many lessons from Vietnam, but perhaps the most important lesson is the fact that the US Army is a people's Army. If the American people do not support what the Army is doing, then the effort is futile and invariably will result in failure. It is arguable as to how best to obtain the people's support over the long term, but it is certain that support will not be given if the people cannot identify with their soldiers. That is why ROTC is critical. It provides leaders from the society the Army serves—that is, ROTC creates a people's Army.

In an oft-quoted remark, "ROTC is not the presence of the military in the university, but rather the presence of the university in the military." All of us in the military, particularly the senior Army leadership, have a vital stake in promoting ROTC. ROTC provides the balance and perspective needed in the US military. It helps prepare us for the future. Our world is not so much inherited from our ancestors as on loan from our children.

### Questions

1. What are some of the reasons for questioning the presence of the ROTC on college campuses? Some people associate the ROTC with their concerns about government defense policies, Pentagon cost overruns and other complaints against the current administration. Do you think this is fair? Why, or why not?

2. Do you think the ROTC represents the presence of the military in the university or the presence of citizens in the military? How do they affect each other?

3. Besides making up for "unmanned spaces" in the officer corps, what other benefits does the author attribute to the ROTC? Do you agree?

4. What changes does Collins call for in the army's attitude toward the ROTC?

5. After reading this article, do you consider the ROTC a bulwark against U.S. militarism or an adjunct to it? Why?

# 9
# War Is No Way To Start a Career

## Peter Passel

This article originally appeared in *The New York Times*, May 23, 1990.

*An economic columnist for The New York Times gives statistical support for the contention that military service does not guarantee any advantages in the civilian job market.*

*Peter Passel first cites traditional studies that point to significant benefits reaped by World War II veterans, and economic disadvantages that accrued to Vietnam War servicepeople. But he qualifies this comparison by attributing the disparity more to recruiting priorities than to the value of military training. He indicates that far more of the poor and untrained saw national duty in the 1960s than in the 1940s.*

*Drawing on a more recent study by Joshua Angrist of Harvard and Alan Krueger of Princeton, the author reexamines the earlier data and finds that most World War II draftees were taken in chronological order. The Angrist-Krueger data was thus able to compare those born in the first six months of 1926 with those who were born near the end of 1928. The older group was much more likely to be drafted than the younger group. It was then possible to compare the lifetime earning history of this composite group. By this measure, those who were drafted did significantly less well than their contemporaries who were passed over by the draft. This discrepancy was even more pronounced during the Vietnam era.*

*The Angrist-Krueger study found that the earning disparity held only for whites. Non-whites appeared not to have been affected by draft status. Even with the help of G.I. Bill educational benefits, white veterans earned about five percent less than non-veterans, thus refuting the earlier findings.*

*As an aside, the more recent findings question the widespread assumption that veterans do not need special help in civilian life. They also cast doubt on the usefulness of skills learned in the military to the poor and untrained. The author's conclusion: "War may make men out of boys. It does not seem to make them better breadwinners.''*

War, as everyone knows, is not good for children and other living things. What is more debatable, however, is war's long-term effect on adults who make it back to civilian life.

Studies after World War II showed that soldiers had served themselves by serving Uncle Sam: on average, male veterans have outearned non-veterans by 10 to 20 percent. But soldiers of the Vietnam years have earned 10 to 20 percent less in the civilian job market.

One often-cited explanation for the contrast is job discrimination. Employers, goes the argument, want nothing to do with those who were exposed to the demoralizing effects of drugs and defeat. Others think the difference in veterans' work experience says more about recruitment than about life in the military. World War II veterans, they argue, were the best and the brightest; in Vietnam the Army was forced to draw disproportionately from the poor and untrained.

Now, two economists, Joshua Angrist of Harvard and Alan Krueger of Princeton, have hit upon an ingenious way to untangle the puzzle. In both wars, they discovered, draft procedures created an arbitrary link between birth dates and the probability of serving in the armed forces. And in both, men with no distinguishing characteristic other than being born on the wrong date earned substantially less in civilian life than men who lucked out.

The Angrist-Krueger analysis of World War II veterans, published as a working paper by the National Bureau of Economic Research, makes use of the fact that draft boards drew on the pool of men in simple chronological order of their birth. Roughly 75 percent of the men born in the first six months of 1926 ended up in the military. Thereafter, the probability declined quarter by quarter. Just 22 percent of those born near the end of 1928 ever served.

It seems unlikely that youth alone was, in itself, a key to success in the postwar labor market. But strikingly, younger workers earned more, strongly suggesting that military service was a handicap. The authors calculate that, adjusted for other factors, World War II veterans have earned about 5 percent less over the decades.

Mr. Angrist's study of Vietnam experience, to be published in June in the American Economic Review, exploits an even sharper statistical distinction. During the Vietnam War, birth-date lotteries were used to set draft priorities within each group coming of draft age. In 1971, for example, 20-year-olds born on the first 125 dates chosen like the numbers in Lotto were eligible; the rest were exempt.

Most draft-eligibles never served. Still, draft status made a big difference: Two eligibles in seven ended up in uniform, compared with just one exempt in seven. By matching birth dates with earnings data, Mr. Angrist figures that military service during Vietnam reduced average earnings for white males by about 15 percent. The earnings of non-whites did not seem to be affected.

The enduring psychological damage from combat may play a role for the relatively small percentage of veterans who were ever under fire. But Mr. Angrist's interpretation of the earnings deficit is more straightforward: Skills acquired in the military do not make up for the lost years of civilian experience. Nor, apparently, does that modest privilege of veteran status, G.I. Bill education subsidies.

The trade-off is closer for non-whites, Mr. Angrist speculates, because they entered the Army with fewer skills and left fewer opportunities behind.

The numbers offer a new perspective on an old issue. Americans have long rationalized tight limits on assistance to war veterans on the ground that the time spent in uniform was an advantage in later life. In fact, it appears to be quite costly, at least for men who were not already victims of poverty or discrimination.

The results might also lead to second thoughts about the use of national service as a means of giving the underclass a second chance to gain the discipline needed to succeed in a middle-class world.

Mr. Angrist's numbers suggest no net benefits for recruits who met the Army's minimum standards. Nor does a recently published analysis of the post-military earnings of low-aptitude recruits, admitted to the Army under a special dispensation during the 1960's and 1970's. Indeed, according to the Human Resources Research Organization in Alexandria, Va., veterans of "Project 100,000" did less well in the civilian job market than comparably skilled non-veterans.

War may make men out of boys. It does not seem to make them better breadwinners.

*Questions*

1. What conclusions do traditional studies come to regarding the peacetime earnings record of veterans? In what way does the Angrist-Krueger study question these conclusions?

2. How would you counsel someone who wishes to join the Armed Forces in order to gain skills valuable to civilian peacetime advancement?

3. What role did Selective Service lotteries play in World War II and the Vietnam War? How did this procedure enable Angrist and Krueger to track the subsequent income history of persons born during these periods?

4. Some have argued against giving generous benefits to ex-GIs because they gained job-related training during their service. Based on recent studies, how would you respond to this contention?

5. How would you evaluate the honesty of military recruiting commercials? Give three examples of such commercials and rate them in the light of the information in this article.

# 10
# War Preparers' Anonymous

## Kurt Vonnegut

This article originally appeared in *The Nation*, January 7, 1984.

*Kurt Vonnegut, author of* Catch 22 *and other popular novels, begins with the surprising opinion that America's most nurturing contribution to the culture of our planet is Alcoholics Anonymous. He finds in this movement a successful method of dealing with addiction, based on honesty, humility, reliance on others and a determination to live one day at a time.*

*From his own experience in World War II, Vonnegut discovers, on the part of many, a parallel addiction to "preparations for war." And he appeals to his readers to treat such persons as they would treat those who suffer from any other addiction. By linking a warlike mentality to alcohol or gambling addiction, he establishes an aesthetic distance from which to view what otherwise might appear to be rational behavior. And, indeed, war and bloated defense budgets may appear rational, until measured against their effects.*

*"If Western Civilization [by which he means just about every world leader] were a person . . . we would be directing it to the nearest meeting of War Preparers' Anonymous." Vonnegut would not treat such persons with contempt. He would only separate them from the levers of power.*

What has been America's most nurturing contribution to the culture of this planet so far? Many would say jazz. I, who love jazz, will say this instead: Alcoholics Anonymous.

I am not an alcoholic. If I were, I would go before the nearest AA meeting and say, "My name is Kurt Vonnegut. I am an alcoholic." God willing, that might be my first step down the long, hard road back to sobriety.

The AA scheme, which requires a confession like that, is the first to have any measurable success in dealing with the tendency of some human beings, perhaps 10 percent of any population, to become addicted to substances that give them brief spasms of pleasure but in the long term transmute their lives and the lives of those around them into ultimate ghastliness.

The AA scheme, which, again, can work only if the addicts regularly admit that this or that chemical is poisonous to them, is now proving its effectiveness with compulsive gamblers, who are not dependent on chemicals from a distillery or a pharmaceutical laboratory. This is no paradox. Gamblers, in effect, manufacture their own dangerous substances. God help them, they produce chemicals that elate them whenever they place a bet on simply anything.

If I were a compulsive gambler, which I am not, I would be well advised to stand up before the nearest meeting of Gamblers Anonymous and declare, "My name is Kurt Vonnegut. I am a compulsive gambler."

Whether I was standing before a meeting of Gamblers Anonymous or Alcoholics Anonymous, I would be encouraged to testify as to how the chemicals I had generated within myself or swallowed had alienated my friends and relatives, cost me jobs and houses, and deprived me of my last shred of self-respect.

I now wish to call attention to another form of addiction, which has not been previously identified. It is more like gambling than drinking, since the people afflicted are ravenous for situations that will cause their bodies to release exciting chemicals into their bloodstreams. I am persuaded that there are among us people who are tragically hooked on preparations for war.

Tell people with that disease that war is coming and we have to get ready for it, and for a few minutes there they will be as happy as a drunk with his martini breakfast or a compulsive gambler with his paycheck bet on the Super Bowl.

Let us recognize how sick such people are. From now on, when a national leader, or even just a neighbor, starts talking about some new weapons system that is going to cost us a mere $29 billion, we should speak up. We should say something on the order of, "Honest to God, I couldn't be sorrier for you if I'd seen you wash down a fistful of black beauties with a pint of Southern Comfort."

I mean it. I am not joking. Compulsive preparers for World War III, in this country or any other, are as tragically and as repulsively addicted as any stockbroker passed out with his head in a toilet in the Port Authority bus terminal.

For an alcoholic to experience a little joy, he needs maybe three ounces of grain alcohol. Alcoholics, when they are close to hitting bottom, customarily can't hold much alcohol.

If we know a compulsive gambler who is dead broke, we can probably make him happy with a dollar to bet on who can spit farther than someone else.

For us to give a compulsive war-preparer a fleeting moment of happiness, we may have to buy him three Trident submarines and a hundred intercontinental ballistic missiles mounted on choo-choo trains.

If Western Civilization were a person—

If Western Civilization, which blankets the world now, as far as I can tell, were a person—

If Western Civilization, which surely now includes the Soviet Union and China and India and Pakistan and on and on, were a person—

If Western Civilization were a person, we would be directing it to the nearest meeting of War Preparers Anonymous. We would be telling it to stand up before the meeting and say, "My name is Western Civilization. I am a compulsive war-preparer. I have lost everything I ever cared about. I should have come here long ago. I first hit bottom in World War I."

Western Civilization cannot be represented by a single person, of course, but a single explanation for the catastrophic course it has followed during this bloody century is possible. We the people, because of our ignorance of the disease, have again and again entrusted power to people we did not know were sickies.

And let us not mock them now, any more than we would mock someone with syphilis or smallpox or leprosy or yaws or typhoid fever or any of the other diseases to which the flesh is heir. All we have to do is separate them from the levers of power, I think.

And then what?

Western Civilization's long, hard trip back to sobriety might begin.

*Questions*

1. Does the author make a convincing case for Alcoholics Anonymous as America's greatest contribution to world civilization? If so, why? If not, why not?

2. What consequences does he describe that flow from addiction to alcohol or gambling? Does his parallel to war preparations hold up, in your mind? Give your reasons, pro or con.

3. How does Vonnegut use humor to make his point? Cite instances.

4. Does the author overstate his case? If so, do you think this detracts from his thesis? Name other authors who have used satire to lampoon evils of their day.

5. In the Bible, it is written: "By their fruits you will know them." Enumerate the fruits of war.

# 11
# "All Quiet on the Western Front"

## Erich Maria Remarque

This excerpt is taken from the novel of the same name, Random House, 1958.

---

*The human face of war, obscured by grand strategies and techno-
logical advances, is poignantly depicted by the author, who was
wounded five times in combat during World War I. Born in Germany,
he worked as a stone cutter and editor, emigrating to the United
States in 1939. He died in Switzerland in 1970.*

*The novel tells the story of Paul Baumer and his generation on
both sides of the war, as the horror of trench warfare overwhelms
their youthful enthusiasm, destroying bodies and souls.*

*In this excerpt, Baumer encounters an enemy soldier: "I strike
madly home." Having assured the death of the man who was probably
already wounded, Baumer has a change of heart. The look of sheer
terror on the dying man's face frightens Baumer, who wants to help.
Through the hours in the heavily bombarded shell-hole, he forgets his
own hunger and thirst enough to study his fellow human being. The
author carefully notes his appearance and learns his identity from the
dead man's wallet. He is "Gérard Duval, printer."*

Already it has become somewhat lighter. Steps hasten over me.
The first. Gone. Again, another. The rattle of machine-guns becomes
an unbroken chain. Just as I am about to turn round a little, something
heavy stumbles, and with a crash a body falls over me into the shell-
hole, slips down, and lies across me—

I do not think at all, I make no decision-I strike madly at home,
and feel only how the body suddenly convulses, then becomes limp,
and collapses. When I recover myself, my hand is sticky and wet.

The man gurgles. It sounds to me as though he bellows, every
gasping breath is like a cry, a thunder—but it is not only my heart
pounding. I want to stop his mouth, stuff it with earth, stab him again,
he must be quiet, he is betraying me; now at last I regain control of
myself, but have suddenly become so feeble that I cannot any more
lift my hand against him.

So I crawl away to the farthest corner and stay there, my eyes glued on him, my hand grasping the knife-ready, if he stirs, to spring at him again. But he won't do so any more, I can hear that already in his gurgling.

I can see him indistinctly. I have but one desire, to get away. If it is not soon it will be too light; it will be difficult enough now. Then as I try to raise up my head I see it is impossible already. The machine-gunfire so sweeps the ground that I should be shot through and through before I could make one jump.

I test it once with my helmet, which I take off and hold up to find out the level of the shots. The next moment it is knocked out of my hand by a bullet. The fire is sweeping very low to the ground. I am not far enough from the enemy line to escape being picked off by one of the snipers if I attempt to get away.

The light increases. Burning I wait for our attack. My hands are white at the knuckles, I clench them so tightly in my longing for the fire to cease so that my comrades may come.

Minute after minute trickles away. I dare not look again at the dark figure in the shell-hole. With an effort I look past it and wait, wait. The bullets hiss, they make a steel net, never ceasing, never ceasing.

Then I notice my bloody hand and suddenly feel nauseated. I take some earth and rub the skin with it; now my hand is muddy and the blood cannot be seen any more.

The fire does not diminish. It is equally heavy from both sides. Our fellows have probably given me up for lost long ago.

It is early morning, clear and grey. The gurgling continues, I stop my ears, but soon take my fingers away again, because then I cannot hear the other sound.

The figure opposite me moves. I shrink together and involuntarily look at it. Then my eyes remain glued to it. A man with a small pointed beard lies there; his head is fallen to one side, one arm is halfbent, his head rests helplessly upon it. The other hand lies on his chest, it is bloody.

He is dead, I say to myself, he must be dead, he doesn't feel anything any more; it is only the body that is gurgling there. Then the head tries to raise itself, for a moment the groaning becomes louder, his forehead sinks back upon his arm. The man is not dead, he is dying, but he is not dead. I drag myself toward him, hesitate, support myself on my hands, creep a bit farther, wait, again a terrible journey. At last I am beside him.

Then he opens his eyes. He must have heard me, for he gazes at me with a look of utter terror. The body lies still, but in the eyes there is such an extraordinary expression of fright that for a moment I think they have power enough to carry the body off with them. Hundreds of miles away with one bound. The body is still perfectly still, without a sound, the gurgle has ceased, but the eyes cry out, yell, all the life is gathered together in them for one tremendous effort to flee, gathered together there in a dreadful terror of death, of me.

My legs give way and I drop on my elbows. "No, no," I whisper.

The eyes follow me. I am powerless to move so long as they are there.

Then his hand slips slowly from his breast, only a little bit, it sinks just a few inches, but this movement breaks the power of the eyes. I bend forward, shake my head and whisper: "No, no, no," I raise one hand, I must show him that I want to help him, I stroke his forehead.

The eyes shrink back as the hand comes, then they lose their stare, the eyelids droop lower, the tension is past. I open his collar and place his head more comfortably.

His mouth stands half open, it tries to form words. The lips are dry. My water bottle is not there. I have not brought it with me. But there is water in the mud, down at the bottom of the crater. I climb down, take out my handkerchief, spread it out, push it under and scoop up the yellow water that strains through into the hollow of my hand.

He gulps it down. I fetch some more. Then I unbutton his tunic in order to bandage him if it is possible. In any case I must do it, so that if the fellows over there capture me they will see that I wanted to help him, and so will not shoot me. He tries to resist, but his hand is too feeble. The shirt is stuck and will not come away, it is buttoned at the back. So there is nothing for it but to cut it open.

I look for the knife and find it again. But when I begin to cut the shirt the eyes open once more and the cry is in them again and the demented expression, so that I must close them, press them shut and whisper: "I want to help you, Comrade, camerade, camerade, camerade—" eagerly repeating the word, to make him understand.

There are three stabs. My field dressing covers them, the blood runs out under it, I press it tighter; there; he groans.

That is all I can do. Now we must wait, wait.

These hours. . . . The gurgling starts again—but how slowly a man dies! For this I know—he cannot be saved, I have, indeed, tried to tell myself that he will be, but at noon this pretence breaks down and melts before his groans. If only I had not lost my revolver crawling about, I would shoot him. Stab him I cannot.

By noon I am groping on the outer limits of reason. Hunger devours me, I could almost weep for something to eat, I cannot struggle against it. Again and again I fetch water for the dying man and drink some myself.

This is the first time I have killed with my hands, whom I can see close at hand, whose death is my doing. Kat and Kropp and Müller have experienced it already, when they have hit someone; it happens to many, in hand-to-hand fighting especially—

But every gasp lays my heart bare. This dying man has time with him, he has an invisible dagger with which he stabs me: Time and my thoughts.

I would give much if he would but stay alive. It is hard to lie here and to have to see and hear him.

In the afternoon, about three, he is dead.

I breathe freely again. But only for a short time. Soon the silence is more unbearable than the groans. I wish the gurgling were there again, gasping hoarse, now whistling softly and again hoarse and loud.

It is mad, what I do. But I must do something. I prop the dead man up again so that he lies comfortably, although he feels nothing any more. I close his eyes. They are brown, his hair is black and a bit curly at the sides.

The mouth is full and soft beneath his moustache: the nose is slightly arched, the skin brownish: it is now not so pale as it was before, when he was still alive. For a moment the face seems almost healthy;—then it collapses suddenly into the strange face of the dead that I have so often seen, strange faces, all alike.

No doubt his wife still thinks of him: she does not know what has happened. He looks as if he would have often have written to her:— she will still be getting mail from him—Tomorrow, in a week's time —perhaps even a stray letter a month hence. She will read it, and in it he will be speaking to her.

My state is getting worse, I can no longer control my thoughts. What would his wife look like? Like the little brunette on the other side of the canal? Does she belong to me now? Perhaps by this act she becomes mine. I wish Kantorek were sitting here beside me. If my mother could see me—. The dead man might have had thirty more years of life if only I had impressed the way back to our trench more sharply on my memory. If only he had run two yards farther to the left, he might now be sitting in the trench over there and writing a fresh letter to his wife.

But I will get no further that way; for that is the fate of all of us: if Kemmerich's leg had been six inches to the right: if Haie Westhus had bent his back three inches further forward—

The silence spreads. I talk and must talk. So I speak to him and to say to him: "Comrade, I did not want to kill you. If you jumped in here again, I would not do it, if you would be sensible too. But you were only an idea to me before, an abstraction that lived in my mind and called forth its appropriate response. It was that abstraction I stabbed. But now, for the first time, I see you are a man like me. I thought of your hand-grenades, of your bayonet, of your rifle; now I see your wife and your face and our fellowship. Forgive me, comrade. We always see it too late. Why do they never tell us that you are poor devils like us, that your mothers are just as anxious as ours, and that we have the same fear of death, and the same dying and the same agony—Forgive me, comrade; how could you be my enemy? If we threw away these rifles and this uniform you could be my brother just like Kat and Albert. Take twenty years of my life, comrade, and stand up—take more, for I do not know what I can even attempt to do with it now."

It is quiet, the front is still except for the crackle of rifle fire. The bullets rain over, they are not fired haphazard, but shrewdly aimed from all sides. I cannot get out.

"I will write to your wife," I say hastily to the dead man. "I will write to her, she must hear it from me. I will tell her everything I have told you, she shall not suffer, I will help her, and your parents too, and your child—"

His tunic is half open. The pocket-book is easy to find. But I hesitate to open it. In it is the book with his name. So long as I do not know his name perhaps I may still forget him, time will obliterate it, this picture. But his name, it is a nail that will be hammered into me and never come out again. It has the power to recall this forever, it will always come back and stand before me.

Irresolutely I take the wallet in my hand. It slips out of my hand and falls open. Some pictures and letters drop out. I gather them up and want to put them back again, but the strain I am under, the uncertainty, the hunger, the danger, these hours with the dead man have made me desperate, I want to hasten the relief, to intensify and to end the torture, as one strikes an unendurably painful hand against the trunk of a tree, regardless of everything.

There are portraits of a woman and a little girl, small amateur photographs taken against an ivy-clad wall. Along with them are let-

ters. I take them out and try to read them. Most of it I do not understand, it is so hard to decipher and I scarcely know any French. But
each word I translate pierces me like a shot in the chest:—like a stab
in the chest.

My brain is taxed beyond endurance. But I realize this much, that
I will never dare to write to these people as I intended. Impossible. I
look at the portraits once more; they are clearly not rich people. I
might send them money anonymously if I earn anything later on. I
seize upon that, it is at least something to hold on to. This dead man is
bound up with my life, therefore I must do everything, promise everything in order to save myself; I swear blindly that I mean to live only
for his sake and his family, with wet lips I try to placate him—and
deep down in me lies the hope that I may buy myself off in this way
and perhaps even get out of this; it is a little stratagem: if only I am
allowed to escape, then I will see to it. So I open the book and read
slowly:—Gérard Duval, compositor.

With the dead man's pencil I write the address on an envelope,
then swiftly thrust everything back into his tunic.

I have killed the printer, Gérard Duval. I must be a printer, I
think confusedly, be a printer, printer—

## Questions

1. How does the author set the scene for his grisly discovery?
2. Why cannot Baumer leave the shell-hole? What effect do the long
   hours with a dying man have on his attitude toward "the enemy"?
3. What happens when the protagonist learns that his enemy is not
   dead? How does he try to comfort him?
4. How does the fact that the two soldiers do not speak the same
   language heighten the tension?
5. Discovering the man's name and occupation deals the final blow to
   any lingering warlike feelings in Paul Baumer. What conclusions
   can the reader draw from this "human face of war"?

---

# SECTION TWO

# Social Justice

# 1
# Pacem in Terris

*Pope John XXIII, #130–145*

---

*Pope John XXIII's encyclical letter "Pacem in Terris" ("Peace on Earth") has been called the Pontiff's "last will and testament." He died less than two months after it was issued "to all men of good will" (a new departure) on April 11, 1963. Written in the heat of the Cuban missile crisis in the fall of 1962, the Pope's letter declared, among other things, that "it is hardly possible to imagine that in the atomic era war could be used as an instrument of justice." John builds on the teachings of his predecessors but he goes beyond them in enumerating the rights of all persons to profess their religion publicly and the rights of newly independent nations to determine their own destinies. Striking a positive note throughout, Pope John lists three characteristics of the modern age: the economic and political gains of the working class, the advances made by women in public life and the passing of colonialism.*

*The selections cited from "Pacem in Terris" (#130–145) call attention to the growing interdependence among the countries of the world. As parts of "one world economy," nation-states' social progress, order, security and peace are "necessarily connected" with those of all other countries. The corollary of this insight is that nations can no longer pursue their own interests "in isolation." By positing a "universal common good," the Pontiff calls on nations to seek this goal in concert, by freely entering into a "public authority of the world community." Nations in isolation or in complete autonomy "are no longer capable of facing the tasks of finding a solution to . . . problems." What this supranational authority will be, the Pope leaves to others to work out.*

*The point of reference of these global efforts is not the nation-state, the Church itself or even God. It is the dignity of the human person. John's view, filled with faith, is clearly anthropocentric. Ignoring those "prophets of doom" who condemn the shortcomings of the United Nations, John emphasizes its achievements and expresses the hope that it "may become ever more equal to the magnitude and nobility of its tasks." In like manner, he praises the U.N. for its Universal Declaration of Human Rights, calling*

107

*it "an important step on the path toward the juridical-political organization of the world community."*

*In the tradition of papal teaching, Pope John stresses the principle of subsidiarity, which states that higher authorities should not take over functions equally well performed by smaller groups. But he applies this principle in the other direction by stating that a supranational authority is needed because "individual states are not in a position to tackle them (problems) with any hope of resolving them satisfactorily."*

## INTERDEPENDENCE BETWEEN POLITICAL COMMUNITIES

130.    Recent progress of science and technology has profoundly affected human beings and influenced men to work together and live as one family. There has been a great increase in the circulation of goods, of ideas and of persons from one country to another, so that relations have become closer between individuals, families and intermediate associations belonging to different political communities, and between the public authorities of those communities. At the same time the interdependence of national economies has grown deeper, one becoming progressively more closely related to the other, so that they become, as it were, integral parts of the one world economy. Likewise the social progress, order, security and peace of each country are necessarily connected with the social progress, order, security and peace of all other countries.

131.    At the present day no political community is able to pursue its own interests and develop itself in isolation, because the degree of its prosperity and development is a reflection and a component part of the degree of prosperity and development of all the other political communities.

## EXISTING PUBLIC AUTHORITY NOT EQUAL
## TO REQUIREMENTS OF THE UNIVERSAL COMMON GOOD

132.    The unity of the human family has always existed, because its members were human beings all equal by virtue of their natural dignity. Hence there will always exist the objective need to promote, in sufficient measure, the universal common good, that is, the common good of the entire human family.

133.    In times past, one would be justified in feeling that the public authorities of the different political communities might be in a position to provide for the universal common good, either through normal diplomatic channels or through top-level meetings, by making use of juridical instruments such as conventions and treaties, for example: juridical in-

struments suggested by the natural law and regulated by the law of nations and international law.

*134.* As a result of the far-reaching changes which have taken place in the relations within the human community, the universal common good gives rise to problems that are very grave, complex and extremely urgent, especially as regards security and world peace. On the other hand, the public authorities of the individual nations—being placed as they are on a footing of equality one with the other—no matter how much they multiply their meetings or sharpen their wits in efforts to draw up new juridical instruments, they are no longer capable of facing the task of finding an adequate solution to the problems mentioned above. And this is not due to a lack of good will or of a spirit of enterprise, but because their authority lacks suitable force.

*135.* It can be said, therefore, that at this historical moment the present system of organization and the way its principle of authority operates on a world basis no longer correspond to the objective requirements of the universal common good.

## RELATIONS BETWEEN THE COMMON GOOD AND PUBLIC AUTHORITY IN HISTORICAL CONTEXT

*136.* There exists an intrinsic connection between the common good on the one hand and the structure and function of public authority on the other. The moral order, which needs public authority in order to promote the common good in civil society, requires also that the authority be effective in attaining that end. This demands that the organs through which the authority is formed, becomes operative and pursues its ends, must be composed and act in such a manner as to be capable of furthering the common good by ways and means which correspond to the developing situation.

*137.* Today the universal common good poses problems of worldwide dimensions, which cannot be adequately tackled or solved except by the efforts of public authorities endowed with a wideness of powers, structure and means of the same proportions: that is, of public authorities which are in a position to operate in an effective manner on a world-wide basis. The moral order itself, therefore, demands that such a form of public authority be established.

## PUBLIC AUTHORITY INSTITUTED BY COMMON CONSENT AND NOT IMPOSED BY FORCE

*138.* A public authority, having world-wide power and endowed with the proper means for the efficacious pursuit of its objective, which is the universal common good in concrete form, must be set up by common accord and not imposed by force. The reason is that such an authority must be in a position to operate effectively; yet, at the same time, its action must be inspired by sincere and real impartiality: in other words, it must be an action aimed at satisfying the objective requirements of the universal common good. The difficulty is that there would be reason to fear that a supranational or world-wide public authority, imposed by force by the more powerful political communities, might be or might become an instrument of one-sided interests; and even should this not happen, it would be difficult for it to avoid all suspicion of partiality in its actions, and this would take from the efficaciousness of its activity. Even though there may be pronounced differences between political communities as regards the degree of their economic development and their military power, they are all very sensitive as regards their juridical equality and their moral dignity. For that reason, they are right in not easily yielding in obedience to an authority imposed by force, or to an authority in whose creation they had no part, or to which they themselves did not decide to submit by conscious and free choice.

## THE UNIVERSAL COMMON GOOD AND PERSONAL RIGHTS

*139.* Like the common good of individual political communities, so too the universal common good cannot be determined except by having regard to the human person. Therefore, the public authority of the world community, too, must have as its fundamental objective the recognition, respect, safeguarding and promotion of the rights of the human person; this can be done by direct action when required, or by creating on a world scale an environment in which the public authorities of the individual political communities can more easily carry out their specific functions.

## THE PRINCIPLE OF SUBSIDIARITY

*140.* Just as within each political community the relations between individuals, families, intermediate associations and public authority are governed by the principle of subsidiarity, so too the relations between the public authority of each political community and the public authority of the world community must be regulated by the light of the same principle. This means that the public authority of the world community must tackle and solve problems of an economic, social, political or cultural character which are posed by the universal common good. For, because of the vastness, complexity and urgency of those problems, the public authorities of the individual States are not in a position to tackle them with any hope of resolving them satisfactorily.

*141.* The public authority of the world community is not intended to limit the sphere of action of the public authority of the individual political community, much less to take its place. On the contrary, its purpose is to create, on a world basis, an environment in which the public authorities of each political community, its citizens and intermediate associations, can carry out their tasks, fulfill their duties and exercise their rights with greater security.[1]

## MODERN DEVELOPMENTS

*142.* As is known, the United Nations Organization (UN) was established on June 26, 1945, and to it there were subsequently added Intergovernmental Agencies with extensive international tasks in the economic, social, cultural, educational and health fields. The United Nations Organization had as its essential purpose the maintenance and consolidation of peace between peoples, fostering between them friendly relations, based on the principles of equality, mutual respect, and varied forms of co-operation in every sector of human society.

*143.* An act of the highest importance performed by the United Nations Organization was the Universal Declaration of Human Rights, approved in the General Assembly of December 10, 1948. In the preamble of that Declaration, the recognition of and respect for those rights and respective liberties is proclaimed as an ideal to be pursued by all peoples and all countries.

*144.* Some objections and reservations were raised regarding certain points in the Declaration. There is no doubt, however, that the document represents an important step on the path towards the juridical-political organization of the world community. For in it, in most solemn form, the dignity of a person is acknowledged to all human beings; and as a consequence there is proclaimed, as a fundamental right, the right of free movement in the search for truth and in the attainment of moral good and of justice, and also the right to a dignified life, while other rights connected with those mentioned are likewise proclaimed.

*145.* It is Our earnest wish that the United Nations Organization—in its structure and in its means—may become ever more equal to the magnitude and nobility of its tasks. May the day soon come when every

---

1. Cf. Pius XII's *Allocution* to youth of Catholic Action from the dioceses of Italy gathered in Rome, September 12, 1948, A.A.S. XL, p. 412.

human being will find therein an effective safeguard for the rights which derive directly from his dignity as a person, and which are therefore universal, inviolate and inalienable rights. This is all the more to be hoped for since all human beings, as they take an ever more active part in the public life of their own political communities, are showing an increasing interest in the affairs of all peoples, and are becoming more consciously aware that they are living members of a universal family of mankind.

*Questions*

1. The world has changed since 1963. Give examples of recent developments in science and technology. Do these developments strengthen or weaken the Pope's assertion that a "one world economy" is emerging? Why?

2. Do you agree with John that no political community can pursue its own interests and develop itself in isolation? Name two nations that developed in isolation in the past. How have conditions changed today?

3. What is one outstanding factor in evaluating the adequacy of a public authority (nation)? Give current examples of the limitations of nation-states in the world today.

4. Which nations was the Pope likely to have had in mind when he warned against imposing a worldwide public authority by force? Give examples.

5. Though issued by a Roman Pontiff, "Pacem in Terris" is addressed to "all men of good will." In what ways is his reasoning apt to be acceptable to persons of different religious and cultural traditions?

2
# Letter from a Birmingham Jail

## Martin Luther King, Jr.

This article originally appeared in *Why We Can't Wait*, Harper & Row, 1963.

---

Many of history's outstanding figures have spent time in jail—Socrates, the Jewish prophets, Jesus, St. Paul, Martin Luther, St. Ignatius Loyola, Gandhi, the Russian dissidents and Martin Luther King. Imprisonment usually strengthens the resolve of people of conscience and gives them time for reflection and expression.

Such was the case with Dr. King, the inspiration and tactical leader of America's black people in the mid-twentieth century. Imprisoned for leading a civil rights demonstration without a permit in April 1963, he sent a reply to eight Alabama clergymen who found his tactics too extreme. In a reply abounding in references to the Jewish and Christian Scriptures and to philosophers ancient and modern, Dr. King met his critics head-on and left a timeless written legacy of his non-violent approach to oppression.

The letter begins with praise for the good will of his detractors and a patient rebuttal of the charge that the writer is an "outside agitator." Not only was he invited by the local chapter of the Southern Christian Leadership Conference, he says, but as a minister of the Gospel he declares his obligation to carry the Christian message to every hamlet where injustice still exists.

With delicacy and tact, Dr. King reminds the ministers that the demonstration he led may be unfortunate, but that "the white power structure of this city left the Negro community with no other alternative." Reviewing the long record of police brutality and unsolved bombings of churches in Birmingham, the author instructs his critics in the four steps of any non-violent campaign: (1) collection of the facts; (2) negotiation; (3) self-purification; (4) direct action. With such arguments, he denies that he acted irresponsibly.

In the crisis created by direct action, Dr. King sees hope for "creative tension"—through the acceptance of beatings and other suffering—which can change an oppressor into an ally. In this, he echoes Gandhi's appeal to "self-suffering." He replies to the charge of being in too much of a hurry by recounting the long centuries of slavery and segregation and their ef-

*fects on black people, especially little children. "I hope, sirs," he says with no little irony, "you can understand our legitimate and unavoidable impatience."*

*Quoting St. Thomas Aquinas, the medieval Catholic philosopher, King distinguishes between just laws and unjust ones, insisting all the while that his followers accept the penalties of even unjust legislation. He expresses his impatience with the "white moderate" who is "more devoted to 'order' than to justice."*

*As to the charge of extremism, King places his movement midway between black nationalist groups which have lost faith in America and segregationists who play into their hands. "If his (the Negro's) repressed emotions do not come out in these non-violent ways," he writes, "they will come out in ominous expressions of violence," a prophecy fulfilled after his own assassination in 1968.*

*By drawing out the implications of traditional Christianity in the turmoil of daily events, King forges a synthesis that challenges those who separate their faith from everyday life.*

April 16, 1963
Birmingham, Alabama
MY DEAR FELLOW CLERGYMEN:

While confined here in the Birmingham city jail, I came across your recent statement calling my present activities "unwise and untimely." Seldom do I pause to answer criticism of my work and ideas. If I sought to answer all the criticisms that cross my desk, my secretaries would have little time for anything other than such correspondence in the course of the day, and I would have no time for constructive work. But since I feel that you are men of genuine good will and that your criticisms are sincerely set forth, I want to try to answer your statement in what I hope will be patient and reasonable terms.

I think I should indicate why I am here in Birmingham, since you have been influenced by the view which argues against "outsiders coming in." I have the honor of serving as president of the Southern Christian Leadership Conference, an organization operating in every southern state, with headquarters in Atlanta, Georgia. We have some eighty-five affiliated organizations across the South, and one of them is the Alabama Christian Movement for Human Rights. Frequently we share staff, educational, and financial resources with our affiliates. Several months ago the affiliate here in Birmingham asked us to be on call to engage in a nonviolent direct-action program if such were deemed necessary. We readily consented, and when the hour came we lived up to our promise. So I, along with several members of my staff, am here because I was invited here. I am here because I have organizational ties here.

But more basically, I am in Birmingham because injustice is here. Just as the prophets of the eighth century B.C. left their villages and carried their "thus saith the Lord" far beyond the boundaries of their home towns, and just as the Apostle Paul left his village of Tarsus and carried the gospel of Jesus Christ to the far corners of the Greco-Roman world, so am I compelled to carry the gospel of freedom beyond my own home town. Like Paul, I must constantly respond to the Macedonian call for aid.

Moreover, I am cognizant of the interrelatedness of all communities and states. I cannot sit idly by in Atlanta and not be concerned about what happens in Birmingham. Injustice anywhere is a threat to justice everywhere. We are caught in an inescapable network of mutuality, tied in a single garment of destiny. Whatever affects one directly, affects all indirectly. Never again can we afford to live with the narrow, provincial "outside agitator" idea. Anyone who lives inside the United States can never be considered an outsider anywhere within its bounds.

You deplore the demonstrations taking place in Birmingham. But your statement, I am sorry to say, fails to express a similar concern for the conditions that brought about the demonstrations. I am sure that none of you would want to rest content with the superficial kind of social analysis that deals merely with effects and does not grapple with underlying causes. It is unfortunate that demonstrations are taking place in Birmingham, but it is even more unfortunate that the city's white power structure left the Negro community with no alternative.

In any nonviolent campaign there are four basic steps: collection of the facts to determine whether injustices exist; negotiation; self-purification; and direct action. We have gone through all these steps in Birmingham. There can be no gainsaying the fact that racial injustice engulfs this community. Birmingham is probably the most thoroughly segregated city in the United States. Its ugly record of brutality is widely known. Negroes have experienced grossly unjust treatment in the courts. There have been more unsolved bombings of Negro homes and churches in Birmingham than in any other city in the nation. These are the hard, brutal facts of the case. On the basis of these conditions, Negro leaders sought to negotiate with the city fathers. But the latter consistently refused to engage in good-faith negotiation.

Then, last September, came the opportunity to talk with leaders of Birmingham's economic community. In the course of the negotiations, certain promises were made by the merchants—for example, to remove the stores' humiliating racial signs. On the basis of these promises, the Reverend Fred Shuttlesworth and the leaders of the Alabama Christian

Movement for Human Rights agreed to a moratorium on all demonstrations. As the weeks and months went by, we realized that we were the victims of a broken promise. A few signs, briefly removed, returned; the others remained.

As in so many past experiences, our hopes had been blasted, and the shadow of deep disappointment settled upon us. We had no alternative except to prepare for direct action, whereby we would present our very bodies as a means of laying our case before the conscience of the local and the national community. Mindful of the difficulties involved, we decided to undertake a process of self-purification. We began a series of workshops on nonviolence, and we repeatedly asked ourselves: "Are you able to accept blows without retaliation?" "Are you able to endure the ordeal of jail?" We decided to schedule our direct-action program for the Easter season, realizing that except for Christmas, this is the main shopping period of the year. Knowing that a strong economic-withdrawal program would be the by-product of direct action, we felt that this would be the best time to bring pressure to bear on the merchants for the needed change.

Then it occurred to us that Birmingham's mayoral election was coming up in March, and we speedily decided to postpone action until after election day. When we discovered that the Commissioner of Public Safety, Eugene "Bull" Connor, had piled up enough votes to be in the run-off, we decided again to postpone action until the day after the run-off so that the demonstrations could not be used to cloud the issues. Like many others, we waited to see Mr. Connor defeated, and to this end we endured postponement after postponement. Having aided in this community need, we felt that our direct-action program could be delayed no longer.

You may well ask, "Why direct action? Why sit-ins, marches, and so forth? Isn't negotiation a better path?" You are quite right in calling for negotiation. Indeed, this is the very purpose of direct action. Nonviolent direct action seeks to create such a crisis and foster such a tension that a community which has constantly refused to negotiate is forced to confront the issue. It seeks so to dramatize the issue that it can no longer be ignored. My citing the creation of tension as part of the work of the nonviolent-resister may sound rather shocking. But I must confess that I am not afraid of the word "tension." I have earnestly opposed violent tension, but there is a type of constructive, nonviolent tension which is necessary for growth. Just as Socrates felt that it was necessary to create a tension in the mind so that individuals could rise from the bondage of myths and half-truths to the unfettered realm of creative analysis and objective appraisal, so must we see the need for nonviolent gadflies to create the kind of tension in society that will help men rise from the dark depths of prejudice and racism to the majestic heights of understanding and brotherhood.

The purpose of our direct-action program is to create a situation so crisis-packed that it will inevitably open the door to negotiation. I therefore concur with you in your call for negotiation. Too long has our beloved Southland been bogged down in a tragic effort to live in monologue rather than dialogue.

One of the basic points in your statement is that the action that I and my associates have taken in Birmingham is untimely. Some have asked: "Why didn't you give the new city administration time to act?" The only answer that I can give to this query is that the new Birmingham administration must be prodded about as much as the outgoing one, before it will act. We are sadly mistaken if we feel that the election of Albert Boutwell as mayor will bring the millennium to Birmingham. While Mr. Boutwell is a much more gentle person than Mr. Connor, they are both segregationists, dedicated to maintenance of the status quo. I have hoped that Mr. Boutwell will be reasonable enough to see the futility of massive resistance to desegregation. But he will not see this without pressure from devotees of civil rights. My friends, I must say to you that we have not made a single gain in civil rights without determined legal and nonviolent pressure. Lamentably, it is an historical fact that privileged groups seldom give up their privileges voluntarily. Individuals may see the moral light and voluntarily give up their unjust posture; but, as Reinhold Niebuhr has reminded us, groups tend to be more immoral than individuals.

We know through painful experience that freedom is never voluntarily given by the oppressor; it must be demanded by the oppressed. Frankly, I have yet to engage in a direct-action campaign that was "well timed" in view of those who have not suffered unduly from the disease of segregation. For years now I have heard the word "Wait!" It rings in the ear of every Negro with piercing familiarity. This "Wait" has almost always meant "Never." We must come to see, with one of our distinguished jurists, that "justice too long delayed is justice denied."

We have waited for more than 340 years for our constitutional and God-given rights. The nations of Asia and Africa are moving with jetlike speed toward gaining political independence, but we still creep at horse-and-buggy pace toward gaining a cup of coffee at a lunch counter. Perhaps it is easy for those who have never felt the stinging darts of segregation to say, "Wait." But when you have seen vicious mobs lynch your mothers and fathers at will and drown your sisters and brothers at whim; when you have seen hate-filled policemen curse, kick, and even kill your black brothers and sisters; when you see the vast majority of your twenty million Negro brothers smothering in an airtight cage of poverty in the midst of an affluent society; when you suddenly find your tongue twisted and your speech stammering as you seek to explain to your six-year-old daughter why she can't go to the public amusement park that has just been advertised on television, and see tears welling up in her eyes when she is told that Funtown is closed to colored children, and see ominous clouds of inferiority beginning to form in her little mental sky, and see her beginning to distort her personality by developing an unconscious bitterness toward white people; when you have to concoct an answer for a five-year-old son who is asking, "Daddy, why do white people treat colored people so mean?"; when you take a cross-country drive and find it necessary to sleep night after night in the uncomfortable corners of your automobile because no motel will accept you; when you are humiliated day in and day out by nagging signs reading "white" and "colored;" when your first name becomes "nigger," your middle name becomes "boy" (however old you are) and your last name becomes "John," and your wife and mother are never given the respected title "Mrs."; when you are harried by day and haunted by night by the fact that you are a Negro, living constantly at tiptoe stance, never quite knowing what to expect next, and are plagued with inner fears and outer resentments; when you are forever fighting a degenerating sense of "nobodiness"—then you will understand why we find it difficult to wait. There comes a time when the cup of endurance runs over, and men are no longer willing to be plunged into the abyss of despair. I hope, sirs, you can understand our legitimate and unavoidable impatience.

You express a great deal of anxiety over our willingness to break laws. This is certainly a legitimate concern. Since we so diligently urge people to obey the Supreme Court's decision of 1954 outlawing segregation in the public schools, at first glance it may seem rather paradoxical for us consciously to break laws. One may well ask: "How can you advocate breaking some laws and obeying others?" The answer lies in the fact that there are two types of laws: just and unjust. I would be the first to advocate obeying just laws. One has not only a legal but a moral responsibility to obey just laws. Conversely, one has a moral responsibility to disobey unjust laws. I would agree with St. Augustine that "an unjust law is no law at all."

Now, what is the difference between the two? How does one determine whether a law is just or unjust? A just law is a man-made code that squares with the moral law or the law of God. An unjust law is a code that is out of harmony with the moral law. To put it in the terms of St. Thomas Aquinas: An unjust law is a human law that is not rooted in eternal law and natural law. Any law that uplifts human personality is just. Any law that degrades human personality is unjust. All segregation statutes are unjust because segregation distorts the soul and damages the personality. It gives the segregator a false sense of superiority and the segregated a false sense of inferiority. Segregation, to use the terminology of the Jewish philosopher Martin Buber, substitutes an "I-it" relationship for an "I-thou" relationship and ends up relegating persons to the status of things. Hence segregation is not only politically, economically, and sociologically unsound, it is morally wrong and sinful. Paul Tillich has said that sin is separation. Is not segregation an existential expression of man's tragic separation, his awful estrangement, his terrible sinfulness? Thus it is that I can urge men to obey the 1954 decision of the Supreme Court, for it is morally right; and I can urge them to disobey segregation ordinances, for they are morally wrong.

Let us consider a more concrete example of just and unjust laws. An unjust law is a code that a numerical or power majority group compels a minority group to obey but does not make binding on itself. This is difference made legal. By the same token, a just law is a code that a majority compels a minority to follow and that it is willing to follow itself. This is sameness made legal.

Let me give another explanation. A law is unjust if it is inflicted on a minority that, as a result of being denied the right to vote, had no part in enacting or devising the law. Who can say that the legislature of Alabama which set up that state's segregation laws was democratically elected? Throughout Alabama all sorts of devious methods are used to prevent Negroes from becoming registered voters, and there are some counties in which, even though Negroes constitute a majority of the population, not a single Negro is registered. Can any law enacted under such circumstances be considered democratically structured?

Sometimes a law is just on its face and unjust in its application. For instance, I have been arrested on a charge of parading without a permit. Now, there is nothing wrong in having an ordinance which requires a permit for a parade. But such an ordinance becomes unjust when it is used to maintain segregation and to deny citizens the First-Amendment privilege of peaceful assembly and protest.

I hope you are able to see the distinction I am trying to point out. In no sense do I advocate evading or defying the law, as would the rabid segregationist. That would lead to anarchy. One who breaks an unjust law must do so openly, lovingly, and with a willingness to accept the penalty. I submit that an individual who breaks a law that conscience tells him is unjust, and who willingly accepts the penalty of imprisonment in order to arouse the conscience of the community over its injustice, is in reality expressing the highest respect for law.

Of course, there is nothing new about this kind of civil disobedience. It was evidenced sublimely in the refusal of Shadrach, Meshach, and

Abednego to obey the laws of Nebuchadnezzar, on the ground that a higher moral law was at stake. It was practiced superbly by the early Christians, who were willing to face hungry lions and the excruciating pain of chopping blocks rather than submit to certain unjust laws of the Roman Empire. To a degree, academic freedom is a reality today because Socrates practiced civil disobedience. In our own nation, the Boston Tea Party represented a massive act of civil disobedience.

We should never forget that everything Adolf Hitler did in Germany was "legal" and everything the Hungarian freedom fighters did in Hungary was "illegal." It was "illegal" to aid and comfort a Jew in Hitler's Germany. Even so, I am sure that, had I lived in Germany at the time, I would have aided and comforted my Jewish brothers. If today I lived in a Communist country where certain principles dear to the Christian faith are suppressed, I would openly advocate disobeying that country's anti-religious laws.

I must make two honest confessions to you, my Christian and Jewish brothers. First, I must confess that over the past few years I have been gravely disappointed with the white moderate. I have almost reached the regrettable conclusion that the Negro's great stumbling block in his stride toward freedom is not the White Citizen's Counciler or the Ku Klux Klanner, but the white moderate, who is more devoted to "order" than to justice; who prefers a negative peace which is the absence of tension to a positive peace which is the presence of justice; who constantly says, "I agree with you in the goal you seek but I cannot agree with your methods of direct action"; who paternalistically believes he can set the timetable for another man's freedom; who lives by a mythical concept of time and who constantly advises the Negro to wait for a "more convenient season." Shallow understanding from people of good will is more frustrating than absolute misunderstanding from people of ill will. Lukewarm acceptance is much more bewildering than outright rejection.

I had hoped that the white moderate would understand that law and order exist for the purpose of establishing justice and that when they fail in this purpose they become the dangerously structured dams that block the flow of social progress. I had hoped that the white moderate would understand that the present tension in the South is a necessary phase of the transition from an obnoxious negative peace, in which the Negro passively accepted his unjust plight, to a substantive and positive peace, in which all men will respect the dignity and worth of human personality. Actually, we who engage in nonviolent direct action are not the creators of tension. We merely bring to the surface the hidden tension that is already alive. We bring it out in the open, where it can be seen and dealt with. Like a boil that can never be cured so long as it is covered up but must be opened with all its ugliness to the natural medicines of air and light, injustice must be exposed, with all the tension its exposure creates, to the light of human conscience and the air of national opinion, before it can be cured.

In your statement you assert that our actions, even though peaceful, must be condemned because they precipitate violence. But is this a logical assertion? Isn't this like condemning a robbed man because his possession of money precipitated the evil act of robbery? Isn't this like condemning Socrates because his unswerving commitment to truth and his philosophical inquiries precipitated the act by the misguided populace in which they made him drink hemlock? Isn't this like condemning Jesus because his unique God-consciousness and never-ceasing devotion to God's will precipitated the evil act of crucifixion? We must come to see that, as the federal courts have consistently affirmed, it is wrong to urge an individual to cease his efforts to gain his basic constitutional rights because the quest may precipitate violence. Society must protect the robbed and punish the robber.

I had also hoped that the white moderate would reject the myth concerning time in relation to the struggle for freedom. I have just received a letter from a white brother in Texas. He writes: "All Christians know that the colored people will receive equal rights eventually, but it is possible that you are in too great a religious hurry. It has taken Christianity almost two thousand years to accomplish what it has. The teachings of Christ take time to come to earth." Such an attitude stems from a tragic misconception of time, from the strangely irrational notion that there is something in the very flow of time that will inevitably cure all ills. Actually, time itself is neutral; it can be used either destructively or constructively. More and more I feel that the people of ill will have used time much more effectively than have the people of good will. We will have to repent in this generation not merely for the hateful words and actions of the bad people, but for the appalling silence of the good people. Human progress never rolls in on wheels of inevitability; it comes through the tireless efforts of men willing to be co-workers with God, and without this hard work, time itself becomes an ally of the forces of stagnation. We must use time creatively, in the knowledge that the time is always ripe to do right. Now is the time to make real the promise of democracy and transform our pending national elegy into a creative psalm of brotherhood. Now is the time to lift our national policy from the quicksand of racial injustice to the solid rock of human dignity.

You speak of our activity in Birmingham as extreme. At first I was rather disappointed that fellow clergymen would see my nonviolent efforts as those of an extremist. I began thinking about the fact that I stand in the middle of two opposing forces in the Negro community. One is a force of complacency, made up in part of Negroes who, as a result of long years of oppression, are so drained of self-respect and a sense of "somebodiness" that they have adjusted to segregation; and in part of a few middle-class Negroes who, because of a degree of academic and economic security and because in some ways they profit by segregation, have become insensitive to the problems of the masses. The other force is one of bitterness and hatred, and it comes perilously close to advocating violence. It is expressed in the various black nationalist groups that are springing up across the nation, the largest and best-known being Elijah Muhammad's Muslim movement. Nourished by the Negro's frustration over the continued existence of racial discrimination, this movement is made up of people who have lost faith in America, who have absolutely repudiated Christianity, and who have concluded that the white man is an incorrigible "devil."

I have tried to stand between these two forces, saying that we need emulate neither the "do-nothingism" of the complacent nor the hatred and despair of the black nationalist. For there is the more excellent way of love and nonviolent protest. I am grateful to God that, through the influence of the Negro church, the way of nonviolence became an integral part of our struggle.

If this philosophy had not emerged, by now many streets of the South would, I am convinced, be flowing with blood. And I am further convinced that if our white brothers dismiss as "rabble-rousers" and "outside agitators" those of us who employ nonviolent direct action, and if they refuse to support our nonviolent efforts, millions of Negroes will, out of frustration and despair, seek solace and security in black-nationalist ideologies—a development that would inevitably lead to a frightening racial nightmare.

Oppressed people cannot remain oppressed forever. The yearning for freedom eventually manifests itself, and that is what has happened to the American Negro. Something within has reminded him of his birthright of freedom, and something without has reminded him that it can be gained. Consciously or unconsciously, he has been caught up by the Zeitgeist, and with his black brothers of Africa and his brown and yellow brothers of Asia, South America, and the Caribbean, the United States Negro is moving with a sense of great urgency toward the promised land of racial justice. If one recognizes this vital urge that has engulfed the Negro community, one should readily understand why public demonstrations are taking place. The Negro has many pent-up resentments and latent frustrations, and he must release them. So let him march; let him make prayer pilgrimages to the city hall; let him go on freedom rides—and try to understand why he must do so. If his repressed emotions are not released in nonviolent ways, they will seek expression through violence; this is not a threat but a fact of history. So I have not said to my people, "Get rid of your discontent." Rather, I have tried to say that this normal and healthy discontent can be channeled into the creative outlet of nonviolent direct action. And now this approach is being termed extremist.

But though I was initially disappointed at being categorized as an extremist, as I continued to think about the matter I gradually gained a measure of satisfaction from the label. Was not Jesus an extremist for love: "Love your enemies, bless them that curse you, do good to them that hate you, and pray for them which despitefully use you, and persecute you." Was not Amos an extremist for justice: "Let justice roll down like waters and righteousness like an ever-flowing stream." Was not Paul an extremist for the Christian gospel: "I bear in my body the marks of the Lord Jesus." Was not Martin Luther an extremist: "Here I stand; I cannot do otherwise, so help me God." And John Bunyan: "I will stay in jail to the end of my days before I make a butchery of my conscience." And Abraham Lincoln: "This nation cannot survive half slave and half free." And Thomas Jefferson: "We hold these truths to be self-evident, that all men are created equal. . . . " So the question is not whether we will be extremists, but what kind of extremists we will be. Will we be extremists for hate or for love? Will we be extremists for the preservation of injustice or for the extension of justice? In that dramatic scene on Calvary's hill three men were crucified. We must never forget that all three were crucified for the same crime—the crime of extremism. Two were extremists for immorality, and thus fell below their environment. The other, Jesus Christ, was an extremist for love, truth, and goodness, and thereby rose above his environment. Perhaps the South, the nation, and the world are in dire need of creative extremists.

I had hoped that the white moderate would see this need. Perhaps I was too optimistic; perhaps I expected too much. I suppose I should have realized that few members of the oppressor race can understand the deep groans and passionate yearnings of the oppressed race, and still fewer have the vision to see that injustice must be rooted out by strong, persistent, and determined action. I am thankful, however, that some of our white brothers in the South have grasped the meaning of this social revolution and committed themselves to it. They are still all too few in quantity, but they are big in quality. Some—such as Ralph McGill, Lillian Smith, Harry Golden, James McBride Dabbs, Ann Braden, and Sarah Patton Boyle—have written about our struggle in eloquent and prophetic terms. Others have marched with us down nameless streets of the South. They have languished in filthy, roach-infested jails, suffering the abuse and brutality of policemen who view them as "dirty niggerlovers." Unlike so many of their moderate brothers and sisters, they have recognized the urgency of the moment and sensed the need for powerful "action" antidotes to combat the disease of segregation.

Let me take note of my other major disappointment. I have been so greatly disappointed with the white church and its leadership. Of course, there are some notable exceptions. I am not unmindful of the fact that each of you has taken some significant stands on this issue. I commend you, Reverend Stallings, for your Christian stand on this past Sunday, in welcoming Negroes to your worship service on a nonsegregated basis. I commend the Catholic leaders of this state for integrating Spring Hill College several years ago.

But despite these notable exceptions, I must honestly reiterate that I have been disappointed with the church. I do not say this as one of those negative critics who can always find something wrong with the church. I say this as a minister of the gospel, who loves the church; who was nurtured in its bosom; who has been sustained by its spiritual blessings and who will remain true to it as long as the cord of life shall lengthen.

When I was suddenly catapulted into the leadership of the bus protest in Montgomery, Alabama, a few years ago, I felt we would be supported by the white church. I felt that the white ministers, priests, and rabbis of the South would be among our strongest allies. Instead, some have been outright opponents, refusing to understand the freedom movement and misrepresenting its leaders; all too many others have been more cautious than courageous and have remained silent behind the anesthetizing security of stained-glass windows.

In spite of my shattered dreams, I came to Birmingham with the hope that the white religious leadership of this community would see the justice of our cause and, with deep moral concern, would serve as the channel through which our just grievances could reach the power structure. I had hoped that each of you would understand. But again I have been disappointed.

I have heard numerous southern religious leaders admonish their worshipers to comply with a desegregation decision because it is the law, but I have longed to hear white ministers declare: "Follow this decree because integration is morally right and because the Negro is your brother." In the midst of blatant injustices inflicted upon the Negro, I have watched white churchmen stand on the sideline and mouth pious irrelevancies and sanctimonious trivialities. In the midst of a mighty struggle to rid our nation of racial and economic injustice, I have heard many ministers say: "Those are social issues, with which the gospel has no real concern." And I have watched many churches commit themselves to a completely otherworldly religion which makes a strange, un-Biblical distinction between body and soul, between the sacred and the secular.

I have traveled the length and breadth of Alabama, Mississippi, and all the other southern states. On sweltering summer days and crisp autumn mornings I have looked at the South's beautiful churches with their lofty spires pointing heavenward. I have beheld the impressive outlines of her massive religious-education buildings. Over and over I have found myself asking: "What kind of people worship here? Who is their God? Where were their voices when the lips of Governor Barnett dripped with words of interposition and nullification? Where were they when Governor Wallace gave a clarion call for defiance and hatred? Where were their voices of support when bruised and weary Negro men and women decided to rise from the dark dungeons of complacency to the bright hills of creative protest?"

Yes, these questions are still in my mind. In deep disappointment I have wept over the laxity of the church. But be assured that my tears have been tears of love. Yes, I love the church. How could I do otherwise? I am in the rather unique position of being the son, the grandson, and the great-grandson of preachers. Yes, I see the church as the body of Christ. But, oh! How we have blemished and scarred that body through social neglect and through fear of being nonconformists.

There was a time when the church was very powerful—in the time when the early Christians rejoiced at being deemed worthy to suffer for what they believed. In those days the church was not merely a thermometer that recorded the ideas and principles of popular opinion; it was a thermostat that transformed the mores of society. Whenever the early Christians entered a town, the people in power became disturbed and immediately sought to convict the Christians for being "disturbers of the peace" and "outside agitators." But the Christians pressed on, in the conviction that they were "a colony of heaven," called to obey God rather than man. Small in number, they were big in commitment. They were too God-intoxicated to be "astronomically intimidated." By their effort and example they brought an end to such ancient evils as infanticide and gladiatorial contests.

Things are different now. So often the contemporary church is a weak, ineffectual voice with an uncertain sound. So often it is an archdefender of the status quo. Far from being disturbed by the presence of the church, the power structure of the average community is consoled by the church's silent—and often even vocal—sanction of things as they are.

But the judgment of God is upon the church as never before. If today's church does not recapture the sacrificial spirit of the early church, it will lose its authenticity, forfeit the loyalty of millions, and be dismissed as an irrelevant social club with no meaning for the twentieth century. Every day I meet young people whose disappointment with the church has turned into outright disgust.

Perhaps I have once again been too optimistic. Is organized religion too inextricably bound to the status quo to save our nation and the world? Perhaps I must turn my faith to the inner spiritual church, the church within the church, as the true ekklesia and the hope of the world. But again I am thankful to God that some noble souls from the ranks of organized religion have broken loose from the paralyzing chains of conformity and joined us as active partners in the struggle for freedom. They have left their secure congregations and walked the streets of Albany, Georgia, with us. They have gone down the highways of the South on tortuous rides for freedom. Yes, they have gone to jail with us. Some have been dismissed from their churches, have lost the support of their bishops and fellow ministers. But they have acted in the faith that right defeated is stronger than evil triumphant. Their witness has been the spiritual salt that has preserved the true meaning of the gospel in these troubled times. They have carved a tunnel of hope through the dark mountain of disappointment.

I hope the church as a whole will meet the challenge of this decisive hour. But even if the church does not come to the aid of justice, I have no despair about the future. I have no fear about the outcome of our struggle in Birmingham, even if our motives are at present misunderstood. We will reach the goal of freedom in Birmingham and all over the nation, because the goal of America is freedom. Abused and scorned though we may be, our destiny is tied up with America's destiny. Before the pilgrims landed at Plymouth, we were here. For more than two centuries our forebears labored in this country without wages; they made cotton king; they built the homes of their masters while suffering gross injustice and shameful humiliation—and yet out of a bottomless vitality they continued to thrive and develop. If the inexpressible cruelties of slavery could not stop us, the opposition we now face will surely fail. We will win our freedom because the sacred heritage of our nation and the eternal will of God are embodied in our echoing demands.

Before closing I feel impelled to mention one other point in your statement that has troubled me profoundly. You warmly commended the Birmingham police force for keeping "order" and "preventing violence." I doubt that you would have so warmly commended the police force if you had seen its dogs sinking their teeth into unarmed, nonviolent Negroes. I doubt that you would so quickly commend the policemen if you were to observe their ugly and inhumane treatment of Negroes here in the city jail; if you were to watch them push and curse old Negro women and young Negro girls; if you were to see them slap and kick old Negro men and young boys; if you were to observe them, as they did on two occasions, refuse to give us food because we wanted to sing our grace together. I cannot join you in your praise of the Birmingham police department.

It is true that the police have exercised a degree of discipline in handling the demonstrators. In this sense they have conducted themselves rather "nonviolently" in public. But for what purpose? To preserve the evil system of segregation. Over the past few years I have consistently preached that nonviolence demands that the means we use must be as pure as the ends we seek. I have tried to make clear that it is wrong to use immoral means to attain moral ends. But now I must affirm that it is just as wrong, or perhaps even more so, to use moral means to preserve immoral ends. Perhaps Mr. Connor and his policemen have been rather nonviolent in public, as was Chief Pritchett in Albany, Georgia, but they have used the moral means of nonviolence to maintain the immoral end of racial injustice. As T. S. Eliot has said, "The last temptation is the greatest treason: To do the right deed for the wrong reason."

I wish you had commended the Negro sit-inners and demonstrators of Birmingham for their sublime courage, their willingness to suffer, and their amazing discipline in the midst of great provocation. One day the South will recognize its real heroes. They will be the James Merediths, with the noble sense of purpose that enables them to face jeering and hostile mobs, and with the agonizing loneliness that characterizes the life of the pioneer. They will be old, oppressed, battered Negro women, symbolized in a seventy-two-year-old woman in Montgomery, Alabama, who rose up with a sense of dignity and with her people decided not to ride segregated buses, and who responded with ungrammatical profundity to one who inquired about her weariness: "My feets is tired, but my soul is at rest." They will be the young high school and college students, the young ministers of the gospel and a host of their elders, courageously and nonviolently sitting in at lunch counters and willingly going to jail for conscience' sake. One day the South will know that when these disinherited children of God sat down at lunch counters, they were in reality standing up for what is best in the American dream and for the most sacred values in our Judaeo-Christian heritage, thereby bringing our nation back to those great wells of democracy which were dug deep by the founding fathers in their formulation of the Constitution and the Declaration of Independence.

Never before have I written so long a letter. I'm afraid it is much too long to take your precious time. I can assure you that it would have been much shorter if I had been writing from a comfortable desk, but what else can one do when he is alone in a narrow jail cell, other than write long letters, think long thoughts, and pray long prayers?

If I have said anything in this letter that overstates the truth and indicates an unreasonable impatience, I beg you to forgive me. If I have said anything that understates the truth and indicates my having a patience that allows me to settle for anything less than brotherhood, I beg God to forgive me.

I hope this letter finds you strong in the faith. I also hope that circumstances will soon make it possible for me to meet each of you, not as an integrationist or a civil-rights leader but as a fellow clergyman and a Christian brother. Let us all hope that the dark clouds of racial prejudice will soon pass away and the deep fog of misunderstanding will be lifted from our fear-drenched communities, and in some not too distant tomorrow the radiant stars of love and brotherhood will shine over our great nation with all their scintillating beauty.

> Yours for the cause of Peace and Brotherhood,
> Martin Luther King, Jr.

*Questions*

1. Explain the importance of the four steps in non-violent action.
2. Critics of Martin Luther King, Jr. have denounced him as a communist. Do you find anything in this letter that supports or rebuts this charge?
3. Why does King sprinkle his letter with citations from so many authorities? Does this strengthen or weaken his case? Why?
4. Given the history of the civil rights movement in the United States since King's death in 1968, do his non-violent methods appear to have been more effective than other forms of protest? Explain.
5. Why do you think that no civil rights leader of comparable stature has come forward since Dr. King's death? What have been the consequences of this fact?

3

# Socialism Informs the Best of Our Politics

## Michael Harrington

This article originally appeared in *In These Times*, February–March 1988.

*Socialism has never had a good press in the United States. According to Michael Harrington, author of The Other America (1962), a book credited with helping launch the Democratic anti-poverty programs of the 1960s, people react to the term "socialist" with misunderstanding at best, and rejection at worst. Until his death, the author was co-chair of the Democratic Socialists of America.*

*Nevertheless, Harrington sees value in the socialist name, the socialist critique and the (indirect) socialist impact on liberal politics.*

*No use changing the name, he argues, because conservatives will not let you get away with it. He feels that a "toning down" of socialist objectives would deprive the movement of its clarity of analysis and program.*

*As part of that analysis, Harrington views homelessness in wider terms than an administrative decision made decades ago to empty mental hospitals. He considers homelessness as a symptom of the nation's failure to provide either a medical or a housing program. Socialism's contribution to economic and political thought is to look for systemic causes, whether it relates to domestic poverty or to hunger in the third world.*

*By frankly admitting the failures of socialists when they were close to power, Harrington comes across as a realistic thinker. He is also a prophet of hope, predicting that change for the better is not far off. As he describes it, this foe of corporate America describes socialism as "the theory and practice which seeks to empower the people . . . to take control of their destiny for the first time."*

Is socialism relevant to the late 20th and 21st centuries? And if so what does one mean by "socialism"? In any case, why identify as a socialist in the United States where the very word invites misunderstanding at best, and a frantic, ignorant rejection at worst? Finally, given all of these problems why build a socialist organization in this country?

First, the socialist critique of power under both capitalism and communism is not only substantial in and of itself; it also makes a significant contribution to the cause of incremental reform as well as to a radical restructuring of society.

Power, that critique argues, is systemic, North, South, East and West, and reproduces itself along with its mutually reinforcing social evils. In the various systems of power in the world today, the control of investment and basic economic allocations, is not the only source of domination—racism and sexism persist in all systems—but it is its single most important constituent. Those in charge of investment, be they corporate executives or commissars, will claim and get unequal treatment for themselves on the grounds that they act in the interest of the future of the entire society and must therefore have the resources to do their job. And those who are excluded from that function will be forced to pay all the social costs of decisions made on high.

## AN UNDERSTANDING OF HOMELESSNESS

In a superficial analysis, the tremendous growth of homelessness in the late 1970s and 1980s is simply a result of the deinstitutionalization of mental patients in the 1960s. But that analysis contradicts the data, which increasingly shows that the homeless are families and that two-thirds of them do not have histories of mental and emotional problems. It also fails to explain why the deinstitutionalization of the 1960s did not lead to a dramatic rise in homelessness until the late 1970s.

A more serious—liberal—analysis would recognize that this homelessness is a function of decreased real income and increased poverty among the wage-earning poor and a decline in the supply of private and government-sponsored affordable housing. From this point of view, one would quite rightly attack New York Mayor Ed Koch for providing tax incentives for the destruction of single-room-occupancy hotels (SROs), while at the same time noting that the SROs themselves were utterly inadequate even if they were better than the streets.

A socialist analysis would deepen those liberal insights. It would see Koch's action as one more example of the system at work: of government policy subsidizing private, profit-making and often anti-social priorities, usually on the grounds of a "trickle-down" theory. It would understand the decline in the real wage and the increase in the poverty of working people as a standard systemic response to the crisis of profitability and productivity in the mid-1970s. And it would stress not simply a program for decent "shelter," but the necessity of democratizing the entire process of investment in this, and other, basic needs of life. It would also show that, had the community health centers projected in the 1960s been built—or more broadly, if America had a national health program—then the problem of the deinstitutionalized mental patients would never have became the outrage it now is.

That socialist conception of a housing program would not, however, simply specify so many "units." It would urge a planned development of racially and socially integrated communities with public spaces and facilities for new institutions of neighborhood democracy and control. And it would try to reach out to build political support for such an undertaking by uniting the homeless in a coalition with young families from the working class and middle class as well as with seniors who do not want to be segregated on the basis of age.

## CHANGING THE DISTRIBUTION OF POWER

The socialist point is that these various reforms, which many liberals would support on an ad hoc basis, must be as coherent as the structures they oppose. What is needed is not simply a new housing bill but a new way of making and designing social investments in areas of critical need. And even if one has to settle politically for something less than that, a proposal designed on the basis of a socialist analysis will be different than one which is the product of liberal concern with a single issue. For example, Representative Ronald Dellums' (D-CA) national health bill gives people at the base a say in non-technical medical decisions; it is not just a matter of "health insurance." And indeed, every socialist program is about changing the distribution of power in the way decisions are made.

## THE SOVIET UNION AND THE THIRD WORLD

Similarly, a socialist response to what is happening under Gorbachev in the Soviet Union would not simply stress the importance of pursuing peace negotiations even more vigorously in order to encourage *Glasnost* and *Perestroika*. It would put Gorbachev's progressive, but technocratic, reforms in the context of an analysis which would see bureaucratic resistance to change in the Soviet Union as a function of an anti-democratic system of power in which even positive initiatives are initiated behind the backs of the people. And it would argue that American unilateral peace initiatives toward verifiable Big

Power agreements may well—and hopefully will—create the long-run conditions for a democratization of Soviet society which goes beyond anything now on the agenda in Moscow.

In the case of the Third World, one can be even more specific. The response to the international debt crisis-and the global structure of inequality underlying it—by the Socialist International, under the leadership of Michael Manley, former Minister of Jamaica and Willy Brandt, former Chancellor of West Germany (and, until his death, of Olof Palme, Prime Minister of Sweden), is a perfect example of what is needed. A major transfer of funds from North to South, the International has shown, could create jobs in the First World as well as the Third. International justice could be an engine of growth for U.S. workers. It could provide an alternative to chauvinist attitudes, which sometimes accompany the justified anger of people under advanced capitalism with the systemic irresponsibility of multi-national corporations.

## NEW DEPARTURES

All these negatives and criticism are well and good, someone might say. But isn't the socialist movement itself in a profound crisis even in those countries where it has a mass base? What about the spectacular failure of the French Socialists when they had an absolute parliamentary majority and control of the presidency as well?

There is no doubt that the "Keynesian" version of social democracy—a mixed corporate economy in which socialist governments extract a surplus for welfare measures, but leave basic investment decisions in private hands—which dominated the European movement from 1950 to about 1975, is in a profound crisis. The French socialists were subjected to the brutal discipline of the world's banks because their socially based Keynesian programs generated more jobs in Japan and Germany than in France. Even as one searches for a new response to this reality, it should be noted that this is one more example of elite corporate power—in this case exercised by multinational banks and corporations. The contemporary challenge to socialism, however, requires new departures, not fatalistic surrender.

At the very origins of the modern socialist movement in the 19th century, there was a basic insight which will be even truer in the 21st century than when it was first formulated. Capitalism was understood as a system of private socialization, creating a genuine world market for the first time in human history, applying science to production, and linking people together in an unprecedented interdependence.

But because that socialization was private, it was pursued at the expense of society. Socialism was conceived of as a program of democratic socialization from below, as a movement to put the people in control of the economic conditions which determine so much about their lives.

That basic goal has been understood over the past century and a half in many, many ways, some of them wrong, some leading to partial victories, none even beginning to achieve the fullness of the original vision. And matters were complicated when, in the Soviet Union, a system of anti-democratic socialization emerged. There the party-state carried out the brutal process of accumulation which was the work of capitalism in the West, and used the rhetoric of socialism to rationalize new forms of class rule.

Now that the Keynesian version of socialism is in crisis, the mass socialist movements of the world are indeed confused and even bewildered about the next steps toward democratic socialization. This is roughly the third time that this has happened: it occurred right after World War I when the socialists suddenly got political power and did not know what to do with it, and at the time of the Depression when, with the exceptions of the Swedes, there was a general programmatic and political failure of the movement.

At the same time, the objective need for socialism has become all the more imperative. The multi-nationalization of the world economy is creating an increasingly interdependent globe, striking at the workers and communities of advanced capitalism as well as at the poor countries. Revolutionary new technologies are undermining even the limited accomplishments of capitalist welfare states.

## THE NEED FOR INTERNATIONAL
## DEMOCRATIC SOCIALIZATION

There is no question now as to whether there will be radical change in the immediate future. It is already under way. The only issue is how it will be carried out. Will it come from on high, at the social and economic cost of the mass of people in every society and through a repression of freedom? Or can socialists, faced with a reality they never imagined, work out effective programs of structural change which move in the direction of a truly democratic socialization of the world?

There is now "too much" food in the world—and people starving to death; "too much" steel capacity and masses desperately in need of housing and transit which use steel. And there will be, within the next year or two, a crisis of the world economy which will not automatically engender a progressive response, but which will make such a political response possible. At that point, some of those who now assume that the determinants of Reagan's America (and Thatcher's Britain, Kohl's Germany, Chirac's France, to cite but a few of the obvious cases) are eternal will look around for a socialist movement with positive answers. These cannot be predicted now, but it is clear that they will be distinctly inter-nationalist, anti-racist, feminist and "green" as well as oriented to the working class, both old and new.

## WHY A SOCIALIST ORGANIZATION?

But why not just insist on the socialist specifics and omit any mention of the socialist name itself? Why not, as Tom Hayden's original Campaign for Economic Democracy of the 1970s proposed, socialism without the "S" word?

It is not just that the right wing will not let you get away with it, although that is true (they routinely denounce liberalism as socialist). It is not even primarily because the historic function of American anti-socialism is to fight liberal reforms, not a non-existent socialist threat, and that an attack on that anti-socialism will broaden the political spectrum in a country which has a right and a center but no real left. Even more important, if one pretends that one is not a socialist, or speaks in euphemisms, all that is lost is the basic clarity of analysis and program. You cannot talk, or think, about the present crisis without understanding its roots in the systemic complex of corporate capitalist power. We can try to communicate that fact in the most effective possible rhetoric-and many socialists do wrongly think that it is "radical" to talk in such a way as to infuriate the average American— but we cannot conceal the basic reality from others and, above all, from ourselves.

Secondly, socialists have had a significant impact upon power in America even if, for complex historic reasons, they have never come close to achieving power. The role of the 1912 Debsian immediate program in introducing the concepts of the welfare state of the New Deal is well known (though it is often not recognized that the 1912 program is still to the left of what has been achieved). So is the critical importance of socialists, communists, Trotskyists and anarchists in struggling for the theory and practice of industrial unionism, which led to the Congress of Industrial Organizations. More recently, David Garrow has documented how Martin Luther King, Jr. saw himself a part of that socialist tradition (a fact that I knew from my own work with Dr. King). And the feminist, anti-interventionist and Citizens' Action movements clearly built upon the radical tradition of the 1960s.

I also think of the generation of economists now in their late thirties and early forties, the men and women who will provide many of the practical ideas of the next mass left. Every one of them comes out of the New Left and the socialist tradition. However they now define themselves, they are a part of that ongoing socialist contribution to practical politics.

But why, then, a socialist organization? Why the backbreaking, frustrating work of building DSA against the tremendous odds of corporate America? Simply put, because there is no individualistic way of showing people that democratic and communitarian action is critical to the future. More broadly, the times are already a-changing. The moral and intellectual fatigue which so many veterans of the past twenty years feel blinds them to the fact that, within a year or two or three, there is going to be a new generation of change in America.

I remember the Eisenhower—and Joe McCarthy—1950s. They were worse than anything that happened in the Reagan 1980s. And when the moment of change came—none of us who had been waiting for years for that blessed break understood that it actually happened on a day in February 1960 when four black students in North Carolina decided to have an integrated cup of coffee—a decimated left was utterly incapable of rising to the enormous new opportunities.

I do not think that the 1960s would have been totally different had there been a continuity with the radicalism of the 1930s, 40s, and 50s—had there been the equivalent of a DSA in February 1960. I do think that there would have been a difference. Perhaps people would not have had to spend so much time reinventing the wheel, sometimes badly, and maybe the histories of Students for a Democratic Society and the Student Non-Violent Coordinating Committee would have benefited.

Right now, the difficult and laborious work of DSA—the struggle to make the anti-intervention movement as broad as possible and to involve the unions and the churches in it; the campaign to make disarmament the beginning of the work of international economic and social justice; the attempt to define the issue of poverty and racism and sexism as problems of economic and social structures rather than discrete evils; the coalition meetings with activists from the unions, the new social strata, the minority movements and all the rest—is going to make a profound contribution to the 1990s left. We are not going to lead the nation and, thank God, have abandoned any Messianic pretense of being the anointed vanguard of history.

## A NEW CIVILIZATION

But when the moment comes, when that pilgrimage of women and men toward the realization of their own humanity begins again, as it will, we will be there. DSA itself may well be transformed at that moment, its cadres and energy and ideas being absorbed into new organizational forms that we cannot now even imagine. And yet it will be there.

Those who lose heart on the very eve of a new generation of change should remember the profound truth Antonio Gramsci articulated from an Italian jail cell in a decade that saw the triumph of fascism—and, with an exception or two, the spectacular failure of socialism and the destruction of the Russian Revolution by Stalinism. Socialism, Gramsci said, was not a matter of a political victory on this or that day, or even this or that decade. It was not an economic program, a recipe. It was a "moral and intellectual reformation," a fight to transform the very culture and will of those who had, since time immemorial, been made subordinate, the epochal work of the creation of a new civilization.

We live today in the most radical of times; humanity is fighting at this very moment over the content of that new civilization—of a new planet, if you will—and that struggle will go on beyond the lifetime of every one of us. There is no guarantee that the vision of a democratic and communitarian socialization will prevail over the bureaucrats and the technocrats who abound in this period. All socialism is—"all"— is the theory and practice which seeks to empower the people of the North, South, East and West to take control of their destiny for the first time.

Those who join the movement for the immediate rewards of power are advised to apply elsewhere. Those who are willing to wager their lives on the possibility of freedom and justice and solidarity should pay their dues.

*Questions*

1. What do you think of when you hear the word socialism? Does the author's description of the movement alter your earlier impressions. In what way?
2. What is the difference between socialism and liberalism, as depicted by the author?

3. The socialist critique focuses on the accumulation of political and economic power in the hands of the few. Is this a necessary part of the capitalist system? Why or why not? Give examples to back up your response.

4. Have the author's predictions about the political climate of the U.S. been borne out? Do you think his optimism was the result of temperament or rigid analysis?

5. In view of the disintegration of the Communist system in Eastern Europe, do you think that the argument for socialism is stronger or less strong? Give your reasons.

4
# The Wail of the Children

## Mother Jones

This article originally appeared in *Mother Jones Speaks*, ed. Philip S. Foner, Monad, 1983.

*Mary Harris Jones ("Mother Jones") was born in County Cork, Ireland, around 1839. Moving to Canada with her family, she married George Jones, an iron union organizer, in 1861. Her husband and four children died in an epidemic in Memphis in 1867. She spent the rest of her life promoting better working conditions for laboring people, especially children, until her death in 1930.*

*Mother Jones traveled the country from New York to Michigan, the south and Arizona to dramatize the exploitation of miners, shirtwaist workers, Mexican immigrants and everyone in need. She was a genius at publicizing her cause, was arrested many times, supported political candidates and appealed directly to Presidents. Her ally was Terence Powderly, founder of the Knights of Labor.*

*The following was taken from a speech she delivered at Coney Island, New York, during a march to the Oyster Bay home of President Theodore Roosevelt in 1903. Her cause on this occasion was the plight of little children required by their parents and employers to work in unsafe mills.*

*Mother Jones died in 1930 expressing the wish, it was reported, "that she could live another hundred years in order to fight to the end that there would be no more machine guns and no more sobbing little children."*

After a long and weary march, with more miles to travel, we are on our way to see President Roosevelt at Oyster Bay. We will ask him to recommend the passage of a bill by Congress to protect children against the greed of the manufacturer. We want him to hear the wail of the children, who never have a chance to go to school, but work from ten to eleven hours a day in the textile mills of Philadelphia, weaving the carpets that he and you walk on, and the curtains and clothes of the people.

Fifty years ago there was a cry against slavery, and the men of the North gave up their lives to stop the selling of black children on the block. To-day the white child is sold for $2 a week, and even by his parents, to the manufacturer.

Fifty years ago the black babies were sold C.O.D. To-day the white baby is sold to the manufacturer on the installment plan. He might die at his tasks and the manufacturer with the automobile and the yacht and the daughter who talks French to a poodle dog, as you can see any day at Twenty-third Street and Broadway when they roll by, could not afford to pay $2 a week for the child that might die, except on the present installment plan. What the President can do is to recommend a measure and send a message to Congress which will break the chains of the white children slaves.

He endorsed a bill for the expenditure of $45,000 to fill the stomach of a Prince who went galivanting about the country.[1] We will ask in the name of the aching hearts of these little ones that they be emancipated. I will tell the President that I saw men in Madison Square last night sleeping on the benches and that the country can have no greatness while one unfortunate lies out at night without a bed to sleep on. I will tell him that the prosperity he boasts of is the prosperity of the rich wrung from the poor.

In Georgia where children work day and night in the cotton mills they have just passed a bill to protect song birds. What about the little children from whom all song is gone?[2]

The trouble is that the fellers in Washington don't care. I saw them last Winter pass three railroad bills in one hour, and when labor cries for aid for the little ones they turn their backs and will not listen to her. I asked a man in prison once how he happened to get there. He had stolen a pair of shoes. I told him that if he had stolen a railroad he could be a United States Senator. One hour of justice is worth an age of praying.

You are told that every American-born male citizen has a chance of being President. I tell you that the hungry man without a bed in the park would sell his chance for a good square meal, and these little toilers, deformed, dwarfed in body, soul, and morality, with nothing but toil before them and no chance for schooling, don't even have the dream that they might some day have a chance at the Presidential chair.

You see those monkeys in the cages.[3] They are trying to teach them to talk. The monkeys are too wise, for they fear that then the manufacturers might buy them for slaves in their factories. In 1860 the workingmen had the advantage in the percentage of the country's wealth. To-day statistics at Washington show that with billions of wealth the wage earners' share is but 10 per cent. We are going to tell the President of these things.

[Brooklyn Daily Eagle, *July 27, 1903;*
New York Times, *July 27, 1903.*]

*Notes*

1. Prince Henry of Germany.
2. Mother Jones had worked in the cotton mills of Alabama and described her experiences in "Civilization in Southern Mills," *International Socialist Review*, March, 1901, pp. 540–41 and reprinted below pp. 453–55. *See also, The Autobiography of Mother Jones*, pp. 117–19.
3. Mother Jones had been invited to visit Coney Island with the children by the owner of the wild-animal show and after the exhibition of the trained animals, he invited Mother Jones to speak to the audience. She placed the children in the empty iron cages of the animals, and they "clung to the iron bars while I talked." (*Autobiography of Mother Jones*, pp. 79–80.)

*Questions*

1. How does Mother Jones compare child labor to slavery? What are the similarities and differences? What forms of exploitation of workers still exist today?
2. With what images does she contrast the rich and the poor?
3. Why does she have a low opinion of lawmakers in Washington?
4. In saying: "One hour of justice is worth an age of praying," is the author belittling prayer? Explain.
5. How does she use statistics to bolster her case?

# 5
# The Case against Helping the Poor

## Garrett Hardin

This article originally appeared in *Psychology Today*, 1974.

*Garrett Hardin, professor of biology at the University of California, Santa Barbara, plays the "devil's advocate" role in opposing an open-handed food and immigration policy on the part of the world's rich nations. By turning the "spaceship earth" metaphor of environmentalists into a "lifeboat ethic," he poses hard questions.*

*The first question is one of capacity. How many "swimmers in the sea" can each lifeboat (rich nation) take in? By following either the Christian or Marxist ethic, he says, the lifeboats will be swamped. If only some are let in, on what basis are the others excluded? The continuing growth of earth's population—principally in the poor nations—only compounds the problem, he says. "The philanthropic load created by the sharing ethic can only increase," he concludes.*

*Switching metaphors, Professor Hardin calls attention to "the tragedy of the commons," in which those who are less responsible will spoil things for everybody else. He enlarges on the perceived shortcomings of Public Law 480, in which "though all U.S. taxpayers were forced to contribute to the cost . . . certain special interests gained handsomely under the program." A World Food Bank, he predicts, would lead to the same problems created by this "combination of silent selfish interests and highly vocal humanitarian apologists." Granting such a bank would be used only for emergencies, what will be the attitude, he asks, of rich nations to those poor ones that did not take prudent steps in normal times?*

*Hardin turns the tables on the "environmentalists" by emphasizing the "draft on all aspects of the environment: food, air, water, forest, beaches, wildlife, scenery and solitude" that every new human being represents. In effect, he makes a strong plea for strict population control. He then moves to the "immigration vs. food supply" dilemma, which makes the same point.*

*In his criticism of the food and immigration solutions for the problems of the world's poor, Hardin is forced to state the need for "a true world government to control reproduction and the use of available resources."*

*Until such time that this becomes a reality, he says, "our survival demands that we (the rich nations) govern our actions by the ethics of a lifeboat, harsh though that may be."*

Environmentalists use the metaphor of the earth as a "spaceship" in trying to persuade countries, industries, and people to stop wasting and polluting our natural resources. Since we all share life on this planet, they argue, no single person or institution has the right to destroy, waste, or use more than a fair share of its resources.

But does everyone on earth have an equal right to an equal share of its resources? The spaceship metaphor can be dangerous when used by misguided idealists to justify suicidal policies for sharing our resources through uncontrolled immigration and foreign aid. In their enthusiastic but unrealistic generosity, they confuse the ethics of a spaceship with those of a lifeboat.

A true spaceship would have to be under the control of a captain, since no ship could possibly survive if its course were determined by committee. Spaceship Earth certainly has no captain; the United Nations is merely a toothless tiger, with little power to enforce any policy upon its bickering members.

If we divide the world crudely into rich nations and poor nations, two-thirds of them are desperately poor, and only one-third comparatively rich, with the United States the wealthiest of all. Metaphorically each rich nation can be seen as a lifeboat full of comparatively rich people. In the ocean outside each lifeboat swim the poor of the world, who would like to get in, or at least to share some of the wealth. What should the lifeboat passengers do?

First, we must recognize the limited capacity of any lifeboat. For example, a nation's land has a limited capacity to support a population and as the current energy crisis has shown us, in some ways we have already exceeded the carrying capacity of our land.

**Adrift in a Moral Sea.** So here we sit, say, 50 people in our lifeboat. To be generous, let us assume it has room for 10 more, making a total capacity of 60. Suppose the 50 of us in the lifeboat see 100 others swimming in the water outside, begging for admission to our boat or for handouts. We have several options: we may be tempted to try to live by the Christian ideal of being "our brother's keeper," or by the Marxist ideal of "to each according to his needs." Since the needs of all in the water are the same, and since they can all be seen as "our brothers," we could take them all into our boat, making a total of 150 in a boat designed for 60. The boat swamps, everyone drowns. Complete justice, complete catastrophe.

Since the boat has an unused excess capacity of 10 more passengers, we could admit just 10 more to it. But which 10 do we let in? How do we choose? Do we pick the best 10, the neediest 10, "first come, first served"? And what do we say to the 90 we exclude? If we do let an extra 10 into our lifeboat, we will have lost our "safety factor," an engineering principle of critical importance. For example, if we don't leave room for excess capacity as a safety factor in our country's agriculture, a new plant disease or a bad change in the weather could have disastrous consequences.

Suppose we decide to preserve our small safety factor and admit no more to the lifeboat. Our survival is then possible, although we shall have to be constantly on guard against boarding parties.

While this last solution clearly offers the only means of our survival, it is morally abhorrent to many people. Some say they feel guilty about their good luck. My reply is simple. "Get out and yield your place to others." This may solve the problem of the guilt-ridden person's conscience, but it does not change the ethics of the lifeboat. The needy person to whom the guilt-ridden person yields his place will not himself feel guilty about his good luck. If he did, he would not climb aboard. The net result of conscience-stricken people giving up their unjustly held seats is the elimination of that sort of conscience from the lifeboat.

This is the basic metaphor within which we must work out our solutions. Let us now enrich the image, step by step, with substantive additions from the real world, a world that must solve real and pressing problems of overpopulation and hunger.

The harsh ethics of the lifeboat become even harsher when we consider the reproductive differences between the rich nations and the poor nations. The people inside the lifeboat are doubling in numbers every 87 years; those swimming around outside are doubling, on the average, every 35 years, more than twice as fast as the rich. And since the world's resources are dwindling, the difference in prosperity between the rich and the poor can only increase.

As of 1973, the U.S. had a population of 210 million people, who were increasing by 0.8 percent per year. Outside our lifeboat, let us imagine another 210 million people (say the combined populations of Colombia, Ecuador, Venezuela, Morocco, Pakistan, Thailand and the Philippines), who are increasing at a rate of 3.3 percent per year. Put differently, the doubling time for this aggregate population is 21 years, compared to 87 years for the U.S.

**Multiplying the Rich and the Poor.** Now suppose the U.S. agreed to pool its resources with those seven countries, with everyone receiving an equal share. Initially the ratio of Americans to non-Americans in this model would be one-to-one. But consider what the ratio would be after 87 years, by which time the Americans would have doubled to a population of 420 million. By then, doubling every 21 years, the other group would have swollen to 354 billion. Each American would have to share the available resources with more than eight people.

But, one could argue, this discussion assumes that current population trends will continue, and they may not. Quite so. Most likely the rate of population increase will decline much faster in the U.S. than it will in the other countries, and there does not seem to be much we can do about it. In sharing with "each according to his needs," we must recognize that needs are determined by population size, which is determined by the rate of reproduction, which at present is regarded as a sovereign right of every nation, poor or not. This being so, the philanthropic load created by the sharing ethic of the spaceship can only increase.

**The Tragedy of the Commons.** The fundamental error of spaceship ethics, and the sharing it requires, is that it leads to what I call "the tragedy of the commons." Under a system of private property, the men who own property recognize their responsibility to care for it, for if they don't they will eventually suffer. A farmer, for instance, will allow no more cattle in a pasture than its carrying capacity justifies. If he overloads it, erosion sets in, weeds take over, and he loses the use of the pasture.

If a pasture becomes a commons open to all, the right of each to use it may not be matched by a corresponding responsibility to protect it. Asking everyone to use it with discretion will hardly do, for the considerate herdsman who refrains from overloading the commons suffers more than a selfish one who says his needs are greater. If everyone would restrain himself, all would be well; but it takes only one less than everyone to ruin a system of voluntary restraint. In a crowded world of less than perfect human beings, mutual ruin is inevitable if there are no controls. This is the tragedy of the commons.

One of the major tasks of education today should be the creation of such an acute awareness of the dangers of the commons that people will recognize its many varieties. For example, the air and water have become polluted because they are treated as commons. Further growth in the population or per-capita conversion of natural resources into pollutants will only make the problem worse. The same holds true for the fish of the oceans. Fishing fleets have nearly disappeared in many parts of the world, technological improvements in the art of fishing are hastening the day of complete ruin. Only the replacement of the system of the commons with a responsible system of control will save the land, air, water, and oceanic fisheries.

**The World Food Bank.** In recent years there has been a push to create a new commons called a World Food Bank, an international depository of food reserves to which nations would contribute according to their abilities and from which they would draw according to their needs. This humanitarian proposal has received support from many liberal international groups, and from such prominent citizens as Margaret Mead, U.N. Secretary General Kurt Waldheim, and Senators Edward Kennedy and George McGovern.

A world food bank appeals powerfully to our humanitarian impulses. But before we rush ahead with such a plan, let us recognize where the greatest political push comes from, lest we be disillusioned later. Our experience with the "Food for Peace Program," or Public Law 480, gives us the answer. This program moved billions of dollars worth of U.S. surplus grain to food-short, population-long countries during the past two decades. But when P.L. 480 first became law, a headline in the business magazine *Forbes* revealed the real power behind it. "Feeding the World's Hungry Millions: How It Will Mean Billions for U.S. Business."

And indeed it did. In the years 1960 to 1970, U.S. taxpayers spent a total of $7.9 billion on the Food for Peace program. Between 1948 and 1970, they also paid an additional $50 billion for other economic-aid programs, some of which went for food and food-producing machinery and technology. Though all U.S. taxpayers were forced to contribute to the cost of P.L. 480, certain special interest groups gained handsomely under the program. Farmers did not have to contribute the grain; the government, or rather the taxpayers, bought it from them at full market prices. The increased demand raised prices of farm products generally. The manufacturers of farm machinery, fertilizers and pesticides benefited by the farmers' extra efforts to grow more food. Grain elevators profited from storing the surplus until it could be shipped. Railroads made money hauling it to ports, and shipping lines profited from carrying it overseas. The implementation of P.L. 480 required the creation of a vast government bureaucracy, which then acquired its own vested interest in continuing the program regardless of its merits.

**Extracting Dollars.** Those who proposed and defended the Food for Peace program in public rarely mentioned its importance to any of these special interests. The public emphasis was always on its humanitarian effects. The combination of silent selfish interests and highly vocal humanitarian apologists made a powerful and successful lobby for extracting money from taxpayers. We can expect the same lobby to push now for the creation of a World Food Bank.

However great the potential benefit to selfish interests, it should not be a decisive argument against a truly humanitarian program. We must ask if such a program would actually do more good than harm, not only momentarily but also in the long run. Those who propose the food bank usually refer to a current "emergency" or "crisis" in terms of world food supply. But what is an emergency? Although they may be infrequent and sudden, everyone knows that emergencies will occur from time to time. A well-run family, company, organization or country prepares for the likelihood of accidents and emergencies. It expects them, it budgets for them, it saves for them.

**Learning the Hard Way.** What happens if some organizations or countries budget for accidents and others do not? If each country is solely responsible for its own well-being, poorly managed ones will suffer. But they can learn from experience. They may mend their ways, and learn to budget for infrequent but certain emergencies. For example, the weather varies from year to year, and periodic crop failures are certain. A wise and competent government saves out of the production of the good years in anticipation of bad years to come. Joseph taught this policy to Pharaoh in Egypt more than 2,000 years ago. Yet the great majority of the governments in the world today do not follow such a policy. They lack either the wisdom or the competence, or both. Should those nations that do manage to put something aside be forced to come to the rescue each time an emergency occurs among the poor nations?

"But it isn't their fault!" some kindhearted liberals argue. "How can we blame the poor people who are caught in an emergency? Why must they suffer for the sins of their governments?" The concept of blame is simply not relevant here. The real question is, what are the operational consequences of establishing a food bank? If it is open to every country every time a need develops, slovenly rulers will not be motivated to take Joseph's advice. Someone will always come to their aid. Some countries will deposit food in the world food bank, and others will withdraw it. There will be almost no overlap. As a result of such solutions to food shortage emergencies, the poor countries will not learn to mend their ways, and will suffer progressively greater emergencies as their populations grow.

**Population Control the Crude Way.** On the average, poor countries undergo a 2.5 percent increase in population each year; rich countries, about 0.8 percent. Only rich countries have anything in the way of food reserves set aside, and even they do not have as much as they should. Poor countries have none. If poor countries received no food from the outside, the rate of their population growth would be periodically checked by crop failures and famines. But if they can always draw on a world food bank in time of need, their population can continue to grow unchecked, and so will their "need" for aid. In the short run, a world food bank may diminish that need, but in the long run it actually increases the need without limit.

Without some system of worldwide food sharing, the proportion of people in the rich and poor nations might eventually stabilize. The overpopulated poor countries would decrease in numbers, while the rich countries that had room for more people would increase. But with a well-meaning system of sharing, such as a world food bank, the growth differential between the rich and the poor countries will not only persist, it will increase. Because of the higher rate of population growth in the poor countries of the world, 88 percent of today's children are born poor, and only 12 percent rich. Year by year the ratio becomes worse, as the fast-reproducing poor outnumber the slow-reproducing rich.

A world food bank is thus a commons in disguise. People will have more motivation to draw from it than to add to any common store. The less provident and less able will multiply at the expense of the abler and more provident, bringing eventual ruin upon all who share in the commons. Besides, any system of "sharing" that amounts to foreign aid from the rich nations to the poor nations will carry the taint of charity, which will contribute little to the world peace so devoutly desired by those who support the idea of a world food bank.

As past U.S. foreign-aid programs have amply and depressingly demonstrated, international charity frequently inspires mistrust and antagonism rather than gratitude on the part of the recipient nation.

**Chinese Fish and Miracle Rice.** The modern approach to foreign aid stresses the export of technology and advice, rather than money and food. As an ancient Chinese proverb goes: "Give a man a fish and he will eat for a day; teach him how to fish and he will eat for the rest of his days." Acting on this advice, the Rockefeller and Ford Foundations have financed a number of programs for improving agriculture in the hungry nations. Known as the "Green Revolution," these programs have led to the development of "miracle rice" and "miracle wheat," new strains that offer bigger harvests and greater resistance to crop damage. Norman Borlaug, the Nobel Prize-winning agronomist who, supported by the Rockefeller Foundation, developed "miracle wheat," is one of the most prominent advocates of a world food bank.

Whether or not the Green Revolution can increase food production as much as its champions claim is a debatable but possibly irrelevant point. Those who support this well-intended humanitarian effort should first consider some of the fundamentals of human ecology. Ironically, one man who did was the late Alan Gregg, a vice-president of the Rockefeller Foundation. Two decades ago he expressed strong doubts about the wisdom of such attempts to increase food production. He likened the growth and spread of humanity over the surface of the earth to the spread of cancer in the human body, remarking that "cancerous growths demand food; but, as far as I know, they have never been cured by getting it."

**Overloading the Environment.** Every human born constitutes a draft on all aspects of the environment: food, air, water, forest, beaches, wildlife, scenery and solitude. Food can, perhaps, be significantly increased to meet a growing demand. But what about clean beaches, unspoiled forests, and solitude? If we satisfy a growing population's need for food, we necessarily decrease its per capita supply of the other resources needed by men.

India, for example, now has a population of 600 million, which increases by 15 million each year. This population already puts a huge load on a relatively impoverished environment. The country's forests are now only a small fraction of what they were three centuries ago, and floods and erosion continually destroy the insufficient farmland that remains. Every one of the 15 million new lives added to India's population puts an additional burden on the environment and increases the economic and social costs of crowding. However humanitarian our intent, every Indian life saved through medical or nutritional assistance from abroad diminishes the quality of life for those who remain, and for subsequent generations. If rich countries make it possible, through foreign aid, for 600 million Indians to swell to 1.2 billion in a mere 28 years, as their current growth rate threatens, will future generations of Indians thank us for hastening the destruction of their environment? Will our good intentions be sufficient excuse for the consequences of our actions?

My final example of a commons in action is one for which the public has the least desire for rational discussion—immigration. Anyone who publicly questions the wisdom of current U.S. immigration policy is promptly charged with bigotry, prejudice, ethnocentrism, chauvinism, isolationism or selfishness. Rather than encounter such accusations, one would rather talk about other matters, leaving immigration policy to wallow in the crosscurrents of special interests that take no account of the good of the whole, or the interests of posterity.

Perhaps we still feel guilty about things we said in the past. Two generations ago the popular press frequently referred to Dagos, Wops, Polacks, Chinks and Krauts, in articles about how America was being "overrun" by foreigners of supposedly inferior genetic stock. But because the implied inferiority of foreigners was used then as justification for keeping them out, people now assume that restrictive policies could only be based on such misguided notions. There are other grounds.

**A Nation of Immigrants.** Just consider the numbers involved. Our government acknowledges a net inflow of 400,000 immigrants a year. While we have no hard data on the extent of illegal entries, educated guesses put the figure at about 600,000 a year. Since the natural increase (excess of births over deaths) of the resident population now runs about 1.7 million per year, the yearly gain from immigration amounts to at least 19 percent of the total annual increase, and may be as much as 37 percent if we include the estimate for illegal immigrants. Considering the growing use of birth control devices, the potential effect of educational campaigns by such organizations as Planned Parenthood Federation of America and Zero Population Growth, and the influence of inflation and the housing shortage, the fertility rate of American women may decline so much that immigration could account for all the yearly increase in population. Should we not at least ask if that is what we want?

For the sake of those who worry about whether the "quality" of the average immigrant compares favorably with the quality of the average resident, let us assume that immigrants and native born citizens are of exactly equal quality, however one defines that term. We will focus here only on quantity; and since our conclusions will depend on nothing else, all charges of bigotry and chauvinism become irrelevant.

**Immigration vs. Food Supply.** World food banks move food to the people, hastening the exhaustion of the environment of the poor countries. Unrestricted immigration, on the other hand, moves people to the food, thus speeding up the destruction of the environment of rich countries. We can easily understand why poor people should want to make this latter transfer, but why should rich hosts encourage it?

As in the case of foreign-aid programs immigration receives support from selfish interests and humanitarian impulses. The primary selfish interest in unimpeded immigration is the desire of employers for cheap labor, particularly in industries and trades that offer degrading work. In the past, one wave of foreigners after another was brought into the U.S. to work at wretched jobs for wretched wages. In recent years the Cubans, Puerto Ricans, and Mexicans have had this dubious honor. The interests of the employers of cheap labor mesh well with the guilty silence of the country's liberal intelligentsia. White Anglo-Saxon Protestants are particularly reluctant to call for a closing of the doors to immigration for fear of being called bigots.

But not all countries have such reluctant leadership. Most educated Hawaiians, for example, are keenly aware of the limits of their environment, particularly in terms of population growth. There is only so much room on the islands, and the islanders know it. To Hawaiians, immigrants from the other 49 states present as great a threat as those from other nations. At a recent meeting of Hawaiian government officials in Honolulu, I had the ironic delight of hearing a speaker, who like most of his audience countered: "How can we shut the doors now? We have many friends and relatives in Japan that we'd like to bring here some day so that they can enjoy Hawaii too." The Japanese-American speaker smiled sympathetically and answered: "Yes, but we have children now, and someday we'll have grandchildren too. We can bring more people from Japan only by giving away some of the land that we hope to pass on to our grandchildren some day. What right do we have to do that?"

At this point, I can hear U.S. liberals asking: "How can you justify slamming the door once you're inside? You say that immigrants should be kept out. But aren't we all immigrants, or the descendants of immigrants? If we insist on staying, must we not admit all others?" Our craving for intellectual order leads us to seek and prefer symmetrical rules and morals: a single rule for me and everybody else; the same rule yesterday, today, and tomorrow. Justice, we feel, should not change with time and place.

We Americans of non-Indian ancestry can look upon ourselves as the descendants of thieves who are guilty morally, if not legally, of stealing this land from its Indian owners. Should we then give back the land to the now living American descendants of those Indians? However morally or logically sound this proposal may be, I, for one, am unwilling to live by it and I know no one else who is. Besides, the logical consequence would be absurd. Suppose that, intoxicated with a sense of pure justice, we should decide to turn our land over to the Indians. Since all our other wealth has also been derived from the land, wouldn't we be morally obliged to give that back to the Indians too?

**Pure Justice vs. Reality.** Clearly, the concept of pure justice produces an infinite regression to absurdity. Centuries ago, wise men invented statutes of limitations to justify the rejection of such pure justice, in the interest of preventing continual disorder. The law zealously defends property rights, but only relatively recent property rights. Drawing a line after an arbitrary time has elapsed may be unjust, but the alternatives are worse.

We are all the descendants of thieves, and the world's resources are inequitably distributed. But we must begin the journey to tomorrow from the point where we are today. We cannot remake the past. We cannot safely divide the wealth equitably among all peoples so long as people reproduce at different rates. To do so would guarantee that our grandchildren, and everyone else's grandchildren, would have only a ruined world to inhabit.

To be generous with one's own possessions is quite different from being generous with those of posterity. We should call this point to the attention of those who, from a commendable love of justice and equality, would institute a system of the commons, either in the form of a world food bank, or of unrestricted immigration. We must convince them if we wish to save at least some parts of the world from environmental ruin.

Without a true world government to control reproduction and the use of available resources, the sharing ethic of the spaceship is impossible. For the foreseeable future, our survival demands that we govern our actions by the ethics of a lifeboat, harsh though they may be. Posterity will be satisfied with nothing less.

*Questions*

1. What are the advantages and disadvantages of using figures of speech like "spaceship" and "lifeboat" in argumentation?
2. Is Hardin correct in stating there are those who favor "uncontrolled immigration and foreign aid"? What reasons might he have had for making this statement?
3. What are the underlying assumptions of the author?
4. How would you respond to Hardin's charge that "international charity frequently inspires mistrust"?
5. Do you think that a "true world government" would solve many of the problems posed by the author? Explain.

# 6
# Chief Seattle's Message

## *Addressed to President Pierce, 1854*

---

*As his tribe, the Coastal Salish of the northwest, was being forced by the U.S. Army to abandon its ancestral lands, Chief Seattle addressed a message to the American President. The actual message, so far as it is known, was much less lofty than the version presented here.*

*The present version, widely used by environmental groups, has a much more recent origin. It was written in 1971 by Ted Perry, a screenwriter in Texas, for a film produced by the Southern Baptist Radio and Television Commision. Mr. Perry, who now teaches at Middlebury College, Vermont, stated that he intended it to be fiction. Nevertheless, the words portray the beliefs and sentiments—if not of Chief Seattle himself—of native Americans in general. In much the same way, the biblical Pentateuch represents the ideas of ancient Judaism, even though not every word attributed to Moses may have been spoken by him.*

*The message shows a fine sense of irony and a realistic appreciation of the military weakness of the Indians' position. In contrast to the white man who uses up the land, the animals and the natural resources in a wasteful manner, the writer states that "every part of the earth is sacred to my people."*

*The writer discerns a divine hand in the power given to the whites to dominate the earth. This is followed by a prediction that the whites too will pass away, "perhaps sooner than all other tribes." The message is clear: humanity is part of the cycle of nature—in despoiling the earth, we hasten to our own destruction.*

The Great Chief in Washington sends word that he wishes to buy our land.

The Great Chief also sends us words of friendship and good will. This is kind of him, since we know he has little need of our friendship in return. But we will consider your offer. For we know that if we do not sell, the white man may come with guns and take our land.

How can you buy or sell the sky, the warmth of the land? The idea is strange to us.

If we do not own the freshness of the air and the sparkle of the water, how can you buy them?

Every part of this earth is sacred to my people. Every shining pine needle, every sandy shore, every mist in the dark woods, every clearing and humming insect is holy in the memory and experience of my people. The sap which courses through the trees carries the memories of the red man.

The white man's dead forget the country of their birth when they go to walk among the stars. Our dead never forget this beautiful earth, for it is the mother of the red man. We are part of the earth and it is part of us. The perfumed flowers are our sisters; the deer, the horse, the great eagle, these are our brothers. The rocky crests, the juices in the meadows, the body heat of the pony, and man—all belong to the same family.

So, when the Great Chief in Washington sends word that he wishes to buy our land, he asks much of us.

So, the Great Chief sends word he will reserve us a place so that we can live comfortably to ourselves. He will be our father and we will be his children.

So we will consider your offer to buy our land. But it will not be easy. For this land is sacred to us.

This shining water that moves in the streams and rivers is not just water but the blood of our ancestors. If we sell you land, you must remember that it is sacred, and you must teach your children that it is sacred, and that each ghostly reflection in the clear water of the lake tells of events and memories in the life of my people. The water's murmur is the voice of my father's father.

The rivers are our brothers, they quench our thirst. The rivers carry our canoes, and feed our children. If we sell you our land, you must remember, and teach your children, that the rivers are our brothers, and yours, and you must henceforth give the rivers the kindness you would give any brother.

The red man has always retreated before the advancing white man, as the mist of the mountain runs before the morning sun. But the ashes of our fathers are sacred. Their graves are holy ground, and so these hills, these trees, this portion of earth is consecrated to us. We know that the white man does not understand our ways. One portion of land is the same to him as the next, for he is a stranger who comes in the night and takes from the land whatever he needs. The earth is not his brother, but his enemy, and when he has conquered it, he moves on. He leaves his fathers' graves behind, and he does not care. He kidnaps the earth from his children. He does not care. His fathers' graves and his children's birthright are forgotten. He treats his mother, the earth, and his brother, the sky, as things to be bought, plundered, sold like sheep or bright beads. His appetite will devour the earth and leave behind only a desert.

I do not know. Our ways are different from your ways. The sight of your cities pains the eyes of the red man. But perhaps it is because the red man is a savage and does not understand.

There is no quiet place in the white man's cities. No place to hear the unfurling of leaves in spring or the rustle of insects' wings. But perhaps it is because I am a savage and do not understand. The clatter only seems to insult the ears. And what is there to life if a man cannot hear the lonely cry of the whippoorwill or the arguments of the frogs around a pond at night? I am a red man and do not understand. The Indian prefers the soft sound of the wind darting over the face of a pond, and the smell of the wind itself, cleansed by a midday rain, or scented with the pinon pine.

The air is precious to the red man, for all things share the same breath—the beast, the tree, the man, they all share the same breath. The white man does not seem to notice the air he breathes. Like a man dying for many days, he is numb to the stench. But if we sell you our land, you must remember that the air is precious to us, that the air shares its spirit with all the life it supports. The wind that gave our grandfather his first breath also receives his last sigh. And the wind must also give our children the spirit of life. And if we sell you our land, you must keep it apart and sacred, as a place where even the white man can go to taste the wind that is sweetened by the meadow's flowers.

So we will consider your offer to buy our land. If we decide to accept, I will make one condition: The white man must treat the beasts of this land as his brothers.

I am a savage and do not understand any other way. I have seen a thousand rotting buffaloes on the prairie, left by the white man who shot them from a passing train. I am a savage and I do not understand how the smoking iron horse can be more important than the buffalo that we kill only to stay alive.

What is man without the beasts? If all the beasts were gone, men would die from a great loneliness of spirit. For whatever happens to the beasts, soon happens to man. All things are connected.

You must teach your children that the ground beneath their feet is the ashes of our grandfathers. So that they will respect the land, tell your children that the earth is rich with the lives of our kin. Teach your children what we have taught our children, that the earth is our mother. Whatever befalls the earth, befalls the sons of the earth. If men spit upon the ground they spit upon themselves.

This we know. The earth does not belong to man; man belongs to the earth. This we know. All things are connected like the blood which unites one family. All things are connected.

Whatever befalls the earth befalls the sons of the earth. Man did not weave the web of life; he is merely a strand in it. Whatever he does to the web, he does to himself.

But we will consider your offer to go to the reservation you have for my people. We will live apart, and in peace. It matters little where we spend the rest of our days. Our children have seen their fathers humbled in defeat. Our warriors have felt shame, and after defeat they turn their days in idleness and contaminate their bodies with sweet foods and strong drink. It matters little where we pass the rest of our days. They are not many. A few more hours, a few more winters, and none of the children of the great tribes that once lived on this earth or that roam now in small bands in the woods will be left to mourn the graves of a people once as powerful and hopeful as yours. But why should I mourn the passing of my people? Tribes are made of men, nothing more. Men come and go like the waves of the sea.

Even the white man, whose God walks and talks with him as friend to friend, cannot be exempt from the common destiny. We may be brothers after all; we shall see. One thing we know, which the white man may one day discover—our God is the same God. You may think now that you own him as you wish to own our land; but you cannot. He is the God of man, and his compassion is equal for the red man and the white. This earth is precious to him, and to harm the earth is to heap contempt on its Creator. The white too shall pass; perhaps sooner than all other tribes. Continue to contaminate your bed, and you will one night suffocate in your own waste.

But in your perishing you will shine brightly, fired by the strength of the God who brought you to this land and for some special purpose gave you dominion over this land and over the red man. That destiny is a mystery to us, for we do not understand when the buffalo are all slaughtered, the wild horses are tamed, the secret corners of the forest heavy with the scent of many men, and the view of the ripe hills blotted by talking wires. Where is the thicket? Gone. Where is the eagle? Gone. And what is it to say goodbye to the swift pony and the hunt? The end of living and the beginning of survival.

So we will consider your offer to buy our land. If we agree, it will be to secure the reservation you have promised. There, perhaps, we may live out our brief days as we wish. When the last red man has vanished from this earth, and his memory is only the shadow of a cloud moving across the prairie, these shores and forests will still hold the spirits of my people. For they love this earth as the newborn loves its mother's heartbeat. So if we sell you our land, love it as we've loved it. Care for it as we've cared for it. Hold in your mind the memory of the land as it is when you take it. And with all your strength, with all your mind, with all your heart, preserve it for your children, and love it . . . as God loves us all.

One thing we know. Our God is the same God. This earth is precious to him. Even the white man cannot be exempt from the common destiny. We may be brothers after all. We shall see.

*Questions*

1. What similarities can you see between Chief Seattle's people and the peoples of the third world?
2. In which passages does Seattle show his dignity and leadership qualities?
3. Describe briefly the worldview of the native American peoples and that of the industrialized West.
4. Which aspects of Seattle's speech are particularly relevant today?
5. Where does Seattle show a profound sense of history?

7

# First Letter to the Delaware Indians

## William Penn

This article originally appeared in *Nonviolence in America: A Documentary History* Staughton Lynd, ed., 1966.

*William Penn (1644–1718) was that exception among European colonizers—a man of peace. An English Quaker who had been imprisoned for his beliefs, Penn never forgot the virtue of tolerance. When King Charles II granted him proprietorship of the colony that was to bear his name, he established it as a haven for those persecuted because of their religious and political beliefs.*

*This letter, written in 1681 to the Native American inhabitants of the new commonwealth, combines faith in a common God with the notion of accountability for human actions. The proposal he makes for rectifying disputes between Indians and colonists springs from his deep adherence to simple justice. Though Penn spent only two three-year periods in the New World, the Quaker settlers maintained peaceful relations with the original inhabitants.*

My Friends—There is one great God and power that hath made the world and all things therein, to whom you and I, and all people owe their being and well-being, and to whom you and I must one day give an account for all that we do in the world; this great God hath written his law in our hearts, by which we are taught and commanded to love and help, and do good to one another, and not to do harm and mischief one to another. Now this great God hath been pleased to make me concerned in your parts of the world, and the king of the country where I live hath given unto me a great province, but I desire to enjoy it with your love and consent, that we may always live together as neighbors and friends; else what would the great God say to us, who hath made us not to devour and destroy one another, but live soberly and kindly together in the world? Now I would have you well observe, that I am very sensible of the unkindness and injustice that hath been too much exercised toward you by the people of these parts of the world, who sought themselves, and to make great advantages by you, rather than be examples of justice and goodness unto you, which I hear hath been a matter of trouble to you, and caused great grudgings and animosities, sometimes to the shedding of blood, which hath made the great God angry. But I am not such a man, as is well known in my own country; I have great love and regard toward you, and I desire to win and gain your love and friendship, by a kind, just and peaceable life, and the people I send are of the same mind, and shall in all things behave themselves accordingly; and if in anything any shall offend you or your people, you shall have a full and speedy satisfaction for the same, by an equal number of just men on both sides, that by no means you may have just occasion of being offended against them. I shall shortly come to you myself, at what time we may more largely and freely confer and discourse of these matters. In the meantime, I have sent my commissioners to treat with you about land, and a firm league of peace. Let me desire you to be kind to them and the people, and receive these presents and tokens which I have sent to you, as a testimony of my good will to you, and my resolution to live justly, peaceably, and friendly with you.

I am your loving friend,

*William Penn*

## Questions

1. What might have been the course of American history had Penn's example been followed by other European settlers?
2. Could Penn's imprisonment in England for his beliefs have influenced him in a direction other than the one he took? Give instances from your knowledge of how imprisonment transformed people, for better or worse.
3. What was Penn's remedy for the injustice imposed on the original inhabitants of the territory?
4. Describe the connection between justice and peace as exemplified in Pennsylvania.
5. In what way do members of the Society of Friends (Quakers) reflect the attitudes of William Penn today?

# 8
## Amnesty International

## A pamphlet

---

To many people, their first knowledge of Amnesty International came through a series of "Conspiracy of Hope" rock concerts held in the United States in the summer of 1986. These events, held in San Francisco, Los Angeles, Denver, Atlanta, Chicago and the New York area, were celebrations of the organization's twenty-fifth anniversary.

The objects of Amnesty International's (AI) concern are men and women in any country imprisoned because of their beliefs, specifically those who have never used or advocated violence. Aware that any nation shrinks from the glare of unfavorable publicity, AI turns the spotlight on government misconduct wherever it may be found and documented. The organization claims 150,000 members and supporters in 150 countries. Meeting in small groups, they "write letters, publicize and organize actions in behalf of prisoners of conscience and work on special campaigns." The effect of such letters and campaigns may be gauged from the following statements made by prisoners who were released through AI's efforts:

"When the first two hundred letters came, the guards gave me back my clothes. Then the next two hundred letters came, and the prison director came to see me. When the next pile of letters arrived, the director got in touch with his superior. The letters kept coming and coming, three thousand of them. The President was informed. The letters still kept arriving, and the President called the prison and told them to let me go." (A released prisoner of conscience from the Dominican Republic)

"We could always tell when international protests were taking place . . . the food rations increased and the beatings were fewer. Letters from abroad were translated and passed around from cell to cell, but when the letters stopped, the dirty food and repression started again." (A released prisoner of conscience from Vietnam)

"For years I was held in a tiny cell. My only human contact was with my torturers. . . . My only company were the cockroaches and mice. . . . On Christmas Eve the door to my cell opened and the guard tossed in a crumpled piece of paper. It said, 'Take heart. The world knows you're

159

*alive. We're with you. Regards, Monica, Amnesty International.' That let-*
*ter saved my life." (A released prisoner of conscience from Paraguay)*

In 1977, the Nobel Peace Prize was awarded to AI for its work on
behalf of 25,000 prisoners around the world.

The following article is taken from a pamphlet describing Amnesty
International's history, purposes and activities.

Thousands of people are in prison because of their beliefs. Many are
held without charge or trial. Torture and the death penalty are widespread. In many countries men, women, and children have "disappeared"
after being taken into official custody. Still others have been killed without
any pretense of legality. These human rights abuses occur in countries of
widely differing ideologies.

Amnesty International is a worldwide movement of people acting on
the conviction that governments must not deny individuals their basic human rights. The organization was awarded the 1977 Nobel Peace Prize for
its efforts to promote global observance of the United Nations' Universal
Declaration of Human Rights.

Amnesty International works specifically for:
- the release of prisoners of conscience—men, women, and children imprisoned for their beliefs, color, sex, ethnic origin, language, or religion; provided they have neither used nor
  advocated violence;
- fair and prompt trials for all political prisoners;
- an end to torture and executions in all cases.

Amnesty International's effectiveness depends on its impartial application of a single standard of human rights to every country in the world.
The organization is independent of all governments, political factions,
ideologies, economic interests, and religious creeds. It accepts no financial
contribution from any government and is funded entirely by donations
from its supporters. To safeguard impartiality, groups do no work for prisoners of conscience held within their own countries.

Amnesty International seeks the most effective means of helping individuals whose rights have been violated. Techniques include long-term
adoption of prisoners of conscience; publicizing patterns of human rights
abuses; meetings with government representatives; and, in cases where
torture or death are feared, a network of volunteers who send urgent telegrams indicating international concern.

Amnesty International·members send letters, cards, and telegrams
on behalf of individual prisoners to government officials. Constant action generates effective pressure. One well-written letter to a minister
of justice is not pressure; ten letters are. Hundreds of letters were sent

on behalf of an adopted prisoner detained for many years in Soviet psychiatric hospitals. Later he said that his release had been a direct result of the letters from Amnesty. He believes they were also the key to better treatment during imprisonment.

Amnesty International members also organize public meetings, collect signatures for petitions, and arrange publicity events, such as vigils at appropriate government embassies. They work on special projects, such as the Campaign to Abolish Torture. At its launching Amnesty members met with more than half of the United States' congressional representatives to voice their concern and outline Amnesty International's program to eradicate torture. Members also raise money to send medicine, food, and clothing to prisoners and their families.

Amnesty International sends missions to countries to appeal in person for the protection of human rights. A medical delegation to Bolivia successfully convinced the government to allow a prisoner to be flown abroad for a lifesaving operation. Another group went to Gambia in response to reports that prisoners were held in leg irons and denied access to friends and relatives. Within months Gambia's President had taken steps to improve conditions.

When Amnesty International hears of political arrests or people facing torture or execution, it concentrates first on getting the facts. At the organization's headquarters in London, the Research Department (with a staff of 150 recruited from over 20 countries) collects and analyzes information from a wide variety of sources. These include hundreds of newspapers and journals, government bulletins, transcripts of radio broadcasts, reports from lawyers and humanitarian organizations, along with letters from and interviews with prisoners and their families. Amnesty International representatives frequently go on missions to collect on-the-spot information. Amnesty legal observers often attend trials where accepted international standards are at issue.

Since it was founded in 1961, Amnesty International has worked on behalf of more than 25,000 prisoners around the world. Last year 150 of the prisoners of conscience adopted by groups in the United States were released. These aren't just numbers. Amnesty members give direct and effective assistance to people who become more than a number and more than a name. A released prisoner from Malaysia wrote to a group member, "Today I took out all the letters and cards you sent me in the past, reread them, looked at them again, and it is hard to describe the feelings in my heart . . . these things I regard as precious jewels."

A released prisoner from Pakistan wrote, "A woman in San Antonio had written some kind and comforting words that proved to be a bombshell for the prison authorities and significantly changed the prisoners' conditions for the better . . . Suddenly I felt as if the sweat drops all over my body were drops from a cool, comforting shower."

## Questions

1. Why does Amnesty International limit its efforts to governments rather than include revolutionary or terrorist groups?
2. How does AI seek to preserve its reputation for impartiality?
3. How does AI describe "pressure"? Why is it sometimes effective?
4. Besides letters and publicity campaigns, how does AI assist prisoners and their families?
5. What are the two goals of AI's health professionals' group?

# 9
# Aims and Means of the Catholic Worker

This article originally appeared in *The Catholic Worker*, May 1987.

*The Catholic Worker movement was founded in New York City in 1933 by Dorothy Day, a newspaper reporter and former communist, and Peter Maurin, a self-taught French peasant with a gift for reducing theological principles to understandable terms. Both embraced Catholicism, pacifism, poverty and a distaste for current economic and political systems. Together they started a movement, a newspaper (The Catholic Worker) and a series of houses of hospitality throughout the country. Though they were devout believers in their Church's teachings, the practical implications they drew from their faith were radical.*

*By condemning both capitalism and communism for neglecting the concerns of the human person, they disturbed the peace of both Church and state. Over the years, hundreds of dedicated people, most of them Catholic and many of them young, were attracted by the lives and writings of these two unusual people. Though most adherents remained at Catholic Worker houses for relatively short periods—studying Gandhi and Catholic social thought, feeding the hungry, befriending the poor and exploited, and occasionally participating in civil disobedience—they remained "Catholic Workers" in their hearts for the rest of their lives.*

*The following article is a distillation of the group's philosophy and goals. The fact that the Catholic Worker outlived its founders (Day died in 1981 and Maurin in 1949), testifies to the power of religious convictions, wedded to poverty and non-violence, to capture the imagination of successive generations of people even in our consumer-oriented society.*

**The aim of the Catholic Worker movement is to live in accordance with the justice and charity of Jesus Christ. Our sources are the Hebrew and Greek Scriptures as handed down in the teachings of the Roman Catholic Church, with our inspiration coming from the lives of the saints, "men and women outstanding in holiness, living witnesses to Your unchanging love." (Eucharistic Prayer)**

This aim requires us to begin living in a different way. We recall the words of our founders, Dorothy Day who said, "God meant things to be much easier than we have made them," and Peter Maurin who wanted to build a society "where it is easier for people to be good."

When we examine our society, which is generally called capitalist (because of its methods of producing and controlling wealth) and is bourgeois (because of a prevailing concern for acquisition and material interests, and its emphasis on respectability and mediocrity), we find it far from God's justice.

**In economics,** private and state capitalism bring about an unjust distribution of wealth, for the profit motive guides decisions. Those in power live off the sweat of another's brow, while those without power are robbed of a just return for their work. Usury (the charging of interest above administrative costs) is a major contributor to the wrong-doing intrinsic to this system. We note especially how the world debt crisis leads poor countries into great deprivation and a dependency from which there is no foreseeable escape. Here at home, the number of hungry and homeless and unemployed people rises in the midst of increasing affluence.

**In labor,** human need is no longer the reason for human work. Instead, the unbridled expansion of technology, necessary to capitalism and viewed as "progress," holds sway. Jobs are concentrated in productivity and administration for a "high-tech," war-related, consumer society of disposable goods, so that laborers are trapped in work that does not contribute to human welfare. Furthermore, as jobs become more specialized, many people are excluded from meaningful work or are alienated from the products of their labor. Even in farming, agribusiness has replaced agriculture, and, in all areas, moral restraints are run over roughshod, and a disregard for the laws of nature now threatens the very planet.

**In politics,** the state functions to control and regulate life. Its power has burgeoned hand in hand with growth in technology, so that military, scientific and corporate interests get the highest priority when concrete political policies are formulated. Because of the sheer size of institutions, we tend towards government by bureaucracy; that is, government by nobody. Bureaucracy, in all areas of life, is not only impersonal, but also makes accountability, and, therefore, an effective political forum for redressing grievances, next to impossible.

**In morals,** relations between people are corrupted by distorted images of the human person. Class, race and sex often determine personal worth and position within society, leading to structures that foster oppression. Capitalism further divides society by pitting owners against workers in perpetual conflict over wealth and its control. Those who do not "produce" are abandoned, and left, at best, to be "processed" through institutions. Spiritual destitution is rampant, manifested in isolation, madness, promiscuity and violence.

**The arms race** stands as a clear sign of the direction and spirit of our age. It has extended the domain of destruction and the fear of annihilation, and denies the basic right to life. There is a direct connection between the arms race and destitution. "The arms race is an utterly treacherous trap for humanity, and one which injures the poor to an intolerable degree." (Vatican II)

\*       \*       \*

In contrast to what we see around us, as well as within ourselves, stands St. Thomas Aquinas' doctrine of the Common Good, a vision of a society where the good of each member is bound to the good of the whole in the service of God. To this end, we advocate:

—**Personalism,** a philosophy which regards the freedom and dignity of each person as the basis, focus and goal of all metaphysics and morals. In following such wisdom, we move away from a self-centered individualism toward the good of the other. This is to be done by taking personal responsibility for changing conditions, rather than looking to the state or other institutions to provide impersonal "charity." We pray for a Church renewed by this philosophy and for a time when all those who feel excluded from participation are welcomed with love, drawn by the gentle personalism Peter Maurin taught.

—**A Decentralized Society** in contrast to the present bigness of government, industry, education, health care and agriculture. We encourage efforts such as family farms, rural and urban land trusts, worker ownership and management of small factories, homesteading projects, food, housing and other cooperatives—any effort in which money can once more become merely a medium of exchange, and human beings are no longer commodities.

—**A "Green Revolution,"** so that it is possible to re-discover the proper meaning of our labor and our true bonds with the land; a Distributist communitarianism, self-sufficient through farming, crafting and appropriate technology; a radically new society where people will rely on the fruits of their own soil and labor; associations of mutuality, and a sense of fairness to resolve conflicts.

We believe this needed personal and social transformation should be pursued by the means Jesus revealed in His sacrificial love. With Christ as our Exemplar, by prayer and communion with His Body and Blood, we strive for the practices of:

—**Nonviolence.** "Blessed are the peacemakers, for they shall be called children of God." (Matt. 5:9) Only through nonviolent action can a personalist revolution come about, one in which one evil will not be replaced simply by another. Thus, we oppose the deliberate taking of life for any reason, and see every oppression as blasphemy. Jesus taught us to take suffering upon ourselves rather than inflict it upon others and He calls us to fight against violence with the spiritual weapons of prayer, fasting and non-cooperation with evil. Refusal to pay taxes for war, to register for conscription, to comply with any unjust legislation; participation in nonviolent strikes and boycotts, protests or vigils; withdrawal of support for dominant systems, corporate funding or usurious practices are all excellent means to establish peace.

—**The works of mercy** (as found in Matt. 25:31-46) are at the heart of the Gospel and they are clear mandates for our response to "the least of our brothers and sisters." Houses of hospitality are centers for learning to do these acts of love, so that the poor can receive what is, in justice, theirs: the second coat in our closet, the spare room in our home, a place at our table. Anything beyond what we immediately need belongs to those who go without.

—**Manual labor** in a society that rejects it as undignified and inferior. "Besides inducing cooperation, besides overcoming barriers and establishing the spirit of brotherhood (besides just getting things done), manual labor enables us to use our body as well as our hands, our minds." (Dorothy Day) The Benedictine motto "Ora et Labora" reminds us that the work of human hands is a gift for the edification of the world and the glory of God.

—**Voluntary Poverty.** "The mystery of poverty is that by sharing in it, making ourselves poor in giving to others, we increase our knowledge and belief in love." (Dorothy Day) By embracing voluntary poverty, that is, by casting our lot freely with those whose impoverishment is not a choice, we would ask for the grace to abandon ourselves to the love of God. It would put us on the path to incarnate the Church's "preferential option for the poor."

We must be prepared to accept seeming failure with these aims, for sacrifice and suffering are part of the Christian life. Success, as the world determines it, is not the final criterion for judgment. The most important thing is the love of Jesus Christ and how to live His truth.

### Questions

1. What does the Catholic Worker mean by private and state capitalism? Why does the movement find these two economic systems repugnant?

2. What is the Catholic Worker's central criticism of bureaucracy?

3. What is unusual about the emphasis on "social relationships" in its statement on morality? Contrast this with the understanding of "morality" that one usually associates with the Christian churches.

4. How do the Houses of Hospitality tie in with the Catholic Worker's dedication to voluntary poverty and social justice?

5. What is the chief source of the Catholic Worker's adherence to non-violence, or pacifism? How does this position differ from the traditional "just war" doctrine of most Christian churches?

# SECTION THREE

## Non-Violence

# 1
# Ahimsa, or the
# Way of Nonviolence

## Mohandas K. Gandhi

This article originally appeared in *All Men Are Brothers*, UNESCO, 1958.

*In these excerpts from Gandhi's writings over many years, the un-wavering consistency of his beliefs comes to the surface. It is well to recall that, at the time of writing these thoughts, Gandhi had no assurance—apart from his own conviction—that "soul force" would eventually lead to a British withdrawal from the subcontinent of India. He wrote in the dark-est days of a forty-year struggle, without the benefit of hindsight.*

*As a product of Eastern thought, Gandhi does not argue with the lin-ear logic of the West. His reasoning, which is more in tune with the ap-proach of the Hebrew and Christian Scriptures, tends to repeat itself in widening circles of insight. One could find many parallels to Jesus' thought in such phrases as "readiness to die" (cf. Jn 10:11), "to love those that hate us" (cf. Mt 5:44), "the impossible ever becoming possible" (cf. Mt 19:20), and others too numerous to mention.*

*From Gandhi's* Autobiography, *we read: "Man and his deed are two distinct things (11), a concept that was taken up by Pope John XXIII in his encyclical "Peace on Earth" (#159), which has been widely interpreted as a reference to communism and its adherents. Ever a realist, Gandhi had little regard for a non-violence that has not been tested in a hostile envi-ronment (12). Somewhat surprisingly, the Indian holy man discounts ahimsa as a "means of personal salvation" (14). Rather, he envisions it as a heartfelt response to "social injustice." (15) One is reminded of the apostle John who wrote: "Anyone who loves God must also love his brother" (1 Jn 4:23).*

*Gandhi distinguishes ahimsa from the utilitarianism made popular by the British philosopher Jeremy Bentham (1748–1832), who sought the "greatest good for the greatest number." Gandhi, on the contrary, says that the followers of ahimsa "will strive for the greatest good of all and die in the attempt to realize the ideal" (17).*

*In a passage that will challenge an age given to hedonism and the avoidance of pain, Gandhi upholds suffering as "the law of human beings"*

*(20). It is suffering that "opens up the inner understanding in man"—this applies to oneself and to one's opponents. We could apply to the current arms race Gandhi's final statement in this section about fear and even cowardice being linked with the possession of arms. The non-violent cannot be true to their calling without "unadulterated fearlessness."*

*Critics have dismissed Gandhi as a dreamer. They argue that successful non-violent action is overly dependent on a charismatic leader. On the other hand, not all critics have studied his philosophy and methods with any seriousness or tried to put them into practice in seemingly hopeless situations.*

Nonviolence is the greatest force at the disposal of mankind. It is mightier than the mightiest weapon of destruction devised by the ingenuity of man. Destruction is not the law of the humans. Man lives freely by his readiness to die, if need be, at the hands of his brother, never by killing him. Every murder or other injury, no matter for what cause, committed or inflicted on another is a crime against humanity. *1*

*Harijan, July 20, 1931*

I claim that even now, though the social structure is not based on a conscious acceptance of nonviolence, all the world over mankind lives and men retain their possessions on the sufferance of one another. If they had not done so, only the fewest and the most ferocious would have survived. But such is not the case. Families are bound together by ties of love, and so are groups in the so-called civilized society called nations. Only they do not recognize the supremacy of the law of nonviolence. It follows, therefore, that they have not investigated its vast possibilities. Hitherto, out of sheer inertia, shall I say, we have taken it for granted that complete nonviolence is possible only for the few who take the vow of non-possession and the allied abstinences. Whilst it is true that the votaries alone can carry on research work and declare from time to time the new possibilities of the great eternal law governing man, if it is a law, it must hold good for all. The many failures we see are not of the law but of the followers, many of whom do not even know that they are under that law willy-nilly. When a mother dies for her child she unknowingly obeys the law. I have been pleading for the past fifty years for a conscious acceptance of the law and its zealous practice even in the face of failures. Fifty years' work has shown marvellous results and strengthened my faith. I do claim that by constant practice we shall come to a state of things when lawful possession will commend universal and voluntary respect. No doubt such possession will not be tainted. It will not be an insolent demonstration of the inequalities that surround us everywhere. Nor need the problem of unjust and unlawful possession appal the votary of nonviolence. He has at his disposal the non-violent weapon of Satyāgraha and non-cooperation which hitherto has been found to be a complete substitute of violence whenever it has been applied honestly in sufficient measure. I have never claimed to present the complete science of nonviolence. It does not lend itself to such treatment. So far as I know, no single physical science does, not even the very exact science of mathematics. I am but a seeker. 8

*Harijan, February 22, 1942*

In the application of Satyāgraha, I discovered in the earliest stages that pursuit of truth did not admit of violence being inflicted on one's opponent but that he must be weaned from error by patience and sympathy. For, what appears to be truth to the one may appear to be error to another. And patience means self-suffering. So the doctrine came to mean vindication of truth, not by infliction of suffering on the opponent, but on one's self. 9

*Young India, November, 1919*

In this age of wonders no one will say that a thing or idea is worthless be-cause it is new. To say it is impossible because it is difficult, is again not in consonance with the spirit of the age. Things undreamt of are daily being seen, the impossible is ever becoming possible. We are constantly being astonished these days at the amazing discoveries in the field of violence. But I maintain that far more undreamt of and seemingly impossible dis-coveries will be made in the field of nonviolence. 10

*Harijan, August 25, 1940*

Man and his deed are two distinct things. It is quite proper to resist and attack a system, but to resist and attack its author is tantamount to resisting and attacking oneself. For we are all tarred with the same brush, and are children of one and the same Creator, and as such the divine powers within us are infinite. To slight a single human being is to slight those divine pow-ers, and thus to harm not only that being but with him the whole world. 11

*An Autobiography*

Nonviolence is a universal principle and its operation is not limited by a hostile environment. Indeed, its efficacy can be tested only when it acts in the midst of and in spite of opposition. Our nonviolence would be a hollow thing and worth nothing, if it depended for its success on the good-will of the authorities. 12

*Harijan, November 12, 1938*

Some friends have told me that truth and nonviolence have no place in politics and worldly affairs. I do not agree. I have no use for them as a means of individual salvation. Their introduction and application in every-day life has been my experiment all along.  *14*

*Harijan, November 12, 1938*

No man could be actively nonviolent and not rise against social injustice no matter where it occurred.  *15*          *Harijan, April 20, 1940*

A votary of ahimsā cannot subscribe to the utilitarian formula (of the greatest good of the greatest number). He will strive for the greatest good of all and die in the attempt to realize the ideal. He will therefore be willing to die, so that the others may live. He will serve himself with the rest, by himself dying. The greatest good of all inevitably includes the good of the greatest number, and, therefore, he and the utilitarian will converge in many points in their career but there does come a time when they must part company, and even work in opposite directions. The utilitarian to be logical will never sacrifice himself. The absolutist will even sacrifice himself.  *17*          *Young India, December 9, 1926*

Suffering is the law of human beings; war is the law of the jungle. But suffering is infinitely more powerful than the law of the jungle for converting the opponent and opening his ears, which are otherwise shut, to the voice of reason. Nobody has probably drawn up more petitions or espoused more forlorn causes than I and I have come to this fundamental conclusion that if you want something really important to be done you must not merely satisfy the reason, you must move the heart also. The appeal of reason is more to the head but the penetration of the heart comes from suffering. It opens up the inner understanding in man. Suffering is the badge of the human race, not the sword.  *20*

*Young India, November 4, 1931*

Nonviolence is a power which can be wielded equally by all—children, young men and women or grown up people—provided they have a living faith in the God of Love and have therefore equal love for all mankind. When nonviolence is accepted as the law of life it must pervade the whole being and not be applied to isolated acts.  *21*

*Harijan, September 5, 1936*

Nonviolence and cowardice go ill together. I can imagine a fully armed man to be at heart a coward. Possession of arms implies an element of fear, if not cowardice. But true nonviolence is an impossibility without the possession of unadulterated fearlessness.  *68*          *Harijan, July 15, 1939*

*Questions*

1. Do you think that every injury, for whatever cause, is a crime against humanity? How should this statement be interpreted in regard to the death penalty imposed by the state? Give your reasons.

2. Can you think of an instance in which your willingness to accept suffering might have changed the attitude of an adversary?

3. Do you agree with Gandhi that *ahimsa* is for everybody and not just for the few? Give your reasons.

4. What consequences do you see in Gandhi's insistence that non-violence is not for individual salvation but rather for "worldly affairs" and "against injustice"? Do you find this viewpoint reflected in your own religious experience? Explain.

5. Do you think that reason alone is sufficient for the resolution of disputes? Give examples where the appeal to the heart is more efficacious.

2
# Letter to Anthony a Bergis

## Desiderius Erasmus

This article originally appeared in *Complaint of Peace*, English edition, 1795, trans. Vicesimus Knox.

*In the heat of the religious wars that marked the sixteenth century, the Dutch Renaissance scholar Erasmus (1466–1536) raised his voice to point out to Europe's leaders the folly of fighting.*

*Erasmus' letter to the abbot of St. Bertin Abbey had two purposes. One was to find a patron who would enable him to leave England to continue his scholarly pursuits on the Continent. The other was to ask the abbot to use his influence with the Emperor Charles to stop the fighting that engulfed Europe.*

*The effects of war, as the author describes them, are familiar: higher prices, rising unrest, terrible loss of human life and property. He contrasts human violence, which knows no limit, with the animal kingdom, where killing is usually "in defense of their young or for food."*

*Erasmus sees a glaring contradiction among those who profess to follow Christ, the Prince of Peace, and then slay their fellow Christians. In the days before citizen armies, soldiers were ruffians who fought for the highest bidder, committing acts that, in peacetime, would land them in jail.*

*Even the winner, he observes, loses more than he gains. And the greatest calamities of all fall upon innocent bystanders who have "no interest . . . in the cause or the success of the war."*

*Erasmus has doubts on the "just war," because he finds that most wars are started on pretexts dreamed up to disguise "the private, sinister, selfish motives of princes." He appeals to the religious authorities (some of whom were warriors themselves) to employ themselves more in keeping with the Gospel by trying to mediate disputes. He even counsels aggrieved leaders to "bear the injury patiently" and thus become a "Christian hero."*

*Another argument against warfare is the effect it has on the non-Christian Turks "when they hear of Christian kings raging against*

*each other." And he lashes out at those Christian leaders who ignore
the positive precepts of Christ and the apostles. Erasmus concludes
by asking the abbot to use his influence with the Emperor Charles to
establish peace.*

Erasmus Roterodamus to Anthony a Bergis,
Abbot of St Bertin, sendeth health.

Most accomplished Father,

From the conversation of the bishop of Durham, and from my
friend Andrew Ammonius the king's secretary, I have learned that
you profess a warmth of affection for me which I may call paternal. It
is this circumstance which makes me rejoice the more at the idea of
returning to my country. I wish I possessed there an independent
income, just enough to support me in a humble state of literary leisure. Not that I dislike England, or have any reason to be dissatisfied
with the patronage of the Maecenas's, whom I have found in it. I have
a great many intimate friends, and experience uncommon instances of
kindness from many of the bishops. The archbishop of Canterbury
fosters me with such peculiar affection, and embraces me with such
cordiality, that he could not shew a greater love towards me if he
were my brother or my father. I enjoy a little pension issuing from a
living which he gave me, and allowed me to resign with an annuity out
of it. My other Maecenas adds an equal sum out of his own purse; and
many of the nobility contribute no inconsiderable addition to my income. I might have a great deal more, if I chose servilely to solicit or
pay my court to great men, which I can by no means prevail upon
myself to do.

But the war which is preparing has altered the very temper and
genius of this island. The price of every necessary of life increases
every day, and the generosity of the people of course decreases. Indeed how can it be otherwise? People that are so often fleeced must
retrench in the liberality of their bounty. I assure you, I lately con-
tracted a severe fit of the gravel, by being under the necessity of
drinking bad beverage through the scarcity of good. Add to this, that
as the whole island may be said, from the circumstance of its being
surrounded by the sea, to be a place of confinement; so we are likely
to be shut up still more closely by the wars. I see great commotions
arising: whither they will tend, or how they will terminate, it is impossible to say. I only wish, God in his mercy would vouchsafe to still the
raging sea which is agitating all Christendom.

I am often struck with astonishment and at a loss to account for the cause which can impel, I do not say Christians, but human creatures to such an extremity of madness and folly, as that they should rush head-long, with such ardour, at so great an expense of treasure, and with such dangers of every kind, to mutual destruction. For what is the business and chief concern of our whole lives, but to wage war with one another?

In the irrational part of the creation it is observable that only those among the beasts who are called wild ever engage in war; and those not with one another, but with brutes of a different species; and they fight only with their own arms, the instruments of offense and defense supplied by nature. They do not attack with engines of destruction, invented by diabolical contrivance, nor on trifling causes and occasions, but either in defense of their young or for food. Our wars, for the most part, proceed either from ambition, from anger and malice, from the mere wantonness of unbridled power, or from some other mental distemper. The beasts of the forest meet not in battle array, with thousands assembled together and disciplined for murder.

To us, glorying as we do in the name of Christ, who taught nothing by his precept, and exhibited nothing in his example, but mildness and gentleness; who are members of one body, all of us one flesh, who grow in grace by one and the same spirit; who are fed by the same sacrament; who adhere to the same head; who are called to the same immortality; who hope for a sublime communion with God, that as Christ and the Father are one, so also we may be one with him; can any thing in this world be of such value as to provoke us to war? A state so destructive, so hideous, and so base, that even when it is founded on a just cause, it can never be pleasing to a good man. Do consider a moment, by what sort of persons it is actually carried into execution; by a herd of cutthroats, debauchees, gamesters, profligate wretches from the stews, the meanest and most sordid of mankind, hireling mankillers, to whom a little paltry pay is dearer than life. These are your fine fellows in war, who commit the very same villainies, with reward and with glory in the field of battle, which in society they formerly perpetrated, at the peril of the gallows. This filthy rabble of wretches must be admitted into your fields and your towns, in order that you may be enabled to carry on war: to these you must yourselves be in a state of subjection, that you may have it in your power to take vengeance of others in war.

Besides all this, consider what crimes are committed under the pretence of war, while the voice of salutary law is compelled to be silent amidst the din of arms; what plunder, what sacrilege, what ravages, what other indecent transactions, which cannot for shame be enumerated. Such a taint of men's morals cannot but continue its influence long after a war is terminated. Compute also the expence, which is so enormous, that even if you come off conqueror, you sit down with more loss than gain: though indeed, by what standard can you appreciate the lives and the blood of so many thousand human creatures?

But the greatest share of the calamities inseparable from a state of war, falls to those persons who have no interest, no concern whatever, either in the cause, or the success of the war: whereas the advantages of peace reach all men of every rank and degree. In war, he who conquers weeps over his triumphs. War draws such a troop of evils in its train, that the poets find reason for the fiction which relates that war was brought from hell to earth by a deputation of devils.

I will not now dwell upon the picking of the people's pockets, the intrigues and collusion of the leading men, the vicissitudes of public affairs, which never can undergo violent revolutions without consequences of a most calamitous nature.

But if it is a desire of glory which drags us to war, be assured that the glory which is eagerly sought after is no glory; that it is impossible to derive real honour from doing mischief; and that, if we must point out something glorious, it is infinitely more glorious to build and establish, than to ruin and lay waste a flourishing community. Now what will you say, when you reflect, that it is the people, yes, the lowest of the people, who build and establish by industry and wisdom, that which kings claim a privilege to subvert and destroy by their folly. If gain rather than glory is the object in view, be it remembered, that no war whatever did, at any time, succeed so fortunately as not to produce more loss than gain, more evil than good: and that no man ever injured his enemy in war, but previously he did many and great injuries to his own people. In short, when I see all human affairs rapidly ebbing and flowing, like the tide of the Euripus, what avails it to establish or extend empire with such vast exertions, when it must very soon, and on very slight occasions, devolve to some other possessor? With how much blood was the Roman empire raised to its exalted pitch of grandeur, and how soon did it decline and fall?

But you will say, the rights of kings must of necessity be prosecuted at all events. It is not for me to speak rashly of the rights of kings; but one thing I know, the strictest right is often the greatest wrong, and that some kings first determine upon a measure, because it accords with their inclination, and then go in quest of some colourable pretence, under which they may cloak their unjustifiable conduct; and amidst so many changes and chances in human affairs, amidst so many treaties made and unmade, what man alive can ever be long at a loss for a colourable pretence? But if it were a nice point in dispute, to whom the right of dominion belonged, what need, in settling a question which requires reason and argument only, what need can there be of spilling human blood? The welfare and happiness of the people have nothing at all to do in the dispute; it is merely a question whether they shall have the privilege of calling this man or that man their king, 'and paying taxes to Thomas instead of John, or to John instead of Thomas'.

There are pontiffs and bishops, there are wise and honest men, who could settle such a trifling and contemptible business as this, without going to war about it, and confounding all things divine as well as human. The pope, the bishops, the cardinals, the abbots, could not employ themselves in any way more consistently with their characters and stations, than in composing the differences of kings: here they ought to exert their authority, and to shew how much the sanctity of their characters and their religion can actually avail.

Pope Julius, a pontiff not of the very best repute in the world, was able to excite the storm of war; and shall Leo, a man of real learning, integrity, and piety, be unable to appease it? The pretext for undertaking the war was, that Pope Julius was in imminent danger. The cause is confessedly removed, but the war does not yet cease.

We ought also to remember, that all men are free, especially all Christian men. Now, when they have been flourishing a long time under any prince, and by this time acknowledge him as their lawful sovereign, what justifiable occasion can there be for disturbing the world, in attempting a revolution? Long consent of the people constituted a lawful sovereign among the heathens, and much more among Christians, with whom the kingly office is a ministerial trust, a chief magistracy, an administration of delegated power, and not a property or absolute dominion; so that if some part of the territory subject to a Christian king were taken away, he is relieved from an onus, a burthensome task, rather than robbed or injured.

But suppose one of the litigant parties will not agree to abide by the arbitration of good men chosen as referees? In this case how would you wish me to act? In the first place, if you are verily and truly a Christian, I would have you bear the injury patiently, sit down with your heart at ease, and give up your right, be it what it will—such would be the conduct of a Christian hero.

In the next place, if, waiving your pretensions of Christianity, you are only a prudent, sensible man of the world; weigh well how much the prosecution of your right will cost you. If it will cost you too dearly, and it certainly will cost you too dearly, if you prosecute it by the sword; then never consent to assert a claim, which perhaps after all is a groundless one, by bringing so much certain mischief to the human race, by so many murders, by making so many childless parents and fatherless children, and by causing the sighs and tears of your own people, who have no concern in your right.

What do you suppose the Turks think, when they hear of Christian kings raging against each other, with all the madness of so many evils let loose? And raging for what? merely on account of a claim set up for power, for empire, and dominion.

Italy is now rescued from the French. And what is the great matter gained by so much blood spilt? what but that, where a Frenchman lately administered the powers of government, there some other man now administers the same powers? And to say the truth, the country flourished more before, than it flourishes now. But I will not enter farther into this part of the subject.

Now, if there are any systems which admit of war, I must maintain that they are founded on a gross principle, and favour of a Christianity degenerating, and likely to be overlaid by worldly influence. I do not know whether these systems, such as they are, justify war in the eyes of some men; but I observe, that whenever, through a zeal for defending the faith, the Christian peace is to be defended against the attack of barbarians, war is not at all opposed by men of acknowledged piety. But why, on these occasions, do a few maxims handed down from one to another by mere men, suggest themselves to our minds, rather than many positive precepts uttered by Christ himself, by the Apostles, by orthodox and approved fathers, concerning peace, and patience under all evil?

As to the usual arguments and means of justifying war, what is there that may not admit of defence in some mode or other; especially when they who have the management of the thing to be defended, are those, whose very villainies are always praised by the adulation of great numbers, and whose errors no man dares openly to reprehend? But in the mean time, it is very clear what all good-hearted men pray for, wish for, sigh for.

If you look narrowly into the case, you will find that they are, chiefly, the private, sinister, and selfish motives of princes, which operate as the real causes of all war.

But pray do you think it a conduct worthy of a rational creature, and not fitter for brutes or devils, to put the world in confusion, whenever one prince takes it into his head to be angry with another prince, or to pretend to be angry?

You and I may wish every thing that would be best, and most conducive to the happiness of the human race, but we can do no more than wish it. For my own part, all the little property I have in the world, I have among the English; and I will resign the whole of it with the greatest pleasure, on condition, that among Christian princes there may be established a Christian peace. Your influence may have considerable weight in accomplishing this end, since you have great interest with one potentate, Charles; a great deal with Maximilian; and stand very well with all the nobility and aristocracy of England. I do not doubt but by this time you have experienced what losses one's own friends may procure one in war; and must be sensible, that it will be doing your own business, and serving your own interest, if you endeavour to prevail with the great ones to put an end to the present war. I mention this, to hint to you that your labour will not be without its reward. I shall make all the haste I can to shake hands with you, as soon as I shall have it in my power to take my flight from this country. In the mean time, most respectable Father, farewel. My best wishes attend Ghilbert the physician, and Anthony Lutzenburg.

*London.*
*Pridie Id. Mart. 1513.*

*Questions*

1. Why is the author writing to Abbott Anthony? How does he try to ensure a favorable response?
2. List the dire effects of war that the author lists. What other effects can you think of that modern warfare has added?
3. How does the author contrast human violence with that of the animal kingdom? Do you find his argument convincing or not? Give your reasons.
4. Does the author's observation on the high price of war hold true today? Give examples from recent history on what has been lost as a result of warfare. What good effects have resulted?
5. How does the author dismiss the usual arguments given for entering into battle? Do you agree with his contention that it is better to bear an injury than to fight back? Give your reasons.

3
# To Oliver Cromwell

## George Fox

This article originally appeared in *Journal*, Dutton, 1924.

---

*George Fox (1624–1691) was founder of the Quakers, one of the
pre-eminent peace churches. He had been thrown into prison by
Oliver Cromwell on suspicion of plotting to overthrow him. In the
first excerpt, written from jail, he declared that, far from fighting
against Cromwell, he stood as "a wittnesse against all violence." The
letter was enough to set him free.*

*Toward the end of his confinement, Fox's fellow prisoners were
so impressed by his goodness that they wanted to elect him their
captain. But this peaceable man would not take up arms against
either Cromwell or his enemy Charles Stuart, whom Cromwell had
deposed as king. For his refusal, Fox was put into "a lousy, stinking place, without any bed, amongst thirty felons . . . almost half
a year."*

*Like Daniel in the lions' den, Fox "had faith in God," and was
eventually freed. True to his pacifist principles, he declared: "All that
pretend to fight for Christ, are deceived." With rhetorical power, he
says in a variety of ways that fighting and the Christian religion have
nothing in common. Throughout the centuries since his time, the
Quakers, though few in number, have never departed from this basic
conviction of their founder.*

### TO OLIVER CROMWELL[1]

I (WHO am of the world called George ffox) doe deny the carrying or drawing of any carnall sword against any, or against thee Oliver
Crumwell or any men in presence of the lord God I declare it (God is

---

1. After being arrested by soldiers of the Protector at a time when it was rumoured
that people were plotting to take Cromwell's life, Fox was set at liberty after affirming
in this letter that his intentions were not violent to Cromwell or any man. The incidents
relating to this letter took place in 1654 and are in the sixth chapter of his *Journal*. The
text of the letter is from the Cambridge edition of the *Journal*.

my wittnesse, by whom I am moved to give this forth for truthes sake, from him whom the world calls George ffox, who is the son of God) who is sent to stand A wittnesse against all violence and against all the workes of darkenesse, and to turn people from the darkenesse to the light, and to bring them from the occasion of the warre, and from the occasion of the Magistrates sword, which is A terrorism to the evill doers which actes contrary to the light of the lord Jesus Christ, which is A praise to them that doe well, which is A protection to them that doe well, and not the evill and such soldiers that are putt in that place no false accusers must bee, no violence must doe, but bee content with their wages, and that Magistrate beares not the sword in vaine, from under the occasion of that sword I doe seeke to bring people, my weapons are not carnall but spirituall, And my Kingdome is not of this world, therefore with the carnall weapon I doe not fight, but am from those things dead, from him who is not of the world, called of the world by the name George ffox, and this I am ready to seale with my blood, and this I am moved to give forth for the truthes sake, who A wittnesse stand against all unrighteousnesse and all ungodlynesse, who A suffrer is for the righteous seed sake, waiteing for the redemption of it, who A crowne that is mortal seeks not for, that fadeth away, but in the light dwells, which comprehends that Crowne, which light is the condemnation of all such; in which Light I wittnesse the Crowne that is Immortall that fades not away, from him who to all your soulls is A friend, for establishing of righteousnesse and cleansing the Land of evil doers, and A wittnesse against all wicked inventions of men and murderous plotts, which Answered shall be with the light in all your Consciences, which makes no Covenant with death, to which light in you all I speake, and am clear.

ff. G.

Who is of the world called George ffox who A new name hath which the world knowes not.

Wee are wittnesses of this Testimony whose names in the flesh is called

THO. ALDAM. ROBERT CREVEN.

### THE TIME OF MY COMMITMENT

Now the time of my commitment to the house of correction being nearly ended, and there being many new soldiers raised, the commissioners would have made me captain over them, and the soldiers said they would have none but me. So the keeper of the house of correc-

tion was commanded to bring me before the commissioners and soldiers in the market-place; and there they offered me that preferment,
as they called it, asking me, if I would not take up arms for the Commonwealth against Charles Stuart? I told them, I knew from whence
all wars arose, even from lust, according to James's doctrine; and that
I lived in the virtue of that life and power that took away the occasion
of all wars. But they courted me to accept their offer, and thought I
did but compliment them. But I told them, I was come into the covenant of peace, which was before wars and strife were. They said, they
offered it in love and kindness to me, because of my virtue; and such
like flattering words they used. But I told them, if that was their love
and kindness, I trampled it under my feet. Then their rage got up, and
they said, 'Take him away, jailer, and put him into the dungeon
amongst the rogues and felons.' So I was had away and put into a
lousy, stinking place, without any bed, amongst thirty felons, where I
was kept almost half a year, unless it were at times; for they would
sometimes let me walk in the garden, having a belief that I would not
go away. Now when they had got me into Derby dungeon it was the
belief and saying of the people that I should never come out; but I had
faith in God, and believed I should be delivered in his time; for the
Lord had said to me before, that I was not to be removed from the
place yet, being set there for a service which he had for me
to do. . . .

. . . All that pretend to fight for Christ, are deceived; for his kingdom is not of this world, therefore his servants do not fight. Fighters
are not of Christ's kingdom, but are without Christ's kingdom; his
kingdom starts in peace and righteousness, but fighters are in the lust;
and all that would destroy men's lives, are not of Christ's mind, who
came to save men's lives. Christ's kingdom is not of this world; it is
peaceable: and all that are in strife, are not of his kingdom. All that
pretend to fight for the Gospel, are deceived; for the Gospel is the
power of God, which was before the devil, or fall of man was; and the
gospel of peace was before fighting was. Therefore they that pretend
fighting, are ignorant of the Gospel; and all that talk of fighting for
Sion, are in darkness; for Sion needs no such helpers. All such as
profess themselves to be ministers of Christ, or Christians, and go
about to beat down the whore with outward, carnal weapons, the
flesh and the whore are got up in themselves, and they are in a blind
zeal; for the whore is got up by the inward ravening from the Spirit of
God; and the beating down thereof, must be by the inward stroke of
the sword of the Spirit within. All such as pretend Christ Jesus, and
confess him, and yet run into the use of carnal weapons, wrestling

with flesh and blood, throw away the spiritual weapons. They that would be wrestlers with flesh and blood, throw away Christ's doctrine; the flesh is got up in them, and they are weary of their sufferings. Such as would revenge themselves, are out of Christ's doctrine. Such as being stricken on one cheek, would not turn the other, are out of Christ's doctrine: and such as do not love one another, nor love enemies, are out of Christ's doctrine. . . .

## Questions

1. What were the circumstances that led to the writing of this letter? What do you think was the reaction of Oliver Cromwell upon reading it?
2. Why did the commissioners try to make Fox captain over them? Why did he refuse?
3. What was the reaction of the commissioners when the author spurned the honor they offered him?
4. What was the mission for which Fox believed God had allowed him to suffer in prison? How do Quakers carry out that mission in modern times?
5. The author's complete rejection of warfare, even in the name of Christ, goes against the practice of the Crusades and other wars in the cause of religion. Which approach strikes you as more in keeping with Christ's teaching? Why?

# 4
# Address to the Congrès de la Paix, Paris, 1851

## Victor Hugo

This article appeared in *The Pacifist Conscience*, Regnery, 1971.

---

*This address to the Peace Congress held in Paris led to the au-thor's exile from France by Napoleon III. As France's leading literary figure, Victor Hugo had much to lose by publicizing his opposition to oppression.*

*Best known in English as author of* The Hunchback of Notre Dame *and* Les Miserables, *Hugo started life as a monarchist but was in-fluenced by the sufferings of the poor under France's monarchy to espouse democratic principles.*

*In this excerpt, the author asks whether the religious idea of universal peace is a practical idea. He asserts that it is not only prac-tical, but inevitable. "Its coming can be delayed or hastened; that is all."*

*With an understanding nod to those who find this concept uto-pian, the author reminds his listeners that, four centuries previous, there were no nations such as France and Italy—only provinces war-ring with one another. He foresees a time—"the radiant door to the future"—when there will be a United States of Europe working in conjunction with the United States of America for world peace.*

*Hugo foresees battlefields replaced by markets for goods and ideas; bullets and bombs replaced by ballots; cannon joining torture instruments in museums. And he predicts that "a great supreme sen-ate," elected by universal suffrage, will be to the peoples of Europe what Parliament is to England.*

*Europe and the United States, he foretells, will exchange their products, their arts, their works of genius to "make the deserts fruit-ful, ameliorating creation under the eyes of the Creator, and joining together to reap the well-being of all. . . ."*

Gentlemen, is this religious idea, universal peace—the linking of the nations together by a common bond, the Gospel to become the supreme law, mediation to be substituted for war—is this religious

187

idea a practical idea? Is this holy thought one that can be realized?
Many practical minds . . . many politicians grown old . . . in the administration of affairs, answer 'No'. I answer with you; I answer unhes-
itatingly; I answer 'Yes', and I will make an attempt to prove my case
later on.

But I will go farther and not only say that it is a realizable end, but
that it is an unavoidable end. Its coming can be delayed or hastened;
that is all.

The law of the world is not nor can it be different from the law of
God. Now, the law of God is not war; it is peace. . . .

When one asserts these high truths, it is quite natural that the
assertion should be met with incredulity; it is quite natural that in this
hour of our trouble and anguish, the idea of a universal peace should
be surprising and shocking, very much like the apparition of the impossible and the ideal. It is quite natural that one should shout 'Uto-
pia'; as for me, modest and obscure worker in this great work of the
nineteenth century, I accept this resistance of other minds without
being either astonished or disheartened by it. It is possible that men's
minds should not be turned and their eyes blink in a kind of dizziness,
when, in the midst of the darkness which still weighs upon us, the
radiant door to the future is suddenly thrust open?

Gentlemen, if someone four centuries ago, at a time when war
raged from parish to parish, from town to town, from province to
province—if someone had said to Lorraine, to Picardy, to Normandy,
to Brittany, to Auvergne, to Provence, to Dauphine, to Burgundy, A
day will come when you will no longer wage war, when you will no
longer raise men of arms against each other, when it will no longer be
said that Normans have attacked the men of Picardy, and the men of
Lorraine have driven back those of Burgundy; that you will still have
differences to settle, interests to discuss, certainly disputes to solve,
but do you know what you will have in place of men on foot and
horseback, in place of guns, falconets, spears, pikes, and swords? You
will have a small box made of wood, which you will call a ballot box.
And do you know what this box will bring forth? An assembly, an
assembly in which you will all feel you live, an assembly which will be
like your own soul, a supreme and popular council which will decide,
judge, and solve everything in law, which will cause the sword to fall
from every hand and justice to rise in every heart. And this event will
say to you, 'There ends your right, here begins your duty. Lay down
your arms! Live in peace!' On that day you will be conscious of a
common thought, common interests, and a common destiny. You will
clasp each other's hands and you will acknowledge that you are sons

of the same blood and the same race. On that day you will no longer be hostile tribes, but a nation. You will no longer be Burgundy, Normandy, Brittany, Provence, you will be France. On that day your name will no longer be war, but civilization.

Well, you say today—and I am one of those who say it with you—all of us here, we say to France, to England, to Prussia, to Austria, to Spain, to Italy, to Russia, we say to them, 'A day will come when your weapons will fall from your hands, a day when war will seem absurd and be as impossible between Paris and London, St Petersburg and Berlin, Vienna and Turin, as today it would seem impossible between Rouen and Amiens, Boston and Philadelphia. A day will come when you France, you Russia, you Italy, you England, you Germany, all you continental nations, without losing your characteristics, your glorious individuality, will intimately dissolve into a superior unity and you will constitute the European brotherhood just as Normandy, Brittany, Burgundy, Lorraine, Alsace, and all our provinces, have dissolved into France. A day will come when there will be no battlefields, but markets opening to commerce and minds opening to ideas. A day will come when the bullets and bombs are replaced by votes, by universal suffrage, by the venerable arbitration of a great supreme senate which will be to Europe what Parliament is to England, the Diet to Germany, and the Legislative Assembly to France. A day will come when a cannon will be a museum-piece, as instruments of torture are today. And we will be amazed to think that these things once existed! A day will come when we shall see those two immense groups, the United States of America and the United States of Europe, stretching out their hands across the sea, exchanging their products, their arts, their works of genius, clearing up the globe, making deserts fruitful, ameliorating creation under the eyes of the Creator, and joining together to reap the well-being of all. . . .

Henceforth the goal of great politics, of true politics, is this: the recognition of all the nationalities, the restoration of the historical unity of nations and the uniting of the latter to civilization by peace, the relentless enlargement of the civilized group, the setting of an example to the still-savage nations; in short, and this recapitulates all I have said, the assurance that justice will have the last word, spoken in the past by might.

*Questions*

1. Why were Victor Hugo's ideas such an affront to the "divine right of kings"?

2. What are some of the author's assumptions about the role of Christianity and European culture in bringing about the betterment of the world? How would his sentiments strike a non-Christian or non-European?

3. What does the author say about rights and duties? Are his comments relevant today? Give examples.

4. What role do visionaries such as the author play in the progress of humanity toward a more just and peaceful world? Which of his predictions have come to pass? Which have not?

5. Are Victor Hugo's ideas relevant today? Why, or why not?

# 5
# Letter to a Non-Commissioned Officer

## Leo Tolstoy

This article originally appeared in Volume 20 of *"The Novels and Other Works of Lyof N. Tolstoy,"* Scribner's, 1902.

---

*Count Leo Tolstoy (1828–1910) was reckoned the most famous man in the world when he died. Born to the Russian nobility, he served briefly in the army and wrote two masterpiece novels, War and Peace and Anna Karenina. In 1885, he underwent a spiritual crisis, which converted him into a "Christian anarchist," irrevocably opposed to the Tsarist government and the Orthodox Church.*

*In this undated letter, Tolstoy responds to an army officer who cannot reconcile his orders to kill with the Christian gospel of love. In true Russian fashion, Tolstoy sees this contradiction as part of a plot by church and state to keep working people in subjection.*

*The plot, as he sees it, began with the emperor Constantine who, in the fourth century, made Christianity the state religion of the Roman empire. Tolstoy regards the Tsarist system as a method for the rich to keep the poor in subjection. To enforce its control over the working classes, the government needs an army. Unlike the sixteenth century, when soldiers were mercenaries, soldiers in the nineteenth century are conscripts who must be taught to kill.*

*The Orthodox Church, in the author's view, is a tool of the state. Instead of insisting on Christ's teaching of the golden rule and the sermon on the mount, the church, he says, subverts Christ's simple teaching with a multitude of superstitious practices. By way of contrast, the author praises the Sectarians, who repudiate Orthodoxy and follow a simpler Christianity.*

*Tolstoy's credo: "The will of God is not that we should fight and oppress the weak, but that we should acknowledge all men to be our brothers and should serve one another."*

*Toward the end of his life, Tolstoy corresponded with Gandhi, who was just beginning his campaigns of non-violent resistance in*

*South Africa. Gandhi often acknowledged his debt to the unorthodox Russian.*

You are surprised that soldiers are taught that it is right to kill people in certain cases and in war, while in the books admitted to be holy by those who so teach, there is nothing like such a permission, but, on the contrary, not only is all murder forbidden but all insulting of others is forbidden also, and we are told not to do to others what we do not wish done to us. And you ask, is not this a fraud? And if it is a fraud, then for whose sake is it done?

Yes, it is a fraud, committed for the sake of those accustomed to live on the sweat and blood of other men, and who have therefore perverted, and still pervert, Christ's teaching, which was given to man for his good, but which has now, in its perverted form, become the chief source of human misery.

The thing has come about in this way:

The government, and all those people of the upper classes that are near the government, and that live by the work of others, need some means of dominating the workers, and this means they find in their control of the army. Defence against foreign enemies is only an excuse. The German government frightens its subjects about the Russians and the French, the French government frightens its people about the Germans, the Russian government frightens its people about the French and the Germans, and that is the way with all governments. But neither the Germans, nor the Russians, nor the French, desire to fight their neighbours and other people; but, living in peace, they dread war more than anything else in the world. The government and the upper governing classes, to excuse their domination of the labourers, behave like a gipsy who whips his horse before he turns a corner and then pretends he cannot hold it in. They provoke their own people and some foreign government, and then pretend that for the well-being or for the defence of their people they must declare war, which again brings profit only to generals, officers, functionaries, merchants, and, in general, to the rich. In reality war is an inevitable result of the existence of armies; and armies are only needed by governments in order to dominate their own working-classes.

The thing is a crime, but the worst of it is that the government, in order to have a plausible basis for its domination of the people, has to pretend that it holds the highest religious teaching known to man (i.e. the Christian), and that it brings up its subjects in this teaching. That teaching, however, is in its nature opposed not only to murder, but to all violence, and, therefore, the governments, in order to dominate the people and to be considered Christian, had to pervert Christianity and to hide its true meaning from the people, and thus deprive men of the well-being Christ brought them.

This perversion was accomplished long ago, in the time of that scoundrel the Emperor Constantine, who for doing it was enrolled among the saints. All subsequent governments, especially our Russian government, do their utmost to preserve this perverted understanding, and not to allow the people to see the real meaning of Christianity; because, having seen the real meaning of Christianity, the people would perceive that the governments, with their taxes, soldiers, prisons, gallows, and false priests, are not only not the pillars of Christianity they profess to be, but are its greatest enemies.

In consequence of this perversion those frauds which have surprised you are possible, and all those terrible misfortunes occur from which people suffer.

The people are oppressed, robbed, poor, ignorant, dying of hunger. Why? Because the land is in the hands of the rich; the people are enslaved in mills and in factories, obliged to earn money because taxes are demanded from them, and the price of their labour is diminished while the price of things they need is increased.

How are they to escape? By taking the land from the rich? But if this is done, soldiers will come and will kill the rebels or put them in prison. Take the mills and factories? The same will happen. Organize and support a strike? But it is sure to fail. The rich will hold out longer than the workers, and the armies are always on the side of the capitalists. The people will never extricate themselves from the want in which they are kept, as long as the army is in the hands of the governing classes.

But who compose these armies that keep the people in this state of slavery? Who are these soldiers that will fire at the peasants who take the land, or at the strikers who will not disperse, and at the smugglers who bring in goods without paying taxes, that put in prison and there guard those who refuse to pay taxes? The soldiers are these same peasants who are deprived of land, these same strikers who want better wages, these same taxpayers who want to be rid of these taxes.

And why do these people shoot at their brothers? Because it has been instilled into them that the oath they were obliged to take on entering the service is binding, and that, though it is generally wrong to murder people, it is right to do so at the command of their superiors. That is to say that that fraud is played off upon them which has occurred to you. But here we meet the question: How is it that sensible people—often people who can read, and even educated people

—believe in such an evident lie? However little education a man may have, he cannot but know that Christ did not sanction murder, but taught kindness, meekness, forgiveness of injuries, love of one's enemies—and therefore he cannot help seeing that on the basis of Christian teaching he cannot pledge himself in advance to kill all whom he may be ordered to kill.

The question is: How can sensible people believe, as all now serving in the army have believed and still believe, such an evident fraud? The answer is that it is not this one fraud by itself that takes people in, but they have from childhood been deprived of the proper use of their reason by a whole series of frauds, a whole system of frauds, called the Orthodox Faith, which is nothing but the grossest idolatry. In this faith people are taught that God is triple, that besides this triple God there is a Queen of Heaven, and besides this queen there are various saints whose corpses have not decayed, and besides these saints there are ikons of the Gods and of the Queen of Heaven, to which one should offer candles and pray with one's hands; and that the most important and holy thing on earth is the pap, which the parson makes of wine and white bread on Sundays behind a railing; and that after the parson has whispered over it, the wine is no longer wine, and the white bread is not bread, but they are the blood and flesh of one of the triple Gods, etc.

All this is so stupid and senseless that it is quite impossible to understand what it all means. And the very people who teach this faith do not tell you to understand it, but only tell you to believe it; and people trained to do it from childhood can believe any kind of nonsense that is told them. And when men have been so befooled that they believe that God hangs in the corner, or sits in a morsel of pap which the parson gives out in a spoon; that to kiss a board or some relics, and to put candles in front of them, is useful for life here and hereafter—they are called on to enter the military service, where they are humbugged to any extent, being made to swear on the Gospels (in which swearing is prohibited) that they will do just what is forbidden in those Gospels, and then taught that to kill people at the word of those in command is not a sin, but that to refuse to submit to those in command is a sin. So that the fraud played off on soldiers, when it is instilled into them that they may without sin kill people at the wish of those in command, is not an isolated fraud, but is bound up with a whole system of fraud, without which this one fraud would not deceive them.

Only a man who is quite befooled by the false faith called Orthodoxy, palmed off upon him for the true Christian faith, can believe that there is no sin in a Christian entering the army, promising blindly to obey any man who ranks above him in the service, and, at the will of others, learning to kill, and committing that most terrible crime, forbidden by all laws.

A man free from the pseudo-Christian faith called Orthodox will not believe that.

And that is why the so-called Sectarians—i.e. Christians who have repudiated the Orthodox teaching and acknowledge Christ's teaching as explained in the Gospels, and especially in the Sermon on the Mount—are not tricked by this deception, but have frequently refused, and still do refuse, to be soldiers, considering such occupation incompatible with Christianity and preferring to bear all kinds of persecution, as hundreds and thousands of people are doing; in Russia among the Dukhobors and Molokans, in Austria the Nazarenes, and in Sweden, Switzerland, and Germany among members of the Evangelical sects. The government knows this, and is therefore exceedingly anxious that the general Church fraud, without which its power could not be maintained, should be commenced with every child from early infancy, and should be continually maintained in such a way that none may avoid it. The government tolerates anything else, drunkenness and vice (and not only tolerates, but even organizes drunkenness and vice—they help to stupefy people), but by all the means in its power it hinders those who have escaped from its trap from assisting others to escape.

The Russian government perpetrates this fraud with special craft and cruelty. It orders all its subjects to baptize their children during infancy into the false faith called Orthodoxy, and it threatens to punish them if they disobey. And when the children are baptized, i.e. are reckoned as Orthodox, then under threats of criminal penalties they are forbidden to discuss the faith into which, without their wish, they were baptized; and for such discussion of that faith, as well as for renouncing it and passing to another, they are actually punished. So that about all Russians it cannot be said that they believe the Orthodox faith—they do not know whether they believe it or not, but were converted to it during infancy and kept in it by violence, i.e. by the fear of punishment. All Russians were entrapped into Orthodoxy by a cunning fraud, and are kept in it by cruel force. Using the power it wields, the government perpetrates and maintains this fraud, and the fraud upholds its power.

And, therefore, the only means to free people from their many miseries lies in freeing them from the false faith instilled in them by government, and in their imbibing the true Christian teaching which is hidden by this false teaching. The true Christian teaching is very simple, clear, and obvious to all, as Christ said. But it is simple and accessible only when man is freed from that falsehood in which we were all educated, and which is passed off upon us as God's truth.

Nothing needful can be poured into a vessel full of what is useless. We must first empty out what is useless. So it is with the acquirement of true Christian teaching. We have first to understand that all the stories telling how God six thousand years ago made the world; how Adam sinned and the human race fell; and how the Son of God, a God born of a virgin, came on earth and redeemed man; and all the fables in the Old Testament and in the Gospels, and all the lives of the saints with their stories of miracles and relics—are nothing but a gross hash of Jewish superstitions and priestly frauds. Only to a man quite free from this deception can the clear and simple teaching of Christ, which needs no explanation, be accessible and comprehensible. That teaching tells us nothing of the beginning, or of the end, of the world, or about God and His purpose, or in general about things which we cannot, and need not, know; but it speaks only of what man must do to save himself, i.e. how best to live the life he has come into, in this world, from birth to death. For this purpose it is only necessary to act to others as we wish them to act to us. In that is all the law and the prophets, as Christ said. And to act in that way we need neither ikons, nor relics, nor church services, nor priests, nor catechisms, nor governments, but on the contrary, we need perfect freedom from all that; for to do to others as we wish them to do to us is only possible when a man is free from the fables which the priests give out as the only truth, and is not bound by promises to act as other people may order. Only such a man will be capable of fulfilling—not his own will nor that of other men—but the will of God.

And the will of God is not that we should fight and oppress the weak, but that we should acknowledge all men to be our brothers and should serve one another.

These are the thoughts your letter has aroused in me. I shall be very glad if they help to clear up the questions you are thinking about.

*Questions*

1. What is the "fraud" that the author thinks is being perpetrated on the working people? How did the Bolsheviks later play on this theme? Do you agree with this interpretation? Why, or why not?
2. What role did the emperor Constantine play in the subjection of

church to state? Are the Christian churches today under the control of the government? Give examples pro or con.

3. In view of the revival of religion in the Soviet Union after seventy years of suppression, would you modify the author's outright condemnation of Orthodoxy? If so, how?

4. What role did universal conscription (the draft) play in the manner in which modern wars are waged?

5. Tolstoy totally opposed the state, while Gandhi was willing to work with governments to accomplish his goals. Which approach strikes you as the more effective? Why?

# 6
# Why I Leave the F.O.R.

## Reinhold Niebuhr

This article originally appeared in *The Christian Century*, January 3, 1934.

*As one of the leading American Protestant theologians of the twentieth century, Reinhold Niebuhr (1892–1971) commanded respect when he expressed—and even when he changed—his opinions. Originally a strict pacifist, he was forced by his experience of worker exploitation in Detroit and elsewhere to modify his opposition to all forms of coercion and violence.*

*This article reflects that change, as he reluctantly takes his leave of the Fellowship of Reconciliation (F.O.R.), a pacifist organization based on Quaker Christianity. Considering himself both a Marxian (though critical of the hatred in communist class war) and a Christian, he tries to balance (1) the Marxian goal of basic economic justice and (2) the Christian ideal of love. As a self-professed pragmatist, he finds himself unable to adhere to absolute nonviolence when faced by the disproportionate economic power of capitalism.*

*Niebuhr carefully distinguishes the various factions within the F.O.R. While conscience forces him to abandon the organization, he expresses deep respect for those whose views he no longer shares.*

*Niebuhr's critique of nonviolence springs from the fear that sometimes it may play into the hands of the exploiters. In this respect, he anticipates by thirty years the strictures of liberation theology against "institutional violence."*

*Following Martin Luther, he holds that Christians may adhere to a strict gospel ethic as individuals, but they may have to compromise those ideals in public life.*

*With the rise of the German invasion of Poland in 1939, Niebuhr —until then a pacifist in international relations—took another step by favoring military means to stop Hitler.*

*Niebuhr's writings do not emanate from an ivory tower. Ever the committed social reformer, he was forced constantly to re-examine his principles in light of the struggle for justice. The evolution of his thought on nonviolence reflects the agony of those who must come to terms with the use of naked and barbaric power in the real world.*

Historically the Fellowship of Reconciliation is an organization of pacifists, born during the war, and holding to the Quaker position on war beyond the confines of the Quaker fellowship. In a sense the Fellowship has been a kind of Quaker conventicle inside of the traditional church. Gradually the effort to present a Christian testimony against war forced an increasingly large number of F.O.R. members to oppose the capitalistic social system as a breeder of war and injustice. As long as they could believe that the injustice of capitalism could be abolished by moral suasion there seemed to be no particular conflict between their pacifism and their socialism. They held to the generally accepted position of Christian socialists who believed that the peculiar contribution of religion to the social struggle must be an insistence upon nonviolent or even noncoercive methods of social change. In the recent poll of the membership it was revealed that 21 per cent of the membership still believed that the Fellowship should endeavor through 'method of love' to bring about a new social order 'without identifying itself with either the underprivileged or the privileged class'.

This position probably mirrors quite accurately the conviction of a very considerable portion of the liberal Protestant Church, which has not yet recognized that it is practically impossible to be completely neutral in a social struggle and that the effort at neutrality is morally more dangerous in a class conflict than in an international war because it works to the advantage of entrenched interests against advancing forces.

## NEUTRALITY IN THE CLASS STRUGGLE

Another 22 per cent of the Fellowship believe in 'identifying itself with the just aims of the workers' but 'without the use of any form of coercion'. Taking these two groups together we find that almost half of the Fellowship disavows any form of coercion. Since this type of ethical perfectionism is not related with any ascetic withdrawal from the world, which might give it consistency, it may be assumed that it is a good revelation of the failure of liberal protestantism to recognize the coercive character of political and economic life. To refuse the use of any coercive methods means that it is not recognized that everyone is using them all the time, that we all live in and benefit or suffer from a political and economic order that maintains its cohesion partially by the use of various forms of political and economic coercion.

## THE DISMISSAL OF MR MATTHEWS

Another group in the Fellowship (47 per cent to be exact) believes in the use of some form of coercion short of violence. One part of the group believes in 'assisting the organization of the workers and in leading them in strikes for a living wage' and also in organizing them into a political party that will use 'nonviolent political and economic coercive measures' and a smaller number in this group go as far as willingness to support the workers in an armed conflict but without themselves participating in the attendant violence in any way.

If the two groups that abjure any form of coercion and those which will not participate in any type of violent coercion are taken together, they represent about 90 per cent of the Fellowship. This is quite natural and logical in an organization of pacifists. It is idle, therefore, to make it appear that the action of the council, which dismissed J. B. Matthews from his position as secretary, was in any sense irregular or unfair. It was the only logical step for the Fellowship to take. Furthermore, though I share, roughly speaking, the political position of Mr Matthews, I do not agree with the publicity that those who are supporting him have released since the dismissal.

I am not a good enough Marxian to declare that convictions are determined purely by class interests and that every pacifist is therefore a conscious or unconscious tool of capitalism. I think it is quite probable that there are wealthy Quakers who abhor all violence without recognizing to what degree they are the beneficiaries of an essentially violent system. In fact, I have known Philadelphia Quakers to give hearty approval to Mr Hoover's treatment of the bonus army. At the same time I am not willing to attribute to men like Nevin Sayre, John Haynes Holmes, and Kirby Page, who represent the middle section of the Fellowship and who believe in the use of nonviolent coercion as a means of attaining social justice, the 'class interests' that have been ascribed to them by those who opposed them.

The pacifist position, whether in its pure form of nonresistance or in the more qualified form of nonviolent resistance, has always been held by a minority in the Christian church. It may be plausibly argued that such pacifism will benefit entrenched interests more than it will help the proponents of a higher social justice when the day of crisis comes. But to suggest that it is dictated by class interests not only does injustice to these courageous champions of justice, but it presses the economic interpretation of history to precisely that point where it becomes absurd. Anyone who recognizes the terrible tension between the Christian ideal of love and the hard realities of life is certainly bound to respect the effort of those who, recognizing the horrors of violence, make non-violence an absolute in their social ethic.

## WE ARE NOT PACIFIST!

While respecting this position of the pure and the qualified pacifists, I am bound to admit that I cannot share their position. For this reason I am forced to associate myself with 20 per cent of the Fellowship who are pacifists only in the sense that they will refuse to participate in an international armed conflict. Perhaps it would clear the issue if we admitted that we were not pacifists at all. We probably all recognize the terrible possibilities of violence. We regard an international armed conflict as so suicidal that we are certain that we will not participate in it.

In the case of the social struggle that is being waged between the privileged and the disinherited classes in every Western nation, some of us, at least, know that there are possibilities that modern civilization will drift into barbarism with the disintegration of the capitalistic system. We believe that not only fascism but communism has the perils of barbarism in it. The peril of the latter arises not so much from its preaching of violence as from its preaching of hatred. Hatred is very blinding; and those who are blind cannot be good enough statesmen to become the instruments of a new unity amid the complexities of Western civilization. We would certainly have as much sense of responsibility toward the avoidance of barbaric civil strife as any other intelligent and responsible person.

The reason we cannot, in spite of our scruples, maintain our connection with the majority of the Fellowship is because we regard all problems of social morality in pragmatic rather than absolute terms. The only absolute law that we recognize is the law of love, and that is an ideal that transcends all law. The purely Marxian section of this 10 per cent minority would probably not recognize the validity of the ideal of love at all. They would think of the social struggle simply as a contest between two classes in which the one class is fated to play the role of creating a classless society. Those of us who are Christian Marxians would renounce some of the utopianism implied in this belief. We believe rather that the world of nature and history is a world in which egoism, collective and individual, will never be completely overcome and in which the law of love will remain both an ideal for which men must strive and a criterion that will convict every new social structure of imperfection.

## A PRAGMATIC PROBLEM

We realize that the problem of social justice is a pragmatic and even a technical one. Modern capitalism breeds injustice because of the disproportions of economic power that it tolerates and upon which it is based. We expect no basic economic justice without a destruction of the present disproportion of power and we do not expect the latter without a social struggle. Once we have accepted the fact of the reality of the social struggle we do not feel that we can stop where the middle portion of the Fellowship has stopped. We are unable to stop there because we can find no stable absolute in the shifting situation of the social struggle where everything must be finally decided in pragmatic terms.

If we should agree with one portion of this middle section that we will use nonviolent coercion in behalf of the disinherited but will discourage any coercion that may issue in violence, we feel that we would give an undue moral advantage to that portion of the community which is always using nonviolent coercion against the disinherited. This is precisely what the liberal church is constantly tempted to do. It is furthermore usually oblivious to the fact that nonviolence may be covert violence. Children do starve and old people freeze to death in the poverty of our cities, a poverty for which everyone who has more than the bare necessities of life must feel some responsibility.

We cannot agree with another group of these qualified pacifists who would participate in an armed social conflict but who would not personally participate in its violence, contenting themselves with non-combatant services, because we have come to believe that such an attitude represents an abortive effort to maintain personal purity while holding an organic relation to a social movement that is bound to result in some degree of violence in the day of crisis.

## IS THIS DIVISION ACADEMIC?

The outsider may think that those careful definitions of just what degree of violence or nonviolence one accepts in a social struggle represent academic hairsplitting. I quite admit that this discussion as to just what any of us would do in the day of crisis is very unrealistic in many ways. As a Marxian and as a Christian it reveals to me the futility of finding a moral absolute in the relativities of politics. If anyone should suggest that those of us who have thus renounced the pacifist position ought not any longer to regard ourselves as Christian, I would answer that it is only a Christianity that suffers from modern liberal illusions that has ever believed that the law of love could be made an absolute guide of conduct in social morality and politics. As a Marxian and as a Christian I recognize the tragic character of man's social life, and the inevitability of conflict in it arising from the inability of man ever to bring his egoism completely under the dominion of conscience.

As a Marxian I will try to guide that conflict to a goal that guarantees a basic economic justice and creates a society that makes modern technical civilization sufferable. As a Christian I will know that even the justice of a socialist commonwealth will reveal the imperfections of natural man and will not destroy the contest of wills and interests which will express itself in every society. As a Christian I will achieve at least enough contrition before the absolute demands that God makes upon me and that I never completely fulfil to be able to deal with those who oppose me with a measure of forgiveness. Christianity means more than any moral attitude that can express itself in social politics. But it must at least mean that the social struggle is fought without hatred. Nonhatred is a much more important sign and symbol of Christian faith than non-violence.

## THE CHOICE OF THE RADICAL

To make the matter short, the Fellowship controversy has revealed that there are radical Christians who can no longer express themselves in pacifist terms. For some of them pacifism was the last remnant of Christianity in their radicalism. With pacifism dissipated they are inclined to disavow their Christian faith or to be quiescent about it. Others of us have merely discovered the profundity of the Christian faith when we ceased to interpret it in merely moralistic demands.

I think we ought to leave the Fellowship of Reconciliation with as good grace as possible. Perhaps we could even prove that there are some of the fruits of the spirit within us by leaving without rancor and without impugning ignoble motives to our comrades to whom we are bound in many cases by inseparable ties of common purpose and affection. In so far as we are radical Christians we must find a more solid ground for the combination of radicalism and Christianity than the creed of pacifism supplied. But we will always maintain our respect for the purity of purpose that animates the men who conceived the Fellowship of Reconciliation and will carry it on in spite of discouragement in these critical days. Perhaps the day will come when we will be grateful for their counsels.

Recognizing, as liberal Christianity does not, that the world of politics is full of demonic forces, we have chosen on the whole to support the devil of vengeance against the devil of hypocrisy. In the day in which we live, a dying social system commits the hypocrisy of hiding its injustices behind the forms of justice, and the victims of injustice express their politics in terms of resentment against this injustice. As Marxians we support this resentment against the hypocrisy. As Christians we know that there is a devil in the spirit of vengeance as well as in the spirit of hypocrisy. For that reason we respect those who try to have no traffic with devils at all. We cannot follow them because we believe that consistency would demand flight to the monastery if all the devils of man's collective life were to be avoided. But our traffic with devils may lead to corruption, and the day may come when we will be grateful for those who try to restrain all demons rather than choose between them.

## Questions

1. The author's departure from the F.O.R. is more in sorrow than in anger. How does he express that sorrow? Give examples. What can be learned from the way in which he states his differences with his opponents?

2. What do you think of Niebuhr's contention that, in some circumstances, "nonviolence may be covert violence"? Explain.

3. Niebuhr considers himself a pragmatist, rather than an absolutist. Explain these terms as they relate to armed conflict, whether they pertain to social groups or nation states.

4. The author says he opts for the "devil of vengeance" over the "devil of hypocrisy." Explain those terms in the context of this article. Are these the only two alternatives? Elaborate on your reply.

5. How does the pacifism that Niebuhr critiques differ from that of Gandhi or Martin Luther King?

# 7
# The Individual Conscience

## A.J. Muste

This article appeared in *Holy Obedience*, Harper 1952.

---

*As Robert Jay Lifton, in another section, gives voice to a secular faith in a non-nuclear world, A.J. Muste here expresses his religious pacifism. When he wrote the following excerpt (taken from his 1952 book, Holy Disobedience), there was much debate in the country about the draft, and certain exceptions to it.*

*Muste, a minister of the Reformed Church, counsels his fellow pacifists not to be taken in by proposed provisions in a draft (conscription) law that would allow alternative service for conscientious objectors. This, he feels, would serve only a narrow attitude, helping only the few who would seek such status.*

*His concern is for the eighteen year olds to be drafted en masse, young men rarely "capable of making a fully rational and responsible choice." He agrees in part with the French author Bernanos who felt that universal conscription, instituted in the French Revolution, pointed to the end of "the man created by western or Christian civilization."*

*While feeling that Bernanos' opinion was oversimplified, Muste points to the linkage between conscription, totalitarianism, depersonalization and war. He calls for resistance (Holy Disobedience) to show the government that not everybody goes along with the exercise of such power. He praises people willing to publicly oppose the draft as the core of any future movement against war and for peace. In the 1960s, those who opposed the Vietnam War—and its conscription policies—looked to Muste for inspiration and support.*

*Drawing on his religious tradition, the author tells the story of St. Stephen who was stoned for his unpopular views. In the crowd that day was Saul, who was converted to Stephen's beliefs and carried on his work. Such is the power, Muste feels, of the individual conscience.*

Participation in alternative service is quite often defended on the ground that our opposition is to war rather than conscription; except in the matter of war we are as ready to serve the nation as anybody; therefore, as long as we are not drafted for combat or forced against our will into the armed services, we are ready to render whatever service of a civilian character may be imposed upon us.

Is this a sound position? Let me emphasize that it is conscription for war under the conditions of the second half of the twentieth century that we are talking about. The question as to whether sometime and under some circumstances we might accept conscription for some conceivable purpose not related to war, is not here at stake. It is academic and irrelevant. The question with which we are dealing is that of conscripting youth in and for modern war.

As pacifists we are opposed to all war. Even if recruitment were entirely on a voluntary basis, we would be opposed. It seems to me we might infer from this that we should be *a fortiori* opposed to military conscription, for here in addition to the factor of war itself, the element of coercion by government enters in, coercion which places young boys in a military regime where they are deprived of freedom of choice in virtually all essential matters. They may not have the slightest interest in the war, yet they are made to kill by order. This is surely a fundamental violation of the human spirit which must cause the pacifist to shudder.

The reply is sometimes made that pacifists are *not* being conscripted for military purposes and therefore—presumably—*they* are not faced with the issue of the nature of military conscription. I shall later contend that it is not really possible to separate conscription and war, as I think this argument does. Here I wish to suggest that even if the question is the conscription of non-pacifist youth, it is a fundamental mistake for pacifists ever to relent in their opposition to this evil, ever to devote their energies primarily to securing provisions for COs in a draft law or to lapse into a feeling that conscription has somehow become more palatable if such provisions are made by the State. It is not our own children if we are pacifist parents, our fellow-pacifist Christians if we are churchmen, about whom we should be most deeply concerned. In the first place, that is a narrow and perhaps self-centered attitude. In the second place, pacifist youths have some inner resources for meeting the issue under discussion. The terrible thing which we should never lose sight of, to which we should never reconcile our spirits, is that the great mass of 18-year-olds are drafted for war. They are given no choice. Few are at the stage of development where they are capable of making fully rational and responsible choice. Thus the fathers immolate the sons, the older generation immolates the younger, on the altar of Moloch. What God centuries ago forbade Abraham to do even to his own son—'Lay not thy hand upon the lad, neither do thou anything unto him'—this we do by decree to the entire youth of a nation.

We need to ask ourselves whether such conscription is in any real sense a lesser evil. As we have already said, the pacifist is opposed to war and we have all sensed the danger of arguing against conscription *on the ground that* the nation could raise all the troops it needed by voluntary enlistment. Nevertheless, there is a point to an impassioned argument which George Bernanos makes in the book we mentioned at the outset, *Tradition of Freedom*. He states that the man created by western or Christian civilization 'disappeared in the day conscription became law . . . the principle is a totalitarian principle if ever there was one—so much so that you could deduce the whole system from it, as you can deduce the whole of geometry from the propositions of Euclid'.

To the question as to whether France, the Fatherland, should not be defended if in peril, he has the Fatherland answer: 'I very much doubt whether my salvation requires such monstrous behavior' as defense by modern war methods. If men wanted to die on behalf of the Fatherland, moreover, that would be one thing but 'making a clean sweep, with one scoop of the hand of an entire male population' is another matter altogether: 'You tell me that, in saving me, they save themselves. Yes, if they can remain free; no, if they allow you to destroy, by this unheard of measure, the national covenant. For as soon as you have, by simple decree, created millions of French soldiers, it will be held as proven that you have sovereign rights over the persons and the goods of every Frenchman, that there are no rights higher than yours and where, then will your usurpations stop? Won't you presently presume to decide what is just and what is unjust, what is Evil and what is Good?'

It is pretty certainly an oversimplification to suggest, as Bernanos here does, that the entire totalitarian, mechanized 'system' under which men today live or into which they are increasingly drawn even in countries where a semblance of freedom and spontaneity remains, can be traced to its source in the military conscription which was instituted by the French Revolution in the eighteenth century. But what cannot, it seems to me, be successfully denied is that today totalitarianism, depersonalization, conscription, war, and the conscripting, war-making power-state are inextricably linked together. They constitute a whole, a 'system'. It is a disease, a creeping paralysis, which affects all nations, on both sides of the global conflict. Revolution and counter-revolution, 'peoples' democracies' and 'western democracies', the 'peace-loving' nations on both sides in the war, are cast in this mold of conformity, mechanization and violence. This is the Beast which, in the language of the Apocalypse, is seeking to usurp the place of the Lamb.

We know that 'war will stop at nothing' and we are clear that as pacifists we can have nothing to do with it. But I do not think that it is possible to distinguish between war and conscription, to say that the former is and the latter is not an instrument or mark of the Beast.

## DISOBEDIENCE BECOMES IMPERATIVE

Non-conformity, Holy Disobedience, becomes a virtue and indeed a necessary and indispensable measure of spiritual self-preservation, in a day when the impulse to conform, to acquiesce, to go along, is the instrument which is used to subject men to totalitarian rule and involve them in permanent war. To create the impression at least of outward unanimity, the impression that there is no 'real' opposition, is something for which all dictators and military leaders strive assiduously. The more it seems that there is no opposition, the less worthwhile it seems to an ever larger number of people to cherish even the thought of opposition. Surely, in such a situation it is important not to place the pinch of incense before Caesar's image, not to make the gesture of conformity which is involved, let us say, in registering under a military conscription law. When the object is so plainly to create a situation where the individual no longer has a choice except total conformity or else the concentration camp or death; when reliable people tell us seriously that experiments are being conducted with drugs which will paralyze the wills of opponents within a nation or in an enemy country, it is surely neither right nor wise to wait until the 'system' has driven us into a corner where we cannot retain a vestige of self-respect unless we can say No. It does not seem wise or right to wait until this evil catches up with us, but rather to go out to meet it—to *resist*—before it has gone any further.

As Bernanos reminds us, 'things are moving fast, dear reader, they are moving very fast'. He recalls that he 'lived at a time when passport formalities seemed to have vanished forever'. A man could 'travel around the world with nothing in his wallet but his visiting card'. He recalls that 'twenty years ago, Frenchmen of the middle class refused to have their fingerprints taken; fingerprints were the concern of convicts'. But the word 'criminal' has 'swollen to such prodigious proportions that it now includes every citizen who dislikes the Régime, the Party, or the man who represents them. . . . The moment, perhaps, is not far off when it will seem natural for us to leave the front-door key in the lock at night so that the police may enter at any hour of the day or night, *as it is to open our pocket-books to every official demand.* And when the State decides that it would be a practical measure . . . to put some outward sign on us, why should we hesitate to have ourselves branded on the cheek or on the buttock, with a hot iron, like cattle? The purges of "wrong-thinkers", so dear to the totalitarian regimes, would thus become infinitely easier.'

To me it seems that submitting to conscription even for civilian service is permitting oneself thus to be branded by the State. It makes the work of the State in preparing for war and in securing the desired impression of unanimity much easier. It seems, therefore, that pacifists should refuse to be thus branded.

In the introductory chapter to Kay Boyle's volume of short stories about occupied Germany, *The Smoking Mountain*, there is an episode which seems to me to emphasize the need of Resistance and of not waiting until it is indeed too late. She tells about a woman, professor of philology in a Hessian university who said of the German experience with Nazism: 'It was a gradual process.' When the first *Jews Not Wanted* signs went up, 'there was never any protest made about them, and, after a few months, not only we, but even the Jews who lived in that town, walked past without noticing any more that they were there. Does it seem impossible to you that this should have happened to civilized people anywhere?'

The philology professor went on to say that after a while she put up a picture of Hitler in her class-room. After twice refusing to take the oath of allegiance to Hitler, she was persuaded by her students to take it. 'They argued that in taking this oath, which so many anti-Nazis had taken before me, *I was committing myself to nothing, and that I could exert more influence as a professor than as an outcast in the town.*'

She concluded by saying that she now had a picture of a Jew, Spinoza, where Hitler's picture used to hang, and added: 'Perhaps you will think that I did this ten years too late, and perhaps you are right in thinking this. *Perhaps there was something else we could all of us have done, but we never seemed to find a way to do it, either as individuals or as a group, we never seemed to find a way.*' A decision by the pacifist movement in this country to break completely with conscription, to give up the idea that we can 'exert more influence' if we conform in some measure, do not resist to the uttermost—this might awaken our countrymen to a realization of the precipice on the edge of which we stand. It might be the making of our movement.

## THE RECONCILING RESISTANCE

Thus to embrace Holy Disobedience is not to substitute Resistance for Reconciliation. It is to practice both Reconciliation and Resistance. In so far as we help to build up or smooth the way for American militarism and the regimentation which accompanies it, we are certainly not practising reconciliation toward the millions of people in the Communist bloc countries against whom American war preparations, including conscription, are directed. Nor are we practising reconciliation toward the hundreds of millions in Asia and Africa whom we condemn to poverty and drive into the arms of Communism by our addiction to military 'defense'. Nor are we practising love toward our own fellow-citizens, including also the multitude of youths in the armed services, if, against our deepest insight, we help to fasten the chains of conscription and war upon them.

Our works of mercy, healing and reconstruction will have a deeper and more genuinely reconciling effect when they are not entangled with conscript service for 'the health, safety and interest' of the United States or any other war-making State. It is highly doubtful whether Christian mission boards can permit any of their projects in the Orient to be manned by men supposed to be working for 'the health, safety and interest' of the United States. The Gospel of reconciliation will be preached with a new freedom and power when the preachers have broken decisively with American militarism. It can surely not be preached at all in Communist lands by those who have not made that break. It will be when we have gotten off the back of what someone has called the wild elephant of militarism and conscription on to the solid ground of freedom, and only then, that we shall be able to live and work constructively. Like Abraham we shall have to depart from the City-which-is in order that we may help to build the City-which-is-to-be whose true builder and maker is God.

It is, of course, possible, perhaps even likely, that if we set ourselves apart as those who will have no dealings whatever with conscription, will not place the pinch of incense before Caesar's image, our fellow-citizens will stone us, as Stephen was stoned when he reminded his people that it was they who had 'received the law as it was ordained by angels, and kept it not'. So may we be stoned for reminding our people of a tradition of freedom and peace which was also, in a real sense, 'ordained by angels' and which we no longer keep. But, it will thus become possible for them, as for Paul, even amidst the search for new victims to persecute, suddenly to see again the face of Christ and the vision of a new Jerusalem.

Some one may at this point reflect that earlier in this paper I counseled against people too readily leaving the normal path of life and that I am now counseling a policy which is certain to create disturbance in individual lives, families and communities. That is so. But to depart from the common way in response or reaction to a conscription law, in the attempt to adapt oneself to an abnormal state of society, is one thing. To leave father, mother, wife, child, yea and one's own life also, at the behest of Christ or conscience is quite another. Our generation will not return to a condition under which every man may sit under his own vine and fig tree, with none to make him afraid, unless there are those who are willing to pay the high cost of redemption and deliverance from a regime of regimentation, terror and war.

Finally, it is of crucial importance that we should understand that for the individual to pit himself in Holy Disobedience against the war-making and conscripting State, wherever it or he be located, is not an act of despair or defeatism. Rather, I think we may say that precisely this individual refusal to 'go along' is now the beginning and the core of any realistic and practical movement against war and for a more peaceful and brotherly world. For it becomes daily clearer that political and military leaders pay virtually no attention to protests against current foreign policy and pleas for peace when they know perfectly well that when it comes to a showdown, all but a handful of the millions of protesters will 'go along' with the war to which the policy leads. All but a handful will submit to conscription. Few of the protesters will so much as risk their jobs in the cause of 'peace'. The failure of the policy-makers to change their course does not, save perhaps in very rare instances, mean that they are evil men who want war. They feel, as indeed they so often declare in crucial moments, that the issues are so complicated, the forces arrayed against them so strong, that they 'have no choice' but to add another score of billions to the military budget, and so on and on. Why should they think there is any reality, hope or salvation in 'peace advocates' who when the moment of decision comes also act on the assumption that they 'have no choice' but to conform?

Precisely in a day when the individual appears to be utterly helpless, to 'have no choice', when the aim of the 'system' is to convince him that he is helpless as an individual and that the only way to meet regimentation is by regimentation, there is absolutely no hope save in going back to the beginning. The human being, the child of God, must assert his humanity and his sonship again. He must exercise the choice which he no longer has as something accorded him by society, which he 'naked, weaponless, armourless, without shield or spear, but only with naked hands and open eyes' must create again. He must understand that this naked human being is the one *real* thing in the face of the mechanics and the mechanized institutions of our age. He, by the grace of God, is the seed of all the human life there will be on earth in the future, though he may have to die to make that harvest possible. As *Life* magazine stated in its unexpectedly profound and stirring editorial of 20 August 1945, its first issue after the atom bombing of Hiroshima: 'Our sole safeguard against the very real danger of a reversion to barbarism is the kind of morality which compels the individual conscience, be the group right or wrong. The individual conscience against the atomic bomb? Yes. There is no other way.'

*Questions*

1. Why does the author advise pacifists not to press for exceptions in the military draft law for conscientious objectors?

2. Has it worked out in practice that draft laws have totally subjected the individual conscience to the state? If not, why not?

3. What evidence do you find for a system in the U.S. that links depersonalization, conscription and war? Give examples of the results to which such a system can lead.

4. Those who publicly protest military operations are accused of having an influence far out of proportion to their numbers. How does this fit in with Muste's views, as expressed in this article?

5. The author repeatedly returns to "the human being, the child of God" as the seed of all human life. What personal consequences could this have on a person opposed to military operations?

# 8

# Are You a Conscientious Objector?

## Pamphlet, Central Committee for Conscientious Objection, April 1986

*With brevity and directness, the authors of this pamphlet ask the young of draft age the question: "Could you kill another person?" Even an uncertain answer, in their view, leaves the door open. Following the prescriptions of draft law and military law, conscientious objection is defined as opposition to "participation in war in any form." Such an attitude does not preclude acceptance of some forms of force, such as that used in law enforcement.*

*The article describes the two types of conscientious objectors (C.O.'s) recognized by the U.S. government: those whose conscience forbids them from serving in any way, and those who "can be part of the military as long as they're not required to kill." Those in the first category are obliged to do civilian work for the duration of a war. Everyone of draft age, C.O. or not, is bound by law to register for the draft.*

*Selective conscientious objection—opposition to some wars but not to all—is not recognized by law. Nevertheless, the authors urge selective objectors to apply for C.O. status. They reason that the law may change and state that it helps to have one's reasons on record.*

*In regard to religious affiliation, say the authors, "The law makes no distinction among religious, moral, and ethical beliefs."*

*This article provides a helpful summary for those liable to draft registration. It spells out the conditions for C.O. status, the penalties for noncompliance and the importance of getting one's convictions on record at the earliest possible date.*

Do you think you'd be willing to fight in a war? Could you kill another person? If you aren't certain, you may be a conscientious objector (CO). A conscientious objector is a man or woman who believes war is wrong and can't be part of it.

To qualify for CO status under draft or military law, you must object to "participation in war in any form" because of your religious or moral beliefs. You don't have to be a member of any special religion—or any religion at all. You don't need to be against all force or violence. The law doesn't even require you to be against all killing. You only need to object to war.

## TWO TYPES OF CONSCIENTIOUS OBJECTORS

Many people cannot serve in the military in any way because for them all military jobs support war. Others find that they can be part of the military as long as they're not required to kill.

The law recognizes both kinds of COs. If you're against all military duty but are willing to do civilian work instead, you can be classified 1-O. If you object to war but are willing to serve as a soldier without using weapons (noncombatant duty), you can be classified 1-A-O.

There's no provision for those who oppose both military and civilian duty. And it's against the law to refuse to register for the draft.

## SELECTIVE OBJECTION

To be a CO under current law, you must be against "war in any form"—meaning all wars which you might be asked to face. If you think you might fight in some wars but not in others, try to be clear about just when you would fight. What makes some wars right and others wrong? Do you think any modern war can meet your standards?

If you find it hard to believe that any war in today's world could be right, you may be opposed to "war in any form," because you are opposed to every war that could really happen. Some COs, for example, base their claims on the Christian "just war theory," which says a war must meet certain moral standards in order to be right. They believe no modern war can meet the just war standards—even though past wars might have met them—because today's weapons would kill too many innocent people.

Some COs would fight in a spiritual war between the powers of good and evil. This is not a "war" under the law. As long as you wouldn't fight in a "flesh and blood war," you can qualify as a CO.

After you've thought about it, you may find that you're opposed to some wars but not to others. This means you probably don't qualify for CO status. You are a "selective conscientious objector." "Selective objectors" believe that sometimes it is necessary and right to take part in war, although they may be strongly opposed to a particular war.

A selective objector can still apply for CO status—and you should do so. Draft or military authorities may decide that you qualify even though you thought you didn't. The law may change. And if you're prosecuted—

for refusing to register, refusing orders, or other offenses—having your views on record can show that there was a moral reason for your actions.

## CONSCIENTIOUS OBJECTION AND RELIGIOUS BELIEF

If you're not a member of a church or synagogue, or if you don't think your beliefs are religious, you can still be a CO. According to the Supreme Court, you need to have a sincere and meaningful belief that occupies a place in your life like that of a more traditional religion. The law makes no distinctions among religious, moral, and ethical beliefs.

COs came from over 230 denominations during World War II. The law has long recognized COs who belong to no religious body. Practically all religious groups—including Protestant, Catholic, Jewish, and many others—recognize and support conscientious objectors.

## CONSCIENTIOUS OBJECTION IN THE MILITARY

If you join the military, the recruiter won't tell you anything about conscientious objection. You'll only hear promises of travel, education, skills training, and interesting jobs. But once you're in you will find that you're being trained to kill. And you may start wondering whether you should really be a soldier.

If your conscience won't let you stay in the military, it's still not too late. You can be honorably discharged or transferred to noncombatant duty as a conscientious objector. Many people have. CCCO can send you more information about applying for CO status. And we can put you in touch with a civilian counselor who can help you with your application.

## DRAFT REGISTRATION

In July, 1980, President Carter ordered men to register for the draft for the first time since 1975. Today the law requires you to register within thirty days before or twenty-nine days after your 18th birthday.

Some men believe that draft registration is wrong. For them, registering for the draft means supporting a system that is part of war. They can't do this. They are conscientious objectors to registration. If you agree and can't register, the law makes no provision for you.

You can't make a formal CO claim when you register for the draft. But you can get your stand on record. If you decide to register, you can write a brief claim on the registration card, make a copy of the card, and keep the copy for your records. Selective Service won't acknowledge your claim or do anything with it, but the fact that you tried to make it may help if you are called under a future draft.

You can also register with CCCO using our Conscientious Objector Card. This isn't an official CO claim, but in a future draft, it will show that your beliefs aren't something new. Filling out a CO card is also a good idea if you decide not to register for the draft. When you register with CCCO, you will receive information on changes in draft law and other issues which you might find helpful.

If you decide not to register, you could face legal charges. The punishment for breaking the draft law is up to five years in prison and up to $250,000 fine. But few non-registrants receive these maximum penalties. From 1980 through 1985, out of over one million men who failed to register, only 20 were charged. As of February, 1986, fourteen had been convicted. None of these received the maximum punishment.

Before you decide whether to register for the draft, try to get counseling so you can be sure you know your choices and what they might lead to. CCCO can help you find a draft counselor. And we can send you information on draft resistance.


## CONSCIENTIOUS OBJECTION UNDER THE DRAFT

Draft calls can't begin again without an act of Congress. But the rest of the draft law remains on the books. So do Selective Service regulations which tell how the draft system might process your CO claim or other claim for deferment or exemption.

As the draft now stands, you can't make any claims until you've been sent an induction order. You'd then have ten days from the issue date of the order to file your claims. In practice, this would mean you might have as few as five or six days to act.

That isn't much time. So it's best for you to decide now what you're going to do. CCCO can give you more information on the draft, conscientious objector status, draft resistance, and other deferments and exemptions. Write for our literature list. And we can refer you to a draft counselor near you so you can talk about your choices and your beliefs.

*Questions*

1. How does the present law distinguish the types of C.O.'s? Do you fit into either category? Briefly explain your reasons.

2. Does the fact that you do not belong to a church or synagogue disqualify you from C.O. status? What is the basis for your reply?

3. Does a person already in the military have any recourse regarding C.O. status? Explain the possible consequences.

4. What advice do the authors have for those whose consciences do not permit them to register for the draft?

5. What are the chances of prosecution for those who do not register? Does this strike you as a sufficient reason for avoiding registration? Explain.

9

# The Challenge of Peace:
## God's Promise and Our Response; A Pastoral Letter on War and Peace

*National Conference of Catholic Bishops,*
*May 3, 1983*

---

*The National Council of Catholic Bishops of the United States, in the section of their pastoral titled "A New Moment," say "no" to nuclear war as a means of resolving international disputes. In hearings that involved the testimony of many experts over a three-year period, the drafting committee listened thoughtfully to a wide range of views, from those of pacifists to those of "just warriors." The result was a 101-page pamphlet which gave a nuanced and detailed but definitive decision against the use of nuclear arms.*

*By going beyond their own previous statements and those of the Holy See and other episcopal conferences on questions of peace and war, the bishops demonstrated courage and sophistication. The section quoted below (#126–138) notes the changed conditions of politics and morals brought about by the nuclear age. They label the nuclear weapons race as "an act of aggression against the poor and a folly which does not provide the security it promises." They praise the Vatican for pointing out the "folly and danger of the arms race," but they give special credit to scientists and physicians for alerting the public to the concrete consequences of nuclear war. They cite a statement by the Pontifical Academy of Sciences as being of particular relevance to the public debate in the United States. The statement, a description of the death and disease that would result from a nuclear exchange, concluded with the words: "Prevention is essential for control."*

*The bishops despair of the possibility of placing political or moral limits on a nuclear war once begun. Before it is too late, they plead not only for "new ideas and a new vision, but (for) what the gospel calls a conversion of the heart." They declare themselves sobered and perplexed by the testimony they have heard. Seeking to do more than restate general moral principles, they try to relate their judgment to the specific elements of the nuclear problem.*

*While showing an awareness of how the nuclear stalemate came about, the bishops express some puzzlement about how to connect their "no" to nuclear war with the "personal and public choices which can move us in a new direction." The very destructiveness of the atom has made it impossible for nation states to protect their own territory and populations, they state. "Threats are made," they say, "which it would be suicidal to implement." Like other human beings caught on the horns of the nuclear dilemma, the prelates ask whether a nation may threaten what it may never do, or possess what it may never use. In the end, the hierarchy shows a commendable willingness to enter into the public debate on the nuclear issue, not from the Olympian heights of moral superiority, but at the tortured level of every other citizen and organization in a threatened world.*

## A. THE NEW MOMENT

*126.*     At the center of the new evaluation of the nuclear arms race is a recognition of two elements: the destructive potential of nuclear weapons, and the stringent choices which the nuclear age poses for both politics and morals.

*127.*     The fateful passage into the nuclear age as a military reality began with the bombing of Nagasaki and Hiroshima, events described by Pope Paul VI as a "butchery of untold magnitude."[56] Since then, in spite of efforts at control and plans for disarmament (e.g., the Baruch Plan of 1946), the nuclear arsenals have escalated, particularly in the two superpowers. The qualitative superiority of these two states, however, should not overshadow the fact that four other countries possess nuclear capacity and a score of states are only steps away from becoming "nuclear nations."

*128.*     This nuclear escalation has been opposed sporadically and selectively but never effectively. The race has continued in spite of carefully expressed doubts by analysts and other citizens and in the face of forcefully expressed opposition by public rallies. Today the opposition to the arms race is no longer selective or sporadic, it is widespread and sustained. The danger and destructiveness of nuclear weapons are understood and resisted with new urgency and intensity. There is in the public debate today an endorsement of the position submitted by the Holy See at the United Nations in 1976: the arms race is to be condemned as a dan-

---

56. Paul VI, "World Day of Peace Message 1976," in *Documents*, p. 198.

ger, an act of aggression against the poor, and a folly which does not provide the security it promises.[57]

129.     Papal teaching has consistently addressed the folly and danger of the arms race; but the new perception of it which is now held by the general public is due in large measure to the work of scientists and physicians who have described for citizens the concrete human consequences of a nuclear war.[58]

130.     In a striking demonstration of his personal and pastoral concern for preventing nuclear war, Pope John Paul II commissioned a study by the Pontifical Academy of Sciences which reinforced the findings of other scientific bodies. The Holy Father had the study transmitted by personal representative to the leaders of the United States, the Soviet Union, the United Kingdom, and France, and to the president of the General Assembly of the United Nations. One of its conclusions is especially pertinent to the public debate in the United States:

> Recent talk about winning or even surviving a nuclear war must reflect a failure to appreciate a medical reality: Any nuclear war would inevitably cause death, disease and suffering of pandemonic proportions and without the possibility of effective medical intervention. That reality leads to the same conclusion physicians have reached for life-threatening epidemics throughout history. Prevention is essential for control.[59]

131.     This medical conclusion has a moral corollary. Traditionally, the Church's moral teaching sought first to prevent war and then to limit its consequences if it occurred. Today the possibilities for placing political and moral limits on nuclear war are so minimal that the moral task, like the medical, is prevention: as a people, we must refuse to legitimate the idea of nuclear war. Such a refusal will require not only new ideas and new vision, but what the gospel calls conversion of the heart.

132.     To say "no" to nuclear war is both a necessary and a complex task. We are moral teachers in a tradition which has always been prepared to relate moral principles to concrete problems. Particularly in this letter we could not be content with simply restating general moral principles or repeating well-known requirements about the ethics of war. We have had

---

57. "Statement of the Holy See to the United Nations" (1976), in *The Church and the Arms Race;* Pax Christi-USA (New York: 1976), pp. 23–24.

58. R. Adams and S. Cullen, *The Final Epidemic: Physicians and Scientists on Nuclear War* (Chicago: 1981).

59. Pontifical Academy of Sciences, "Statement on the Consequences of the Use of Nuclear Weapons," in *Documents,* p. 241.

to examine, with the assistance of a broad spectrum of advisors of varying persuasions, the nature of existing and proposed weapons systems, the doctrines which govern their use, and the consequences of using them. We have consulted people who engage their lives in protest against the existing nuclear strategy of the United States, and we have consulted others who have held or do hold responsibility for this strategy. It has been a sobering and perplexing experience. In light of the evidence which witnesses presented and in light of our study, reflection, and consultation, we must reject nuclear war. But we feel obliged to relate our judgment to the specific elements which comprise the nuclear problem.

133.    Though certain that the dangerous and delicate nuclear relationship the superpowers now maintain should not exist, we understand how it came to exist. In a world of sovereign states, devoid of central authority and possessing the knowledge to produce nuclear weapons, many choices were made, some clearly objectionable, others well-intended with mixed results, which brought the world to its present dangerous situation.

134.    We see with increasing clarity the political folly of a system which threatens mutual suicide, the psychological damage this does to ordinary people, especially the young, the economic distortion of priorities—billions readily spent for destructive instruments while pitched battles are waged daily in our legislatures over much smaller amounts for the homeless, the hungry, and the helpless here and abroad. But it is much less clear how we translate a "no" to nuclear war into the personal and public choices which can move us in a new direction, toward a national policy and an international system which more adequately reflect the values and vision of the kingdom of God.

135.    These tensions in our assessment of the politics and strategy of the nuclear age reflect the conflicting elements of the nuclear dilemma and the balance of terror which it has produced. We have said earlier in this letter that the fact of war reflects the existence of sin in the world. The nuclear threat and the danger it poses to human life and civilization exemplify in a qualitatively new way the perennial struggle of the political community to contain the use of force, particularly among states.

136.    Precisely because of the destructive nature of nuclear weapons, strategies have been developed which previous generations would have found unintelligible. Today military preparations are undertaken on a vast and sophisticated scale, but the declared purpose is not to use the weapons produced. Threats are made which would be suicidal to implement. The key to security is no longer only military secrets, for in some instances security may best be served by informing one's adversary publicly what weapons one has and what plans exist for their use. The presumption of the nation-state system, that sovereignty implies an ability to

protect a nation's territory and population, is precisely the presumption denied by the nuclear capacities of both superpowers. In a sense each is at the mercy of the other's perception of what strategy is "rational," what kind of damage is "unacceptable," how "convincing" one side's threat is to the other.

137.    The political paradox of deterrence has also strained our moral conception. May a nation threaten what it may never do? May it possess what it may never use? Who is involved in the threat each super-power makes: government officials? or military personnel? or the citizenry in whose defense the threat is made?

138.    In brief, the danger of the situation is clear; but how to pre-vent the use of nuclear weapons, how to assess deterrence, and how to delineate moral responsibility in the nuclear age are less clearly seen or stated. Reflecting the complexity of the nuclear problem, our arguments in this pastoral must be detailed and nuanced; but our "no" to nuclear war must, in the end, be definitive and decisive.

## Questions

1. The bishops state that "nuclear escalation has been opposed sporadic-ally and selectively but never effectively." Cite several instances of this opposition and give your reasons why they have not succeeded.

2. Describe several non-religious organizations, such as those of physi-cians and scientists, which have alerted the public to the effects of nu-clear war on civilian populations.

3. Why do the bishops endorse the statement that "prevention is essential for control"?

4. Do you think that the bishops make a convincing case against nuclear war? Why, or why not?

5. Do you think the section on deterrence (#137) takes an unequivocal position on the question? Why, or why not?

# 10
# The Techniques of Nonviolent Action

## Gene Sharp

This article originally appeared in *Exploring Nonviolent Alternatives*, 1970.

---

*The largely non-violent revolution in the Philippine Islands in February 1986 demonstrates how even a powerful autocrat like Ferdinand Marcos could be toppled when the people and their organizations rise up against him. In this excerpt from his 1970 book, Gene Sharp, a proponent and tactician of non-violent popular action, explains some of the basic principles of this strategy. It is significant that the U.S. Catholic bishops, in their 1983 pastoral letter, "The Challenge of Peace: God's Promise and Our Response," call for the training of citizens in "peaceable non-compliance" as a means of deterring an invading force.*

*Sharp distinguishes between military and non-violent action. He describes the purpose of military action as that of "inflicting heavy destruction" on an enemy. Non-violent action, on the other hand, seeks "to deny the enemy the human assistance and cooperation which are necessary if he is to exercise control over the population."*

*The author points out that a ruler—even a dictatorial one—must depend on the populace for such services as business, transportation, the bureaucracy and the police to make his rule effective. He further explains that the strategy consists of non-cooperation in those matters in which they are expected to obey and the performance of actions they are not expected to do. He insists that this is action, not inaction, passivity, submission or cowardice. Sharp also says that the strategies he recommends are different from pacifism, although he does not explain how. Perhaps the answer may be found in the fact that such actions may be motivated by religious or ethical motives, or purely pragmatic ones.*

*Sharp states that there are no less than 197 forms of non-violent action. He puts them into three categories: non-violent protest and persuasion, non-cooperation and non-violent intervention.*

*In the first category, he lists such things as marches, picketing, "haunting" officials, public meetings, distribution of literature and even humorous pranks. One thinks of the partially successful but ultimately defeated actions by members of the Solidarity Union in Poland.*

223

The second category involves non-cooperative actions such as social and economic boycotts, strikes of all sorts and political non-cooperation. These are designed to deny the oppressor the ordinary activities of governance. For success, Sharp warns, sufficient numbers of people must take part.

The third method, non-violent intervention, challenges the opponent more directly, through sit-ins, fasts, non-violent obstruction and parallel government. Assuming "fearlessness and discipline," he says that relatively small numbers of people may have a "disproportionately large impact."

Such actions, states the author, may lead to conversion of the opponent, who may "come around to a new point of view." Failing this, the opponent may decide "to grant the demands of the nonviolent activists in a situation where he still has a choice of action." "Nonviolent coercion" goes beyond the first two steps. The ruler's power begins to disintegrate and he is no longer able to control the situation. This is eventually what happened to Marcos, though not without the help of the army.

Sharp states that repression may actually function as a "jiu-jitsu" tactic, in which the opponent is thrown off balance and manages to alienate the main population. If repression produces large numbers of adversaries to the regime "it will have clearly rebounded against the opponent."

The unique value of Sharp's analysis is that it provides suitable alternatives to submission and open warfare. However, it requires clearheaded leadership and discipline among the followers, qualities that are hard to maintain in many instances.

It is widely believed that military combat is the only effective means of struggle in a wide variety of situations of acute conflict. However, there is another whole approach to the waging of social and political conflict. Any proposed substitute for war in the defense of freedom must involve wielding power, confronting and engaging an invader's military might, and waging effective combat. The technique of nonviolent action, although relatively ignored and undeveloped, may be able to meet these requirements, and provide the basis for a defense policy.

## ALTERNATIVE APPROACH TO THE CONTROL OF POLITICAL POWER

Military action is based largely on the idea that the most effective way of defeating an enemy is by inflicting heavy destruction on his armies, military equipment, transport system, factories, and cities. Weapons are designed to kill or destroy with maximum efficiency. Nonviolent action is based on a different approach: to deny the enemy the human assistance and cooperation which are necessary if he is to exercise control over the population. It is thus based on a more fundamental and sophisticated view of political power.

A ruler's power is ultimately dependent on support from the people he would rule. His moral authority, economic resources, transport system, government bureaucracy, army, and police—to name but a few immediate sources of his power—rest finally upon the cooperation and assistance of other people. If there is general conformity, the ruler is powerful.

But people do not always do what their rulers would like them to do. The factory manager recognizes this when he finds his workers leaving their jobs and machines, so that the production line ceases operation; or when he finds the workers persisting in doing something on the job which he has forbidden them to do. In many areas of social and political life comparable situations are commonplace. A man who has been a ruler and thought his power secure may discover that his subjects no longer believe he has any moral right to give them orders, that his laws are disobeyed, that the country's economy is paralyzed, that his soldiers and police are lax in carrying out repression or openly mutiny, and even that his bureaucracy no longer takes orders. When this happens, the man who has been ruler becomes simply another man, and his political power dissolves, just as the factory manager's power does when the workers no longer cooperate and obey. The equipment of his army may remain intact, his soldiers uninjured and very much alive, his cities unscathed, the factories and transport systems in full operational capacity, and the government buildings and offices unchanged. Yet because the human assistance which had created and supported his political power has been withdrawn, the former ruler finds that his political power has disintegrated.

## NONVIOLENT ACTION

The technique of nonviolent action, which is based on this approach to the control of political power and the waging of political struggles, has been the subject of many misconceptions. . . .

The term nonviolent action refers to those methods of protest, non-cooperation and intervention in which the actionists, without employing physical violence, refuse to do certain things which they are expected, or required, to do; or do certain things which they are not expected, or are forbidden, to do. In a particular case there can of course be a combination of acts of omission and acts of commission. . . .

While it is not violent, it is action, and not inaction; passivity, submission, and cowardice must be surmounted if it is to be used. It is a means of conducting conflicts and waging struggles, and is not to be equated with (though it may be accompanied by) purely verbal dissent or solely psychological influence. It is not pacifism, and in fact has in the vast majority of cases been applied by nonpacifists. The motives for the adoption of nonviolent action may be religious or ethical, or they may be based on considerations of expediency. Nonviolent action is not an escapist approach to the problem of violence, for it can be applied in struggles against opponents relying on violent sanctions. The fact that in a conflict one side is nonviolent does not imply that the other side will also refrain from violence. Certain forms of nonviolent action may be regarded as efforts to persuade by action, while others are more coercive.

## METHODS OF NONVIOLENT ACTION

There is a very wide range of methods, or forms, of nonviolent action, and at least 197 have been identified. They fall into three classes—nonviolent protest and persuasion, noncooperation, and nonviolent intervention.

Generally speaking, the methods of nonviolent protest are symbolic in their effect and produce an awareness of the existence of dissent. Under tyrannical regimes, however, where opposition is stifled, their impact can in some circumstances be very great. Methods of nonviolent protest include marches, pilgrimages, picketing, vigils, "haunting" officials, public meetings, issuing and distributing protest literature, renouncing honors, protest emigration, and humorous pranks.

The methods of nonviolent noncooperation, if sufficient numbers take part, are likely to present the opponent with difficulties in maintaining the normal efficiency and operation of the system; and in extreme cases the system itself may be threatened. Methods of nonviolent noncooperation include various types of social noncooperation (such as social boycotts), economic boycotts (such as consumers' boycott, traders' boycott, rent refusal, and international trade embargo), strikes (such as the general strike, strike by resignation, industry strike, go-slow, and economic shutdown), and political noncooperation (such as boycott of government employment, boycott of elections, administrative noncooperation, civil disobedience, and mutiny.

The methods of nonviolent intervention have some features in common with the first two classes, but also challenge the opponent more directly; and, assuming that fearlessness and discipline are maintained, relatively small numbers may have a disproportionately large impact. Methods of nonviolent intervention include sit-ins, fasts, reverse strikes, nonviolent obstructions, nonviolent invasion, and parallel government. . . .

Just as in military battle weapons are carefully selected, taking into account such factors as their range and effect, so also in nonviolent struggle the choice of specific methods is very important.

## MECHANISMS OF CHANGE

In nonviolent struggles there are, broadly speaking, three mechanisms by which change is brought about. Usually there is a combination of the three. They are conversion, accommodation, and nonviolent coercion.

George Lakey has described the conversion mechanism thus: "By conversion we mean that the opponent, as the result of the actions of the nonviolent person or group, comes around to a new point of view which embraces the ends of the nonviolent actor." This conversion can be influenced by reason or argument, but in nonviolent action it is also likely to be influenced by emotional and moral factors, which can in turn be stimulated by the suffering of the nonviolent actionists, who seek to achieve their goals without inflicting injury on other people.

Attempts at conversion, however, are not always successful, and may not even be made. Accommodation as a mechanism of nonviolent action falls in an intermediary position between conversion and nonviolent coercion, and elements of both of the other mechanisms are generally involved. In accommodation, the opponent, although not converted, decides to grant the demands of the nonviolent actionists in a situation where he still has a choice of action. The social situation within which he must operate has been altered enough by nonviolent action to compel a change in his own response to the conflict; perhaps because he has begun to doubt the rightness of his position, perhaps because he does not think the matter worth the trouble caused by the struggle, and perhaps because he anticipates coerced defeat and wishes to accede gracefully or with a minimum of losses.

Nonviolent coercion may take place in any of three circumstances. Defiance may become too widespread and massive for the ruler to be able to control it by repression; the social and political system may become paralyzed; or the extent of defiance or disobedience among the ruler's own soldiers and other agents may undermine his capacity to apply repression. Nonviolent coercion becomes possible when those applying nonviolent action succeed in withholding, directly or indirectly, the necessary sources of the ruler's political power. His power then disintegrates, and he is no longer able to control the situation, even though he still wishes to do so.

## NONVIOLENT ACTION VERSUS VIOLENCE

There can be no presumption that an opponent, faced with an opposition relying solely on nonviolent methods, will suddenly renounce his capacity for violence. Instead, nonviolent action can operate against opponents able and willing to use violent sanctions, and can counter their violence in such a way that they are thrown politically off balance in a kind of political jiu-jitsu.

Instead of confronting the opponent's police and troops with the same type of forces, nonviolent actionists counter these agents of the opponent's power indirectly. Their aim is to demonstrate that repression is incapable of cowing the populace, and to deprive the opponent of his existing support, thereby undermining his ability or will to continue with the repression. Far from indicating the failure of nonviolent action, repression often helps to make clear the cruelty of the political system being opposed, and so to alienate support from it. Repression is often a kind of recognition from the opponent that the nonviolent action constitutes a serious threat to his policy or regime, one which he finds it necessary to combat.

Just as in war danger from enemy fire does not always force front line soldiers to panic and flee, so in nonviolent action repression does not necessarily produce submission. True, repression may be effective, but it may fail to halt defiance, and in this case the opponent will be in difficulties. Repression against a nonviolent group which persists in face of it and maintains nonviolent discipline may have the following effects: it may alienate the general population from the opponent's regime, making them more likely to join the resistance; it may alienate the opponent's usual supporters and agents, and their initial uneasiness may grow into internal opposition and at times into noncooperation and disobedience; and it may rally general public opinion (domestic or international) to the support of the nonviolent actionists; though the effectiveness of this last factor varies greatly from one situation to another, it may produce various types of supporting actions. If repression thus produces larger numbers of nonviolent actionists, thereby increasing the defiance, and if it leads to internal dissent among the opponent's supporters, thereby reducing his capacity to deal with the defiance, it will clearly have rebounded against the opponent.

### Questions

1. How does military action differ from non-violent action? Do you think this distinction holds up in real situations? Why, or why not?

2. Do you think that non-violent action is different from pacifism? If so, in what ways? Are the two compatible or incompatible? Explain.

3. Briefly describe conversion, accommodation and non-violent coercion, as used by the author. In which situations is each most appropriate?

4. What does Sharp mean by describing non-violent action as "a kind of political jiu-jitsu?"

5. Can you think of any situations besides the peaceful revolution in the Philippines where non-violent action has led to the removal of repressive regimes?

# 11
# The Holocaust as a Problem in Moral Choice

## Robert McAfee Brown

This article originally appeared in *"Dimensions of the Holocaust,"* Northwestern
University (undated).

---

*In confronting issues of war and peace, the "monstrous evil" of
the Holocaust challenges our humanity and belief in God.*

*So says Robert McAfee Brown, echoing the views of other
thinkers who have reflected on Nazi Germany's systematic liquida-
tion of six million Jews in World War II.*

*The author, a Christian theologian and peace activist, takes as his
guide Elie Wiesel, who survived Auschwitz and writes unceasingly
about it. Brown traces Wiesel's thought through five novels, in which
the roles of victim, executioner, suicide, madman and participant are
explored.*

*Wiesel's conclusion is that the only way to defeat evil is to help
one's fellow man, the only way to defeat death is to serve one's
brother. Though Wiesel finds no easy answers, he continues to ask the
hard question: Why did God permit such an obscenity?*

*Brown notes that Wiesel's way of confronting the Holocaust is by
writing about it. "Perhaps," says Brown, "we must also passionately
exhort people to repudiate dark events, to put them so far off that
they can never be repeated."*

*The author seeks to unite the pain of the Holocaust victims with
that of other peoples suffering today. "We know that pain everywhere must be combatted."*

*He gives Elie Wiesel the last word in a passage that states: to be a
Jew is to have reasons to destroy, and not to destroy; to have reasons
to hate the Germans, and not to hate them; to have reasons to mistrust
the church, and not to hate it. "To be a Jew is to have all the reasons in
the world not to have faith in language, in singing, in prayers, and in
God, but to go on telling the tale, to go on carrying on the dialogue,
and to have my own silent prayers and quarrels with God."*

I approach this occasion with a mixture of eagerness and healthy
dread. Eagerness because the occasion is an important one and I am

deeply honored to have been asked to share in it; dread because the assignment outstrips my ability to deal with it, or indeed the ability of any theologian, however well-versed or eminent, to unravel the mystery of this most monstrous of all events in the annals of human evil; but healthy dread, as well, since an audience that has successively been exposed to Elie Wiesel, Lucy Dawidowicz and Dorothy Rabinowitz will already have gained enough insight to be generous toward the failings of anyone cast in the difficult position of following them.

## HOW CAN ONE DARE TO SPEAK?

How does one approach even the outer precincts of "The Holocaust as a Problem in Moral Choice"? How, particularly, does a Christian find an explanation when he remembers that Christians were among the chief participants, almost invariably on the wrong side? I have tried to expose myself to some of the literature and some of the persons for whom the Holocaust has been the normative event of our time, and have tried to enter into that experience in ways that on any human level I would have preferred to avoid. Yet, of course, both as a non-Jew and as a non-inhabitant of the camps, I cannot really "enter into" that experience at all. I can therefore hardly claim the right to speak about it. To some it may even seem a blasphemy that I dare to try.

This is a dilemma that has faced even those most personally involved in the Holocaust: how can one speak about the unspeakable? After having written half a dozen novels on the Holocaust, Elie Wiesel wrote a book called *The Oath*, in which he examined the notion that it might have been better to remain silent in the face of such evil than attempt to speak at all. The issue was a genuine one for him; if, after writing half a dozen novels, nothing seemed to have changed in human perceptions about the Holocaust, perhaps silence might have been the more powerful witness. *The Oath* chronicles his realization that if, by the telling of the story of countless deaths, one life can be saved, the story must be told, no matter how painful. If a single life can be saved, one must speak, even if in so doing one breaks (as did the narrator in *The Oath*) a sacred oath made half a century before.

That conclusion indicates why we must dare to speak of events our words will seem to trivialize if not distort. We must do so not only so that the dead are not forgotten; not only as a reminder that we, too, might have been able to play the role of SS guards and feel no inner laceration of the spirit; we must also do so as a way of seeking to ensure that such events can never happen again. For we must face the painful reality that there is that in our nature that could allow it to happen again, that could even will its repetition. And if retelling the story can alert us to such possibilities, and increase our resolve that they must be avoided, the retelling, however painful, must take place.

## A VARIETY OF RESPONSES

I have discovered that there are many kinds of responses to the Holocaust among both Jews and Christians. For Richard Rubenstein, the reality of Auschwitz has destroyed the reality of God. For him, no other conclusion is possible. God, if God existed after Auschwitz, could only be a moral monster. For Emil Fackenheim, on the other hand, to engage in such a denial of God in the face of Auschwitz would be, as he says in *God's Presence in History,* to grant Hitler a posthumous victory: setting out in his lifetime to destroy the Jews, Hitler would finally have succeeded beyond his lifetime in destroying Judaism. For Elie Wiesel, to whom I shall shortly turn, the greatest problem posed by the Holocaust seems to be the silence of God. One may not have expected much from man; one surely could have expected more from God. Why did God not speak or act? Why did God seemingly remain indifferent? How can one do other than contend with a God so apparently callous?

There are also varieties of Christian responses to the Holocaust. These have been longer in coming and are only now beginning to receive significant articulation. Some Christians are not even willing to confront the issue; it is absent from their deliberation in ways that are harder and harder to understand. Others are so devastated by their discovery of Christian complicity in the event that they are immobilized by guilt. Still others react defensively, seeking to exonerate themselves and their Christian heritage from any responsibility, usually by blaming it on others or letting a few brave Christians go bail for the massive numbers of indifferent and complicit. A few go so far as to assert that there has been an in-built anti-Semitism in historical Christianity that must be purged and replaced by a radical theological reconstruction.

## TWO OVERALL PROBLEMS

In all these responses, and others that could be noted if space permitted, there are at least two widely-shared problems. The first of these is the problem of *responsibility.* Who is to be held accountable?

How widely must the net of accountability be spread? It includes Hitler. It includes Eichmann. Does it include the guards in the camps, the "good Germans" who only "followed orders"? Does it include those who knew what was going on and chose to remain silent? Does it include those who feared what was going on and took special pains not to find out? Does it include the Allied high command who, when told what was going on in Auschwitz, still would not give the order to bomb the railroad tracks leading to the death camp? Does it include the churches and the leaders of the churches who were silent even when many facts were known? This question of responsibility is a particularly burning one for non-Jews, though Wiesel and others have demonstrated that in this period there were even some Jews who preferred not to get involved—a fact I cite as a tribute to Jewish honesty rather than as a means of assuaging Christian consciences.

The second problem is one that all of us share—Jews and Christians alike—even though we approach it in different ways. This is the crisis of *belief* that the Holocaust forces on us. For who, whether Jew or Christian, can believe in a God in whose world such things take place? The perennial mystery of evil, the source of our greatest vulnerability as believers, reaches unique expression in the Holocaust. No theodicy can encompass this event so that its wounds are closed or its scars healed. It forever precludes easy faith in God or in humanity. Both are placed under judgment, and a verdict of acquittal may not be lightly rendered, if at all, to either party. (To this theme of the crisis of belief I will return toward the end of the present essay.)

## THE DISCIPLINE OF LISTENING

How, then, are we to approach the Holocaust as "a problem of moral choice"? My first task as a Christian must be to listen, and to ask, "Who has the authority to command my ear?" Not the one who says it did not happen. Not the one who says it happened long ago, and we now have more pressing problems. Not the one who says it was only a temporary deviation from an otherwise reliable human norm. Not the one who simply theorizes. No, the one to whom I must first listen is the one who was there, the survivor, the one who knows it happened because he bears forever the scars, both physical and psychic, of the ordeal. In my case, listening to one particular survivor has been particularly important. He has been perhaps the most important single theological influence on me in the last four or five years, even though he makes no claim to be a theologian and prefers to call himself a teller of tales. He is Elie Wiesel. He has been wres-

tling with the moral dilemma of the Holocaust for a third of a century
—he was deported to Auschwitz in 1944. He writes as a Jew and he
insists that the more he speaks out of his own particularity, out of his
Jewishness, the more he speaks universally to non-Jews as well. I can
testify to that. He speaks to me.

His words are written out of fire and blood, the fire of the crema-
toria and the blood of the victims. So they destroy. Just as fire and
blood are symbols of destruction, words nurtured by them produce
destruction. They destroy illusions, complacency, indifference. But
in both the Jewish and Christian traditions, fire and blood have creative possibilities as well. For fire can purge and blood can cleanse;
they are symbols of new beginnings as well. So also with Wiesel's
words. When their surgery has been accomplished—even while it is
being accomplished—they become instruments of healing, reaching
out over deep chasms of pain, not to anesthetize or to hide but to
transform. Elie Wiesel's pilgrimage through his own "valley of the
shadow of death" and beyond, through his series of wrestlings with
the question of what we do in the face of the greatest moral obscenity
of history—constitutes for me both a searing and a healing experience. As one who has first been called upon to listen, I propose to
share some reflections on that listening, as I have had to walk, imagi-
natively, the path that for Wiesel was not imagination but ugly reality.

## WIESEL'S RESPONSES TO MONSTROUS MORAL EVIL

How does one respond, then, in the face of monstrous moral evil?
We can distinguish at least five stages in Wiesel's pilgrimage.

The first response is the response not of a choice inwardly made
but of a decision outwardly imposed. In the face of monstrous evil it
may be that we are simply cast in the role of *victims*. This role is
described in Wiesel's first book, *Night*, the autobiographical account
of a boy of fifteen, loaded with friends and family onto cattle cars,
experiencing the tortures of thirst and hunger and madness, the splitting up of families at the entrance to the camps, and the subsequent
dehumanization to which all the "survivors" were subjected. Wiesel
had been a pious Hasidic Jew, and on the very first night his Hasidic
faith was destroyed. After being parted from his mother and sister
forever, he walked into the camp with his father and discovered a
large ditch from which giant flames were leaping. Wiesel writes,
"They were burning something. A lorry drew up and delivered its
load—little children. Babies!" (*Night*, p. 42). He knows that this is a
nightmare, that it is not to be believed, that the terrible dream will

come to an end. And it is indeed a nightmare, but it is in fact true, and Elie Wiesel will never wake up to find that its truth has been negated. And so, on that night, his childhood faith was destroyed: "Never shall I forget those flames which consumed my faith forever." (*Night*, p. 44). When morning came, he writes, "A dark flame had entered into my soul and devoured it." And the evening and the morning were the first day. Only the first day.

The rest of the journal italicizes the powerless and helpless role of a victim, the unwilling recipient of actions over which he has no control, in this case given unbearable poignancy because they are being etched in the life of a fifteen-year-old boy.

When the war ends, and he is finally released, Wiesel spends the first weeks of his liberation in the hospital at the point of death because, as he writes with crushing honesty, when the prisoners were released, all they could think about was food—and so got stomach poisoning.

> One day I was able to get up, after gathering all my strength. I wanted to see myself in the mirror hanging on the opposite wall. I had not seen myself since the ghetto. From the depths of the mirror, a corpse gazed back at me. (*Night*, p. 127)

One may unwillingly be cast in the role of victim. If there are any choices, it would seem preferable to be the *executioner* rather than the victim, and that role is explored in Wiesel's second book, a powerful short novel, *Dawn*. The narrator, Elisha, has "survived" the concentration camps at the end of the war, and while living in Paris is urged by Gad, a leader of Palestinian guerrilla forces, to go to Palestine to work for the establishment of the state of Israel.

Gad pleads all night long with Elisha. No longer, he argues, can Jews simply be the passive victims of historical fate. They must seize their fate in their own hands. He argues convincingly that the only thing to do is to go to Palestine with the guerrilla forces and engage in whatever terrorist activities are necessary to drive out the British and ensure the establishment of a Jewish state. And as dawn is rising in Paris, described as "a pale, prematurely weary light, the color of stagnant water," Gad looks out and says, "Here is the dawn. In our land it is very different. Here the dawn is gray; in Palestine it is red like fire." (*Dawn*, p. 31) Elisha accepts.

They go to Palestine. Elisha is trained, participates in a raid and then, still very young, is chosen to shoot a hostage, John Dawson, who has been seized in reprisal for the seizure of one of the Palestinian leaders. The execution is to take place at dawn. Here is a reversal of roles; as Elisha goes down into the cell under the ground to do the deed, he can almost feel the Nazi swastika on his arm, as though he were now part of the SS troops he had abhorred. He would like to be able to hate John Dawson, because that might give moral meaning to the act, but he cannot whip up a frenzy. When the time comes that he must calculatingly pull the trigger, the shot goes through John Dawson's skull and Elisha comments, "That's it. It's done. I've killed. I've killed . . ." And then he says not "I've killed John Dawson," but rather, "I've killed Elisha." (*Dawn*, p. 126) Although the victim has become an executioner, the execution turns out to be a self-execution. Murder is a form of suicide.

When Elisha goes upstairs to the Palestinian dawn, the dawn is not the dawn that Gad has promised, a dawn "red like fire." Instead, "The night left behind it a grayish light the color of stagnant water." It is still the dawn of Paris, not the dawn of the new country and the new hope.

So if it will not solve anything to accept the role of victim, neither will it solve anything to switch roles and become an executioner.

In a third book, which in the original French was called *Le Jour* (Day) but in English is called *The Accident*, we have another young survivor of the Holocaust, this time named Eliezer, Wiesel's own name, who is still trapped in a past he cannot escape. The "accident" is his being run over by a taxi, although he sees in retrospect that it was an accident only in the most euphemistic sense, since he realizes that he had willed not to step out of the taxi's way, and had welcomed the possibility of death as a possible escape from the past. He has seen himself only as a "messenger from the dead," among the living. He feels that he brings only death to those whom he confronts. He cannot find a way to escape from the past and affirm the present. He cannot bring himself to engage in a genuine act of love or sharing or commitment.

He has an artist friend, Guyula, who desperately tries to persuade him that this must be done—that he must choose the living rather than the dead, and ruthlessly, if necessary, stamp out the past. As Eliezer is recuperating in the hospital after the accident, Guyula paints his portrait. When the portrait is shown to Eliezer, it is clear that Guyula has ferreted out Eliezer's secret, his will to die. He pleads with Eliezer to love Kathleen and to let her love him; and then, to dramatize the need for a real break with the past, he lights a match to the portrait and burns it.

But it doesn't quite work. For when Guyula goes out, he leaves the ashes. The past is still there. The past is only destructive. There seems no way to stamp it out and begin again, free of its destructive grip.

Each of these first three books, then, leads into a cul-de-sac. It is only in the fourth book, *The Town Beyond the Wall*, that a new set of possibilities emerges. In this work, perhaps the most fruitful of all of Wiesel's writings, there are three further probings of the question. One of the options, madness, is creatively ambiguous; another, the option of spectator, must be utterly rejected; while the third, the option of participant, provides the beginnings of an extraordinary breakthrough.

On the flyleaf of *The Town Beyond the Wall* is a statement by one of Dostoevski's characters, "I have a plan—to go mad." And *madness* is explored as another way to deal with monstrous moral evil. Mad people are found in all of Wiesel's novels, often as the purveyors of the only true wisdom to be found within the works themselves. On close examination there seem to be two kinds of madness under discussion. (For this distinction, and many other insights within the present essay, I am indebted to a number of articles by Byron L. Sherwin.) There is what could be called "clinical madness," which describes those who simply give up, throw in the towel, and insulate themselves from the rest of the world, refusing to relate at all, living finally in total isolation. That, of course, is another cul-de-sac, a way without promise or hope.

But there is another kind of madness portrayed by Wiesel, what some have called "moral madness." This is the madness of those who said, in effect, "If this world of the Holocaust is to be described as a world of sanity, give me madness any day." When Wiesel himself went to the Eichmann trial in Jerusalem after the war, he was staggered with the ease with which it was possible to certify to the court that Eichmann was "sane." Wiesel wrote, in his *One Generation After*:

> It occurred to me that if he were sane, I should choose madness. It was he or I. For me, there could be no common ground with him. We could not inhabit the same universe or be governed by the same laws. (p. 6)

By the same logic, who in the world of the 1930's and the 1940's was sane and who was mad? Were those who were burning babies the ones who were sane, or were those who, for whatever reason, refused to sanction or be part of such actions, the ones who were truly sane?

Mosche, the "madman," was so described because he told people that Jews were being cremated, when everybody knew that such things don't happen in the twentieth century. Wiesel suggests, in other words, that the attitude which the world calls madness may in fact be the true sanity, seeing things as they really are, refusing to accept the values and patterns and standards that were regnant in Europe at that time. Such persons may have had a higher degree of sanity than those around them who called them mad.

So the response of madness, while ambiguous, is an ongoing response that needs increasing attention as a possible moral stance in the face of monstrous evil. For we too, in our era, have burned babies in the name of the American way of life—the napalm of the U.S. Air Force in southeast Asia is simply a more sophisticated weapon than the gasoline of the funeral pyres of Auschwitz.

Another role, one which Michael, the protagonist of *The Town Beyond the Wall*, rejects unambiguously, is the role of *spectator*. After the war, Michael returns to his home town of Szerencsevaros not quite sure why he does so but knowing that he must make his peace with the past in that place from which he had been deported by the Nazis a few years earlier. (Here is a significant advance beyond *The Accident*. Instead of trying to destroy the past, as Guyula had urged, Michael must find what salvation he can by confronting the past and meeting it head on.) Not until he revisits the town square, the scene of the earlier deportation, does the reason for his need to return become clear. Suddenly it clicks. He remembers that there was a face in one of the windows, an impassive face that watched the deportation with no sense of engagement, no sense of involvement. The face of a spectator. And Michael reflects:

> This, this was the thing I had wanted to understand ever since the war. Nothing else. How a human being can remain indifferent. The executioners I understood; also the victims, though with more difficulty. For the others, all the others, those who were neither for nor against, those who sprawled in passive patience, those who told themselves, "The storm will blow over and everything will be normal again," those who thought themselves above the battle, those who were permanently and merely spectators—all those were closed to me, incomprehensible. (p. 159)

The spectator still lives in Szerencsevaros. Michael talks to him and can discover no sense of passion or concern even after the event. And he makes an awesome discovery about himself. He discovers that he cannot hate the spectator, for, as he says, "Hatred implies human-

ity." All he can feel is contempt, a contempt which implies not humanity but something less than humanity, something decadent. It is noteworthy that the spectator realizes this and seeks desperately to be
hated, because hatred will at least be an acknowledgment of his humanity and personhood. But Michael refuses to give him even that
satisfaction.

For Wiesel, remaining a spectator is the most morally reprehen-
sible response of all. The one who simply opts out, the one who will
take no part, the one who will be neither for nor against, is not only
inhuman, but is in reality *against*, for the spectator by his lack of
involvement casts his vote for those who are doing the dirty work.

Where beyond these roles can one go? Wiesel develops a creative alternative in the latter part of *The Town Beyond the Wall*. It is a
role that cannot be described by a single word like "victim," "executioner," "madman" or "spectator." But it is a role that can at least be
pointed to by such words as "reciprocity," "identification," "sharing," perhaps even "love." Let us call it the role of *participant*, of one
who decides, even in the face of terrible risk, to make an act of identification with another, to side with the victim.

This role is powerfully illustrated in two relationships in *The
Town Beyond the Wall*. The first is the relationship between Michael
and Pedro, a man with whom Michael begins to be able to relate as
they build up a sense of mutual trust for one another—a quality that
Michael, as a survivor of the death camps, had never since been able
to feel toward another person. Pedro and Michael begin to discover
that they can share, and that in sharing, their own identities become
bound up with one another. As they are parting, Pedro says to Michael of their previous conversation, "I won't forget last night. From
now on you can say, 'I am Pedro,' and I, 'I am Michael.' " (*The Town
Beyond the Wall*, p. 131) Pedro can henceforth be identified only in
relation to Michael, and Michael only in relation to Pedro. It is this
sense of reciprocity, of participation, that frees Michael to be able to
look at and engage in the human venture once again. He is soon called
upon to test its reality.

Michael carries this precious truth with him into the prison cell in
which he shortly finds himself incarcerated with a prisoner who has
gone mad, totally cut off from the world, incapable of initiating any
response whatsoever. Michael realizes that relationship must be established, or in a short time both of them will be mad. In an imaginary
conversation, Pedro says to him, "Re-create the universe. Restore
that boy's sanity. Cure him. He'll save you." (*The Town Beyond the
Wall*, p. 182) This is the creative possibility that Pedro has offered to

Michael in a compressed juxtaposition of five words: "Cure him. He'll save you." The mad prisoner needs Michael. Michael needs the mad prisoner. They must find one another, enter into relationship with one another. And so Michael sets out to break through the recesses of madness to discover a point at which relationship can begin. For, as he says, "One of us will win and if it isn't me we're both lost!" (*The Town Beyond the Wall*, p. 185.) By various devices Michael begins to elicit little flickers of response from the other, enough so that he can say to the one who is as yet uncomprehending:

> One day the ice will break . . . You'll tell me your name and you'll ask me 'Who are you?' and I'll answer, 'I'm Pedro.' And that will be a proof that man survives, that he passes himself along. Later, in another prison, someone will ask your name and you'll say, 'I'm Michael.' And then you will know the taste of the most genuine of victories. (*The Town Beyond the Wall*, pp. 188–189)

And as the book ends, Wiesel writes of the prison counterpart to Michael, "The other bore the biblical name of Eliezer, which means *God has granted my prayer*." (*The Town Beyond the Wall*, p. 189) It is highly significant that Wiesel gives to "the other" his own name—a clear affirmation that for Wiesel himself it is in relationship with another, in participation in the lot of the victim or potential victim, that a meaning can begin to be found that draws one out of the shell of isolation and depersonalized existence represented by the roles of victim, executioner and spectator.

At the end of this book night is receding and dawn is breaking, not the false dawn that greeted Elisha after he shot John Dawson, but the true dawn, full of fresh promise for a new day.

A way to summarize the extraordinary progression that has taken place in these books is to compare their endings. At the conclusion of *Night*, Wiesel looks into a mirror and sees himself as a corpse. At the end of *Dawn* Elisha looks out a window and likewise sees only a reflection of himself. He knows what this means, for he has been told by an old man ("mad," naturally) that if he looked in a window and saw a face, he could know that it was night—not dawn, not day, but night. At the end of *The Accident* Eliezer is looking only at a portrait of himself.

In all of those situations, the protagonist is still locked into himself, *seeing only himself.* But at the end of *The Town Beyond the Wall* he is looking into *the face of another*, and in that reciprocity, in that sharing, it is clear that creativity and healing have truly begun. Let us further note, as a transition to what follows, that at the end of the next book, *The Gates of the Forest,* the protagonist is in Williamsburg as part of a group that has formed a minyan for a service. He has found his way back to the midst of the Hasidic community. As the book ends, Gavriel is saying kaddish for his dead friend, giving expression to a relationship that extends beyond himself, beyond even another human being, to the God to whom the prayer is being offered.

## IS THERE STILL A ROLE FOR GOD?

I have tried to suggest that within the arena of the re-creation of human relationship and trust, Wiesel sees the possibility of rebuilding a life that has been destroyed by the Holocaust, and that in such sharing the reality of God begins once again to intrude.

But we must not jump to easy formulas or answers. It still remains difficult to talk about the Holocaust, difficult to talk about God, and even more difficult to talk about these together, without seeming to blaspheme. How can this ever be done?

Let us recall that for Wiesel it is the questions that count, not the answers. He is rightly suspicious of those who offer answers. He re- calls a question to one of the participants in the Eichmann trial, in which the participant was asked if he could now discern a meaning in Auschwitz. The reply came, "I hope I never do. To understand Auschwitz would be even worse than not to understand it." Such a response is important. If we have a view of God into which Auschwitz somehow "fits," if we can conceive of a universe congruent with Auschwitz, then such a God must be a moral monster and such a universe a nightmare beyond imagination.

Nevertheless, for Wiesel and for many others the issue will not go away. He must *contest* with God, concerning the moral outrage that somehow seems to be within the divine plan. How can one affirm a God whose "divine plan" could include such barbarity? For Wiesel, the true "contemporary" is not the modern skeptic, but the ancient Job, the one who dared to ask questions of God, even though Wiesel feels that Job gave in a little too quickly at the end.

There is another way to approach the relation of God to the Holocaust. We must note that when Wiesel is writing about the rela- tionship between person and person, he is also writing about the relationship between persons and God. Each relationship sheds light upon the other. The Hasidic tale with which he concludes *The Town Beyond the Wall* shows how this double dimension suffuses his writing:

Legend tells us that one day man spoke to God in this wise:
"Let us change about. You be man, and I will be God. For only one second."
God smiled gently and asked him, "Aren't you afraid?"
"No. Are you?"
"Yes, I am," God said.
Nevertheless he granted man's desire. He became a man, and the man took his place and immediately availed himself of his omnipotence: he refused to revert to his previous state. So neither God nor man was ever again what he seemed to be.
Years passed, centuries, perhaps eternities. And suddenly the drama quickened. The past for one, and the present for the other, were too heavy to be borne.
As the liberation of the one was bound to the liberation of the other, they renewed the ancient dialogue whose echoes come to us in the night, charged with hatred, with remorse, and most of all, with infinite yearning. (*The Town Beyond the Wall*, p. 190)

What happens (in Buber's phrase) "between man and man," also happens between man and God. And the qualities of the one relationship are likewise true of the other. In both relationships there is hatred. In both relationships there is remorse. In both relationships, also, there is infinite yearning.

Menachem, the believing Jew who was for awhile in Michael's prison cell in Szerencsevaros, is surely echoing Wiesel's own yearning question when he asks, "Why does God insist that we come to him by the hardest road?" (*The Town Beyond the Wall*, p. 146) Wiesel (who lived through Auschwitz) once had an exchange with Richard Rubenstein (who did not, but for whom Auschwitz meant the death of God and the consequent difficulty of living in a world where belief in God is no longer possible). Wiesel said:

I will tell you, Dick, that you don't understand those in the camps when you say that it is more difficult to live today in a world without God. NO! If you want difficulties, choose to live *with* God . . . The real tragedy, the real drama, is the drama of the believer. (Littell and Locke, eds., *The German Church Struggle and the Holocaust*, p. 274)

So if it is true that when Wiesel is writing about man he is writing about God, and when he is writing about God he is writing about man, we may retrace the human pilgrimage we took a few moments ago, and make the fascinating discovery that the roles Wiesel attributes to human beings in responding to monstrous evil are similar to the roles human beings have frequently attributed to God.

It is clear, for example, that many today believe with Rubenstein that in the face of the reality of the Holocaust, God has become a *victim*. A survey of the Holocaust and post-Holocaust world leads them to proclaim that "God is dead." The phrase, to be sure, was initiated long before the Holocaust, but the Holocaust has put the final seal upon the verdict; a God worthy of the name has not survived. God is victim.

There are others who, whether they intended it or not, come perilously close to describing God as *executioner*, God as the one who is finally the author of evil. This is a difficult conclusion for orthodox Christian theology to avoid, at least to the degree that logic inhabits orthodox formulations, for any theology that postulates belief in an omnipotent God has a difficult time evading the conclusion that an all-powerful God is ultimately responsible for evil. Such a God seems either to have willed, or decreed, or at the very least, "permitted" it.

There are some who would say that God is *mad*, a diabolical creator, or at least (in the other notion of madness we examined) a God who, like some of those who are humanly denominated as mad, has a totally different set of priorities and criteria for action. Wiesel, indeed, has written a play called *Zalman, or The Madness of God*, in which he sets forth the notion of a response to a God who makes demands so different from those of the world that those who respond will find themselves in grave difficulty with the world. Perhaps God and the world are simply incommensurate. That could be a consolation. It could also be a new source of despair.

The notion of God as *spectator* has frequently characterized human thinking about God; whatever else we affirm about God, we find that God seems to be aloof and removed from where we are. Either God can do nothing about evil in the world, or refuses to do anything about it. In either case, God becomes a spectator to evil. This, I think, is what Wiesel is wrestling with when he talks about the silence of God in the face of cries for meaning. And just as the human role of spectator seems the most morally culpable, so also would the divine role of spectator seem to be the most damaging charge we could lay against God—that the God who knew what was going on did nothing.

There remains the possibility of describing God as *participant* in the struggle with evil. This seems to me a possibility toward which Wiesel's thought has been moving. In the account of the reciprocity between Michael and Pedro, and between Michael and the silent prisoner, in *The Town Beyond the Wall*, we sense that in that give and take, that sharing, that risk-in-love, whatever has been meant by the word "God" is broodingly and hauntingly present. The theme is further pursued by Wiesel, not only in *The Gates of The Forest* and *A Beggar in Jerusalem*, but also in a yet later writing, *Ani Maamin*, which employs an even more direct use of Messianic imagery as a way of stating a demand that God share, at least, in the plight of creation. While we cannot pursue the themes of this remarkable poem in detail, we must note certain things that Wiesel emphasizes.

*Ani Maamin* is the libretto for a cantata Wiesel wrote that was set to music by Darius Milhaud shortly before his death. The words come from Maimonides' statement of faith, "Ani maamin beviat ha-ma-shiah"—"I believe in the coming of the Messiah." How, Wiesel asks, can a Jew still sing that song? Was it not lost in the camps? How is it that those who have hoped for a Messiah, who have hoped for a divine vindication in history, can continue to believe, when such belief has received no vindication? Could one *still* hope for a vindication? What does it take to bring the Messiah, if God really cares?

With such questions in mind, Wiesel retells the old Midrashic tale of Abraham, Isaac and Jacob going down from heaven to earth to find out what was going on, and reporting back to the divine throne. In Wiesel's version of the story, the terrestrial visitation occurs during the time of the Holocaust. The patriarchs report back to God. But no matter how loudly they talk, no matter how painfully they describe the horror, there is nothing but silence from the divine throne. Nothing but silence.

So the Messianic question for Wiesel becomes the question: *The world is so evil, why does the Messiah not come?* What does it take to bring him? Are not six million dead enough? And even if he came after six million deaths, would that not already be too late? That is the Jewish form of the question. But let us note that there is a Christian form of the question which is just the reverse. If the Jewish form of the question is, "The world is so evil, why does the Messiah not come?" the Christian form of the question is surely: *The Messiah has come, why is the world so evil?* In a presumably redeemed world, redemption is not so evident. Perhaps a time is coming when, at this point of their greatest division, namely their conflicting interpretations of the Messianic claim, Jews and Christians can begin to acknowledge that they are, among all the religions of the world, at least dealing with the same problem. Both acknowledge that a spectator God would indeed be a moral obscenity; that, somehow, to talk of love must mean to talk about participation and sharing.

And the extraordinary thing that happens at the end of Wiesel's drama is this: when the patriarchs have exhausted their patience and elect to return to the children of earth with a report of divine indifference, each tells the story of a Jew who continued to believe—who continued to believe *in spite of* everything, against all odds, with no conceivable reason to do so. And *this*, so the narrator informs us, breaks through the divine impassivity. The cumulative impact of the three stories reduces God to tears, tears of love. And as Abraham, Isaac and Jacob turn to go to earth, we are told:

> They leave heaven and do not, cannot, see that they are no longer alone: God accompanies them, weeping, smiling, whispering: *Nitzhuni banai*, my children have defeated me, they deserve my gratitude. (*Ani Maamin*, p. 105)

This is no *deus ex machina* victory that ties everything together. Wiesel immediately writes, "The Word of God continues to be heard. *So does the silence of his dead children.*" (*Ani Maamin*, p. 105, italics added) But it is a powerful evocation of the theme of participant as a role we can be audacious enough to ascribe to God as well.

## HOW, FINALLY, DO WE "RESPOND"?

We have looked at some of Wiesel's responses to monstrous evil: some may have no choice but to be victims; others, seeing evil's immensity, may capitulate and become evil's enablers, opting for the role of executioners; some may choose suicide or madness as attempts to cope with the problem; others may elect the ultimate cop-out of being spectators, or even the worse cop-out of pretending that the evil didn't really happen. Finally, some may insist that however feeble the effort may seem, it is crucial to side with those who are victims or potential victims and to do so in actions of participation, identification, and sharing, believing that only thus can there be created a counterforce whose very power, whose very unexpected power, may lie in its seeming fragility. Those who do so may or may not acknowledge that whatever terms they use, they will be wrestling with God, posing questions and remaining unsatisfied with answers, particularly answers that seem to satisfy and relieve them of further responsibility.

Woven into all those responses is a further response, mentioned early in these pages and so patent that we may almost have overlooked it. For we can also respond to monstrous evil by *chronicling it,* reporting it, reminding all listeners that whatever else they forget they may not forget *that* evil, lest they make its repetition possible.

Can one, however, chronicle a unique event—an event incommensurate with all other events—in such a way that it speaks to those in other situations? Some would argue that the very uniqueness of the Holocaust renders inappropriate any attempt to relate it to other events, lest it seem to be scaled down to just another instance of moral perversity.

I disagree. I want to test the reason for my disagreement, so that if I am wrong I can be further instructed. Start with the patent truth that we can never "justify" the Holocaust or, indeed, any instance of evil. We must always remain outraged, and resist the drift toward complacency that time and distance so easily induce. But continue with a recognition that we not only have an opportunity, but an obligation, to make use of the Holocaust for some kind of creative end. We point to good and positive events of the past as events that cast light on the rest of experience: Moses before Pharoah saying, "Let my people go!" The Exodus and the giving of the Law, the prophet of the Exile singing "Comfort, comfort my people, says your God." Perhaps we need to point also to evil and dark events of the past. If we passionately exhort people to emulate great events, perhaps we must also passionately exhort people to repudiate dark events, to put them so far off that they can never be repeated.

It may be that the fires of Auschwitz are powerful enough to illumine otherwise dark corners of our moral landscape, making us aware of present acts of human demonry we would not otherwise see. Those fires have served a sensitizing purpose for Jews in relation to subsequent Jewish persecution in Russia, in relation to threats against the survival of Israel, in relation to anti-Semitic remarks that have recently emanated from the Pentagon. I think they can serve that purpose for the rest of us as well.

I have recently returned from a visit to Chile, Argentina and other Latin American countries. On the surface all seems well—just as on the surface all seemed well in Germany in 1933. But in the light of the fires of Auschwitz it was clear to me that all was *not* well in Chile and Argentina—just as all was not well in Germany in 1933. Arrests, "disappearances," confiscation, torture, all the marks of diabolical cunning, are present just below the surface, but not below the surface to those who can see. I think we are finally challenged by the Holocaust to the daring and frightening notion that an obscenity can be used as a way of forestalling other obscenities. If we can so affirm, then there is hope that the Holocaust, unredeemably evil in itself, could be a grotesque beacon, in the light of which we could gird ourselves against its repetition toward any people, in any time, in any place. *And I believe that unless we can use it as such a beacon, the Nazis have finally won.*

Wiesel and other Jews look to Israel as they make this point, but they look elsewhere as well—to Vietnam, to Chile, to the Sohel, to Bangladesh, to any place where people are suffering. I do not believe there exists a people who wants to say, "Only our pain is important." I believe there exists a people who not only wants to say, but does say, "Because of the magnitude of the pain we have suffered, we know that there is no pain anywhere that can be ignored. We know that pain everywhere must be combatted."

There is great wisdom in some advice offered by Azriel in *The Oath:* "So you hope to defeat evil? Fine. Begin by helping your fellow man. Triumph over death? Excellent. Begin by saving your brother." (*The Oath,* p. 14) For, as the narrator later says to us all, "Every truth that shuts you in, that does not lead to others, is inhuman." (*The Oath,* p. 73)

Can one, then, out of ashes and bitterness, affirm more than ashes and bitterness? Wiesel himself is proof that one can. He has earned the right to be heard. In the passage with which I conclude (from Littell and Locke, op. cit., pp. 276–77), Wiesel speaks to Jews, but as always, in such a way as to include the rest of us as well:

> When Rabbi Ishmael, one of the ten martyrs of the faith in Roman times, was led to his death, a heavenly voice was heard, saying, "Ishmael, Ishmael, should you shed one tear I shall return the universe to its primary chaos." And the Midrash says that Rabbi Ishmael was a gentleman and did not cry. And I couldn't understand that for quite awhile. Why didn't he cry? The hell with it! If this is the price to pay, who needs it? Who wants this kind of world? Who wants to live in it? Yet there are many reasons why he didn't cry.
>
> One, he was a martyr. Two, he obeyed. Three, the last and most poetic ultimate reason why he didn't cry was because he wanted to teach us a lesson in Judaism . . . Even while dying, he wanted to teach us a lesson: Yes, I could destroy the world and the world deserves to be destroyed. But to be a Jew is to have all the reasons in the world to destroy and *not to destroy!* To be a Jew is to have all the reasons in the world to hate the Germans and *not to hate them!* To be a Jew is to have all the reasons in the world to mistrust the church and *not to hate it!* To be a Jew is to have all the reasons in the world not to have faith in language, in singing, in prayers, and in God, but *to go on telling the tale, to go on carrying*

*on the dialogue,* and to have my own silent prayers and quarrels with God.

Amen.

## Questions

1. Why is the author reluctant to approach the question of the Holocaust? Why does he decide to do so?
2. Summarize the progression of Elie Wiesel's thought in the five novels cited in this article. What is the key event in the final novel that constitutes a breakthrough?
3. Why does Wiesel consider questions more important than answers? Do you agree, or disagree? Why?
4. How do Jews and Christians differ in their approach to evil, in the light of their differing views on the Messiah?
5. Wiesel comes to terms with the evil of the Holocaust by telling the story over and over. Do you think it would be better simply to put that event aside? Why, or why not?

# 12
# Those Who Said 'No' to the Holocaust

## David Kitterman

This article originally appeared in *Nonviolent Sanctions*, Spring 1991.

*Is it possible to refuse cooperation with a murderous regime and still survive? Contrary to popular—and even scholarly—belief, even those under the direct control of Nazi Germany during World War II were able to ignore or even sabotage the systematic killing of Jews and others—and live to tell about it.*

*David Kitterman, associate professor of history at Northern Arizona University, gives examples of Germans who would not go along with the Holocaust. His prime example is that of Dr. Albert Battel, a lawyer and army lieutenant who used his troops to prevent Jews from being transported to the Belzec extermination camp. He could not save them all from the dreaded SS, but several hundred persons survived because of his heroic efforts. Despite threats of arrest, he received only a reprimand and was later promoted.*

*Others simply refused to carry out orders. In more than half the cases, no negative consequences were suffered by those who would not kill unarmed civilians.*

*The author concludes on the mournful note that, given more instances of non-violent resistance, the Holocaust might have been prevented.*

This is Holocaust Remembrance Week. It is a time to remember the millions who were killed by the Nazis in World War II. It is also a time to remember those courageous individuals who saved lives by refusing to participate in Hitler's genocide.

Well-known are the stories of those who hid Jews or helped them escape from the Nazis. Virtually unknown, however, are the cases of resistance by Germans inside the Nazi extermination apparatus.

Historical research has revealed at least 100 documented cases of German soldiers, policemen, or members of the SS refusing orders to kill Jews, other unarmed civilians, or POWs. Not one of these Germans was killed for refusing orders and few suffered serious consequences.

249

These facts contradict the conventional wisdom held during the war by German combatants that any order given by a superior officer had to be obeyed or drastic consequences would follow. Many students of Nazi history have held the same view.

One dramatic case involved Dr. Albert Battel, a lawyer and first lieutenant in the army. His troops were stationed in Przemysl, Poland, where Jewish ghetto laborers were working for the army. On July 26, 1942, Battel used his troops to seal off a bridge, preventing the SS from taking the Jews to the Belzec extermination camp. He and his unit then forced entrance to the ghetto, which had been surrounded by police and SS troops, and relocated 80–100 laborers and their families to army headquarters.

The next day Battel was forced to allow the SS into the Jewish ghetto, with tragic results. The Jews were sent on death trains to Belzec, all but the few hundred Battel had managed to save. His actions constituted direct armed resistance to SS orders. SS leader Himmler threatened to arrest him. However, he received only a reprimand and was subsequently promoted before being sent to a frontline unit. Battel survived the war and was honored in Israel for his efforts to save the Jews.

What other tactics did Germans employ in refusing orders to kill? Unlike Battel, virtually all others used nonviolent methods. The majority simply stated their refusal to carry out such orders. Others protested to their superiors, which was especially effective when police or army units not under the direct control of the SS were asked to assist. A few cited damage to their emotional, psychological, or physical health. Others refused on grounds of conscience, religion, or moral scruples. Still others asked for transfers or feigned madness.

One army officer in Poland told Jewish captives to escape when his colleague, the security officer in charge of their roundup, was absent. The guards assumed it was approved and allowed the Jews to leave.

Some threw away or "lost" their weapons. One shot wildly, deliberately missing an old man in a ditch. Others overlooked women and children hiding from search details. In one case, two men raised their loaded rifles in self-defense against their drunken officer. He had drawn his pistol to kill them when they wouldn't shoot twenty women and children encountered on a road.

What were the consequences of these acts? Each of the refusers I interviewed had felt certain they would be shot or placed in a concentration camp for refusing to obey orders. But surprisingly, in 58% of the cases, those who refused suffered no negative consequences.

In only eight percent were there serious consequences. Two men were court-martialed and sent to concentration camps. Others were forced to participate in some minor way, such as driving officers to the execution site or digging the execution pit.

Lesser consequences happened in about one third of the cases. Some were transferred back to Germany (hardly a punishment) or to another unit. Such transfers sometimes resulted in demotions with lower salary, but several of those transferred were later promoted. Verbal or written reprimands, transfer to a combat unit, demotion in rank, and slower promotions were most common.

The Holocaust was an unparalleled tragedy. But in the midst of the horror heroes emerged, those who said "No!", those who overcame fear, indoctrination, and peer pressure to refuse participation in crimes against humanity. Their stories show that it was possible to refuse participation in Holocaust killings. Contrary to popular belief, there was not an effective automatic system of "terror-justice" operating against those who refused. Indeed, the coercive powers of the wartime Nazi system proved to be impotent or ineffective in nearly every documented case of refusal to murder unarmed people.

If only more Germans had said "No!", perhaps the Holocaust might have been prevented.

## Questions

1. Picture yourself in the situation of someone who is ordered to participate in the killing of the innocent. List the consequences of your refusal to act. What would you do in such a situation? Why?

2. Why do you think none of the one hundred German soldiers and others who disobeyed orders were put to death? What does that tell you about the real power of a dictatorial regime?

3. Why did so many collaborate with the Nazis?

4. How does fear play into the hands of a tyrant or a bully? Give examples from your own experience.

5. What lessons do the example of these courageous Germans have for people in today's world who are told to carry out acts that are destructive to human dignity?

# SECTION FOUR

## Conflict Resolution

# 1
# A Nuclear Age Ethos:
# Ten Psychological-Ethical Principles

## Robert Jay Lifton

This article originally appeared in *Journal of Humanistic Psychology*, Fall 1985.

*Human beings live by faith, whether religious or secular. Robert Jay Lifton of John Jay College, City University of New York, proposes ten principles to live by in our nuclear age.*

*The author begins with the nuclear dimension of war—not massive destruction, but the end of human civilization. He makes an act of the will to reject that possibility, committing himself to "the flow and continuity of human life." In this endeavor he recognizes that technology has imposed a unity on all humankind: survive or die.*

*In an expression of his secular faith, Lifton places his trust in the "collective human power in behalf of change" leading to survival. For this is required the renunciation of anything that has to do with nuclear weapons. This profound change he sees as each individual's decision to step away from "waiting for the bomb" and toward eliminating it. He includes members of every profession and form of work or thought to take part in this enterprise.*

*Rather than approach this new task with "doom and gloom," the author calls for a turn to "beauty, love, spirituality and sensuality." He concludes with a "renewed sense of human possibility in general."*

(1) We face a new dimension of destruction—not a matter of disaster or even of a war but, rather, of an end: an end to human civilization and perhaps humankind. We therefore speak of a "nuclear end."

Our imaginations and training enable us to recognize the truth of this principle precisely because of the helplessness of the helping professions in the face of nuclear holocaust.

(2) We reject that nuclear end. We believe in—commit ourselves to—the flow and continuity of human life, and to the products of the human imagination.

We find little solace, for instance, in the idea of a "divine spirit" or a "Buddha mind" continuing after a nuclear war. These are sublime concepts, but are themselves products of the human imagination.

(3) Nuclear weapons create a universally shared fate—a technologically imposed unity of all of humankind. We may say that humankind—all of it, or almost all of it—either survives or dies.

(4) We believe in the possibility of collective human power on behalf of change, awareness, and ultimately on behalf of human survival. We believe, that is, that human beings are able to mobilize the collective capacity to "imagine the real" (in Martin Buber's phrase).

(5) We believe that a key to that life—power lies in the renunciation of nuclearism—of the dependency on and even worship of, nuclear weapons. This includes renunciation of nuclear illusions having to do with foreknowledge, preparation, protection, stoic behavior under attack, recovery, security, and rational behavior in connection with the weapons in general. False concepts of "security" must especially be renounced.

(6) We believe in the possibility of a nonnuclear world—a world that reasserts the great chain of being and directs its energies toward humane goals, toward meeting human needs, toward genuine human security.

(7) We recognize that our lives must be inevitably and profoundly bound up with this struggle. So we take that step away from resignation—from "waiting for the bomb"—toward commitment to eliminating it. And we question again and again what we can do, how we can live, toward that end.

(8) In these personal, individual efforts, we seek to connect our everyday working professional existence—our creative concerns—with the antinuclear-weapons struggle. In this way we unify our own lives. And we believe that every group—members of every profession and form of work or thought—has some special knowledge, some special quality of imagination, that it can bring to this struggle for survival.

(9) In participating in this struggle, we do not embrace doom and gloom—not hopelessness and despair—but, rather, a more full existence. In confronting a genuine threat, rather than numbing ourselves to it, we experience greater vitality. We feel stronger human ties. We turn to beauty, love, spirituality, and sensuality. We touch the earth and we touch one another.

(10) Finally, in struggling to preserve humankind, we experience a renewed sense of human possibility in general. We feel part of

prospective historical and evolutionary achievements. We feel not only ourselves but our species, and relationship to that species, to be newly alive.

## Questions

1. What does the author mean by "the helplessness of the helping professions in the face of nuclear holocaust"? Give specifics.

2. Why does the author reject the idea of a "divine spirit" continuing after nuclear war? Do you agree or disagree? Why?

3. If nuclear weapons impose a collectively shared fate on humankind, what role does Lifton see in collective human power to bring about change? On what does he base his belief? Do you share it? Why or why not?

4. What role does the author see in human responsibility in the creation of a more humane, non-nuclear world?

5. Do you find the author's expression of faith convincing? Why, or why not?

2

# Communication and Conflict— Management Skills: Strategies for Individual and Systems Change

## Neil H. Katz and John W. Lawyer

This article originally appeared in *National Forum*, Fall 1983.

*Like the U.S. cavalry riding to the rescue, Katz and Lawyer were brought into a conflict-ridden school problem. Unlike the cavalry, the authors—a professor at Syracuse University and the head of Henneberry Hill Consultants—brought with them peaceful ways of change.*

*After extensive interviews, they proposed a collaborative (win/win) model of action based on "trust, honesty and mutual respect" in the course of a two-day, off-site seminar. Out of this emerged a transition team to meet weekly throughout the school year, temporary task forces to deal with specific problems and a skills training course for all parties to the negotiations.*

*The authors define communication as "an exchange of meaning between persons that allows each to influence the other's experience." They lay stress on conflict management, a process which reveals the existence and causes of basic disagreements, followed by problem-solving methods in a manner that respects the rights and feelings of everybody. To bring out the best ("actualizing values") in the participants, Katz and Lawyer concentrate on developing a set of skills: instrumental (competence); interpersonal (generosity); imaginal (generation of ideas); systems (relating parts to the whole).*

*The skills training course runs from 30 to 36 hours and covers six areas: information sharing, reflective listening, problem solving, assertiveness, conflict management and skill selection. Examples illustrate the uses to which these skills are put. The authors also go into detail on how they conduct these sessions so as to increase their effectiveness.*

*As a consequence of such training programs, organizations usually experience a growth in the quality and quantity of work done, better use of resources, a spirit of cooperation, improved planning and other desirable outcomes. In the particular school system studied, the atmosphere im-*

*proved markedly. The same might be said for other organizations, large and small, that devote similar efforts to peaceful change.*

Smarting from two painful contract negotiations, the teachers' association, administrative staff, and board of education in a large public school system were confused about what to do next. They faced yet another round of negotiations, this time in an atmosphere of heightened alienation, with each group holding the others accountable for the difficult situation in which they found themselves as individuals and as a school system.

At this point, the system's superintendent invited us as consultants to help the school move from its present adversarial (win/lose) model of dealing with conflict to a collaborative (win/win) model based on trust, honesty, and mutual respect.

Our response was to begin by conducting an organizational diagnosis. This involved one-on-one interviews with members of the executive committee of the teachers' association, with a sampling of the teachers, with the school's administrative staff, and with the school board members. After analyzing the resulting data, we decided to engage the members of the board of education, the administrative staff, and the executive board of the teachers' association in a two-day, off-site experience. Its design involved activities that would help surface the conflict, heal some of its scars, and develop a concrete action plan to bring about systemwide change, leading to a collaborative model of dealing with differences. The action plan involved three phases:

1. The creation of a transition team to facilitate change in the system toward win/win outcomes. Its membership consisted of two persons each from the board of education and the administrative staff as well as four persons from the teachers' association. This group agreed to meet weekly throughout the school year.

2. The creation of temporary task forces to deal with specific problems identified in the off-site experience. Their work is coordinated by the transition team.

3. Skills training in communication and conflict management, presented in both a five-day design offered during the summer or a two-weekend design offered during the school year. All members of the school's administrative, teaching, and noninstructional staff, and the board of education were invited to participate.

As a consequence of these efforts—specifically employing methods to enhance communication and conflict-management skills to bring about significant change in individuals and in organizations—this school system is moving rapidly toward a collaborative model of managing disputes. It is a model that allows all involved parties to experience positive outcomes, with their basic individual needs and interests satisfied.

Before considering the specifics of the content and process of communication and conflict-management skills training such as that offered in the polarized school system discussed above, we must briefly examine the basic concepts involved and the broader principles of values acquisition in which the skills training is grounded.

In our work, we define communication as an exchange of meaning between persons that allows each to influence the other's experience. Communication takes place at both conscious and unconscious levels. Conflict management is the process of becoming aware of a conflict, diagnosing its nature, and employing an appropriate problem-solving method to enable the persons involved to get their own needs met without infringing on the rights of others (that is, to simultaneously achieve their personal goals and enhance their relationships). As constructive techniques are engaged to manage conflict, feelings of self-confidence, competence, self-worth, and power increase, thereby enhancing the overall capacity of the system to respond to conflict in positive ways.

We believe that positive change can occur in a system when a significant number of its members are functioning at a level of development that enables them to make decisions based on an internal set of moral (other-regarding) principles rather than looking outside themselves for guidance and direction. This presupposes that the people in the system are largely engaged in the pursuit of their personal needs to be themselves, direct their own lives, and express creative insight. It also presupposes that their physical needs for safety and security as well as their needs for acceptance, affirmation, approval, and achievement are largely met. When people are developmentally able to make decisions independently, they can choose to meet not only their own needs but the needs of the system which includes other people as well.

Achieving this level of development requires that the system's members acquire such values as assertion, empathy, mutual accountability, flexibility, honesty, expressiveness, and initiation. Brian Hall and Helen Thompson, in their book *Leadership Through Values* (New York: Paulist Press, 1980), have defined values as priorities we choose and act upon that creatively enhance our own lives and the lives of those around us. Our lives are, in fact, motivated by values.

Integrating and actualizing values in our lives requires the development of skills (a skill being defined in this context as an internalized ability to actualize a value in behavior). For integrated development to occur, growth must take place in four skill areas:

• Instrumental skills: the ability to act with intelligence, using both mind and body to be competent in a chosen endeavor.

• Interpersonal skills: the ability to act with generosity and understanding toward others, which flows from self-knowledge, together with ability to represent one's experience to another with accuracy and clarity.

• Imaginal skills: the ability to initiate new ideas and use data-based information to develop new concepts and courses of action, including the ability to create by integrating instrumental and interpersonal skills in innovative ways.

• Systems skills: the ability to plan and design changes in whole systems and act based on a capacity to see how the parts relate to the whole. These skills combine a blend of imagination, sensitivity to others, and competence and they help to integrate instrumental, interpersonal, and imaginal skills.

For personal and systems growth to occur, members of the system must develop these skills in an integrated way and incorporate them into their everyday behavior.

The learning experience in communication and conflict management we have developed provides participants the opportunity to refine and integrate these skills. It focuses on the following specific interpersonal and imaginal skills that, when mastered, will enable the participants to communicate and manage conflict effectively and participate productively in systems change:

• Expressing and sharing emotions.

• Expressing anger and resentment in nonharmful ways.

• Identifying and expressing their own and others' thoughts and feelings accurately in both interpersonal and group settings.

• Using imagination, fantasy, and reflection.

• Listening to others attentively, with empathy and respect, thereby hearing and understanding more clearly what others are communicating.

• Enabling others to see and hear themselves accurately.

• Articulating needs, interests, and personal goals clearly.

• Clarifying and solving problems.

• Using creativity to imagine new and innovative outcomes for problems.

• Asserting in a straightforward manner to ensure that their basic human rights are secured without infringing on the rights of others.

• Affirming others for the positive impact they have had on the participants.

• Remaining calm under stress and in high-anxiety situations.

• Settling disputes involving both needs and values in constructive, resourceful, and collaborative ways.

• Negotiating differences in interests.

The specific skills listed above are grouped into the following six skill areas, designed for presentation during a 30- to 36-hour learning experience:

Information sharing. This involves expressing one's thoughts and feelings to another with clarity and accuracy and helping another do likewise. It involves representing one's experience to another without deleting, generalizing, or distorting information. Information sharing is enhanced by improving one's ability to establish and maintain rapport through increased sensory acuity, appropriate pacing, and selecting a manner of communicating that effectively mirrors the other's frame of reference.

Reflective listening. This entails following the thoughts and feelings of another and understanding what the other is saying from his or her point of view. It involves respectfully hearing both the thoughts and feelings of the other and then expressing (reflecting) them succinctly to him or her in one's own words to capture the essence of what the other is communicating. This skill is fundamental in constructive communication and is an essential ingredient in effective problem solving, assertion, and conflict management.

Problem solving. The ability to clarify another's problem and then use a problem-solving process to help the other generate a number of possible creative outcomes and select and commit to a constructive solution is an important skill for participants to develop.

Assertion. Everyone must develop the ability to express his/her thoughts, feelings, and opinions without infringing on the rights of another. Assertiveness involves achieving one's personal goals without damaging one's relationship with the other or injuring his or her self-esteem. Participants learn to formulate and send assertion messages that enable them to get their needs and interests met in effective ways.

Conflict management. Conflict management is a process of diagnosing a conflict situation and engaging the appropriate problem-solving approach to generate a solution that satisfies the interests of all parties involved. The learning experience introduces two strategies for producing mutually acceptable outcomes: one for conflicts involving mutually exclusive needs, goals, means, and scarce resources and another for conflicts involving fundamental differences in values, beliefs, and preferences.

Skill selection. We have found that it is also important to know when to use which skill.

In the ordinary communication situation, the feeling or energy level of both persons involved in the relationship is normal, with both usually being able to adequately represent their experience. Information-sharing skills are especially useful in this situation to prevent the generalization, distortion, or deletion of information.

The second situation is where another person has a problem or a pressing need or is feeling a particularly high level of positive or negative energy on an issue. In this case, the skills of reflective listening and problem solving are required. Within this area, three specific applications emerge. The first involves reflective listening where the problem or issue presented has no solution—for example, the death of a loved one. In this instance, reflective listening skills provide an accepting and supportive presence to the other person. The second application occurs when a person is presenting a problem or need for which a solution is possible. By using reflective-listening skills, one can commit to be with the other person as he or she discusses the pressing issue. In talking the matter through, the other can acquire new insight and become able to move directly to his or her own solution. A third application involves a situation where a person has correctly identified a problem but is unable to resolve the matter and is seeking assistance. In this case, both reflective listening and problem-solving skills are used to appropriately help the other.

A third situation emerges when you are the one who has a problem or a pressing need or you are experiencing especially high emotional energy or strong feelings about an issue. In this case, the skill of assertion is most appropriate.

In the fourth situation, the parties involved are experiencing strong feelings regarding opposing needs or values, requiring the skills of conflict management.

In short, knowing when to use which of these skills requires the ability to carefully observe from moment to moment where the energy in the relationship is and identify who has the pressing need. Once one is clear about who has the high energy or a pressing need, one can more readily select the appropriate skill.

In presenting communication and conflict-management skills, we have adapted an approach developed by Allen Ivey called microskill training. Ivey divides skills into small components, called microskills, which can more easily be presented and acquired than a skill in its entirety. In learning to play tennis, for example, we might first learn to hold the racket, then to place the ball, and finally to serve the ball using the racket. The skill components are acquired and added one-by-one, so that finally the entire skill area is mastered.

In our work we believe that the process used in training is fundamental to success in the acquisition of skills. We have found that effective delivery of communication and conflict-management skill learning involves the following process elements:

Modeling. Modeling the use of the skills we teach throughout the learning experience is critical to skill development. Each question is appropriately paraphrased. Each challenge is carefully heard nondefensively, using reflective listening skills.

Theory presentation. Each skill is introduced in simple language, using visual aids and examples from our personal and professional lives. The examples enable participants to relate the skill to real-life experience.

Demonstration. Each skill presented is demonstrated, usually using a volunteer participant who offers to share with us a concrete problem to enable everyone to see the skill in use in a real-life situation. Each demonstration is critiqued to extract maximum learning from the experience.

Practice. Since we believe that skills are acquired through use, a good portion of the learning experience involves skill practice. For skill-practice sessions, we use a small-group model involving three persons. In a reflective-listening practice, for instance, Person A describes a real-life concern or problem while Person B listens using the skill; Person C observes the process and leads a critique at the end of the session.

Feedback. Following each segment of the learning experience, we invite feedback about both its process and its content, in the belief that every learning experience is enhanced by periodic reflections and conversations around those aspects of the training that are going well and those that need to be adjusted in order to facilitate the participants' skill development. During those times set aside for discussion, each person is invited to share his or her thoughts and feelings about the experience as it is progressing.

The workbook. The workbook performs two functions: It provides a reference for material presented in the learning experience, and it includes written exercises that allow participants to practice responses to communication situations. These exercises are especially useful in the reflective listening and assertion components of the learning experience.

Personal documentation. At the beginning of each segment of the learning experience, participants are invited to write their current perspectives on the particular subject being presented. Later, after learning has occurred, participants are invited to capture another perspective, compare the two, and identify the new insights acquired.

Role-plays. Role-playing exercises are presented to permit effective skill practice in the conflict-management section of the learning experience. In each role-playing exercise, two roles are established—one for a skilled party and the other for an unskilled party. The role-plays allow participants to practice conflict-management skills in a safe, supportive environment.

In our consulting experience, we have found when individuals undertake training in communication and conflict-management skills, the systems in which they function experience significant improvement in the effectiveness of their members and their organization. As appropriate reflective listening, problem solving, assertion, and conflict-management skills are used, individuals communicate and deal with differences more constructively. Moreover, the health of the entire system is enhanced, as measured by improvements in such factors as:

• Overall performance of individuals and work groups, in terms of both quality and quantity of output;

• Organizational efficiency: the relationship of resources used by the organization to the quality of the product or services produced;

• Cooperation and coordination between individuals and work groups;

• Action planning and decision making, in terms of quality and timeliness;

• Organizational effectiveness: the degree to which the organization reaches its goals;

• The organization's climate and the level of morale and creativity exhibited by its members.

In short, the acquisition of communication and conflict-management skills empowers individuals with concrete strategies that enable them to help one another and attend to their own needs and interests in ways that enhance their self-esteem and improve their interpersonal relationships. More constructive interactions then impact favorably on the performance of the organization as a whole.

The school system we described at the beginning of this article has already experienced some of these benefits. As more and more people in the system have completed the basic communication and conflict-management learning experience, the quality of their interactions and the performance of the school as a whole has improved. Conflicts that were previously handled in adversarial terms are now being addressed in collaborative ways, with attempts being made to negotiate disputes so that all parties involved experience win/win outcomes with their basic needs and interests met. Skill training in communication and conflict management has indeed been the foundation of this system's broad-based change effort.

*Questions*

1. What are the advantages and disadvantages of bringing outside consultants into a dispute?
2. The authors give their definition of "communication." Can you think of any others?
3. What steps would you recommend to keep "conflict management" from being manipulated in favor of one party?
4. How would you react to the statement that all the authors are doing is putting common sense into fancy language? State your reasons.
5. The article speaks of feedback as part of the learning process. Define feedback and explain its significance.

3

# Identifying Alternatives to Political Violence: An Educational Imperative

## *Christopher Kruegler and Patricia Parkman*

This article originally appeared in *Harvard Educational Review*, February 1985.

*Somewhat like the weather, violence is something everybody complains about, but few do much to change. The authors ask themselves—and the reader—why governments and movements still "cling to its use." They conclude that the efficacy of violence as a means of resolving disputes is overrated and they give their reasons why they believe this to be so.*

*Kruegler and Parkman cite the world's current trouble spots as instances of the stalemate and simmering revolts that remain even after the introduction of massive force—Vietnam and Afghanistan being two outstanding examples.*

*The authors develop their thesis for non-violent problem-solving from the history of successful political change through other than military means: the 1944 general strike in El Salvador, the 1905 "first" Russian revolution and the Danish resistance to Nazism during World War II. Though each of these movements had its mixture of success and failure, the authors issue this reminder: "When violent sanctions fall short of achieving their objectives, we do not usually conclude that violence has been tried and found wanting." They ask for equal treatment of non-violence.*

*Their final plea is for educators to do far more empirical research on the strategy and tactics of non-violence, with the goal of helping people to "envision credible alternatives to armed conflict."*

Few would disagree that organized political violence has had disastrous consequences for human life and civilization in this century. War, dictatorship, terrorism, genocide, and systems of social oppression have conspired to take millions of lives, divert precious economic resources from other human enterprises, and place the continued existence of humanity in question.[1]

Yet, while we conclude rationally that we may not survive our collective dependence on violence, both nation-states and insurgent movements

267

cling to its use. In the absence of the international rule of law or a just world order, organized violence appears to be the ultimate recourse against intolerable conditions and grave threats to our lives, interests, and values. It persists, on the one hand, because of a widespread but largely unexamined belief that it "works" and, on the other, because there are no generally recognized alternative means of resolving those critical conflicts in which one or both parties perceive the stakes as too high to permit compromise.[2]

In this article, we argue that the efficacy of organized violence is overrated and, more important, that nonviolent sanctions offer a greatly underrated and underdeveloped source of political power which could replace armed force and free humanity from its heavy costs and incalculable dangers. We see a major role for educators in breaking down the cultural conditioning that perpetuates reliance on violence and in making nonviolent sanctions more effective, and therefore, more relevant to the critical conflicts of our time.

To say that the efficacy of organized violence is overrated is not to say that it never works, but merely that its recent history is not one of unqualified success. On a tactical level, superior armed force can control many, if not all, situations. Any act of resistance that is limited in time and place can be negated by sufficiently ruthless opponents. On the strategic and political levels, however, the probable effects of violence become less easy to calculate. Most armed struggles involve at least one clear loser. Moreover, victory is often achieved at terribly high or unanticipated costs. Finally, stalemate must be considered as a possible outcome. These less desirable outcomes for one or both protagonists waging violent struggle have been frequent enough to warrant a serious investigation of nonviolent alternatives.

Political scientist John Stoessinger has observed that "no nation that *began* a major war in this century emerged a winner."[3] Aside from possible disagreement over which wars should be classified as "major," it is correct that those powers which have struck first in the larger wars of this century have met military defeat, despite the range of possible outcomes described above. Stoessinger analyzes the moments of decision when statesmen chose either war or escalation and finds that these moments were almost always characterized by mutual misperception of each other's intentions and capabilities and the potential risks of armed conflict. Thus, he suggests, war functions as a sort of reality therapy in which expectations are most often adjusted in a context of defeat or stalemate.[4]

The complete failure of military power to secure policy objectives is perhaps best typified by the U.S. experience in Vietnam, and the same fate may well await the Soviet Union in Afghanistan. These are examples of asymmetrical conflicts: the vast preponderance of power, conventionally understood, appears to be on one side. In such conflicts, the ostensibly weaker parties are sometimes able to control the political aspects of the conflict and turn even military defeats to their own advantage. Thus the Tet offensive of 1968, technically a military victory for the United States, became a watershed for American antiwar sentiment simply because the opponent was still able to mount a major offensive at that point in the struggle. The My Lai massacre stands as another tactical "victory," whose counterproductive political effects far outweighed its military value.

If the Vietnam War demonstrates the limits of military methods for a superpower like the United States, does it not conversely support a case for successful use of unconventional warfare by Vietnam? Here, the question of costs becomes relevant. Although Vietnam can claim that it won, as many as two million of its people died. Its countryside is poisoned with chemical toxins and defaced by some twenty million bomb craters.[5] Independence of a sort was achieved, but for the foreseeable future Vietnam will probably be a military, economic, and political dependent of the Soviet Union. Vietnam's authoritarian regime, a product of thirty years of warfare, has alienated many of its citizens. Continuing regional conflict is another legacy of this war.

Hidden costs may also accrue to the winners of less significant conflicts. Both the British victory in the Falklands/Malvinas crisis and the recent invasion of Grenada by the United States were hailed by their architects as unequivocal triumphs. The former victory, however, obliged the Thatcher government to commit itself to an indefinite and expensive military presence in another hemisphere, while the latter reaped for the United States the dubious political prestige that results from defeating such a small opponent.

Stalemate is an outcome that appears to be occurring with increasing frequency. The Korean War is probably the clearest example of a large-scale, painful struggle that ended in the frustration of both sides' objectives. The interminable wars of the Middle East, in which the local participants draw encouragement and support from their big-power sponsors, have also been inconclusive. Fifteen years of paramilitary struggle in Northern Ireland have not significantly changed the balance of power in favor of the separatist forces in that country, while military occupation, special police powers, and other repressive measures on the part of the British government have failed either to restore the status quo ante or to remove the threat of terror.

Despite this record, news media, history books, and popular culture consistently focus on the results achieved by violence. Moreover, they give more attention to violent struggles that fail to achieve their objectives than to nonviolent struggles that succeed. Hence, few people are aware of the alternative ways to wage serious conflict that have been widely used for centuries.

## THE HIDDEN HISTORY OF NONVIOLENT SANCTIONS

Nonviolent sanctions are those punishments and pressures which do not kill or threaten physical harm but which, nonetheless, thwart opponents' objectives and cause them to alter their behavior.[6] The power of nonviolent sanctions is essentially that of denying opponents the support or cooperation which they need to attain their objectives. Many people associate nonviolent action exclusively with the work of Mohandas Gandhi and Martin Luther King, Jr. While the contributions of these men and their followers are extremely important, they do not encompass or exhaust the potential of this form of power. Its use does not require a commitment to nonviolence as an ethical principle, although its most effective deployment does require an understanding of the special dynamics of nonviolent struggle.

There is, in fact, a vast hidden history of nonviolent sanctions.[7] Much of this history has simply been overlooked because of the selective perception noted above. Nonviolent sanctions have also gone unrecognized because they were not consciously chosen and identified as such. In many cases they have been used side by side with violent sanctions. Lacking a conceptual framework from which to do so, historians have often failed to ask questions or collect data that would enable us to assess the significance of the nonviolent facets of a conflict.

Of the hundreds of conflicts in which nonviolent action has played a significant role, only a few have been sufficiently researched to assess the strategic effect of nonviolent sanctions. The three cases that follow are among those which have received such study. They challenge common stereotypes about the conditions under which nonviolent sanctions can be effective. In none of the three were the nonviolent protagonists committed to nonviolence as an ethical principle, nor were their opponents liberal democratic governments. On the contrary, the opponent in each case was a dictatorship with a record of ruthlessness, and in two cases the opponent responded to the nonviolent action with violent repression.

Maximiliano Hernández Martínez was El Salvador's most notorious dictator, best known for the massacre of 1932 which followed a brief, easily suppressed peasant uprising. Estimates of the number of people executed in cold blood range from eight thousand to thirty thousand in a country that, at the time, had a total population of about one million. The Martínez regime then suppressed the fledgling labor movement and all political parties except its own.

Twelve years of one-man rule gradually alienated many people who initially supported Martínez, including the majority of the big landowners, businessmen, professionals, and junior military officers. On April 2, 1944, the small Salvadoran air force and two army regiments took up arms against the government. The revolt quickly became a tragicomedy of overconfidence, bungling, and division among the insurgent leaders. Troops loyal to the president crushed the revolt within forty-eight hours.

Two weeks later, with the surviving opposition leaders imprisoned, in exile, or in hiding, university students, women, and collaborators in various occupational groups began to organize a completely nonviolent general strike that escalated rapidly from May 5–8. At the height of the action, buses and taxis disappeared from the streets of the capital city. Market stalls, shops, banks, and professional offices were closed. Government employees abandoned their work. The nation's railroads stopped running, and the strike began to spread to other cities.

Taken by surprise, divided, and demoralized, the government took no effective action to counter the strike. When a frightened or trigger-happy policeman shot and killed a boy on May 7, angry, though peaceful, crowds filled the streets. Martínez' cabinet panicked and resigned. After hours of negotiations on May 8, Martínez announced his decision to give up the presidency. The next morning the National Assembly received the president's resignation and named his successor.[8]

How has the memory of these events been preserved in El Salvador? April 2—not May 9—was declared a national holiday. As late as 1976, ceremonies still commemorated a botched military coup. Salvadoran periodical literature abounds with memoirs by participants of the April 2 uprising and gives detailed reconstructions of the fighting, while the civilian movement which actually dislodged Martínez is rarely mentioned. The only book on the revolution of 1944 devotes thirty-five pages to the events of April 2–4, another twenty-two to the trials and executions of a number of the participants, and eight to a woefully inaccurate and incomplete account of the general strike.[9]

The first Russian Revolution of 1905 is not commonly understood as nonviolent. Indeed, it was accompanied by a great deal of politically motivated violence, mostly in the form of assassinations and peasant riots. On October 17, 1905, however, it was not violence that forced Tsar Nicholas II of Russia to take an unprecedented and, for him, repugnant step.[10] When Nicholas created Russia's first representative assembly, or Duma, he did so in response to a massive general strike, which has been described as one of the most complete in history, and a campaign of public defiance of civil laws that mobilized nearly the entire urban population of Russia.[11]

In addition to strikes, the nonviolent methods employed in this movement included the holding of political banquets during which petitions were drafted; mass demonstrations, processions, and demonstration funerals; the withholding of taxes; the usurpation of governmental prerogatives by illegal bodies; defiance of censorship laws; refusal of conscription; and the refusal of troops to carry out orders. Most of these methods were used in an improvised fashion. In the course of the struggle, new organizations such as unions, soviets, or workers' councils, and illegal political parties with a variety of orientations were formed. These gained invaluable experience during the revolution, and many of them persisted after it had run its course. Labor unions, for example, won the right to exist legally as a result of the struggle and continued to function openly for several years.

The Duma, which Nicholas called for in his manifesto of October 17, represented the first legal limitation on the autocratic power of the tsar. Its creation did not by any means constitute a complete victory over the tsarist system, but it was certainly a major step toward the disintegration of that system.[12]

The Danish response to occupation by Nazi Germany from 1940 to 1945 employed various forms of social, political, and economic noncooperation to preserve the integrity of Danish life and institutions in the face of a concerted attempt to integrate them into Hitler's New Order. Open resistance was not initially condoned by the Danish government, which remained nominally in power until August 28, 1943. Instead, the civil service and government officials who retained their positions worked to mitigate the effects of the occupation on the Danish people.

In this period, resistance mainly took the form of *schweikism*, or obstructionism disguised as apparent cooperation.[13] Government officials, for example, concealed increases in food production from the German authorities, leaked information about repressive actions to the intended victims, and generally slowed down orders which might have hampered other resistance activities.[14] German concerts were boycotted in favor of community songfests featuring traditional Danish music. German soldiers and their collaborators were ostracized. Danish national symbols and pro-Allied symbols became widely used as a means of expressing opposition at comparatively little risk.[15] Subtle forms of noncooperation prevented Nazi penetration of Danish governmental institutions for three years, during which time a psychological climate conducive to open resistance, by both violent and nonviolent means, was developed.

In August of 1943, an industrial strike movement, accompanied by widespread sabotage, provoked a crisis. Government officials resigned rather than implement the severe repressive measures demanded by German authorities. The Danish government dissolved, leaving no legitimate authority in its place and removing the legal barrier to open resistance. Among the most notable achievements of the nonviolent branch of the resistance was the rescue of approximately seven thousand Danish Jews from Nazi persecution by means of clandestine evacuation routes to Sweden, thus frustrating the implementation of Hitler's "final solution."[16] Later, early in the summer of 1944, the German occupation authorities gave in to demands to revoke a series of repressive measures when they found that they could not control a general people's strike in Copenhagen, although they had killed over one hundred Danes in the attempt to do so.[17]

It is important to note the catalytic role played by violent sabotage in eliciting the repression which stimulated the governmental crisis of August 1943. This illustrates the sometimes complex relationship between violent and nonviolent sanctions when they are used in the same conflict by the same protagonists.[18] The degree to which the two types of sanctions are, or are not, compatible under specific circumstances is a matter which has yet to receive serious and systematic study.[19]

In these three cases, nonviolent sanctions achieved a great deal. These examples do not, however, lead to the conclusion that nonviolent sanctions offer a ready-made panacea to those looking for a means of waging conflict. Indeed, examination of the outcomes brings to light the limitations of these and many similar movements.

While the Danish resistance made Germany's military and economic exploitation of Denmark less efficient than it would otherwise have been, neither the nonviolent sanctions nor the combination of violent and nonviolent sanctions stopped that exploitation. The opposition to Martínez failed in its attempt to establish democratic government in El Salvador, which soon succumbed to a new military dictatorship. Similarly, analysts of the 1905 general strike in Russia have pointed out that the coalition of forces which frightened the tsar into issuing the manifesto of October 17 did not act effectively to consolidate its new position. Instead, it became embroiled in its own internal struggles for power and ideological leadership. It was unable to respond with a unified program when the autocracy began to renege on promised reforms, to limit the powers of the Duma, and to invoke harsh repressive measures in the months that followed.[20]

When violent sanctions fall short of achieving their objectives we do not usually conclude that violence has been tried and found wanting. We ask what conditions favored the winner and what did the loser do wrong. Nonviolent struggle should be judged by the same standards. Given the nature of the forces involved in the examples above, there is no reason to think that the nonviolent protagonists would have achieved more with violent sanctions. We can, on the other hand, see their weaknesses. In each case nonviolent sanctions were improvised under harsh conditions with little or no advance preparation on the part of those using them. The Salvadoran opponents of Martínez had no strategy for pursuing longer-range goals beyond his resignation, and the opposition to the tsar suffered from lack of agreed-upon leadership and mechanisms for decision making.

Analysis of these and other cases of nonviolent struggle ought to suggest ways in which nonviolent sanctions could be made more effective, just as military strategists learn from the study of past victories and defeats. Over the past three decades a small group of researchers has begun a systematic study of nonviolent sanctions which should lead to a much better understanding of both their limits and their potential.[21]

## POTENTIAL OF NONVIOLENT SANCTIONS

Nonviolent sanctions are already used with great regularity and proficiency in certain types of conflicts. Both sides in most labor disputes, for example, are skilled in the use of a variety of coercive yet nonviolent methods for attaining their ends. Domestic protest movements and civil rights movements in many countries rely heavily on nonviolent sanctions to advance their causes. The question before us now is whether, on the basis of historical experience and creative new thinking, it is possible to extend deliberately the range of issues and problems for which they are relevant and to which they can be applied with confidence.

It has been suggested that nonviolent sanctions might provide the basis of an alternative means of national defense.[22] This possibility was recently explored in a three-year study conducted by Britain's Alternative Defence Commission. The Commission's report, *Defence without the Bomb,* argues that British national security would be enhanced by a reduced role in NATO, unilateral nuclear disarmament, and the adoption of a two-tiered defense system, combining elements of both conventional military defense and prepared nonviolent resistance by civilians. The sixteen-member commission felt that conventional coastal and anti-aircraft defenses could extract a high entry price from a hypothetical invader, and that this might have some dissuasive power. Should an invasion be accomplished, however, the best defense might be achieved by withholding any form of cooperation from the opponent and waging a protracted resistance against the invaders by exclusively nonviolent means.[23]

For many small countries, any degree of armed resistance against their prospective opponents might be futile, if not suicidal. For these countries, a purely "civilian-based defense" may well offer the best alternative to surrender, on the one hand, and devastating armed conflict against much larger powers, on the other.[24] Such a defense policy would entail, in times of national crisis, the transformation of all of society's ordinary institutions and organizations into resistance organizations, thus denying the opponents effective political control and ultimately forcing them to withdraw. Naturally, the adoption of a civilian-based defense policy would imply considerable knowledge of, and confidence in, the nonviolent sanctions that would be its principal weapons.

Nonviolent sanctions are also being looked at with renewed interest by people who find themselves faced with various forms of social, political, and economic oppression. The assertion that armed struggle is the only effective method of changing or removing oppressive regimes is open to question. As the cases described above demonstrate, even the most repressive governments are dependent to some degree on the cooperation and acquiescence of the people they rule. When this cooperation is withdrawn in a systematic way, the power base of the oppressive authorities may erode very quickly. A struggle of this type inevitably involves violent repression against those wielding the nonviolent sanctions. Thus, participants must organize themselves at the outset to endure hardships and to continue the resistance despite repression, as they would have to do in a violent struggle. Nonviolent struggles are currently being waged in a number of repressive states, including Poland, Chile, and the Philippines. Nonviolent sanctions might also play a meaningful role in many other societies if their dynamics were better understood.

## AN AGENDA FOR EDUCATORS

Developing the potential of nonviolent sanctions requires much more empirical research on their successes and failures, as well as theoretical work on questions of strategy and tactics. This is a task for institutions of higher learning. At the present time, Harvard University's Program on Nonviolent Sanctions in Conflict and Defense is the only program in the world, of which the authors are aware, that is specifically dedicated to research in this field, and it has only two full-time researchers. A handful of students have produced useful case studies as theses and dissertations, but many more are needed.

One reason for the paucity of research is lack of attention to nonviolent sanctions in the instructional programs of colleges and universities. While the World Policy Institute's curriculum guide, *Peace and World Order Studies*, does not necessarily give a complete picture of what is offered, it is probably representative. Of the thirty-one undergraduate peace studies programs surveyed, only eight appear to offer one or more courses on nonviolent action.[25]

The need is not simply to increase course offerings, however. As educators at all levels have become sensitive to the presence of race and gender stereotypes in what is taught—often implicitly rather than explicitly—we should ask how the existing curriculum perpetuates the assumption that violence "works" and how it treats the role of nonviolent sanctions in human life. A critical examination of curriculum guides, textbooks, and audiovisual materials from this point of view would show us where the deficiencies are and what is needed in the way of new materials. To our knowledge no such study has been proposed or undertaken. This is new subject matter for most teachers, which again argues for course offerings on nonviolent sanctions in colleges and universities, as well as in in-service training programs.

Education is not only what goes on in schools. A total of perhaps two-dozen informal study groups have used either a draft study guide on civilian-based defense or *U.S. Defense Policy: Mainstream Views and Nonviolent Alternatives*, which gives substantial attention to civilian-based defense.[26] The fall 1984 catalogue of the Pittsburgh Peace Institute offers an imaginative workshop on "The Nonviolent Defense of Pittsburgh." Interest in such adult education offerings is clearly growing and presents a challenge for the development of more and better materials.

To meet this interest, library holdings on nonviolent sanctions must be expanded. There is an urgent need for the translation of the best literature into languages other than the original, and for publication of new literature as it is developed.

The entertainment industry also has a role to play. Nonviolent struggle is drama. Its history abounds in stories of courage, suspense, and victory against formidable odds. Yet for every *Gandhi*, how many fantasies like *Red Dawn* unrealistically glorify violence? Why should films and television not bring us the excitement of, say, the rescue of the Danish Jews from Nazi persecution? And why should fiction not explore the as yet untried possibilities of the eminently human power of nonviolence?

We began by citing the threat to human survival posed by the technology of organized violence. That threat poses a challenge to educators, and central to the challenge is the need to help people envision credible alternatives to armed conflict. The development of nonviolent sanctions points the way to one such alternative.

*Notes*

1. This assessment of the problem, and much of the analysis which follows, draws heavily on Gene Sharp's *Social Power and Political Freedom* (Boston: Porter Sargent, 1980), ch. 9 and 11 in particular.

2. This point was first made by Walter Lippmann in "The Political Equivalent of War," *Atlantic Monthly*, Aug. 1928, p. 181.

3. Stoessinger, *Why Nations Go to War* (New York: St. Martin's Press, 1978), p. 123. Emphasis added.

4. Stoessinger, *Why Nations Go to War*, pp. 227–231.

5. Stoessinger, *Why Nations Go to War*, p. 136.

6. Sharp, *Social Power and Political Freedom*, p. 289.

7. For a list of eighty-five major cases, see Sharp, *Exploring Nonviolent Alternatives* (Boston: Porter Sargent, 1971), pp. 115–123.

8. For a detailed reconstruction and analysis of this case, see Patricia Parkman, "Insurrection Without Arms: The General Strike in El Salvador, 1944" Diss. Temple University, 1980.

9. Francisco Morán, *Las jornadas cívicas de abril y mayo de 1944*. (San Salvador: Editorial Universitaria, Universidad de El Salvador, 1979), pp. 61–96, 105–127, 127–136.

10. By the Julian calendar, used in Russia until 1918, thirteen days behind the Gregorian calendar used in the West.

11. Alan Moorhead, *The Russian Revolution* (New York: Harper, 1958), p. 58.

12. Only Peter Ackerman's "Strategic Aspects of Nonviolent Resistance Movements," Diss. Tufts University, 1976, and Sharp's, *The Politics of Nonviolent Action* (Boston: Porter Sargent, 1973), pp. 78–79, treat the specifically nonviolent character of this revolution.

13. This technique takes its name from the bungling soldier in Jaroslav Hasek's *The Good Soldier Schweik* (Harmondsworth: Penguin, 1951). This is a reprint of the posthumously published work, which Hasek had not completely finished at the time of his death in 1923.

14. Paul Wehr, "Aggressive Nonviolence," in *Response to Aggression*, ed. Arnold P. Goldstein, Edward G. Carr, William S. Davidson II, and Paul Wehr (New York: Pergamon Press, 1981), p. 485.

15. Jeremy Bennett, "The Resistance Against the German Occupation of Denmark 1940–1945," in *Civilian Resistance as a National Defence*, ed. Adam Roberts (Baltimore: Penguin Books, 1969), pp. 187–189.

16. Wehr, "Aggressive Nonviolence," p. 488. It is estimated that only 450 of Denmark's 8,000 Jews were actually apprehended.

17. Wehr, "Aggressive Nonviolence," pp. 489–490.

18. There is a lively discussion in the literature as to whether sabotage is by definition violent, and whether it is ever compatible with nonviolent struggle. See esp. Sharp, *The Politics of Nonviolent Action*, pp. 608–611; and Bennett, "The Resistance Against the German Occupation of Denmark 1940–1945," pp. 190–197. In this context, we refer primarily to bombings at industrial and military sites.

19. In addition to the sources cited above, further material on nonviolent resistance in Denmark can be found in Jorgen Haestrup's *European Resistance Movements, 1934–45: A Complete History* (Westport: Meckler, 1981).

20. Ackerman, "Strategic Aspects of Nonviolent Resistance Movements," pp. 371–376.

21. See esp. the work of Sharp, Adam Roberts, Theodor Ebert, Johan Galtung, Anders Boserup, and Andrew Mack on this subject. Boserup and Mack's *War without Weapons* (New York: Schocken, 1975) provides a useful bibliography of the major works.

22. The National Conference of Catholic Bishops, to cite one example, called for the development of nonviolent means of national defense in its 1983 pastoral letter, *The Challenge of Peace: God's Promise and Our Response* (Washington: United States Catholic Conference, 1983).

23. The Alternative Defence Commission, *Defence Without the Bomb* (London, Taylor & Francis, 1983), pp. 11, 204–205, 243.

24. Sharp, *Social Power and Political Freedom*, p. 232 ff., offers a definition and thorough discussion of this policy.

25. Barbara J. Wein, ed., *Peace and World Order Studies* (New York: World Policy Institute, 1984), pp. 629–667. Sample syllabuses can be found on pp. 70–126, although these are not all clearly focused on nonviolent sanctions as an alternative form of power.

26. Bob Irwin, *U.S. Defense Policy: Mainstream Views and Nonviolent Alternatives (A Macro-Analysis Seminar Manual)* (Waltham, MA: International Seminars on Teaching for Nonviolent Action, 1982).

## Questions

1. How great a role does cultural conditioning play in the common acceptance of violence as an acceptable way of resolving conflicts? Give examples from your everyday experience.

2. Why do the authors say that violence is overrated? Do you agree or disagree? State your reasons.

3. What were some of the factors in the limited success of the three nonviolent movements cited by the authors?

4. What is the authors' assessment of peace studies programs? How could they be strengthened?

5. What role does the entertainment industry play in the promotion of the cult of violence? Give examples from your own experience.

# 4
# You Be the Arbitrator

## American Arbitration Association

---

*Each case story is a capsule version taken from a real case adminis-
tered under the Voluntary Labor Arbitration Rules of the Association, and
each was reported in AAA's monthly award reporting service, Summary of
Labor Arbitration Awards. Naturally, this brief, popular presentation does
not permit full analysis of all the important details involved in the case.
These stories should therefore be used not for in-depth examination of the
issues, but as a training aid to give the reader an opportunity for a quick,
superficial judgment. A synopsis of the decision by the arbitrator in the
real case will be found at the end of this chapter.*

*Most educators find "You Be the Arbitrator" useful for the practical
insight it affords into day-to-day problems arising in the application and
interpretation of collective bargaining agreements. The popular format
helps stimulate discussion, and the student, whether in the academic environment or in industry, is brought to see that issues must be resolved
within a general contractual framework.*

*Teachers, training specialists and discussion leaders naturally apply
their own methods in using this pamphlet. Some consult the source (the
Summary of Labor Arbitration Awards) for a somewhat more comprehensive analysis of the case. Others may want the full text of the arbitrator's
award, which can be purchased from AAA's Publications Department at
30 cents per page. (The typical labor arbitration award and opinion is about
ten pages long.)*

*No exact statistics are available, but it appears that a rather large per-
centage of those who read these stories, regardless of how limited their
experience might be, come to the same conclusion the arbitrator reached
in the real case. One can only speculate as to the reason. Perhaps it is that,
underlying the many complicated and often difficult problems of contract
interpretation, the arbitrator's task calls for plain common sense, of which
an abundance is found among "amateurs" as well as professional arbitrators.*

## THE CASE OF THE HUMANE DEMOTION

John V. was promoted to a better job, which he performed competently as far as quality was concerned. But he never produced enough, mostly because he just couldn't or wouldn't resist the temptation to chat with everyone within earshot. Unfortunately, his work required him to be in constant touch with other employees, which made matters worse. The foreman spoke to John about this fault many times. In fact, the company was later able to produce a dossier showing oral reprimands and even warnings to the union.

Finally John was demoted to a lower-rated job, in a more isolated area. The difference in pay was not great—only five cents an hour. But a grievance was filed promptly. "You can't demote a man all of a sudden without warning," the shop steward said. "You have a disciplinary system that calls for oral warnings, written warnings, and other disciplinary action, but you never used it."

"If we followed the letter of that disciplinary system," the personnel manager replied, "John would have been tossed out long ago. By demoting him, we're being more humane. We're preserving his job."

Eventually the case went to arbitration. Suppose you were the arbitrator. How would you rule?

## THE CASE OF WHO CAME FIRST

One Friday in February 1956, two men appeared at the personnel office of an appliance manufacturing company looking for work. Both were hired and instructed to start the following day. One was assigned to the 7 a.m.–4 p.m. shift, the other to the 4 p.m.–11 p.m. shift. Some years later, the two men were still with the company but on the same shift. Work became slack and employees had to be laid off in accordance with plant-wide seniority. It became a question of letting one of the two go. The man notified that he was to be laid off happened to be the one who had started on the first shift. This led to a grievance.

"It's true the other man and I were hired on the same day and started work on the same Monday," he argued. "But I started on an earlier shift. That gives me an edge over him."

"Not at all," answered the personnel manager. "The contract defines seniority as starting on the employee's original 'date of hire.' You two men have identical seniority. I can select either one of you for layoff when your date of hire is reached on the seniority list."

Eventually the case went to arbitration. Suppose you were the arbitrator. How would you rule?

## THE CASE OF THE INNOCENT VICTIM

Tom K., a laborer in a nonferrous foundry, was picked up by the police one day on suspicion that he had passed a bad check during a night of overindulgence in a tavern. Bail was set, but Tom didn't have the money. He was kept in jail until his case was tried. The tavern owner withdrew charges; Tom was acquitted.

But that was not the end of his troubles. When Tom showed up for work, he was told he had been fired for unauthorized absence. "I couldn't help it," he explained. "They held me in jail until the trial. Besides, I was found not guilty. What kind of justice are you handing out when you fire an innocent man?"

"You may have been found innocent as far as the law is concerned," answered the company, "but the contract gives us the right to discharge men who are absent without good reason. Your reasons for absence aren't excusable. Besides, why didn't you get in touch with us right away and let us know the situation?"

Eventually the case went to arbitration. Suppose you were the arbitrator. How would you rule?

## THE CASE OF THE NEAT NUT

Joe Lupo, a mechanic in a machine-building plant, came to work one day and found that someone—probably a fellow employee—had tampered with his tool box and broken the hinges. This would have been mildly distressing for anyone, but for Joe it was a calamity. As everyone in the shop knew, he was very fussy about the orderliness of his tools.

Unable to repair the tool box, Joe bought a new one and presented the bill to the company. "The contract requires all employees to furnish their own tools," he said. "That makes the company liable for damages and losses on company property."

The general foreman refused to okay the bill. The matter went through all the steps of grievance procedure without agreement. Finally, the union demanded arbitration.

Management appeared before the arbitrator, but the preliminary question of arbitrability was the main issue. The company's position was that the dispute was not arbitrable because there was nothing in the contract to require the company to reimburse employees for such damages. The union answered that the grievance was made arbitrable by the fact that employees were required to provide their own "tools of the trade" and by the fact that the company had reimbursed employees for losses in the past.

Eventually the case went to arbitration. Suppose you were the arbitrator. How would you rule?

## THE CASE OF THE OVERTIME HOGS

Toward the end of the year, the foreman of a small appliance assembly department decided to keep his men on overtime to complete orders for the Christmas trade. There were 30 employees under his supervision, and he offered each of them five hours' overtime during a certain week. It didn't occur to him that a plan so obviously fair to all could ever possibly be the basis of a union grievance. But a grievance nevertheless resulted.

"Ten of these men are probationers," the shop steward reminded the foreman. "A right to share in overtime is not one of the privileges of seniority," the foreman replied. "As long as we give all employees an equal opportunity we're conforming to the agreement."

Eventually the case went to arbitration. Suppose you were the arbitrator. How would you rule?

## THE CASE OF THE "SICK" MEN

Management of a furniture plant suspected that employees were pretending sickness to escape unpleasant tasks. It seemed that every time one of those assignments came up, the man who was supposed to do it would go to the first aid room with a headache or some other complaint not easy to diagnose and get a pass to leave the plant.

To control the situation, a new rule was established. It required an employee with such a pass to get a doctor's certificate of "fitness to work" before he could return. The union didn't protest.

One day, however, two men, after completing their regular eight-hour shift, begged off continuing for eight hours more with the excuse that they were "too tired and sick."

Their foreman wouldn't let them start next day without doctors' certificates. They got the statements, but the union filed a grievance.

Eventually the case went to arbitration. Suppose you were the arbitrator. How would you rule?

## THE CASE OF THE FIRST-TIME LOSER

In negotiating a new contract with the union, management of an industrial equipment company insisted on a strong clause to cope with a serious problem of workers absenting themselves without calling in. The parties agreed to a series of penalties, ranging from reprimand for the first offense to discharge after the fifth violation.

Some months later, one employee failed to show up for work on a Monday and stayed out all week without getting any message to the personnel office. At the end of the fifth day, he was notified of his discharge as a fifth offender. When the union learned of this, a grievance was filed.

"Fifth offender nothing," said the shop steward. "The five days of absence were consecutive—one offense. The grievant can get a reprimand, that's all."

"Show me where the contract says that consecutive days of absence count as one day," replied the company. "He committed five offenses and got what the contract says was coming to him."

Eventually the case went to arbitration. Suppose you were the arbitrator. How would you rule?

## THE CASE OF THE EDUCATED FOREMEN

The first problem following delivery of computers to an eastern company was to educate foremen and supervisors in their use. Management's solution was to close down the entire plant for a day so that all foremen and supervisors concerned with the new equipment could be sent to the computer manufacturer for a brief but intensive course of instruction. No doubt the supervisory staff was paid for this time, but hourly-rated employees were not. This led to a grievance.

"This is a lockout," the business agent said. "There's work to be done, and the employees are willing to do it. You can close the plant if you want to, but you have to pay them for the time."

"Since when?" the industrial relations director demanded to know. "Our contract does not contain a guaranteed workweek. We can close the plant if we have a good reason, and training supervisors is the best of reasons. If a senior man lost time while a junior worked, you would have a case. But we laid off the whole bargaining unit for one day, so you have no basis for objecting."

Eventually the case went to arbitration. Suppose you were the arbitrator. How would you rule?

## THE CASE OF THE LATE SLEEPER

Thanksgiving day was a paid holiday in an auto parts manufacturing company. Management decided that the plant might just as well be closed the next day too. But one man, a maintenance mechanic, was ordered to report on Friday.

The mechanic had overeaten on Thanksgiving, then overslept on Friday. The result was that he punched in an hour and a half late for his holiday maintenance work in the plant.

The lateness wasn't held against him as a matter of discipline, but when he got his next paycheck he saw he wasn't paid for the holiday. "The union contract requires that you work the full regularly scheduled workdays surrounding the holiday as a condition for receiving holiday pay," the plant manager explained. "You forfeited holiday pay by reporting late."

The mechanic didn't think this was fair—neither did the shop steward.

Eventually the case went to arbitration. Suppose you were the arbitrator. How would you rule?

## THE CASE OF THE UNWILLING TRAVELER

A company manufacturing electronic equipment often had to send its repairmen to distant cities to help install or repair pieces of apparatus. Some of the repairmen were glad to do this kind of work, others were reluctant to travel. When a union contract was negotiated, it was therefore agreed that "no employee will be required to go on an out-of-plant assignment unless he voluntarily accepts such assignment."

One summer, when management decided to add to the repair crew, the plant manager was very careful to hire a man who said he would like to travel. For several months, the new repairman worked in the plant, with no travel assignments coming his way. When the first out-of-plant assignment did come up, the repairman refused it.

"I know I agreed to travel," he admitted. "But that was before my wife had a baby. It's not convenient now and I refuse."

"If you won't travel you're not conforming to the terms of your employment," answered the personnel manager. "I'm giving to you two weeks' notice of dismissal beginning right now."

Eventually the case went to arbitration. Suppose you were the arbitrator. How would you rule?

## THE ARBITRATORS' AWARDS

*Caution: These awards do not indicate how other arbitrators might rule in apparently similar cases. Arbitrators do not follow precedents. Each case is decided on the basis of the contract, evidence, past practice and other facts involved.*

**THE HUMANE DEMOTION**—John was ordered back on the

higher-rated job. The arbitrator admitted that this might result in John's dismissal altogether, because he was now officially warned that discharge would follow if he continued to perform less than the proper quantity of work. But this was the risk John must take. This conclusion, the arbitrator pointed out, followed from the fact that John was able to do his job properly. If he lacked ability the problem would not have been a disciplinary one and a different outcome would be indicated.

**WHO CAME FIRST**—The arbitrator wrote: "Dictionary definition and industrial usage agree that date of employment refers to the calendar day and not to the hour or minute when the employee began work." And so the grievance was denied.

**THE INNOCENT VICTIM**—The arbitrator wrote: "If the grievant had been found guilty, one might argue that he brought this period of imprisonment on himself and that his imprisonment was not a just cause for absence within the meaning of the contract. However, this cannot be validly argued in the face of the grievant's acquittal." But since Tom didn't do all he could to notify the company of his reason for absence, reinstatement was directed without back pay.

**THE NEAT NUT**—The arbitrator dismissed the grievance on the grounds that the dispute was not arbitrable. He wrote: "I cannot relate, directly or indirectly, the practice upon which the union relies to any express provision of the contract . . . I cannot decide a controversy entirely upon practices and customs outside of the obligations assumed in the written agreement."

**THE OVERTIME HOGS**—Reading the contract as a whole, the arbitrator said that the right to share in overtime was no more linked to seniority than was the right to a paid holiday. Both were privileges that accrue to employees, regardless of their length of service. The company won the case.

**THE "SICK" MEN**—The company was upheld in its right to promulgate the rule, but was not sustained in its application in this case. The proper application of the rule, the arbitrator said, was to discourage malingering. It even could be invoked to discourage refusal of reasonable overtime assignments. But there was nothing in the contract or the practice in this shop to require employees to work sixteen hours at a time.

**THE FIRST-TIME LOSER**—The arbitrator upheld the union. "The basic purpose of the warning system," he wrote, "is to advise the employee of his unsatisfactory behavior." If the grievant had been notified of the lesser forms of discipline, it would have been different. As it was, the five days counted as one offense and the discharge was reduced to a reprimand.

**THE EDUCATED FOREMEN**—Management won. The arbitrator said this was no lockout within the "normal meaning" of the word, because there had been no dispute between the parties and management was not trying to use economic pressure against employees in order to accomplish some purpose. Although the company might have managed the training some other way, he concluded, the manner it chose was within its "exclusive responsibility," and it was not for him to direct some other form of training.

THE LATE SLEEPER—The arbitrator observed that the holiday clause required work on the "full scheduled workdays" before and after the holiday. As the plant was shut down on the Friday in question, except for one man, it was not a "regularly scheduled" day within the meaning of the contract. The tardiness could not be used to deprive the man of holiday pay.

THE UNWILLING TRAVELER—The arbitrator sympathized with the company's position but said: "As the collective bargaining agreement is presently written, the company is obliged to abide with the vagaries of its employees. It was within the repairman's contractual rights to proceed as he did."

*Questions*

1. Explain the difference between arbitration and negotiation.

2. Is arbitration limited to labor-management disputes? Can you think of any international body that employs voluntary arbitration of disputes? Name a recent example.

3. How did your answers compare with those given at the end of the article? In the cases where you gave a different reply, were you convinced by the "official" answer? Why or why not?

4. What are the strengths and weaknesses of voluntary arbitration?

# 5
# Conflict Resolution:
# Isn't There a Better Way?

## Warren E. Burger

This article originally appeared in *National Forum*, Fall 1983.

*The former Chief Justice of the United States Supreme Court is a voice that cannot be ignored. When he asks whether our civil administration of justice has become obsolete, the problem must be serious indeed. To some extent, the roots of the problem—"in fees, expenses and waste of time"—go back to the adversarial (win/lose) tradition in which lawyers have been trained, according to Burger.*

*"Only very few law schools," says Burger, "have significant focus on arbitration." Even fewer, in his informed view, emphasize the art and skills of negotiation. Such "non-judicial" routes to conflict resolution could help ease the backlog of litigation as "Americans are increasingly turning to the courts for relief from a range of personal distresses and anxieties." Burger also recommends a "third" approach (in addition to arbitration and negotiation) exemplified in the administrative process used under the workers' compensation acts.*

*Justice Burger builds his case for "non-judicial" settlements by citing the growth of litigation in the federal district courts over a forty-year period at a rate six times that of the nation's population increase. And the rate is nearly tripled in the Court of Appeals over a shorter period as more litigants want a "second bite of the apple."*

*The justice points to the natural competitiveness of lawyers and business executives "to win using every tactic available." The time consumed, he says, runs "not weeks or months, but years" with corresponding expenditure of money.*

*The cases Burger suggests moving to the "non-judicial" process of mediation and arbitration include "divorce, child custody, personal injury, landlord and tenant cases and probate of estates." He gives historical examples of arbitration from the days of Homer in ancient Greece to the seventeenth century Dutch and other colonial procedures in America. He seeks to allay lawyerly fears of loss of business by reminding such advocates that they "are not excluded from that process."*

*Recent developments give Justice Burger some reason for hope. He lists the advantages of arbitration in terms of expertise, the absence of stress, cost and limitation of abuses. To be effective, he cautions, arbitration "should be final and binding." He notes with approval a recent step taken by the American Bar Association but calls for bolder moves. While praising the ABA, at whose 1982 convention in Chicago he delivered this address, Burger proposes a "commission of distinguished leaders" to study and recommend a wide-ranging series of steps to get many forms of litigation out of the courts and into a system "aimed at delivering justice in the shortest possible time and at the least expense."*

The obligation of our profession is, or has long been thought to be, to serve as healers of human conflicts. To fulfill our traditional obligation means that we should provide mechanisms that can produce an acceptable result in the shortest possible time, with the least possible expense and with a minimum of stress on the participants. That is what justice is all about.

The law is a tool, not an end in itself. Like any tool, our judicial mechanisms, procedures, or rules can become obsolete. Just as the carpenter's handsaw was replaced by the power saw, and his hammer was replaced by the stapler, we should be alert to the need for better tools to serve the ends of justice.

Many thoughtful people, within and outside our profession, question whether that is being done today. They ask whether our profession is fulfilling its historical and traditional obligation of being healers of human conflicts and whether we are alert in searching for better tools. Although it may be too much to say that we lawyers are becoming part of the problem instead of the means to a solution, I confess there is more to support our critics than I would have thought 15 or 20 years ago.

## LITIGATION AND THE ADVERSARY TRADITION

I address the administration of justice in civil matters, which shares with criminal justice both delay and lack of finality. Even when an acceptable result is finally achieved in a civil case, that result is often drained of much of its value because of the time-lapse, the expense, and the emotional stress inescapable in the litigation process.

Abraham Lincoln once said: "Discourage litigation. Persuade your neighbors to compromise whenever you can. Point out to them how the nominal winner is often a real loser—in fees, expenses, and waste of time." In the same vein, Judge Learned Hand commented: "I must say that, as a litigant, I should dread a lawsuit beyond almost anything else short of sickness and of death."

I was trained, as many of you were, with that generation of lawyers taught that the best service a lawyer could render a client was to keep away from the courts. Obviously that generalization needs qualifying, for often the courts are the only avenue to justice. In our search for "better ways," we must never forget that.

Law schools have traditionally steeped the students in the adversary tradition rather than in other skills of resolving conflicts. And various factors in the past 20–25 years—indeed increasingly—have combined to depict today's lawyer in the role of a knight in shining armor, whose courtroom lance strikes down all obstacles. But the emphasis on that role can be carried too far. Only very few law schools have significant focus on arbitration. Even fewer law schools focus on training in the skills—the arts—of negotiation that can lead to settlements. Of all the skills needed for the practicing lawyer, skill in negotiation must rank very high.

It is refreshing to note that the dean of a new law school recently said he hoped the school would play a leading role in preparing lawyers to find fresh approaches to resolving cases outside the courtroom. He said:

> The idea of training a lawyer as a vigorous adversary to function in the courtroom is anachronistic. With court congestion and excessive litigiousness drawing increasing criticism, it is clear that lawyers in the future will have to be trained to explore nonjudicial routes to resolving disputes. (Dean Charles Halpern, Law School, City University of New York.)

This echoed the theme of the 1976 Pound Conference of which this Association was a cosponsor. Obviously two of those "non-judicial routes" are arbitration and negotiation, and it is very encouraging to find a new law school opening with this fresh approach. A third approach is greater use of the techniques of the administrative process exemplified by the traditional workmen's compensation acts. The adversary process is expensive. It is time-consuming. It often leaves a trail of stress and frustration.

One reason our courts have become overburdened is that Americans are increasingly turning to the courts for relief from a range of personal distresses and anxieties. Remedies for personal wrongs that once were considered the responsibility of institutions other than the courts are now boldly asserted as legal "entitlements." The courts have been expected to fill the void created by the decline of church, family, and neighborhood unity.

Possibly the increased litigiousness that court dockets reflect simply mirrors what is happening worldwide. The press, TV, and radio, for hours every day, tell us of dire events in Asia, Africa, Europe, and Latin America where there is seething political, social, and economic turmoil. It is not surprising that our anxieties are aggravated and we have a few problems of our own.

In 1975, Professor John Barton of Stanford cautioned that:

> As implausible as it may appear, . . . increases over the last decade suggest that by the early 21st century—18 years hence—the federal appellate courts alone will decide approximately 1 million cases each year. That bench would include over 5,000 active judges, and the Federal Reporter would expand by more than 1,000 volumes each year.

We do not need to accept this scholar's perception to know that the future prospects are neither comfortable nor comforting.

## COSTS OF LITIGATION

Our litigation explosion during this generation is suggested by a few figures: from 1940 to 1981, annual Federal District Court civil case filings increased from about 35,000 to 180,000. This almost doubled the yearly case load per judgeship from 190 to 350 cases. The real meaning of these figures emerges when we see that federal civil cases increased almost six times as fast as our population.

From 1950 to 1981, annual Court of Appeals filings climbed from about 2,800 to more than 26,000. The annual case load per Circuit judgeship increased from 44 to 200 cases. That growth was 16 times as much as the increase in population. A similar trend took place in the state courts from 1967 to 1976, where appellate filings increased eight times as fast as the population, and state trial court filings increased at double the rate of population growth.

It appears that people tend to be less satisfied with one round of litigation and are demanding a "second bite at the apple," far more than in earlier times.

We, as lawyers, know that litigation is not only stressful and frustrating, but expensive and frequently unrewarding for litigants. A personal injury case, for example, diverts the claimant and entire families from their normal pursuits. Physicians increasingly take note of "litigation neuroses" in otherwise normal, well-adjusted people. This negative impact is not confined to litigants and lawyers. Lay and professional witnesses, chiefly the doctors who testify, are also adversely affected. The plaintive cry of many frustrated litigants echoes what Learned Hand implied: "There must be a better way."

A common thread pervades all courtroom contests: lawyers are natural competitors and once litigation begins they strive mightily to win using every tactic available. Business executives are also competitors and when they are in litigation they often transfer their normal productive and constructive drives into the adversary contest. Commercial litigation takes business executives and their staffs away from the creative paths of development and production and often inflicts more wear and tear on them than the most difficult business problems.

We read in the news of cases that continue not weeks or months, but years. Can it be that the authors of our judicial system, those who wrote constitutions 200 years ago, ever contemplated cases that monopolize one judge for many months or even years? A case recently terminated has been in court 13 years, and has largely occupied the time of one judge for half that time, with total costs running into hundreds of millions of dollars.

I doubt the Founding Fathers anticipated such results. That these cases are infrequent is not the whole story. In 1960, there were only 35 federal trials that took more than one month. By 1981, these protracted cases multiplied five times, and that is not the end of the story. All litigants standing in line behind a single protracted case—whether it is a one-month, a three-month or a longer case—are denied access to that court. This becomes more acute if that litigant cannot recover interest on the award, or is allowed interest at 8 percent while paying double or more on a home mortgage or other debts.

## MODERN APPLICATION OF ARBITRATION

We must now use the inventiveness, the ingenuity, and the resourcefulness that have long characterized the American business and legal community to shape new tools. The paradox is that we already have some very good tools and techniques ready and waiting for imaginative lawyers to adapt them to current needs. We need to consider moving some cases from the adversary system to administrative processes like workmen's compensation or to mediation, conciliation, and especially arbitration. Divorce, child custody, adoptions, personal injury, landlord and tenant cases, and probate of estates are prime candidates for some form of administrative or arbitration processes.

Against this background I focus now on arbitration, not as the answer or cure-all for the mushrooming case loads of the courts, but as one example of "a better way to do it."

If the courts are to retain public confidence, we cannot let disputes wait two, three, or five years to be disposed of, as is so often the situation. The use of voluntary private binding arbitration has been neglected. Lawyers in other countries, who admire the American system in general, are baffled that we use arbitration so little and use courts so much.

There is, of course, nothing new about the concept of arbitration to settle controversies. The concept of mediation and arbitration preceded by many centuries the creation of formal and organized judicial systems and codes of law. Ancient societies, more than 25 centuries ago, developed informal mechanisms, very much like mediation and arbitration, to resolve disputes.

In the time of Homer, for example, the community elders served as civil arbitrators to settle disputes between private parties. By the fourth century B.C., this practice was a settled part of Athenian law. Commercial arbitration was a common practice among Phoenician traders and the desert caravans of Marco Polo's day, and later in the Hanseatic League.

An early use of arbitration in America was of Dutch origin. In 1647, in what is now New York City, an ordinance created the "Board of Nine," which arbitrated minor civil and mercantile disputes. In colonial Connecticut, Pennsylvania, Massachusetts, and South Carolina, various arbitration mechanisms were established to deal with debt or trespass and boundary disputes. As early as 1682, the Assembly of West New Jersey enacted a law which provided:

> And for the preventing of needless and frivolous Suits. Be it Hereby Enacted . . . that all Accounts of Debt . . . of Slander . . . and Accounts whatsoever not exceeding Twenty Shillings, . . . Arbitration of two [neutral] Persons of the Neighbourhood, shall be tendered by some one Justice of the Peace who shall have Power to summon the Parties. . . .

Despite the early use of arbitration in this country, and despite legislative efforts to expand that process in this country, two strong adversaries emerged: first, some judges, fearing that arbitration would deprive them of their jurisdiction, jealously guarded their powers and resisted arbitration; second, lawyers, mistakenly fearing that arbitration would adversely affect their practice, zealously pursued court litigation. Ironically, experience has shown that litigants can secure acceptable arbitration results and lawyers are not excluded from that process.

More than 50 years ago the American Bar Association had a large part in drafting the United States Arbitration Act, which called for binding arbitration to cut delay and expense. Yet for all that early support of arbitration, it has not developed as an alternative to adversary litigation in the courts. Old attitudes and old habits die hard.

## RECENT DEVELOPMENTS

It is often difficult to discern the precise time when new developments occur relating to the human condition, but I think that for at least the past 20 years there has been a slowly—all too slowly—developing awareness that the traditional litigation process has become too cumbersome, too expensive, and also burdened by many other disadvantages.

In 1976 we took note of these growing problems in commemorating the 70th Anniversary of Roscoe Pound's indictment of the American judicial and legal systems. That Conference brought arbitration sharply into focus. In opening the Pound Conference, I urged that we make a "reappraisal of the values of the arbitration process. . . . " The American Bar Association responded promptly to the Pound Conference and there are now committees taking a fresh look at alternative means of dispute resolution. Our President, David Brink, has given the broad subject priority status.

What we must have, I submit, is a comprehensive review of the whole subject of alternatives, with special emphasis on arbitration. It is now clear that neither the federal nor the state court systems are capable of handling all the burdens placed upon them. Surely the avalanche that is bound to come will make matters worse for everyone.

I do not suggest in any sense that arbitration can displace the courts. Rather, arbitration should be an alternative that will complement the judicial systems. There will always be conflicts which cannot be settled except by the judicial process.

Let me suggest some of the important advantages in private arbitration, especially in large, complex commercial disputes:
- Parties can select the arbitrator, taking into account the special experience and knowledge of the arbitrator.
- A privately selected arbitrator can conduct all proceedings in a setting with less stress on the parties; confidentiality can be preserved where there is a valid need to protect trade secrets, for example.
- Arbitration can cope more effectively with complex business contracts, economic and accounting evidence, and financial statements. A skilled arbitrator acting as the trier can digest evidence at his own time and pace without all the expensive panoply of the judicial process. (To operate a U.S. District Court with a jury costs approximately $350.00 per hour.)
- Parties to arbitration can readily stipulate to discovery processes in

a way that can control, if not eliminate, abuses of discovery processes.

One example of an effective statutory, although not binding, arbitration program is found in Pennsylvania. The impact upon court backlogs in that state has been significant. In Philadelphia, in the first two years after the jurisdictional level was increased to $10,000, the entire civil calendar backlog was reduced from 48 months to 21 months. In 1974, more than 12,000 of approximately 16,000 civil cases were resolved through arbitration.

Several federal courts have experimented with similar procedures established under local rules that refer certain types of civil suits seeking damages, in some cases up to $100,000, to an arbitration panel of three attorneys. The results indicate that arbitration could well shorten the disposition of most cases by two to four months, and that the counsel in the cases hold a generally favorable view of the procedure. Perhaps most important, preliminary evidence suggests that arbitration may reduce by as much as half the number of such cases that otherwise would go to trial.

We must, however, be cautious in setting up arbitration procedures to make sure they become a realistic alternative rather than an additional step in an already prolonged process. For this reason, if a system of voluntary arbitration is to be truly effective, it should be final and binding, without a provision for de novo trial or review. This principle was recognized centuries ago by Demosthenes, who, in quoting the law, told the people of Athens:

> [W]hen [the parties] have mutually selected an arbiter, let them stand
> fast by his decision and by no means carry on appeal from him to another
> tribunal; but let the arbiter's [decision] be supreme.

Anything less than final and binding arbitration should be accompanied by some sanctions to discourage further conflict. For example, if the claimant fails to increase the award by 15 percent or more over the original award, he should be charged with the costs of proceedings plus the opponent's attorney fees. Michigan is one of the states that has experimented with this kind of sanction and such programs deserve close study.

## THE ABA PROGRAMS

The Association has taken a positive step by broadening the jurisdiction of the "Special Committee on Resolution of Minor Disputes" and it is now designated the "Special Committee on Alternative Means of Dispute Resolution."

That was a good step, but with all deference, I suggest we need more. Either the existing committee should be altered or an enlarged commission should be created. Such a commission could well include not only distinguished leaders of the Bar, but also distinguished representatives of business and other disciplines.

The Association should now proceed carefully with an indepth examination of these problems. This cannot be done routinely or casually. Rather, it must be done on the scale of the 1969 monumental work of the American Law Institute experience of such groups as the American Arbitration Association.

If there are objectors, as there may be, to broadening arbitration, objections will serve to sharpen the analysis of the alternatives and guide us in making arbitration effective.

For 200 years, our country has made progress unparalleled in human history. We have done this by virtue of a willingness to combine ancient wisdom with innovation and with what was long called "Yankee ingenuity."

The American Bar Association has been a leader in virtually every major improvement in the administration of justice in the past quarter of a century. During my tenure in office, alone, their support made possible the Institute for Court Management, the Circuit Executives for Federal Courts, the Code of Judicial Conduct, the National Center for State Courts, expanded continuing education for lawyers and judges, and training of paralegals. All of these were aimed at delivering justice in the shortest possible time and at the least expense.

This proposal could well be another major contribution to make our system of justice work better for the American people.

## Questions

1. Why should the Chief Justice be concerned about the time and expense involved in litigation?

2. What factors in the past twenty-five years "have combined to depict today's lawyer in the role of a knight in shining armor"? What factors tend to portray the lawyer as a villain?

3. What does Burger mean when he says that "the courts have been expected to fill the void created by the decline of church, family and neighborhood unity"?

4. What effect does the competitive nature of our national ethos have on litigation and foreign policy?

5. Why does Burger insist that arbitration should be "final and binding"?

# 6
# Arbitration vs. Mediation—
# Explaining the Differences

## John W. Cooley

This article originally appeared in *Judicature*, February–March 1986.

*There are many pathways to peace and the just settlement of disputes. Arbitration and its cousin mediation are two of the most effective tools available for bringing about solutions to human conflict. Yet, as the author—a lawyer and a former U.S. magistrate—declares, "an amazing number of lawyers and business professionals are unaware of the differences between arbitration and mediation." He finds this confusion understandable.*

*Even history is no sure guide, according to Cooley, because the two words have been used interchangeably. And the distinction between arbitration and mediation has not been much clarified in modern times, as can be seen by looking at the terminology in current labor relations statutes. Even libraries get into the act with imprecise cross-references to arbitration and mediation.*

*Cooley puts the distinction between the two means of resolving disputes into its simplest terms: "Arbitration involves a decision by an intervening third party or 'neutral'; mediation does not." He amplifies on this by describing arbitration as a "left brain" or "rational mental process" (analytical, logical, administrative); and mediation as a "right brain" or "creative process" (intuitive, artistic, symbolic, emotional). "The arbitrator," he explains, "deals largely with the objective; the mediator, the subjective."*

*Moreover, the two processes are usually employed to settle different types of disputes. Arbitration works best, says the author, when there is no reasonable likelihood of a negotiated settlement and the disputants will not have a continuing relationship. Mediation is employed in exactly the reverse conditions. "Mediation occurs first," he explains, "and if unsuccessful, resort is made to arbitration."*

*Cooley launches into the history of the arbitration process and the various stages it involves (initiation, preparation, prehearing conferences, the hearing and decision-making). To this he compares the stages of me-*

296

*diation (initiation, preparation, introduction, problem statement, gener-*
*ation and evaluation of alternatives and selection of alternatives). He adds:*
*"A mediator's patience, flexibility and creativity throughout this entire*
*process are necessary keys to a successful solution."*

*Drawing on legal precedents, Cooley further explains the differences*
*between the two processes in terms of function and power. He concludes*
*with the assertion that the benefits of arbitration and mediation "are just*
*beginning to be recognized by lawyers and business professionals alike."*
*His lucid explanation of the entire matter is likely to assist both legal*
*professionals and litigants to become more comfortable with the two meth-*
*ods of dispute resolution.*

An amazing number of lawyers and business professionals are unaware of the differences between arbitration and mediation. Their confusion is excusable.

In the early development of the English language, the two words
were used interchangeably. The *Oxford English Dictionary* provides as
one historical definition of arbitration: "to act as formal arbitrator or um-
pire, to mediate (in a dispute between contending parties)." The Statutes
of Edward III (1606) referring to what today obviously would be called a
commercial *arbitration* panel, provided: "And two Englishmen, two of
Lombardie and two of Almaigne shall (be) chosen to be mediators of questions between sellers and buyers."[1]

Modern labor relations statutes tend to perpetuate this confusion. As
one commentator has observed:

> Some statutes, referring to a process as "mediation" describe formal
> hearings, with witnesses testifying under oath and transcripts made, re-
> quire reports and recommendations for settlement to be made by the
> neutral within fixed periods, and either state or imply the finality of the
> "mediator's recommendations." In one statute the neutral third parties
> are called, interchangeably, mediators, arbitrators and impasse panels.[2]

The Federal Mediation and Conciliation Service (note the absence of
"arbitration" in its title) performs a basic arbitration function by maintaining a roster from which the Service can nominate arbitrators to the parties
and suggest "certain procedures and guides that [the Service believes] will
enhance the acceptability of arbitration."[3]

The National *Mediation* Board (emphasis added) performs important
functions in the promotion of arbitration and the selection of arbitrators for
the railroad and airline industries.[4]

Libraries also assist in perpetuating the arbitration/mediation definitional charade. Search under "mediation" and you will invariably be referred to "arbitration." In the midst of this confusion—even among congressional draftsmen—it is time to explain the differences between the processes.

The most basic difference between the two is that arbitration involves a *decision* by an intervening third party or "neutral"; mediation does not.

Another way to distinguish the two is by describing the processes in terms of the neutral's mental functions. In arbitration, the neutral employs mostly "left brain" or "rational" mental processes—analytical, mathematical, logical, technical, administrative; in mediation, the neutral employs mostly "right brain" or "creative" mental processes—conceptual, intuitive, artistic, holistic, symbolic, emotional.

The arbitrator deals largely with the objective; the mediator, the subjective. The arbitrator is generally a passive functionary who determines right or wrong; the mediator is generally an active functionary who attempts to move the parties to reconciliation and agreement, regardless of who or what is right or wrong.

Because the role of the mediator involves instinctive reactions, intuition, keen interpersonal skills, the ability to perceive subtle psychological and behavioral indicators, in addition to logic and rational thinking, it is much more difficult than the arbitrator's role to perform effectively.[5] It is fair to say that while most mediators can effectively perform the arbitrator's function, the converse is not necessarily true.

Besides these differences the two processes are generally employed to resolve two different types of disputes. Mediation is used where there is a reasonable likelihood that the parties will be able to reach an agreement with the assistance of a neutral. Usually, mediation is used when parties will have an ongoing relationship after resolution of the conflict. Arbitration, on the other hand, is generally appropriate for use when two conditions exist: there is no reasonable likelihood of a negotiated settlement; and there will not be a continuing relationship after resolution.[6]

If the two processes are to be used in sequence, mediation occurs first, and if unsuccessful, resort is made to arbitration.[7] Viewed in terms of the judicial process, arbitration is comparable to a trial and mediation is akin to a judicial settlement conference. They are as different as night and day.[8] The differences can best be understood by discussing them in terms of the processes of arbitration and mediation.

## THE ARBITRATION PROCESS

Arbitration has had a long history in this country, going back to procedures carried over into the Colonies from mercantile England. George

Washington put an arbitration clause in his last will and testament to resolve disputes among his heirs. Abraham Lincoln urged lawyers to keep their clients out of court and himself arbitrated a boundary dispute between two farmers. Today, arbitration is being used more broadly for dispute settlement both in labor-management relations and in commercial transactions.

Aside from its well-known use in resolving labor disputes, arbitration is now becoming widely used to settle inter-company disputes in various industries, including textile, construction, life and casualty insurance, canning, livestock, air transport, grain and feed and securities.[9]

Simply defined, arbitration is a process in which a dispute is submitted to a third party or neutral (or sometimes a panel of three arbitrators) to hear arguments, review evidence and render a decision.[10] Court-annexed arbitration, a relatively new development, is a process in which judges refer civil suits to arbitrators to render prompt, non-binding decisions. If a particular decision is not accepted by a losing party, a trial *de novo* may be held in the court system. However, adverse decisions sometimes lead to further negotiation and pre-trial settlement.[11]

The arbitration process, court-annexed or otherwise, normally consists of six stages: initiation, preparation, prehearing conferences, hearing, decisionmaking, and award.

**Initiation.** The initiation stage of arbitration consists of two substages: initiating the proceeding, and selecting the arbitrator. An arbitration proceeding may be initiated either by: submission; "demand" or "notice"; or, in the case of a court-annexed proceeding, court rule or court order.

A submission must be signed by both parties and is used where there is no previous agreement to arbitrate. It often names the arbitrator (or method of appointment), contains considerable detail regarding the arbitrator's authority, the procedure to be used at the hearing, statement of the matter in dispute, the amount of money in controversy, the remedy sought and other matters.

On the other hand, where the description of a dispute is contained in an agreement and the parties have agreed in advance to arbitrate it, arbitration may be initiated unilaterally by one party serving upon the other a written "demand" or "notice" to arbitrate.

However, even where an agreement contains a "demand" or "notice" arbitration clause, parties sometimes choose also to execute a submission after the dispute has materialized. In the court-annexed situation, a lawsuit is mandatorily referred to an arbitration track and the parties must select an arbitrator from a court-maintained roster or otherwise by mutual agreement.[12]

Several types of tribunals and methods of selecting their membership are available to parties who wish to arbitrate. Parties may choose between the use of a "temporary" or "permanent" arbitrator. They can also choose to have single or multiple arbitrators. Since success of the arbitration process often hinges on the expertise of the tribunal, parties generally select a tribunal whose members possess impartiality, integrity, ability and experience in the field in which the dispute arises. Legal training is often helpful but not indispensable.

Information concerning the qualifications of some of the more active arbitrators is contained in the *Directory of Arbitrators*, prepared by the Bureau of National Affairs, Inc., and in *Who's Who* (of arbitrators) published by Prentice-Hall, Inc. Also, the Federal Mediation and Conciliation Service (FMCS), the National Mediation Board (NMB) and the American Arbitration Association (AAA) provide biographical data on arbitrators.[13]

**Preparation.** The parties must thoroughly prepare cases for arbitration. Obviously, a party must fully understand its own case to communicate effectively to the arbitrator. Depending on the nature of the case, prehearing discovery may be necessary and its permissible extent is usually determined by the arbitrator. The advantages of simplicity and utility of the arbitration mode normally weigh against extensive discovery. During this stage, the parties also enter into fact stipulations where possible.[14]

Ordinarily, most or all of the arbitrator's knowledge and understanding of a case is based upon evidence and arguments presented at the arbitration hearing. However, the arbitrator does have some "preparation" functions. Generally, where no tribunal administrator (such as AAA) is involved, the arbitrator, after accepting the office, designates the time and place of the hearing, by mutual agreement of the parties if possible. The arbitrator also signs an oath, if required in the particular jurisdiction, and determines whether the parties will have representation, legal or otherwise, at the hearing.[15]

**Prehearing conferences.** Depending on the complexity of the matter involved, the arbitrator may wish to schedule a prehearing conference, which is normally administrative in nature.[16] Briefing schedules, if necessary, are set on motions attacking the validity of claims or of the proceeding. But generally, briefing is minimized to preserve the efficiency of the process. Discussion of the underlying merits of claims or defenses of the parties is avoided during a prehearing conference. *Ex parte* conferences between the arbitrator and a party are not permitted.[17]

**The hearing.** Parties may waive oral hearing and have the controversy determined on the basis of documents only. However, an evidentiary-type hearing in the presence of the arbitrator is deemed imperative in virtually all cases. Since arbitration is a private proceeding, the hearing is not open to the public as a rule but all persons having a direct interest in the case are ordinarily entitled to attend.

A formal written record of the hearing is not always necessary; use of a reporter is the exception rather than the general practice. A party requiring an interpreter has the duty to arrange for one. Witnesses testifying at the hearing may also be required to take an oath if required by law, if ordered by the arbitrator, or on demand of any party.[18]

Opening statements are made orally by each party in a brief, generalized format. They are designed to acquaint the arbitrator with each party's view of what the dispute is about and what the party expects to prove by the evidence. Sometimes an arbitrator requests each party to provide a short written opening statement and issue statement prior to the hearing. Occasionally, a respondent opts for making an opening statement immediately prior to presenting initial evidence.[19]

There is no set order by which parties present their cases in arbitration, although in practice the complaining party normally presents evidence first. The parties may offer any evidence they choose, including personal testimony and affidavits of witnesses. They may be required to produce additional evidence the arbitrator deems necessary to determine the dispute. The arbitrator, when authorized by law, may subpoena witnesses or documents upon his or her own initiative or by request of a party. The arbitrator also decides the relevancy and materiality of all evidence offered. Conformity to legal rules of evidence is unnecessary. The arbitrator has a right to make a physical inspection of premises.[20]

The parties make closing arguments, usually limited in duration. Occasionally, the arbitrator requests post hearing briefs. When this occurs, the parties usually waive oral closing arguments.[21]

**Decisionmaking.** When the issues are not complex, an arbitrator may render an immediate decision. However, when the evidence presented is voluminous and/or time is needed for the members of an arbitration panel to confer, it might require several weeks to make a decision.

The award is the arbitrator's decision. It may be given orally but is normally written and signed by the arbitrator(s). Awards are normally short, definite, certain and final as to all matters under submission. Occasionally, they are accompanied by a short well-reasoned opinion. The award is usually issued no later than 30 days from the closing date of the hearing. When a party fails to appear, a default award may be entered.[22] Depending on the nature of the award (i.e., binding), it may be judicially enforceable and, to some extent, reviewable. The losing party in a court-annexed arbitration is entitled to trial *de novo* in court.

## THE MEDIATION PROCESS

Mediation is a process in which an impartial intervenor assists the disputants to reach a voluntary settlement of their differences through an agreement that defines their future behavior.[23] The process generally consists of eight stages: initiation, preparation, introduction, problem statement, problem clarification, generation and evaluation of alternatives, selection of alternative(s), and agreement.[24]

**Initiation.** The mediation process may be initiated in two principal ways: parties submit the matter to a public or private dispute resolution organization or to a private neutral; or the dispute is referred to mediation by court order or rule in a court-annexed mediation program.

In the first instance, counsel for one of the parties or, if unrepresented, the party may contact the neutral organization or individual and the neutral will contact the opposing counsel or party (as the case may be) to see if there is interest in attempting to mediate the dispute.

**Preparation.** As in arbitration, it is of paramount importance that the parties to a dispute in mediation be as well informed as possible on the background of the dispute, the claims or defenses and the remedies they seek. The parties should seek legal advice if necessary, and although a party's lawyer might attend a typical nonjudicial mediation, he or she normally does not take an adversary role but is rather available to render legal advice as needed.

The mediator should also be well-informed about the parties and the features of their dispute and know something about:

• the balance of power;
• the primary sources of pressure exerted on the parties;
• the pressures motivating them toward agreement as well as pressures blocking agreement;
• the economics of the industry or particular company involved;
• political and personal conflicts within and between the parties;
• the extent of the settlement authority of each of the parties.

The mediator sets the date, time and place for the hearing at everyone's convenience.[25]

**Introduction.** In the mediation process, the introductory stage may be the most important.[26] It is in that phase, particularly the first joint session, that the mediator establishes his or her acceptability, integrity, credibility and neutrality. The mediator usually has several objectives to achieve initially. They are: establish control of the process; determine issues and positions of the parties; get the agreement-forging process started; and encourage continuation of direct negotiations.[27]

Unlike a judge in a settlement conference or an arbitrator who wields the clout of a decision, a mediator does not, by virtue of position, ordinarily command the parties' immediate trust and respect; the mediator earns them through a carefully orchestrated and delicately executed ritual of rapport-building. Every competent mediator has a personal style. The content of the mediator's opening remarks is generally crucial to establishing rapport with the parties and the respectability of the mediator and the process.

Opening remarks focus on: identifying the mediator and the parties; explaining the procedures to be followed (including caucusing),[28] describing the mediation function (if appropriate) and emphasizing the continued decisionmaking responsibility of the parties; and reinforcing the confidentiality and integrity of the process.[29] When appropriate, the mediator might invoke the community and public interest in having the dispute resolved quickly and emphasize the interests of the constituents in the successful conclusion of the negotiations.[30]

Finally, the mediator must assess the parties' competence to participate in the process. If either party has severe emotional, drinking, drug, or health problems, the mediator may postpone the proceeding. If the parties are extremely hostile and verbally abusive, the mediator must endeavor to calm them, by preliminary caucusing if necessary.[31]

**Problem statement.** There are essentially two ways to open a discussion of the dispute by the parties: Both parties give their positions and discuss each issue as it is raised; or all the issues are first briefly identified, with detailed exposition of positions reserved until all the issues have been identified. The second procedure is preferred; the first approach often leads to tedious time-consuming rambling about insignificant matters, sometimes causing the parties to become more entrenched in their positions.[32]

Generally, the complaining party tells his or her "story" first. It may be the first time that the adverse party has heard the full basis for the complaint. The mediator actively and empathically listens, taking notes if helpful, using listening techniques such as restatement, echo and non-verbal responses. Listening is the mediator's most important dispute-resolving tool.[33]

The mediator also:
• asks open-ended and closed-ended questions at the appropriate time and in a neutral fashion;
• obtains important "signals" from the behavior and body movements of the parties;
• calms a party, as necessary;
• clarifies the narration by focused questions;
• objectively summarizes the first party's story;

- defuses tensions by omitting disparaging comments from the summary;
- determines whether the second party understands the first party's story;
- thanks the first party for his or her contribution.

The process is repeated with the second party.[34]

**Problem clarification.** It is in this stage that the mediator culls out the true underlying issues in the dispute. Often the parties to a dispute intentionally obfuscate the core issues. The mediator pierces this cloud-cover through separate caucuses in which he or she asks direct, probing questions to elicit information which one party would not disclose in the presence of the other party. In a subsequent joint session, the mediator summarizes areas of agreement or disagreement, being careful not to disclose matters which the parties shared with the mediator in confidence. They are assisted in grouping and prioritizing issues and demands.[35]

**Generation and evaluation of alternatives.** In this stage, the mediator employs two fundamental principles of effective mediation: creating doubt in the minds of the parties as to the validity of their positions on issues; and suggesting alternative approaches which may facilitate agreement.[36] These are two functions which parties to a dispute are very often unable to perform by themselves. To carry out these functions, the mediator has the parties separately "brainstorm" to produce alternatives or options; discusses the workability of each option; encourages the parties by noting the probability of success, where appropriate; suggests alternatives not raised by the parties and then repeats the three previous steps.[37]

**Selection of alternative(s).** The mediator may compliment the parties on their progress and use humor, when appropriate, to relieve tensions; assist the parties in eliminating the unworkable options; and help the parties determine which of the remaining workable solutions will produce the optimum results with which each can live.[38]

**Agreement.** Before the mediation is terminated, the mediator summarizes and clarifies, as necessary, the terms of the agreement reached and secures the assent of each party to those terms; sets a follow-up date, if necessary; and congratulates the parties on their reasonableness.

The mediator does not usually become involved in drafting a settlement agreement. This task is left to the parties themselves or their counsel. The agreement is the parties', not the mediator's.[39]

A mediator's patience, flexibility and creativity throughout this entire process are necessary keys to a successful resolution.

## THE "NEUTRAL'S" FUNCTIONS

To fully appreciate the differences (or the similarities) between the two processes, and to evaluate the appropriate use of either process, it is instructive to focus on considerations which exist at their interface—the function and power of the "neutral." This is a particularly important exercise to acquire a realistic expectation of the result to be obtained from each process.

The arbitrator's function is quasi-judicial in nature and, because of this, an arbitrator is generally exempt from civil liability for failure to exercise care or skill in performing the arbitral function.[40] As a quasi-judicial officer, the arbitrator is guided by ethical norms in the performance of duties. For example, an arbitrator must refrain from having any private (*ex parte*) consultations with a party or with an attorney representing a party without the consent of the opposing party or counsel.[41]

Moreover, unless the parties agree otherwise, the arbitration proceedings are private and arbitrators must take appropriate measures to maintain the confidentiality of the proceedings.[42] It has generally been held that an arbitrator may not testify as to the meaning and construction of the written award.[43]

In contrast, a mediator is not normally considered to be quasi-judicial, unless he or she is appointed by the court as, for example, a special master. Some courts have extended the doctrine of immunity to persons termed "quasi-arbitrators"—persons empowered by agreement of the parties to resolve disputes arising between them.[44] Although the law is far from clear on this point, a very persuasive argument may be advanced that mediators are generally immune from lawsuits relating to the performance of their mediation duties where the agreement under which they perform contains a hold-harmless provision or its equivalent.

In absence of such contractual provision, it would appear that a functionary such as a mediator, selected by parties to perform skilled or professional services, would not ordinarily be immune from charges of negligence but rather is required to work with the same skill and care exercised by an average person engaged in the trade or profession involved.[45]

Of course, weighing heavily against a finding of negligence on the part of a mediator is the intrinsic nature, if not the essence, of the mediation process which invests the parties with the complete power over their destiny; it also guarantees any party the right to withdraw from the process and even to eject the mediator during any pre-agreement stage.[46]

Also, in contrast to arbitrators, certain ethical restrictions do not apply to mediators. Mediators are permitted to have *ex parte* conferences with the parties or counsel. Indeed, such caucuses, as they are called, are the mediator's stock-in-trade. Furthermore, while one of the principal advantages of a privately-conducted mediation is the non-public or confidential nature of the proceedings, and although Rule 408 of the Federal Rules of Evidence and public policy considerations argue in favor of confidentiality, the current state of the law does not provide a guarantee of such confidentiality.[47] However, in most cases a strong argument can be made that the injury from disclosure of a confidential settlement proceeding is greater than the benefit to be gained by the public from nondisclosure.[48]

Finally, unlike the arbitrator, the performance of whose function may be enhanced by knowledge, skill, or ability in a particular field or industry, the mediator need not be an expert in the field which encompasses the subject of the dispute. Expertise may, in fact, be a handicap, if the parties look wrongly to the mediator as an advice-giver or adjudicator.[49]

## COMPARATIVE POWER

The arbitrator derives power from many sources. The person may be highly respected in a particular field of expertise or widely renowned for fairness. But aside from these attributes which emanate from personal talents or characteristics, the arbitrator operates within a procedural and enforcement framework which affords considerable power, at least from the perspective of the disputants. Under certain circumstances, arbitrators may possess broad remedy powers, including the power, though rare, to grant injunctive relief.[50] They normally have subpoena power, and generally they have no obligation to anyone, not even "to the court to give reasons for an award."[51]

In general, a valid arbitration award constitutes a full and final adjustment of the controversy.[52] It has all the force and effect of an adjudication, and effectively precludes the parties from again litigating the same subject.[53] The award can be challenged in court only on very narrow grounds. In some states the grounds relate to partiality of the arbitrator or to misconduct in the proceedings, such as refusal to allow the production of evidence or to grant postponements, as well as to other misbehavior in conducting the hearings so as to prejudice the interests of a party.[54]

A further ground for challenge in some states is the failure of the arbitrator to observe the limits of authority as fixed by the parties' agreement—such as determining unsubmitted matters or by not dealing definitely and finally with submitted issues.[55] In Illinois, as in most states, a judgment entered on an arbitration award is enforceable "as any other judgment."[56] Thus, from a systemic perspective, the arbitrator is invested with a substantial amount of power.

In striking contrast, with the exception of a special master appointed by the court or a neutral appointed by some governmental body, the mediator has little if any systemic-based power. Most if not all of a mediator's power is derived from experience, demonstrated skills and abilities, and a reputation for successful settlements.

Any particular mediator may wield power by adopting a particular role on what might be described as a continuum representing the range of strengths of intervention: from virtual passivity, to "chairman," to "enunciator," to "prompter," to "leader," to virtual arbitrator.[57] The mediator who can adopt different roles on this continuum, changing strategies to fit changing circumstances and requirements of both the disputants and himself, is inevitably more effective in accumulating and wielding power which is real, yet often not consciously perceptible by the disputants themselves.[58]

Since, in the ordinary case, the result of the mediation process is an agreement or contract not reduced to a court judgment,[59] the result is binding on the parties only to the extent that the law of contracts in the particular jurisdiction requires. And to the same extent, the result is enforceable by one party against another. As a practical matter, where a party breaches an agreement or contract which is the product of mediation and the agreement is not salvageable, prudence would seem to dictate that in most cases the underlying dispute—and not the breach of agreement— should be litigated.

## SUMMARY

It is clear that both the functions and the levels of power of the arbitrators and mediators are dramatically different. Counsel must assess the nature of the dispute and the personalities of the disputants prior to determining which process, arbitration or mediation, has the best chance to achieve a successful resolution of the particular conflict.

For example, arbitration would probably prove to be the better dispute resolution choice where the dispute involves highly technical matters; a long-standing feud between the disputants; irrational and highstrung personalities; and no necessity of a continued relationship after resolution of the conflict.

On the other hand, mediation may prove to be the most effective choice where disputants are stubborn but basically sensible; have much to gain from a continued relationship with one another; and conflict resolution is time-critical.

Table 1  **A comparison of arbitration/meditation processes**

| Arbitration | Meditation |
| --- | --- |
| **1. Initiation** | **1. Initiation** |
| Submission | Submission |
| Demand or notice | Court rule or order |
| Court rule or order | Assignment or selection of mediator |
| Selection of arbitrator | |
| | |
| **2. Preparation** | **2. Preparation** |
| Discovery | Usually, no discovery |
| Prehearing conference | Parties obtain background information on claims, defenses, remedies |
| Motions | |
| Stipulations | Mediator obtains information on parties and history of dispute |
| Arbitrator's oath | |
| Arbitrator's administrative duties | Usually, no mediator oath |
| Arbitrator does not seek out information about parties or dispute | |
| | |
| **3. Prehearing conference** | **3. Introduction** |
| Administrative | Mediator: |
| Scheduling | Conducts *ex parte* conferences, if necessary, for calming |
| No discussion of underlying merits of claims or defenses | Gives opening descriptive remarks |
| No *ex parte* conferences | Develops trust and respect |
| | Emphasizes importance of successful negotiations |
| | Helps parties separate the people from the problem |
| | |
| **4. Hearing** | **4. Problem statement** |
| Not generally open to public | Confidential proceeding, no written record |
| Written record, optional | |
| Witnesses and parties testify under oath | Parties do not speak under oath |
| **Opening statement** | Issues identified |
| Made orally | Issues discussed separately; stories told |
| Sometimes also in writing | Mediator listens; takes notes |
| **Order of proceedings and evidence** | Mediator asks questions; reads behavioral signals |
| Complaining party usually presents evidence first | Mediator calms parties; summarizes stories; defuses tensions |
| Arbitrator may subpoena witnesses | |
| Evidence rules relaxed | Mediator determines whether parties understand stories |
| Arbitrator rules on objections to evidence; may reject evidence | Mediator usually has no subpoena power |

Table 1   A comparison of arbitration/meditation processes *(continued)*

| Arbitration | Meditation |
| --- | --- |
| **Closing arguments** | **5. Problem clarification** |
| Oral arguments normally permitted for clarification and synthesis | Mediator: |
| | Culls out core issues in caucus |
| Post-hearing briefs sometimes permitted | Asks direct, probing questions |
| | Summarizes areas of agreement and disagreement |
| | Assists parties in grouping and prioritizing issues and demands |
| | Helps parties focus on interests, not positions |
| **5. Decisionmaking** | **6. Generation and evaluation of alternatives** |
| If issues non-complex, arbitrator can issue an immediate decision | Mediator: |
| If issues complex, or panel has three members, extra time may be required | Creates doubts in parties' minds as to validity of their positions |
| | Invents options for facilitating agreement |
| | Leads "brainstorming;" discusses workability; notes probability of success of options |
| | **7. Selection of alternative(s)** |
| | Mediator: |
| | Compliments parties on progress |
| | Assists parties in eliminating unworkable options |
| | Helps parties to use objective criteria |
| | Helps parties determine which solution will produce optimum results |
| **6. Award** | **8. Agreement** |
| Normally in writing, signed by arbitrator(s) | Mediator: |
| Short, definite, certain and final, as to all matters under submission | Summarizes and clarifies agreement terms |
| | Sets follow-up date, if appropriate |
| Occasionally a short opinion accompanies award | Congratulates parties on their reasonableness |
| Award may be judicially enforceable or reviewable | Usually does not draft or assist in drafting agreement |
| | Agreement is enforceable as a contract and subject to later modification by agreement |

Arbitration and mediation are two separate and distinct processes having a similar overall goal (terminating a dispute), while using totally different methods to obtain dissimilar (decisional vs. contractual) results. These differences are best understood by viewing the processes side-by-side in Table 1.

The benefits of arbitration and mediation to litigants, in terms of cost and time savings, are just beginning to be recognized by lawyers and business professionals alike. It is hoped that this discussion of the arbitration and mediation processes and their differences will help lawyers feel more comfortable with these two methods of dispute resolution and to use them to their clients' advantage in their joint pursuit of swift, inexpensive, simple justice.

## Notes

1. Robins, *A Guide for Labor Mediators* 6 (Honolulu: University Press of Hawaii, 1976).

2. *Id.*

3. Elkouri and Elkouri, *How Arbitration Works* 24 (Washington, D.C.: BNA, 3rd ed. 1973).

4. *Id.* at 25.

5. As one American professional mediator put it, the mediator "has no science of navigation, no fund inherited from the experience of others. He is a solitary artist recognizing, at most, a few guiding stars and depending mainly on his personal power of divination." Meyer, *Function of the Mediator in Collective Bargaining*, 13 *Indus. & Lab. Rel. Rev.* 159 (1960).

6. In labor relations arbitrations, of course, condition (2) is normally not present. Labor disputes are generally divided into two categories: rights disputes and interest disputes. Disputes as to "rights" involve the interpretation or application of existing laws, agreements or customary practices, disputes as to "interests" involve controversies over the formation of collective agreements or efforts to secure them where no such agreement is yet in existence. Elkouri and Elkouri, *supra* n. 3, at 47.

7. Because of ethical considerations, the arbitrator and mediator normally are different persons. It should also be noted that mediation is frequently effective when it is attempted, with the concurrence of the parties, during the course of an arbitration with a neutral other than the arbitrator serving as the mediator. Often the unfolding of the opponent's evidence during the course of arbitration leads to a better appreciation of the merits of their respective positions and hence an atmosphere conducive to settlement discussions.

8. The stark distinction between mediation and arbitration was well made by a professional mediator who became chairman of the New York State Mediation Board: "Mediation and arbitration . . . have conceptually nothing in common. The one [mediation] involves helping people to decide for themselves, the other

involves helping people by deciding for them." Meyer, *supra* n. 5, at 164, as quoted in Gulliver, *Disputes and Negotiations, a Cross-cultural Perspective*, 210 (New York: Academic Press, 1979).

9. Cooley, *Arbitration as an Alternative to Federal Litigation in the Seventh Circuit, Report of the Subcommittee on Alternatives to the Present Federal Court System, Seventh Circuit Ad Hoc Committee to Study the High Cost of Litigation*, 2 (July 13, 1978).

10. *Paths to Justice: Major Public Policy Issues of Dispute Resolution, Report of the Ad Hoc Panel on Dispute Resolution and Public Policy*, Appendix 2 (Washington, D.C.: National Institute for Dispute Resolution, October, 1983).

11. *Id. See also Evaluation of Court-Annexed Arbitration in Three Federal District Courts* (Washington, D.C.: Federal Judicial Center, 1981).

12. Cooley, *supra* n. 9, at 4, Elkouri and Elkouri, *supra* n. 3, at 183–86. Domke on Commercial Arbitration. §§14:00–14:05 (Rev. Ed. 1984). Arbitrators, if chosen from a list maintained by an arbitration organization or court-maintained roster, are normally compensated at the daily rate fixed by the organization or the court. Arbitrators selected independently by the parties are compensated at the daily or hourly rate at which they mutually agree. In such cases, the parties equally share the expense of the arbitrator's services.

13. Elkouri and Elkouri, *supra* n. 3, at 24–25.

14. Elkouri and Elkouri, *supra* n. 3, at 197; (for preparation checklist *see* pp. 198–199); Domke, *supra* n. 12, §§24:01 and 27:01.

15. *Id.*

16. Some of the matters which might be discussed at a prehearing conference are: whether discovery is needed and, if so, scheduling of same; motions that need to be filed and briefed or orally argued, and the setting of firm oral argument and hearing dates.

17. Cooley, *supra* n. 9, at 4–5; Elkouri and Elkouri, *supra* n. 3, at 186–90.

18. Cooley, *supra* n. 9, at 5.

19. Elkouri and Elkouri, *supra* n. 3, at 224–25.

20. Cooley, *supra* n. 9, at 5; Elkouri and Elkouri, *supra* n. 3, at 223–28.

21. Elkouri and Elkouri, *supra* n. 3, at 225.

22. Cooley, *supra* n. 9, at 6.

23. Salem, *Mediation—The Concept and the Process*, in *Instructors Manual for Teaching Critical Issues* (1984, unpublished). *See generally* Simpkin, *Mediation and the Dynamics of Collective Bargaining* 25 (BNA, 1971). Court-annexed mediation is a process in which judges refer civil cases to a neutral (mediator or master) for settlement purposes. It also includes in-court programs in which judges perform the settlement function full-time.

24. *See generally* Ray, *The Alternative Dispute Resolution Movement*, 8 *Peace and Change* 117 (Summer 1982). The process of mediation and the roles and strategies of mediators have been generally neglected in studies of negotiation. As one author remarked, "Mediation still remains a poorly understood process." Gulliver, *supra* n. 8.

25. Meagher, "Mediation Procedures and Techniques," 18–19 (unpublished

paper on file in the Office of the General Counsel, FMCS, Washington, D.C.). Mr. Meagher is a former commissioner of FMCS.

26. The success of the introductory stage is directly related to two critical factors: (1) the appropriate timing of the mediator's intervention, and (2) the opportunity for mediator preparation. A mediator's sense of timing is the ability to judge the psychological readiness of an individual or group to respond in the desired way to a particular idea, suggestion or proposal. Meagher, *supra* n. 25, at 5, *see also* Maggiolo, *Techniques of Mediation in Labor Disputes* 62 (Dobbs Ferry, NY: Oceana Publications, 1971). The kinds of preparatory information needed by the mediator are discussed in the text *supra*. In many instances, such information is not available prior to intervention and thus it must be delicately elicited by the mediator during the introductory stage.

27. Meagher, *supra* n. 25, at 26–27. Wall, *Mediation, An Analysis, Review and Proposed Research*, 25 *J. Conflict Res.* 157, 161 (1981).

28. Caucusing is an *ex parte* conference between a mediator and a party.

29. Meagher, *supra* n. 25, at 28; Maggiolo, *supra* n. 26, at 42–44.

30. *Id.*

31. Ray, *supra* n. 24, at 121; Maggiolo, *supra* n. 26, at 52–54.

32. Meagher, *supra* n. 25, at 30; Maggiolo, *supra* n. 26, at 47.

33. Ray, *supra* n. 24, at 121; Salem, *supra* n. 23, at 4–5; Robins, *supra* n. 1, at 27; Maggiolo, *supra* n. 26, at 48–49.

34. Ray, *supra* n. 24, at 121.

35. *Id.* at 121–22; Meagher, *supra* n. 25, at 57–58; Robins, *supra* n. 1, at 43–44; Maggiolo, *supra* n. 26, at 49–50.

36. Maggiolo, *supra* n. 26, at 12. Other basic negotiation principles which some mediators use to advantage throughout the mediation process are found in Fisher and Ury, *Getting to Yes* (New York: Penguin Books, 1983). Those principles are: (1) separate the people from the problem; (2) focus on interests, not positions; (3) invent options of mutual gain; (4) insist on using objective criteria.

37. Ray, *supra* n. 24, at 122. Meagher, *supra* n. 25, at 48–49, describes additional techniques of "planting seeds," "conditioning," and "influencing expectations."

38. Ray, *supra* n. 24, at 122.

39. *Id.*

40. Domke, *supra* n. 12, §23:01, at 351–53.

41. *Id.* §24:05, at 380.

42. *Id.*

43. *Id.* §23:02, at 355.

44. See Craviolini v. Scholer & Fuller Associated Architects, 89 Ariz. 24, 357 P.2d 611 (1960), where an architect was deemed to be a "quasi-arbitrator" under an agreement with the parties and therefore entitled to immunity from civil liability in an action brought against him by either party in relation to the architect's dispute-resolving function. *Compare* Gammell v. Ernst & Ernst, 245 Minn. 249,

72 N.W.2d 364 (1955), where certified public accountants, selected for the specific purpose of making an examination and of auditing the books of a corporation to ascertain its earnings, were held not to have acquired the status of arbitrators so as to create immunity for their actions in the performance of such service, simply because the report was to be binding upon the parties.

45. Domke, *supra* n. 12, §23:01, at 352–53.

46. As two professional mediators have poignantly commented: "Unlike arbitration and other means of adjudication, the parties retain complete control . . . If they do not like the mediator, they get another one. If they fail to produce results, they may end the mediation at any time." Phillips and Piazza, *How to Use Mediation*, 10 *A.B.A.J. of Sect. of. Lit.* 31 (Spring, 1984).

47. *See* Grumman Aerospace Corp. v. Titanium Metals Corp., 91 F.R.D. 84 (E.D. N.Y. 1981) (Court granted a motion to enforce a subpoena *duces tecum* involving a report prepared by a neutral fact-finder on the effects of certain price-fixing activities). *See generally* Restivo and Mangus, *Alternative Dispute Resolution: Confidential Problem-Solving or Every Man's Evidence? Alternatives to the High Cost of Litigation*, 2 *Law & Bus. Inc./Ctr. for Public Resources*, 5 (May, 1984). Parties can assist the preservation of confidentiality of their mediation proceedings by reducing to writing any expectations or understanding regarding the confidentiality of the proceedings and by being careful to protect against unnecessary disclosure both within their respective constituencies and the outside world, *id.* at 9.

48. *See, e.g.*, NLRB v. Joseph Macaluso, 618 F.2d 51 (9th Cir. 1980); Pipefitters Local 208 v. Mechanical Contractors Assn. of Colorado, 90 Lab. Cas. (CCH) ¶ 12,647 (D. Colo. 1980).

49. Phillips and Piazza, *supra* n. 46, at 33.

50. In re Ruppert, 29 LA 775, 777 (N.Y. Ct. App. 1958); In re Griffin, 42 LA 511 (N.Y. Sup. Ct. 1964). *See generally* Elkouri and Elkouri, *supra* n. 3, at 241–51.

51. Domke, *supra* n. 12, §29:06, at 436.

52. Donoghue v. Kohlmeyer & Co., 63 Ill. App. 3d 979, 380 N.E.2d 1003, 20 Ill. Dec. 794 (1978).

53. Borg, Inc. v. Morris Middle School Dist. No. 54, 3 Ill. App. 3d 913, 278 N.E.2d 818 (1972).

54. Domke, *supra* n. 12, §33:00, 463.

55. *Id.* In Illinois, the court's power to vacate or modify arbitration awards is narrowly circumscribed. *See Ill. Rev. Stat.* ch. 10, ¶¶ 112, 113 (1981).

56. *Ill. Rev. Stat.* ch. 10, ¶ 114 (1981).

57. Gulliver, *supra* n. 8, at 220.

58. *Id.* at 226.

59. Where a settlement agreement is reduced to a judgment, for example, through intervention and assistance of a special master, the "consent judgment" is generally enforceable, if necessary, before the court in which the consent judgment is entered.

*Questions*

1. Explain in your own words the differences between arbitration and mediation.
2. What kinds of skills does the mediator need that the arbitrator does not require?
3. What are the main features of the decision-making stage of arbitration?
4. How does the generation and evaluation of alternatives work in mediation?
5. Give some of the roles a mediator may adopt to help settle disputes.

# 7
# Getting to "Yes" in a Nuclear Age

## Roger Fisher

This article originally appeared in *Getting to 'Yes': Negotiating Agreement without Giving In*, 1981.

*Roger Fisher, a Harvard University specialist in international affairs, observes in his 1981 article that current U.S. foreign policy seeks peace through belligerent behavior toward the Russians. He bids us to consider how America reacts when the Soviets do the same thing. One-sidedness, he says, makes the superpower negotiators much like drug addicts unable to shake their addiction.*

*Before World War II, Fisher says, "Political power was directly related to military power." With the atom bomb, this is no longer the case. He envisions the problem of getting agreements to be more psychological than military: "the balance between the consequences they see in saying 'yes' and the consequences they see of saying 'no'." In Table 1, Fisher lays out these consequences in regard to Russia's response to martial law in Poland.*

*The author argues that cutting off communication with the Soviets actually decreases our ability to influence their behavior. Also important is how we negotiate. At some length, he contrasts "hard" and "soft" negotiating stances, and compares them with what he calls "principled negotiation." (See Tables 2 and 3.) Since "principled negotiation" is his brain child, he dwells on it at length, calling it an attempt to "change the game." It involves: (1) separating the people from the problem; (2) focusing on interests, not positions; (3) generating a variety of possibilities before deciding what to do; (4) insisting that the result be based on an objective standard.*

*Each of these four principles is subject to three stages in negotiation: analysis, planning and discussion. The finished product, in Fisher's view, "typically results in a wise agreement." He cites the success of Salt I and even the unratified Salt II agreement which have generally been observed by both superpowers. As with international conventions that pertain to shipping, it is advance knowledge, convergence of interests and mutual*

315

*understanding that count for more than the legally binding nature of an*
*agreement.*

The political and military intentions of the Soviet Union are of utmost
concern to American officials. Since World War II, a central task of United
States foreign policy has been to influence Soviet decisionmaking. To this
end the United States has employed a variety of approaches, ranging from
arms limitation agreements and the expansion of East-West trade, to economic sanctions, geopolitical confrontations, and the pursuit of nuclear
superiority.

Recently, the United States has been looking especially hard to do
something. Faced with a continuous Soviet arms buildup, the military
domination of Afghanistan, the presence of Cuban and East German
forces in Africa, the potential invasion of Poland, and Soviet failures to
comply with the human rights provisions of the Helsinki Accords,
Washington has taken a decidedly military approach toward influencing
the Soviet Union. Strategic and theatre-level nuclear forces have been
upgraded toward a first-strike capability; "rapid deployment" forces
have been expanded; overall military spending has been vastly increased. There also has been tough talk about American resolve and
willingness to fight a nuclear war, variously accompanied by public de-
nunciations, a boycott of the Olympics, and on-again/off-again grain em-
bargoes. And all too often, Washington has placed tight restrictions on
communication. We have tended not only to hang up the phone, but
to cut the line. For nine months the United States had no ambassador
in Moscow. At every level, contacts with Soviet officials have tended to
be stiff, peremptory, and minimal.

The underlying assumption is clear enough: the way to make the Soviets more peaceful is for the United States to behave more belligerently.
The idea is that by engaging in a massive military buildup, and threatening
to use it, we will scare the Soviet Union into being more peaceful.

But let us stop and think. How do we react when the Soviets build
more weapons and threaten us? Do we ask ourselves whether U.S. policies
have looked unduly aggressive? Do officials suggest that we show restraint
by slowing down our military spending and behaving in more peaceful
ways? No. When the Soviets build SS-20 missiles by the score, we become
more bellicose. And we step up our military spending.

Knowing how we react, common sense tells us how the Soviet Union
will react to our bellicosity. We react belligerently to the fact that the Soviets outspent the United States during the past decade by some $300 bil-
lion for military purposes. We should well understand why the Soviet
Union reacts similarly to the fact (equally true) that during that same

decade we and our NATO allies outspent the Soviets and their allies by some $280 billion for military purposes.

Of course, throwing our arms away cannot be expected to cause the Soviets to lie down like lambs, no more than the United States would do so were the Soviet Union to pursue the same course. But now that each of us has more than enough military hardware to serve as a deterrent, now that both sides have roughly comparable military forces (all the talk about a "missile gap" or a "window of vulnerability" to the contrary notwithstanding), more U.S. weapons will hardly cause the Soviets to produce less.

In sum, the suggestion that being more belligerent will cause the Soviets to behave less belligerently is contrary to both experience and common sense. And the companion notion that we make the world safer for the United States by acquiring weapons that make it more dangerous for the Soviet Union is far worse. So far as nuclear war is concerned, we are in the same boat. We cannot make our end of the boat safer by making the Soviet end more likely to tip over. And to diminish Soviet confidence in the physical security of their nuclear forces only increases the pressure to use them.

Thus, while the original international problem for which we got our nuclear weapons was fear of aggression by another Hitler, the cure has now become more dangerous than the disease. Like drugs to which we have become addicted, our nuclear weapons have become habit-forming and dangerous. Designed to protect us from other countries that legitimately give us cause for concern, they themselves have become a threat to national survival; and a failure to appreciate this blunt fact indicates a failure to comprehend the radical change from the days when there were only conventional weapons available. We can boldly say: "Better dead than Red." But, honestly, each of us would prefer to have our children in Havana, Belgrade, Beijing, Warsaw, or Leningrad today than in Hiroshima or Nagasaki when the nuclear bombs went off. A general nuclear war would be far more damaging to our national interest than even the most outrageous political domination.

I

Before World War II, superior military force was persuasive indeed. Defensively, if a country had the clear physical ability to protect itself, then others could be persuaded not to attack: since an attack would fail, why try? Offensively too, if a country had the clear ability physically to impose its will and to produce the result it desired, then why resist? In an era which considered both colonialism and war legitimate, the political

cost of imposing a desired result was likely to be modest. The power to
bring about a result by self-help if negotiations should fail made it far more
likely that a weaker country would agree to the result requested by a
stronger country. A country that could not prevent a given result by fighting might just as well agree without a fight. Political power was directly
related to military power.

Despite our nuclear age, some military weapons still do enhance the
power to persuade. Having enough "smart" anti-tank weapons helps persuade an adversary not to launch a tank attack. A strong physical barrier,
a mine field, an anti-submarine net, or anti-aircraft batteries may effectively persuade an opposing country not to attempt a particular military
action. Such weapons deter action because they have the power to prevent
it. Offensively, too, where the desired result is to occupy and maintain
control over nearby territory, the physical power to do so greatly enhances
a State's negotiating power. The situation of Israel and the Golan Heights
is a case in point.

But in the world today, most foreign policy objectives—particularly
those of the United States and the Soviet Union toward one another—cannot be accomplished by military means. There is no way we can physically
impose freedom upon the Soviet Union, and no way they can physically
impose their values upon us. We cannot physically impose self-government on some country that does not have it. The United States has found
that its possession of vast military forces has not given it the power to persuade Vietnam, Libya, South Africa, Syria, or Iran to make the decisions
we want them to make. And the Soviet Union has discovered that the billions of rubles it has spent on arms have not given it the power to influence
others either. Ten years ago, Egypt had 17,000 Soviet troops. Today those
troops have been expelled and American and Egyptian troops conduct
joint maneuvers.

This point—that the power to persuade and military power are no
longer necessarily synonymous or coextensive—is especially important in
the context of nuclear confrontation. The consequences of a nuclear war
would be catastrophic. And they would be worse for some countries than
for others. But unless a real prospect of nuclear war appears on one side
of the choice a country faces, the consequences of a nuclear war are irrelevant to that choice. For example, as we press the Soviet Union to bring
about an end to martial law in Poland, the Soviet Union might see their
choice as depicted in Table 1. If this is the way the Soviet Union sees its
choice, our military weapons, including our nuclear weapons, are irrelevant to their decision. Equally so our nuclear superiority has been irrelevant to our negotiations with Iran over the hostages, to our efforts to
persuade Israel to stop building settlements in the West Bank, to our

**Table 1**
Today's Context: Where Military Power Is Not the Power to Persuade

| QUESTION: SHALL WE, THE SOVIET UNION, PRESS FOR THE END OF MARTIAL LAW IN POLAND? | |
|---|---|
| If "Yes" | If "No" |
| − We accept full responsibility for the mess in Poland. | + We limit our responsibility for Poland. |
| − We risk instability in Eastern Europe. | + Eastern Europe is likely to remain stable. |
| − We antagonize Poland nationalists of all kinds in the military, in Solidarity, in the Church, and in the Party. | + We buy time. |
| | + We stand up to the United States. |
| − Both the economy and the political situation are likely to become worse. | + The Polish Army may bring the situation under control. |
| − We look weak in backing down to a US demand. | + We limit our confrontation with the Poles. |
| | + We keep our options open (we can always do something later if it appears desirable). |

efforts to moderate Libya's behavior, or to persuade our European allies to support sanctions against the Soviet Union.

True, our nuclear weapons do serve one important function. They make it extremely dangerous for the Soviet Union to do outrageous things such as bomb Pearl Harbor or New York, or land forces in Florida or Britain, or try a blitzkrieg attack across Western Europe. But once we have enough strategic forces to make any such action extremely risky, additional nuclear forces do not improve our negotiating position on the daily problems we have with the Soviet Union and with other governments of the world. If having a superior power to destroy gave one the power to persuade, then the Soviet Union—and the rest of the world, for that matter—would have been dancing to our tune for the last 30 years.

In sum, diplomatic success today depends less upon what can be produced by physical means than upon what takes place in somebody else's head; "our" success depends upon "their" decision. And in all such cases the critical balance is not the balance of destructive power, but, rather, the balance sheet of the presently perceived choice: how do the consequences of "their" deciding as "we" wish compare in their minds with the consequences of not doing so? The critical balance, in other words, is not that between our military force and the force on the other side, but the balance between the consequences they see of saying "yes" and the consequences they see of saying "no."

Of course, beyond an analysis of Soviet decisionmaking, we can see that our choice also is subject to influence. Indeed, the major case for an enormous strategic weapons buildup rests on the premise that those weapons will protect us against a Soviet demand that is backed up with a nuclear threat. But just as a large number of nuclear weapons provides no protection against attempted extortion by a lone terrorist, they cannot protect us from attempted extortion by a Soviet leader who might be equally indifferent to the fate of others. The outcome of such attempted blackmail is not determined by counting potential casualties; the numbers are all but irrelevant. In such an exchange of unprincipled threats, the advantage goes to the leader who is least concerned with human life, is more ruthless, is more willing to gamble for high stakes, is less vulnerable to criticism by a free press, and has fewer constituents to whom he must later answer. But there is no way in which our acquiring additional nuclear warheads will make it wise policy for an American President to compete in ruthlessness with a leader of the Soviet Union.

Our ability to influence the Soviet Union depends, then, upon our ability to affect the way they see a future choice, independent of the nuclear threat; and this is as true in the realm of arms control and disarmament as it is in any other. To persuade the Soviet Union to agree to meaningful arms limitation and reduction proposals, we need to formulate and present a series of choices where each time the consequences of deciding as we would like are more attractive to them as well as to us than their proceeding down the road toward a deteriorating relationship.

## II

Of the many variables that enhance such negotiating power, one of the most important is effective two-way communication. If we are to change Soviet minds, we need to know what is on those minds; we need to listen. Whatever Soviet officials may try to conceal, the more extensive our discussions, the more we can listen "between the lines," the better will be the intelligence we can glean.

There are those who favor breaking or reducing diplomatic relations as a response to outrageous conduct. They suggest that talking under such circumstances looks "soft," that it implies approval, and that actions speak louder than words. Actions do speak loudly. But our purpose is not simply to express ourselves. It is to affect Soviet behavior, and to this end communication is more powerful if it is two-way, precise, and continuous. To close down the Soviet purchasing office, to suspend talks on wheat sales and merchant marine matters, or to reduce scientific exchange, tends to decrease our ability to influence the Soviet Union, not increase it. Such actions suggest that we are enemies no matter what the other side does, thus eliminating any incentive for change. With continuous talks, however, we learn more and there is more time for good ideas to prevail. We also avoid the unfortunate result that if stopping talks is used to signal disapproval, then resuming talks—as we did over wheat sales—implies approval, it implies for instance, that Soviet conduct, even in Afghanistan, is not so bad after all.

The model for good communication is not a "high-noon" confrontation between gunslingers, but the kind of intensive talks that produced the treaty banning atmospheric nuclear tests. We exert influence most effectively when the other side knows exactly what is expected, why it is legitimate, and what we will do next. These are conditions that are hard to meet without talking extensively and in detail. We can be just as firm in a meeting as elsewhere—and a great deal clearer. Our negotiating power is enhanced by maintaining the maximum amount of two-way communication at all levels. Without effective two-way communication there is no successful negotiation.

### III

Another key variable to successful negotiation is how we negotiate. Our purpose is to work out with the Soviet Union a way to live together on this precarious globe. We want to clarify existing restraints and develop additional ones because it is in our mutual interest to do so. But to increase the chance of our devising wise restraints in time to avoid disaster, we should stop bargaining over positions as though haggling over the price of a rug; we should use a method more likely to serve our shared interests. The process of negotiation itself is critical.

The traditional mode of conducting a two-party international conference is well illustrated by the SALT—now START—process, and has three key features:

*Decide first, talk later.* Each side unilaterally develops and decides upon its proposed solution before talking with the other side.

*Argue about positions.* Most of the discussion among negotiators is devoted to explaining and defending one's own one-sided position and attacking that of the other side.

*Make concessions slowly.* As time goes by, one side or the other reluctantly makes a small concession to keep the talks from breaking down.

This is a poor method of negotiating.

First, this approach is unlikely to produce optimal results: with it more time is spent arguing over extreme positions than in trying to develop creative solutions. When negotiators bargain over positions, they tend to lock themselves into those positions. The more often they restate a position and defend it against attack, the more committed they become to it. The more they try to convince the other side of the impossibility of changing their opening position, the more difficult it becomes to do so. Egos become identified with positions. There develops a new interest in "saving face"—in reconciling future action with past positions. This process makes it less and less likely that any agreement will wisely reconcile the parties' original concerns.

The danger that positional bargaining will impede a negotiation was well illustrated by the breakdown of talks under President Kennedy for a comprehensive ban on nuclear testing. A critical question arose: how many on-site inspections per year should the Soviet Union and the United States be permitted to make within the other's territory to investigate suspicious seismic events? The Soviet Union finally agreed to three inspections. The United States insisted on no less than ten. And there the talks broke down—over positions—despite the fact that no one understood whether an "inspection" would involve one person looking around for one day, or a hundred people prying indiscriminately for a month. The parties had made little attempt to design an inspection procedure that would reconcile the United States's interest in verification with the desire of both countries for minimal intrusion.

As more attention is paid to positions, less attention is devoted to meeting the underlying concerns of the parties. Agreement becomes less likely. Any agreement reached may reflect a mechanical splitting of the difference between stated positions rather than a solution carefully crafted to meet the legitimate interests of the parties. The result is frequently an agreement less than satisfactory to each side than it could have been.

Second, this "bazaar" or "haggling" approach to negotiation tends to be extremely inefficient; it takes a lot of time. The United States devoted a full year to producing preliminary agreement among Army, Navy, Air Force, State Department, Arms Control Agency, and White House officials, as well as our NATO allies, merely on an opening SALT/START position—which everyone knew had no chance of being accepted by the Soviet Union. Now, over the months and years ahead, we will have to get similar agreement on each of many concessions arising from this maximum position.

Bargaining over positions creates incentives that stall settlement. In positional bargaining we try to improve the chance that any settlement reached be favorable to us by starting with an extreme position, by stubbornly holding to it, by deceiving the other party as to our true views, and by making small concessions only as necessary to keep the negotiation going. The same is true for the other side. Each of those factors tends to interfere with reaching a settlement promptly. The more extreme the opening positions and the smaller the concessions, the more time and effort it will take to discover whether or not agreement is possible.

The standard minuet also requires a large number of individual decisions as each negotiator decides what to offer, what to reject, and how much of a concession to make. Decisionmaking in this fashion is difficult and time-consuming at best. Where each decision not only involves yielding to the other side but the possibility of having to yield further, a negotiator has little incentive to move quickly. Dragging one's feet, threatening to walk out, stonewalling, and other such tactics become commonplace. They all increase the time and costs of reaching agreement as well as the risk that no agreement will be reached at all.

Finally, in addition to producing unwise agreements and to being time-consuming, positional bargaining is politically costly, endangering ongoing relationships. During the entire process there is an incentive for everyone to be stubborn, hoping that someone else will yield first. In the East-West context, the contest of will that this process involves can be expected to exacerbate relations not only with the Soviet Union but among our allies as well.

Each negotiator asserts what he will and won't do. The task of jointly devising an acceptable solution becomes a battle. Each side tries through sheer will power to force the other to change its position. "We're not going to give in. If you want to limit or reduce arms, it's our way or nothing." Anger and resentment often result as one side sees itself bending to the rigid will of the other while its own legitimate concerns go unaddressed.

Positional bargaining thus strains and sometimes shatters the relationship between the parties. This has happened between the United States and the Soviet Union on numerous occasions, and the world is not a safer place for it.

On the other hand, being "nice" is no answer either. Many people recognize the high costs of hard positional bargaining, particularly on the parties and their relationship. They hope to avoid them by following a more gentle style of negotiation. Instead of seeing the other side as adversaries, they prefer to see them as friends. Rather than emphasizing a goal of victory, they emphasize the necessity of reaching agreement. In a soft negotiating game the standard moves are to make offers and concessions, to trust the other side, to be friendly, and to yield as necessary to avoid confrontation.

Table 2 illustrates two styles of positional bargaining: soft and hard. Most people see their choice of negotiating strategies as between these two styles. Looking at the table as presenting a choice, should the United States or the Soviet Union be a soft or a hard positional bargainer?

The soft negotiating game emphasizes the importance of building and maintaining a relationship. Within families and among friends much negotiation takes place in this way. The process tends to be efficient, at least to the extent of producing results quickly. As each party competes with the other in being more generous and more forthcoming, an agreement becomes highly likely. But the agreement may not be wise. Any negotiation primarily concerned with the relationship runs the risk of producing a sloppy agreement.

**Table 2**

| PROBLEM | |
| --- | --- |
| Positional Bargaining: Which Game Should You Play? | |

| SOFT | HARD |
| --- | --- |
| Participants are friends. | Participants are adversaries. |
| The goal is agreement. | The goal is victory. |
| Make concessions to cultivate the relationship. | Demand concessions as a condition of the relationship. |
| Be soft on the people and the problem. | Be hard on the problem and the people. |
| Trust others. | Distrust others. |
| Change your position easily. | Dig in to your position. |
| Make offers. | Make threats. |
| Disclose your bottom line. | Mislead as to your bottom line. |
| Accept one-sided losses to reach agreement. | Demand one-sided gains as the price of agreement. |
| Search for the single answer: the one *they* will accept. | Search for the single answer: the one *you* will accept. |
| Insist on agreement. | Insist on your position. |
| Try to avoid a contest of will. | Try to win a contest of will. |
| Yield to pressure. | Apply pressure. |

Further, pursuing a soft form of positional bargaining makes us vulnerable to someone who plays a hard game of positional bargaining. In positional bargaining, a hard game dominates a soft one. If the hard bargainer insists on his position while the soft bargainer insists on agreement, the negotiating game is biased in favor of the hard player. Any agreement reached will be more favorable to the hard positional bargainer than to the soft one.

## IV

Fortunately, the "bazaar" approach to negotiation is not the only way to seek agreement. If we do not like the choice between hard and soft positional bargaining, we can change the game.

A more efficient and effective approach to negotiation, a method explicitly designed to produce wise outcomes efficiently and amicably, is called principled negotiation or negotiation on the merits. Based on the principle of talking first and deciding later, it can be boiled down to four basic points.

These four points define a straightforward method of negotiation that can be used under almost any circumstance. Each point deals with a basic element of negotiation, and suggests what you should do about it.

*People:* Separate the people from the problem.
*Interests:* Focus on interests, not positions.
*Options:* Generate a variety of possibilities before deciding what to do.
*Criteria:* Insist that the result be based on some objective standard.

The first point responds to the fact that human beings, including representatives of national governments, are not computers. We are creatures of strong emotions who often have radically different perceptions and have difficulty communicating clearly. Emotions typically become entangled with the objective merits of the problem. Taking positions just makes this worse because people's egos become identified with their positions. Hence, before working on the substantive problem, the "people problem" should be disentangled from it and dealt with separately. Figuratively if not literally, the participants should come to see themselves as working side by side attacking the problem, not each other. Hence the first proposition: Separate the people from the problem.

The second point is designed to overcome the drawback of focusing on stated positions when the object of a negotiation is to satisfy underlying interests. Since any norm we might later agree upon must be in the interests of the Soviet Union and the United States, we should learn as much as possible about Soviet needs and wants, and we should make sure that Moscow is equally clear about ours. We should ignore any declared position except as evidence of some underlying interest. Compromising between positions is unlikely to produce an agreement which will effectively take care of the human needs that lead people to adopt those positions. The second basic element of the method thus is: Focus on interests, not positions.

The third point responds to the difficulty of designing optimal solutions while under pressure. Trying to decide in the presence of an adversary narrows one's vision. Having a lot at stake inhibits creativity. So does searching for the one right solution. A major aim, therefore, is to invent, without commitment, different ways of possibly reconciling conflicting interests. We can offset the constraints of pressured circumstance by setting aside designated occasions within which to think up a wide range of possible solutions that advance shared interests and creatively reconcile differing interests. During the SALT I talks, two members of each delegation (called "the wizards" by the Russians) used to meet for the purpose of creative brainstorming, understood to be without commitment on behalf of either government. Some such process is extremely valuable, permitting the Soviet Union and the United States to devise norms of behavior, both for weapons and for military-political activity, that are in the interest of each country to respect so long as the other is demonstrably doing so. Hence the third basic point: Before trying to reach agreement, invent options for mutual gain.

Some negotiators obtain a favorable result simply by being stubborn. To allow that to happen rewards intransigence and produces arbitrary results. It is possible to counter such a negotiator by insisting that his single say-so is not enough and that any agreement must reflect some fair standard independent of the naked will of either side. This does not mean insisting that the terms be based on the standard we select, but only that some fair standard determine the outcome. In negotiating arms limitations, there are many possible objective standards to assure fairness or rough equivalence in arms reductions, in force levels, or in military vulnerability. By discussing such criteria rather than what the parties are willing or unwilling to do, neither party need give in to the other; both can defer to a fair solution. Hence the fourth basic point: Insist on using objective criteria.

The method of principled negotiation is contrasted with hard and soft positional bargaining in Table 3, which shows the four basic points of the method in boldface type. With a good understanding of each other's interests, with multiple options that have been designed to meet them, and with the principle of reciprocity as a guide, there is an optimal chance that negotiators can produce recommendations for official decision.

It is important to note also that the four basic propositions of principled negotiation are relevant from the time one begins to think about negotiating until the time either an agreement is reached or a decision is

**Table 3**

| PROBLEM | | SOLUTION |
|---|---|---|
| Position Bargaining: Which Game Should You Play? | | Change the Game— Negotiate on the Merits |
| **SOFT** | **HARD** | **PRINCIPLED** |
| Participants are friends. | Participants are adversaries. | Participants are problem-solvers. |
| The goal is agreement. | The goal is victory. | The goal is a wise outcome reached efficiently and amicably. |
| Make concessions to cultivate the relationship. | Demand concessions as a condition of the relationship. | Separate the people from the problem. |
| Be soft on the people and the problem. | Be hard on the problem and the people. | Be soft on the people, hard on the problem. |
| Trust others. | Distrust others. | Proceed independent of trust. |
| Change your position easily. | Dig in to your position. | Focus on interests, not positions. |
| Make offers. | Make threats. | Explore interests. |
| Disclose your bottom line. | Mislead as to your bottom line. | Avoid having a bottom line. |
| Accept one-sided losses to reach agreement. | Demand one-sided gains as the price of agreement. | Invent options for mutual gain. |
| Search for the single answer: the one *they* will accept. | Search for the single answer: the one *you* will accept. | Develop multiple options to choose from; decide laters. |
| Insist on agreement. | Insist on your position. | Insist on objective criteria. |
| Try to avoid a contest of will. | Try to win a contest of will. | Try to reach a result based on standards independent of will. |
| Yield to pressure. | Apply pressure. | Reason and be open to reasons; yield to principle, not pressure. |

made to break off the effort. That period can be divided into three stages: analysis, planning, and discussion.

During the analysis stage one is simply trying to diagnose the situation—to gather information, organize it, and think about it. Negotiators will want to consider the people problems of partisan perceptions, hostile emotions, and unclear communication, as well as to identify their interests and those of the other side. They will want to note options already on the table and identify any criteria already suggested as a basis for agreement.

During the planning stage negotiators deal with the same four elements a second time, both generating ideas and deciding what to do. How do they propose to handle the people problems? Of their interests, which are most important? And what are some realistic objectives? They will want to generate additional options and additional criteria for deciding among them.

Again during the discussion stage, when the parties communicate back and forth, looking toward agreement, the same four elements are the best subjects to discuss. Differences in perception, feelings of frustration and anger, and difficulties in communication can be acknowledged and addressed. Each side should come to understand the interests of the other. Both can then jointly generate options that are mutually advantageous and seek agreement on objective standards for resolving opposed interests.

To sum up, in contrast to positional bargaining, the principled negotiation method of focusing on basic interests, mutually satisfying options, and fair standards typically results in a wise agreement. The method permits reaching a gradual consensus on a joint decision efficiently without all the transactional costs of digging in to positions only to have to dig out of them. And separating the people from the problem allows dealing directly and empathetically with the other negotiator as a human being, thus making possible an amicable agreement. If all this is possible, an actual commitment becomes less important. The provisions of SALT I have expired and those of SALT II never have come into effect. Yet, except for the dismantling provisions, both the Soviet Union and the United States are respecting those terms. Even nonbinding norms can establish a modus vivendi. As with an unmarried couple sharing an apartment, it may be easier for both countries to live together than to enter into major commitments.

We and the Soviet Union have good reason to be skeptical about each other's intentions. Yet however high our level of mutual distrust, we share an enormous interest in avoiding a calamitous collision. On the high seas the danger of ships colliding is reduced through international agreement on a system of signals and evasive turns. What matters is not that the signals are legally binding but that they have been worked out in advance and have become well understood.

The danger of a military collision between the Soviet Union and the United States is both far more dangerous and far more difficult to avoid. The fact that we distrust each other makes joint planning for crisis management both more important and more urgent. As disastrous as any nuclear war would be, it would be tragic indeed to have a nuclear war which both sides wanted at the last minute to avoid, but didn't know how. Maintaining effective two-way communication and adopting techniques of principled negotiation in the pursuit of common interests are among the first prerequisites for overcoming mutual distrust and avoiding such a calamity.

*Questions*

1. Why does Fisher say that cutting off contacts with the Soviets does little to influence them to move in our direction?

2. How can U.S. policymakers "read between the lines" to determine Soviet intentions?

3. Why does the author compare most international negotiations with "haggling over the price of a rug"? Why does he find this method counterproductive?

4. How does "principled negotiation" differ from "hard" and "soft" negotiation?

5. What would be one example of an objective standard on which to evaluate the results of a negotiation?

# SECTION FIVE

# World Order

# 1
# Universal Declaration of Human Rights

*United Nations General Assembly, Dec. 10, 1948*

---

*The Universal Declaration of Human Rights, adopted by the United Nations General Assembly in 1948, is a remarkable document. Assuming the sincerity of its signatory states, it represents a level of agreement on fundamental issues that few would have predicted in the years preceding its adoption. From one perspective, it is a compilation of the political wisdom of the Western world. But the U.N. also included states from the officially atheistic Soviet bloc and non-Western nations. While disputes could arise on the origin of the rights of the human person (whether from the Creator or from natural evolutionary processes, for example), the declaration provided a platform from which has been proclaimed the fact that such rights do exist without distinction. In a divided world, that in itself is no small achievement.*

*Based loosely on such documents as the Magna Carta (1215) in England, the U.S. Declaration of Independence (1776) and Constitution (1787) and the French Declaration of the Rights of Man (1789), the Universal Declaration reaches back to the "common sense" of all humanity, which thinkers such as Pope John XXIII would equate with the natural moral law. The declaration goes beyond these previous documents in specifying the rights which belong to every member of humanity.*

*Cynics may affirm that, in most countries, these rights are ignored when reasons of state find them inconvenient. To be sure, laws were not made to be broken, but their very existence holds individuals and nations to a higher standard that would otherwise be possible.*

*The declaration itself is relatively short and unambiguous. It deserves to be read slowly and thoughtfully. Many of its thirty short articles point an accusing finger at present-day abuses—slavery and torture, detention and exile, deprivation of nationality, to mention a few. Quite a few have legal overtones, because it is in the administration of justice—or of its opposite—that dedication to human rights is tested. Nor are the rights of the family—especially mothers and children—neglected. Primary education is affirmed as a natural human right, as is participation in government. Economic rights, such as the right to a job, to decent compensation and other social benefits, are up-held.*

*Even though the Universal Declaration's noble aims have been ig-nored or abused—and the Helsinki Accords of 1976 have not fared any better—nevertheless this document forms the proximate basis for most of the human rights organizations and activities in today's world.*

## PREAMBLE

**Whereas** recognition of the inherent dignity and of the equal and in-alienable rights of all members of the human family is the foundation of freedom, justice and peace in the world,

**Whereas** disregard and contempt for human rights have resulted in barbarous acts which have outraged the conscience of mankind, and the advent of a world in which human beings shall enjoy freedom of speech and belief and freedom from fear and want has been proclaimed as the highest aspiration of the common people,

**Whereas** it is essential, if man is not to be compelled to have recourse, as a last resort, to rebellion against tyranny and oppression, that human rights should be protected by the rule of law,

**Whereas** it is essential to promote the development of friendly rela-tions between nations,

**Whereas** the peoples of the United Nations have in the Charter re-affirmed their faith in fundamental human rights, in the dignity and worth of the human person and in the equal rights of men and women and have determined to promote social progress and better standards of life in larger freedom,

**Whereas** Member States have pledged themselves to achieve, in co-operation with the United Nations, the promotion of universal respect for and observance of human rights and fundamental freedoms,

**Whereas** a common understanding of these rights and freedoms is of the greatest importance for the full realization of this pledge,

*Now, Therefore,*

## THE GENERAL ASSEMBLY
### *proclaims*

THIS UNIVERSAL DECLARATION OF HUMAN RIGHTS as a common standard of achievement for all peoples and all nations, to the end that every individual and every organ of society, keeping this Declaration constantly in mind, shall strive by teaching and education to promote respect for these rights and freedoms and by progressive measures, national and international, to secure their universal and effective recognition and observance, both among the peoples of Member States themselves and among the peoples of territories under their jurisdiction.

**Article 1.** All human beings are born free and equal in dignity and rights. They are endowed with reason and conscience and should act towards one another in a spirit of brotherhood.

**Article 2.** Everyone is entitled to all the rights and freedoms set forth in this Declaration, without distinction of any kind, such as race, colour, sex, language, religion, political or other opinion, national or social origin, property, birth or other status.

Furthermore, no distinction shall be made on the basis of the political, jurisdictional or international status of the country or territory to which a person belongs, whether it be independent, trust, non-self-governing or under any other limitation of sovereignty.

**Article 3.** Everyone has the right to life, liberty and security of person.

**Article 4.** No one shall be held in slavery or servitude; slavery and the slave trade shall be prohibited in all their forms.

**Article 5.** No one shall be subjected to torture or to cruel, inhuman or degrading treatment or punishment.

**Article 6.** Everyone has the right to recognition everywhere as a person before the law.

**Article 7.** All are equal before the law and are entitled without any discrimination to equal protection of the law. All are entitled to equal protection against any discrimination in violation of this Declaration and against any incitement to such discrimination.

**Article 8.** Everyone has the right to an effective remedy by the competent national tribunals for acts violating the fundamental rights granted him by the constitution or by law.

**Article 9.** No one shall be subjected to arbitrary arrest, detention or exile.

**Article 10.** Everyone is entitled in full equality to a fair and public hearing by an independent and impartial tribunal, in the determination of his rights and obligations and of any criminal charge against him.

**Article 11.** (1) Everyone charged with a penal offence has the right to be presumed innocent until proved guilty according to law in a public trial at which he has had all the guarantees necessary for his defence.

(2) No one shall be held guilty of any penal offence on account of any act or omission which did not constitute a penal offence, under national or

international law, at the time when it was committed. Nor shall a heavier penalty be imposed than the one that was applicable at the time the penal offence was committed.

**Article 12.** No one shall be subjected to arbitrary interference with his privacy, family, home or correspondence, nor to attacks upon his honour and reputation. Everyone has the right to the protection of the law against such interference or attacks.

**Article 13.** (1) Everyone has the right to freedom of movement and residence within the borders of each state.

(2) Everyone has the right to leave any country, including his own, and to return to his country.

**Article 14.** (1) Everyone has the right to seek and to enjoy in other countries asylum from persecution.

(2) This right may not be invoked in the case of prosecutions genuinely arising from non-political crimes or from acts contrary to the purposes and principles of the United Nations.

**Article 15.** (1) Everyone has the right to a nationality.

(2) No one shall be arbitrarily deprived of his nationality nor denied the right to change his nationality.

**Article 16.** (1) Men and women of full age, without any limitation due to race, nationality or religion, have the right to marry and to found a family. They are entitled to equal rights as to marriage, during marriage and at its dissolution.

(2) Marriage shall be entered into only with the free and full consent of the intending spouses.

(3) The family is the natural and fundamental group unit of society and is entitled to protection by society and the State.

**Article 17.** (1) Everyone has the right to own property alone as well as in association with others.

(2) No one shall be arbitrarily deprived of his property.

**Article 18.** Everyone has the right to freedom of thought, conscience and religion; this right includes freedom to change his religion or belief, and freedom, either alone or in community with others and in public or private, to manifest his religion or belief in teaching, practice, worship and observance.

**Article 19.** Everyone has the right to freedom of opinion and expression; this right includes freedom to hold opinions without interference and to seek, receive and impart information and ideas through any media and regardless of frontiers.

**Article 20.** (1) Everyone has the right to freedom of peaceful assembly and association.

(2) No one may be compelled to belong to an association.

**Article 21.** (1) Everyone has the right to take part in the government of his country, directly or through freely chosen representatives.

(2) Everyone has the right of equal access to public service in his country.

(3) The will of the people shall be the basis of the authority of government; this will shall be expressed in periodic and genuine elections which shall be by universal and equal suffrage and shall be held by secret vote or by equivalent free voting procedures.

**Article 22.** Everyone, as a member of society, has the right to social security and is entitled to realization, through national effort and international co-operation and in accordance with the organization and resources of each State, of the economic, social and cultural rights indispensable for his dignity and the free development of his personality.

**Article 23.** (1) Everyone has the right to work, to free choice of employment, to just and favourable conditions of work and to protection against unemployment.

(2) Everyone, without any discrimination, has the right to equal pay for equal work.

(3) Everyone who works has the right to just and favourable remuneration ensuring for himself and his family an existence worthy of human dignity, and supplemented, if necessary, by other means of social protection.

(4) Everyone has the right to form and to join trade unions for the protection of his interests.

**Article 24.** Everyone has the right to rest and leisure, including reasonable limitation of working hours and periodic holidays with pay.

**Article 25.** (1) Everyone has the right to a standard of living adequate for the health and well-being of himself and of his family, including food, clothing, housing and medical care and necessary social services, and the right to security in the event of unemployment, sickness, disability, widowhood, old age or other lack of livelihood in circumstances beyond his control.

(2) Motherhood and childhood are entitled to special care and assistance. All children, whether born in or out of wedlock, shall enjoy the same social protection.

**Article 26.** (1) Everyone has the right to education. Education shall be free, at least in the elementary and fundamental stages. Elementary education shall be compulsory. Technical and professional education shall be made generally available and higher education shall be equally accessible to all on the basis of merit.

(2) Education shall be directed to the full development of the human personality and to the strengthening of respect for human rights and fundamental freedoms. It shall promote understanding, tolerance and friend-

ship among all nations, racial or religious groups, and shall further the activities of the United Nations for the maintenance of peace.

(3) Parents have a prior right to choose the kind of education that shall be given to their children.

**Article 27.** (1) Everyone has the right freely to participate in the cultural life of the community, to enjoy the arts and to share in scientific advancement and its benefits.

(2) Everyone has the right to the protection of the moral and material interests resulting from any scientific, literary or artistic production of which he is the author.

**Article 28.** Everyone is entitled to a social and international order in which the rights and freedoms set forth in this Declaration can be fully realized.

**Article 29.** (1) Everyone has duties to the community in which alone the free and full development of his personality is possible.

(2) In the exercise of his rights and freedoms, everyone shall be subject only to such limitations as are determined by law solely for the purpose of securing due recognition and respect for the rights and freedoms of others and of meeting the just requirements of morality, public order and the general welfare in a democratic society.

(3) These rights and freedoms may in no case be exercised contrary to the purposes and principles of the United Nations.

**Article 30.** Nothing in this Declaration may be interpreted as implying for any State, group or person any right to engage in any activity or to perform any act aimed at the destruction of any of the rights and freedoms set forth herein.

*Questions*

1. What is the underlying assumption of the declaration regarding the relation of the individual to the nation-state? Does it favor any particular form of government? Explain.
2. Enumerate the benefits noted in the preamble that flow from respect for personal rights.
3. List some of the rights that the declaration upholds in common with the U.S. Constitution. Name some that are not mentioned in the American document.
4. Why does the declaration single out marriage and the family unit for special mention?
5. Why does the declaration urge "teaching and education" as means of promulgating knowledge of human rights? Think of some of the implications of your answer.

# 2
# Redefining National Security

## Lester R. Brown

This article originally appeared in *Nuclear Times*, June 1986

---

*Lester Brown of the Worldwatch Institute, a Washington think tank, sheds light on a factor not discussed in the previous article—the emergence of Japan as an economic superpower. The principal reason for this emergence is not hard to find: Japan spends less than one percent of its Gross National Product on the military while the U.S. lavishes seven percent and the U.S.S.R. pours fourteen percent of its GNP into armaments. For many countries, he says, the era of guns-and-butter has come to an end.*

*Brown repeats, in concise form, some of the economic woes facing both military superpowers as recorded by Dumas in Section One. While the U.S. and the Soviets suffer economic setbacks for their weapons expenditures, Brown fears that too little attention is paid to such major matters as third world debt, the international financial system and the deterioration of the world's natural resources.*

*Yet he finds some hope in the fact that military expenditures are actually going down in such countries as China, Argentina and Peru. Brown does not go so far as to predict that other countries will follow suit, but there is no doubt where his heart is. In the nettlesome area of superpower arms reduction, "the likelihood of reducing tensions may be improving." Even in the Soviet Union, he discerns signs that pragmatism may win out over ideology.*

*Future world leadership for both the U.S. and the U.S.S.R., he says, "may now depend on reducing military expenditures to strengthen their faltering economies."*

Preoccupied with each other, the United States and the Soviet Union have apparently failed to notice that global geopolitics are being reshaped in a way that defines security more in economic than in traditional military terms. Now, quite apart from the positive contributions of the peace movement, worsening economic conditions may become the key motivation for reversing the militarization of the past generation.

Throughout most of the post-war period, an expanding economy permitted the world to have more guns and more butter. For many countries, however, this age has come to an end. Governments can no longer both boost expenditures on armaments and deal effectively with the forces that are undermining their economies.

The choices now are between continued militarization of the economy and restoration of its environmental support systems; between continued militarization and attempts to halt growth of the U.S. debt; between continued militarization and new initiatives to deal with the dark cloud of Third World debt. The world has neither the financial resources nor the time to militarize and to deal with these new threats to security.

## DEBTS OF DESPAIR

"National security" has become a commonplace expression, a concept regularly appealed to. It is used to justify the maintenance of armies, the development of new weapon systems, and the manufacture of armaments. One-fourth of all the federal taxes in the United States and at least an equivalent amount in the Soviet Union are levied in its name.

Since World War II, the concept of national security has acquired an overwhelmingly military character, rooted in the assumption that the principal threat to security comes from other nations. Commonly veiled in secrecy, consideration of military threats has become so dominant that new threats to the security of nations—threats with which military forces cannot cope—are being ignored.

For the United States and the Soviet Union, the cost of the arms race goes beyond mere fiscal reckoning. It is draining their treasuries, weakening their economies, and lowering their positions in the international economic hierarchy. This long, drawn-out conflict is contributing to a realignment of the leading industrial countries, with Japan assuming a dominant position in the world economy. One of the keys to Japan's emergence as an economic superpower is its negligible military expenditures—less than one percent of its gross national product (GNP), compared with seven percent of the GNP in the United States and 14 percent in the Soviet Union.

The doubling of the U.S. national debt, from $914 billion in 1980 to $1,841 billion in 1985, is due more to the growth of military expenditures than to those of any other sector. The growing federal debt is mortgaging the country's economic future and, consequently, its position in the world economy.

An overvalued dollar and the lack of investment in new industrial capacity have dramatically altered America's position in world trade. As recently as 1975, the United States had a small trade surplus. In 1980, it registered a trade deficit of $36 billion. The trade deficit climbed to $70 billion in 1983, and to a staggering $150 billion in 1985.

This ballooning trade deficit and the associated borrowing abroad to finance the federal debt have cost the country its position as the world's leading international investor. While Japan's external holdings during this decade have grown from $12 billion to more than $120 billion, the net foreign assets of the United States have plummetted to *minus* $120 billion. Almost overnight, the United States has become a debtor nation—a precipitous, and unprecedented, fall from leadership.

This is a worrisome shift for a country whose international leadership role since World War II has derived in large part from its economic strength and prestige. The military expenditures that are weakening the United States economically are diminishing both its stature within the international community and its capacity to lead.

The Soviet Union, too, is paying a heavy price for its role in the arms race, retaining second-class economic status despite its wealth of natural resources. Military spending channels roughly one-seventh of the nation's resources to nonproductive uses. From the early 1950s through the late 1970s the Soviet economy grew at roughly five percent annually, a rate of expansion that brought progress on many fronts. Today, Soviet industrial growth has slowed to a crawl. In agriculture, less grain is being produced now than in the late 1970s.

While the United States and the Soviet Union have been preoccupied with each other militarily, Japan has been moving to the fore economically. By some economic indicators, it now leads both military superpowers. In a world where the enormous investment in nuclear arsenals has no practical use, the terms denoting leadership and dominance are shifting in Japan's favor. Governors and mayors in the United States now compete vigorously for Japanese investment. And Third World delegations seeking investment and technology from abroad regularly journey to Tokyo. For developing countries, the Japanese model is far more attractive than either the problem-ridden Soviet economy or the debt-ridden American one.

The U.S. economy is still twice as large as Japan's, and the country has a vastly superior indigenous resource base of land, energy fuels, minerals, and forest products. Nonetheless, a country that is a net debtor, borrowing heavily from the rest of the world, cannot effectively exercise economic or political leadership.

Unfortunately, the two superpowers that are perpetuating the arms race are not its only victims. To the extent that the arms competition diverts attention from the Third World debt that is weakening the international financial system, or from the ecological deterioration that is undermining the global economy, the entire world suffers. The extensive deterioration of national support systems and the declining economic conditions evident in much of the Third World pose threats to national and international security that now rival the traditional military ones.

## HOPEFUL SIGNS

Yet, a few governments have begun to redefine national security, putting more emphasis on economic progress and less on buying arms. At a time when global military expenditures are rising, some countries are actually cutting military outlays. A handful are reducing them sharply, not only as a share of GNP, but in absolute terms as well. Among these are China, Argentina, and Peru.

As recently as 1972, China was spending 14 percent of its GNP for military purposes, one of the highest rates in the world at the time. Beginning in 1975, however, China systematically began to reduce its military expenditures, and except for 1979 has done so for the last eight years. By 1985, military spending had fallen to 7.5 percent of its gross national product.

There are indications that this trend may continue throughout the 1980s. In July 1985, Beijing announced a plan to invest $360 million over two years to retrain one million soldiers for return to civilian life. Such a move would cut the armed forces in China from 4.2 million in 1985 to 3.2 million in 1987, a drop of 24 percent. At the same time, the leaders in Beijing have stepped up the effort to restore and protect the economy's environmental support systems by increasing expenditures on agriculture, reforestation and desert reclamation. In effect, China is defining security in economic and ecological terms.

In Argentina, one of the first things that Raul Alfonsin did as newly elected president in late 1983 was to announce a plan to steadily lower military spending. When he took office there was broad public support for a reduction in arms expenditures, partly because of the ill-fated Falklands War, which undermined the military's credibility. By 1984, arms outlays had been cut to half the peak level of 1980, earning Alfonsin a well-deserved reputation for reordering priorities and shifting resources to social programs.

More recently, Peru has joined the ranks of those announcing plans to cut military expenditures. One of the first actions of President Alan Garcia on taking office in the summer of 1985 was a call to halt the regional arms race. Garcia is convinced of the need to reduce the five percent of Peru's GNP allotted to the military, a sum that consumed one-fourth of its federal budget. As an indication of his sincerity, President Garcia announced that he was cancelling half of an order for 26 French Mirage fighter planes.

Encouragingly, the reductions in military expenditures undertaken by these three governments were independent of any negotiated reductions in neighboring countries. China lowered military outlays unilaterally, despite its 3000 kilometer border with the Soviet Union, which has continued to increase its military might. Over the next few years, as governments everywhere face difficulties in maintaining or improving living standards, others may also choose to reduce military expenditures.

## RESHAPING GEOPOLITICS

Understanding the new threats to security and economic progress will challenge the analytical skills of governments. Sadly, the decision-making apparatus in most governments is not organized to balance threats of a traditional military nature with those of an ecological and economic origin. Non-military threats are much less clearly defined. And national defense establishments are useless against them.

The key to demilitarizing the world economy and shifting resources is defusing the arms race between the United States and the Soviet Union. Whether this can be achieved in the foreseeable future remains to be seen. But as the costs of maintaining the arms race multiply, both for the superpowers and for the world at large, the likelihood of reducing tensions may be improving.

In East Asia, for example, traditional adversaries China and Japan appear to be in the process of establishing strong economic ties. In contrast to the United States, China appears to be abandoning military competition with the Soviet Union. With Japan showing little interest in becoming a military power, the stage is being set for peace in the region. Both countries have redefined security and reshaped their geopolitical strategies.

If ideology gives way to pragmatism, as it is doing in China, then the conflicts and insecurities bred by the ideological distinctions between East and West can lessen. If the Soviet Union adopts the reforms needed to get its economy moving again, a similar ideological softening may result. Turning more towards a market-oriented economy to allocate resources and boost productivity could not only restructure the Soviet economy, but also reorient Soviet politics. Although pragmatism has typically taken a back seat to ideology in the Soviet Union, the leaders have demonstrated that they can be pragmatic when circumstances require, as when they import grain from the United States, their ideological rival.

For the world as a whole, the past generation has seen an overwhelming movement toward militarization. Apart from the heavy claim on public resources, the East-West conflict contributes to a psychological climate of suspicion and distrust that makes the cooperative, international assessment of new threats to the security of nations next to impossible. China, Argentina and Peru may provide the models for the future. If demilitarization could replace militarization, national governments would be free to reorder their priorities, and could return to paths of sustained progress.

Ironically, for the United States and the Soviet Union, maintaining a position of leadership may now depend on reducing military expenditures to strengthen their faltering economies. Acting thus in their own interest, they could set the stage for demilitarizing the world economy. Once it starts, demilitarization—like militarization—could feed on itself.

## Questions

1. What effect does militarization have on the world environment, the U.S. budget deficit and third world debt?
2. Name some threats to the security of the U.S. that cannot be coped with by the armed forces.
3. What are some consequences of the fact that the U.S. is now a debtor nation?
4. Is the author too optimistic in his estimate that the cost of the arms race may help reduce East-West tensions? Give your reasons.
5. What effects are the lowered military outlays by China likely to have on the U.S.S.R.?

3

# Foreign Aid and U.S. National Interests

## George Shultz

This article originally appeared in *Current Policy No. 457* U.S. Department of State, February 24, 1983.

*Realism, strength and negotiation are the foundations of the conduct of American foreign policy, according to Secretary of State Shultz. In his address to the Southern Center for International Studies, the Secretary enunciates President Reagan's policy "to reduce a decade's accumulation of doubt about U.S. commitments and staying power."*

*Realism, he says, involves calling aggression, chemical and biological warfare and economic problems by their right names, "whether it happens to be in a country that is friendly to us or not." Shultz's interpretation of strength begins with military force, but he qualifies that by saying that "military strength rests on a strong economy." In this connection, he cites the control of inflation, increased productivity and a rising standard of living as American accomplishments. Above all, he invokes the importance of maintaining confidence in "our own beliefs and ideals." In regard to negotiations, he makes reference to American efforts toward "saving the city of Beirut from complete destruction," in addition to trying to resolve the difficulties in such places as Kampuchea (Cambodia), Afghanistan and southern Africa. He expresses the wish that the U.S. be conceived "as part of the solution and not part of the problem."*

*With this background, Shultz turns to relations with the third world. His two basic assumptions are that economic growth in the developing nations is essential to a strong American economy and that the same applies to security and peace in these countries. With statistical evidence, he asserts that, until the recent recession, the third world accounted for forty percent of U.S. exports—a factor in saving American jobs. He concedes that the worldwide recession of 1982 has hurt the U.S. economy and adds that American dependence on third world countries for strategic minerals and other goods emphasizes the interrelatedness of the world economy. To this he pledges his Administration to fight for the reduction of trade barriers and to oppose protectionism.*

*In regard to peace and security, the Secretary asserts that the main challenges in recent years have come from unrest and warfare in third world countries, a development he blames on "the Soviet Union and its allies." Like his predecessors going back to World War II, Secretary Shultz emphasizes the need for military support for friendly countries around the world. Complementing such activities are U.S. foreign aid programs which, he is quick to say, are not a "giveaway." This too places the Reagan Administration, in its stated goals, in the mainstream of U.S. postwar foreign policy.*

*In conclusion, Shultz compares the small amount spent each year on foreign aid with the amount Americans spend on luxuries. Above all, he calls for perseverance so that "we will be able to brighten the future for ourselves and for others throughout the world."*

A speech such as today's provides an opportunity for me to use a wide-angle lens. Although the broad picture is ever in our mind, the day-to-day business of the State Department generally finds us using not the broad brush but the jeweler's glass as we examine the myriad individual issues on which our foreign relations turn. So today I want to begin by opening the lens full scope. I will describe the fundamental tenets which underlie President Reagan's foreign policy.

Then I'd like to turn the lens down in two successive notches: first, a moderate turn to discuss the importance to our foreign policy of the more than 100 developing countries of the Third World—Asia, Africa, and South America.

Finally, I plan to focus way down and—in this time of tight budgets—discuss the funds which the United States must expend to achieve its objectives. Contrary to popular opinion, the currency of foreign affairs is not cookies. It takes resources—modest but sustained, applied credibly over time—to secure international peace, foster economic growth, and help insure the well-being of each of our citizens. But we'll start with the broader view.

## FUNDAMENTAL TENETS OF U.S. FOREIGN POLICY

Since his inauguration 2 years ago, President Reagan has sought to revitalize U.S. foreign policy. He is resolved to reduce a decade's accumulation of doubt about the U.S. commitment and staying power. Our watchwords in doing this are four ideas:

**First,** we start with realism.

**Second,** we build our strength.

**Third,** we stress the indispensable need to negotiate and to reach agreements.

**Fourth,** we keep the faith. We believe that progress is possible even though the tasks are difficult and complex.

Let me take each of these very briefly in turn. I'm very conscious of them, because as I get caught up in the day-to-day details of foreign policy and go over to the White House to discuss my current problems with the President, he has the habit of bringing me back to these fundamentals. And I believe they are truly fundamental.

**Realism.** If we're going to improve our world, we have to understand it. And it's got a lot of good things about it; it's got a lot of bad things about it. We have to be willing to describe them to ourselves. We have to be willing if we see aggression to call it aggression. We have to be willing if we see the use of chemical and biological warfare contrary to agreements to get up and say so and document the point. When we see persecution, we have to be willing to get up and say that's the reality, whether it happens to be in a country that is friendly to us or not.

When we look at economic problems around the world, we have to be able to describe them to ourselves candidly and recognize that there are problems. That's where you have to start, if you're going to do something about them. So, I think realism is an essential ingredient in the conduct of our foreign policy.

**Strength.** Next, I believe, is strength. We must have military strength, if we're going to stand up to the problems that we confront around the world and the problems imposed on us by the military strength of the Soviet Union and the demonstrated willingness of the Soviet Union to use its strength without any compunction whatever.

So, military strength is essential, but I think we delude ourselves if we don't recognize—as we do, as the President does—that military strength rests on a strong economy; on an economy that has the capacity to invest in its future, believe in its future—as you do here in Atlanta; an economy that brings inflation under control and that stimulates the productivity that goes with adequate savings and investment and has given us the rising standard of living and remarkable economic development that our country has known. But more than that, we have to go back to our own beliefs and ideals and be sure that we believe in them. And there is no way to do that better than to live by them ourselves. So, we have to maintain our own self-confidence and our own will power and our own notion that we are on the right track to go with the strength in our economy and our military capability.

**Negotiation.** Of course, beyond this, if we are realistic and we are strong, I believe it is essential that we also are ready to go out and solve problems, to negotiate with people, to try to resolve the difficulties that we see all around the world—not simply because in doing so we help the places where those difficulties are but because in doing so we also help ourselves, we further our own interests. So, negotiation and working out problems has got to be a watchword for us, and we do that all around the world. I think it is no exaggeration to say that the efforts of the United States resulted in saving the city of Beirut from complete destruction. We are active in trying to resolve difficulties in Kampuchea. We have called attention to the problems in Afghanistan. We're working in southern Africa in a most difficult situation to bring about a resolution of the Namibia issues, and so on around the world. But I like to think that the United States must be conceived of as part of the solution and not part of the problem. That's where we want to be standing.

Finally, if we can achieve these things, if we can be strong enough so that people must take us seriously, and put our ideas forward in a realistic manner, then we will be able to solve problems and have some competence to be successful, and, if we're successful, certainly the world can be better.

## RELATIONS WITH THE THIRD WORLD

Against that background, let me turn to the problems of the Third World and our dealings with them and our stake in doing so successfully. Many of our citizens still see the developing countries as accessories to our basic interests. But over the past two decades, these countries have increasingly moved to the front of the stage where issues of peace and prosperity are played out. I believe this trend has assumed such proportions that I can advance two fundamental propositions.

**First,** there will be no enduring economic prosperity for our country without economic growth in the Third World.

**Second,** there will not be security and peace for our citizens without stability and peace in developing countries.

Let me explain these propositions. For the past 15 years, until the current recession took its toll, the developing countries as a whole have been growing more rapidly than the United States and Europe. As they have grown, they have become increasingly important as customers and suppliers for ourselves and other industrial nations.

In 1980, developing countries purchased about 40% of U.S. exports—more than bought by Western Europe, Eastern Europe, the

Soviet Union, and China combined. These countries have accounted for more than half the growth in U.S. exports since 1975. At this juncture, approximately 1 out of every 20 workers in our manufacturing plants and 1 out of every 5 acres of our farmland produce for Third World markets. I might say that 2 out of every 5 acres of our farmland produce for export. That's how interrelated our farm community is with the international community.

The current worldwide recession has vividly—if painfully—highlighted these relationships. In the past several years, growth rates in the developing countries have dropped from over 5% per year to around 2%. Partly as a result, our exports to these countries—which were increasing at more than 30% a year in the late 1970s—have tapered off. For example, in the first 8 months of 1982, U.S. exports to Mexico dropped 26%; to Chile, 59%; and to Thailand, 25%. According to estimates, every $1 billion decline in U.S. exports erases 60,000–70,000 U.S. jobs after multiplier effects are taken into account. There's a direct correlation. Today some of the workers in our unemployment lines and some of the businesses and farms on the auction block are living, if unwanted, proof that the well-being of our citizens is linked to the well-being of citizens in the Third World.

On the other side of the trade ledger, the developing countries supply about 40%–45% of the goods which we import for our factories and consumers. Although we are richer in minerals than most industrialized countries, the Third World supplies more than half the bauxite, tin, and cobalt used by U.S. industry. For some 11 other strategic metals and minerals, the developing countries supply more than half of our imports. For some natural products, such as rubber, coffee, cocoa, and hard fibers, the Third World supplies everything we use.

This intertwining of the European and our economy with those of the Third World will increase in the 1980s and 1990s. As the recession fades, we can expect the faster growing countries—particularly in Asia but also in South America—to resume their role as engines of growth in the world economy. They will open up new opportunities for our exports and jobs for our citizens. We have an abiding interest in fostering this growth.

It is for this reason that we are joining with other industrial nations to add funds to the International Monetary Fund. These funds are critical to helping debt-plagued developing countries make painful but unavoidable adjustments in their economies and thereby resume healthy growth rates. We have a direct stake in their success.

For this reason, also, we resist—and call on all Americans to resist—pleas for further protectionism. Putting up barriers to imports will only result in losing markets for our exports and paying higher prices for goods. Resorting to protectionism as an antidote to recession is like turning to alcohol to ward off the cold. It may feel good at first, but it shortly becomes corrosive. The tonic for our ills is noninflationary growth, not stiff draughts of old Smoot-Hawley.

Beyond the demands of economies, the Third World is fundamental to our aspirations for security and peace. Since 1950, most of the major threats to international stability, and the chief opportunities for expansion of the Soviet Union's political reach, have come in the Third World. The headlines have rung with now familiar names: Korea in 1950; Dienbienphu in 1954; Suez, Cuba, and more recently Iran, Angola, Afghanistan, Kampuchea, El Salvador, and Ethiopia.

A study by the Brookings Institution has identified no fewer than 185 incidents in developing countries since the end of World War II when U.S. military forces were used in situations which threatened our political or economic interests. As we speak today, 1,200 Marines are on duty in Lebanon helping again to patch the torn fabric of peace.

The point is clear. The fault line of global instability runs strongly across the continents of the Third World. This instability is inimical to our security in many ways. Small incidents can flare into larger conflagrations and potentially into confrontations between the superpowers. Korea and Cuba teach this lesson well.

More subtly, the Soviet Union and its allies are able to feed on political instability. Some of the most significant uses by the Soviets of military power since World War II have been in the developing world. The Soviet deployment of a deepwater navy, an airlift capacity, and mobile ground forces has given them the ability to intervene when they perceive opportunities.

In addition, the Soviet Union supports 870,000 troops in North Korea—60% more than maintained by South Korea. It bankrolls the Vietnamese Army, which has positioned 180,000 troops directly on the border of Thailand. It supports about 40,000 Cuban troops in Angola, Ethiopia, and Mozambique. In 1981, the Soviet Union supplied about three times as many tanks, aircraft, and artillery pieces as did the United States.

We cannot ignore these realities as they challenge our national interests. Strategically, some of the least secure Third World countries are sources of critical raw materials or lie astride sealanes which carry our military forces and world commerce. The premier example is the Persian Gulf. About 32% of the free world's oil supplies is pumped there. The region is vital to the economic and political security of Europe, Japan, and the United States. It is in our interest to build stability in this region and thereby help assure access to those supplies.

As a parenthetical remark, I want to mention my belief that the recent decline in oil prices—and the possibility of further declines—will spur the free world's economic recovery. For some countries—such as Venezuela and Mexico—cheaper oil surely means tougher times. But it will be good for most of us. I have seen one illustrative estimate that a decline in oil prices to $20 per barrel would boost real growth rates in the industrial countries by up to 1.5%. A less steep decline would have proportionately positive effects. So, I have the sense that as people contemplate the declines in oil prices, there's a tendency for people to wring their hands about what happened to this or that business or financial institution or country— and there are problems and we need to look at them, all right. But let's not forget the main point, it's going to be good for us and good for economic growth, which we need.

The job of building our security also requires that we maintain military facilities and strengthen indigenous defense forces around the world. This includes U.S. bases in the Philippines and in Turkey, the Azores, Morocco, and other strategically placed countries.

The United States cannot defend its interests by operating out of the United States and Europe alone. We need the cooperation of countries in the Third World to grant transit, refueling, and base rights. Otherwise, while we may wish to build up a rapid deployment force, we will be unable to deploy it without Third World friends who will allow us to use their facilities. We must be prepared, in turn, to help these key countries achieve their aspirations for security and economic growth. This is not just a short-term proposition. The process of mutual cooperation weaves ties of interdependence and friendship which will redound to our benefit in years to come.

It goes without saying that the least desirable method for preserving our strategic interests and insuring stability in the developing countries is by sending in U.S. forces. The 185 incidents which I mentioned earlier represent, in essence, 185 failures to resolve problems by more measured means. If we are to reduce incidents in the future, we need a significant program—sustained over time—to secure peace and economic well-being in regions vital to our security.

## U.S. SECURITY AND DEVELOPMENT COOPERATION PROGRAM

In fact, we have such a program. It is called the U.S. Security and Development Cooperation Program. Although our Administration has clarified its goals and sharpened its focus, it is essentially the same program endorsed by every U.S. President since Harry Truman. It's sometimes called foreign aid and all too often depicted as a giveaway. But that is a misnomer. The program's purpose is to create those conditions of growth, security, and freedom in developing countries which serve the fundamental interests of each U.S. citizen.

Let me give some examples of how it works. Our highest priority in this program is bringing peace to the Middle East. Because of the ties between the United States and Israel, a crisis in this region has always placed us in the center of a potentially serious world confrontation. This has been so for more than 25 years. Achieving a lasting peace in the Middle East will not only benefit each and every citizen in those lands but will ease one of the fundamental threats to world peace and our own security.

Making peace there means more than holding talks, as vital as these are. Sustained economic growth is needed in Egypt, Israel, and Jordan. Lebanon needs to open roads, restore electrical service, restart its economic engines, and resume its place as a stable and friendly nation in that part of the world. These countries also need to be able to defend themselves against those they see as aggressors. In this circumstance, we and other nations provide both economic and military aid. This aid is indispensable to the peace process.

Another program—with particular bearing here in the south—is the President's Caribbean Basin initiative. Some of you have dealt directly with the consequences of poverty, political turmoil, and Soviet/Cuban interventionism near our shores. These have come in human form—off airplanes and out of boats—to present in person their claims for a better deal. For the south, the need to help the Caribbean and Central American nations grow economically and build democratic institutions is not an abstract issue. It is one which can directly affect your economy and society.

Another part of our program is helping curb the rampant population growth which underlies much of the Third World's poverty and threatens our planet's resource base. The arithmetic is inexorable. Before World War II there were more than 2 billion people in the world. Now there are 4.3 billion. Even though growth rates have slowed in recent years, 17 years from now, in the year 2000, there will be 6 billion. If we act effectively, the world population may stabilize at between 12 and 16 billion in the last half of the next century. That's 12–16 billion people to feed, clothe, and provide jobs for.

To bring it closer to home, Mexico currently has 62 million people. If they are able to lower their birth rate to the two-children-per-family level in the first 20 years of the next century, they will have "only" about 250 million people when their population stops growing.

Faced with these numbers, the United States provides direct technical advice and training to 27 countries to assist them to mount voluntary family planning programs. It's been an effective effort. We have a deep interest in continuing it.

Similarly, we provide funds for U.S. agricultural universities to help developing countries grow more food. Although there are food surpluses now, population increase, plus growth in the world economy, means that food production in the developing countries must keep growing at 3%–4% per year, or we may all face shortages and rising prices again by the end of the decade.

So with U.S. funds, Mississippi State is introducing improved seed in Thailand. The University of Florida is increasing crop production in Ecuador. Auburn is working in Jamaica and Indonesia on fish production. It is in all our interests that these universities, and others across our agricultural heartland, continue with our support to devote some of their considerable talents to building secure food supplies in the world.

Let me give one more example, this time on the security side. A glance at a map indicates the importance of Turkey to our strategic interests. It sits like a wedge between the Soviet Union, the Middle East, and the western flank of the Persian oil fields. With Iran and Iraq in turmoil, the importance of an economically and militarily strong Turkey has increased. In the last few years, the Russians have increased the size of their forces stationed north of Turkey.

Hence, we and other countries of Europe, led by the Germans, are helping the Turks spur their economy and replace obsolete tanks and other equipment in their armed forces. The cost to us of assisting Turkey maintain strong defense forces between Russia and the Middle East is less than one-sixth of the cost of maintaining U.S. soldiers overseas for the same purpose.

These are examples of how an investment of our resources contributes to the well-being and security of each of us in this room. The cost is modest. For the coming fiscal year, the amounts we've requested from the Congress for the examples I've given work out as follows for each U.S. citizen:

For building peace in the Middle East ......... $12.35 per person
For the Caribbean Basin ...................... $3.84 per person
For curbing population growth.................. 92¢ per person
For building secure food supplies.............. $3.15 per person
For helping Turkey ........................... $1.78 per person

The total request for all our security and economic assistance programs in the developing countries is $43.91 per person.[1] By contrast, we Americans spend $104 per person a year for TV and radio sets, $35 per person per year for barbershops and beauty parlors, $97 per person per year for soap and cleaning supplies, and $21 per person per year for flowers and potted plants.

I'm not belittling any of these expenses. That's not my intent. They're part of our commerce, which provides us with jobs as producers and satisfies us as consumers. I am simply trying to establish some relative values.

Every American must understand that it's necessary to spend a fraction of our collective resources to secure our most precious goals of freedom, economic well-being, and peace. An esteemed son of Georgia and predecessor of mine, Dean Rusk, said it succinctly: "Freedom is not free."

## PROGRESS IS POSSIBLE

Let me close by opening my lens back up and reverting to the fourth of the tenets which guide our conduct of foreign affairs: namely, our conviction that progress is possible. We Americans have lived for over 40 years in a tumultuous world in which we have pursued four basic goals:

**First,** building world peace and deterring war—above all, nuclear war which would threaten human existence;

**Second,** containing the influence of nations which are fundamentally opposed to our values and interests—notably the Soviet Union and its allies;

**Third,** fostering a growing world economy and protecting U.S. access to free markets and critical resources; and

**Fourth,** encouraging other nations to adopt principles of self-determination, economic freedom, and the rule of law which are the foundation stones of American society.

In these endeavors, we have had some signal successes. Some formerly troubled countries of the world—for instance, the countries of East Asia—are now relatively strong and prosperous. Western Europe, a cock-

---

1. The figures cited are derived by dividing the Administration's FY 1984 request for development assistance, PL 480, economic support funds, military education and training program, military assistance and foreign military grants by the U.S. population of approximately $230 million. The figures *do not include* foreign military sales guaranteed loans which are extended at market or near-market rates to foreign governments. These loans by law are not included in the U.S. budget.

pit of warring nationalities for a century, has been at peace for 37 years. Progress has been made in fundamental areas affecting the mass of mankind: better health, longer life expectancy, more schooling, increased income. We have a chance in the coming year to make major strides in fashioning peace in the Middle East.

Americans as a people are pragmatists, suspicious of grand assurances or easy promises. But I'm convinced that if we persevere—proceeding realistically, backed by strength, fully willing to negotiate and search for agreement—we will be able to brighten the future for ourselves and for others throughout the world.

*Questions*

1. If the basic principles of U.S. foreign policy, as enunciated by Secretary Shultz, are consistent with those of previous Administrations, how do you explain the partisan debates about foreign policy in Congress?

2. Do you think Shultz's statement on realism in foreign policy can be taken at face value? Give examples.

3. Does Shultz's assertion of U.S. economic growth in the post-war period stand up to scrutiny? Why, or why not?

4. The Secretary puts the blame for unrest in the third world squarely on the shoulders of the U.S.S.R. How might the Russians respond to this charge?

5. Shultz calls for military and economic support for friendly countries. Can you think of any qualifications to that statement?

4

# Arbitration:
# An International Wallflower

## *Robert Coulson*

This article originally appeared in *National Forum*, Fall 1983.

*Robert Coulson, president of the American Arbitration Association, raises his voice for the settlement of disputes between nations by means of arbitration. He refers to the widespread practice even today of resolving international commercial problems by this means. In view of arbitration's success in cases where it has been used, Coulson wonders why "impartial, binding arbitration of nonbusiness disputes between nations (has) become an international wallflower."*

*For one thing, he says, arbitration provides "a rational alternative to the threat of force" as exemplified by the Algerian Accords which settled monetary claims between the United States and Iran. Like Burger, Coulson has recourse to historical examples of arbitration, which were "discarded" during the Civil War and "overwhelmed" by World War I. He cites with approval the non-violent efforts of Gandhi and Martin Luther King, Jr.*

*Given the troubles of the American delegation to the United Nations, Coulson reflects on the common public attitude: "In America, real men don't mediate." Such "macho" attitudes, he says, make the future dim for international arbitration. He appeals for "a more acute understanding of the mutual dependence of all peoples" in accordance with concepts of international justice.*

*Coulson admits that high hopes for the Permanent Court of Arbitration set up at the Hague earlier in the century have not lived up to expectations. But he says that multinational cooperation has worked in communications, air travel and space. Coulson suggests that "the potential causes of war (economic and social differences) could be the subject of mediation (non-binding) or arbitration (binding)." In the dance of nations, he concludes: "It is time to invite arbitration to the party."*

Long before laws were memorialized or formal courts of justice were created, people resorted to arbitration for the resolution of disputes. For adjusting obscure tribal discords, for settling sordid business squabbles among dusty traders, for resolving border disputes between angry nation-states, arbitration was the remedy of choice throughout the ancient world. (See also Warren E. Burger's article for further documentation of this historical precedent.)

Today, multitudes of business controversies are resolved by arbitration in preference to court litigation. In the United States, arbitration tribunals resolve a substantial percentage of commercial cases because many executives are convinced that such tribunals composed of their peers will make informed decisions. Elsewhere in the world, arbitration is frequently used for both domestic and transnational business disputes. Arbitration clauses are placed in virtually all contracts between Western corporations and socialist foreign trade organizations. In international commercial transactions, where neither party wants to submit to the other's courts, the parties' use of arbitration clauses in contracts has become almost universal. The convenience and informality and privacy of arbitration appeal to business firms and their attorneys.

Arbitration is used in the United States for a wide variety of noncommercial matters. Arbitrators resolve labor-management grievances and collective-bargaining impasses. They settle minor criminal matters. They adjust family disputes. They have even been installed in correctional institutions to settle confrontations between inmates and the prison administration.

In arbitration, a neutral person or panel is selected to hear the parties and, having gained an understanding of the dispute, that person is authorized to issue a binding award. Most legal systems recognize the arbitration process and enforce parties' agreements to arbitrate and give force and effect to any award rendered by the arbitrator. Arbitration provides a practical, alternative, dispute-resolution process.

One party to an arbitration may be a government entity. In labor arbitration, the "employer" may be a local municipality, county, state, or even a federal agency. In building construction, the "owner" may be a governmental agency. In international commercial arbitration, the contract may pit a multinational investment firm against a foreign state or instrumentality. A substantial body of law has developed around the question of whether government entities can submit their disputes to arbitration and whether, once having done so, such a party can repudiate its agreement. With relatively few exceptions, courts have held governments to their agreements.

International commercial arbitration has become a well-recognized mode of settlement of international trade and investment disputes. The United Nations Convention on the Recognition and Enforcement of Foreign Arbitral Awards has only confirmed this trend. In view of the broad acceptance of arbitration as a method for resolving commercial disputes, one must wonder why arbitration seems to have lost its early popularity as a method for fixing other disagreements between nations. Why has impartial, binding arbitration of nonbusiness disputes between nations become a wallflower?

From time to time, arbitration continues to be used to fix some international border, particularly where the participants are minor powers. The impasse over the United States employees held by Iran was resolved by the Algerian Accords which created an arbitration tribunal to process monetary claims. Arbitration clauses are frequently inserted in international conventions, dealing with quasi-commercial matters. But, in general, arbitration has not been selected as the remedy of choice in international affairs. Why not?

I will discuss some problems that seem to stand in the way of a broader use of arbitration for resolving disputes between nations. At the outset, arbitration is regarded as a "soft" or "weak" form of dispute settlement. Military force, in contrast, is highly regarded by the major powers. Arbitration provides a rational alternative to the threat of force. Unfortunately, arbitration has become identified with pacifism in the political mind. In the United States, the peace movement always played a relatively minor role in national politics. For example, an American Peace Society was founded in 1828 but was virtually swept aside by the Civil War. In that frenzy of hostilities, rational alternatives were discarded for fear that they would weaken the public's commitment to armed conflict.

In the postwar period, arbitration had another passing vogue. In 1874, both houses of Congress passed a resolution that arbitration clauses be incorporated in treaties. Arbitration groups were formed to encourage the idea: the National Arbitration League (1882), the Christian Arbitration Association (1886), and the Lake Mohonk Conference (1895-1916). The American Arbitration Association, itself, received inspiration from such efforts and continues its support of research in the field of international arbitration.

World War I overwhelmed whatever chance there might have been for arbitration to replace the major powers' reliance upon the threat of violence, supplemented by diplomacy. From time to time, world leaders came to the surface, like Gandhi, who espoused arbitration and nonviolence, or Martin Luther King, Jr., who created a social movement using similar ideas. Both men were representatives of a large, emerging population, confronting a powerful national interest. For their time and purpose, arbitration provided an appropriate part of their strategy. The justice of their cause was so persuasive that an impartial tribunal would be likely to decide in their favor.

Encouraging the United States to make broader use of arbitration agreements presents a different challenge. On many issues, Americans find themselves in the minority. The General Assembly of the United Nations is not always an accurate guide to world opinion, but our experience there has been unfortunate. Our wealth and potential power make us the envy of other nations, creating a climate that does not encourage us to submit vital issues to arbitration tribunals selected from the nationals of other countries. American leaders may legitimately doubt whether the public would support the submission of important matters to a neutral tribunal. Our society seems committed to adversarial competition. The American public expects to win; to field a winning team; to overwhelm its enemies. What politician would act in denial of such expectations?

Some internationalists believe that, through better communication, by building trust and trying to understand mutual needs, it becomes possible to resolve international disputes through mediation. In mediation, a skillful third party helps the parties to reach their agreement through bilateral negotiations. But, as someone succinctly stated at a recent conference, "In America, real men don't mediate." The machismo of our leaders and of our mass media limits the potential of third-party intervention. In those areas where it has become part of the system, such as labor relations for local and state employees, the use of arbitration results from statutory law. As long as nations refuse to relinquish their autonomous power to defend vital interests through force, the future of international arbitration seems dim.

Arbitration has become popular in international commercial agreements, because the parties can select their own system of dispute settlement, avoiding national courts that one or another may suspect of bias. In international political disputes, national leaders may find it difficult to trust anyone's impartiality. And yet we find examples of such trust as Iran and the United States agreeing to arbitrate substantial investment claims.

At home, the federal government is reluctantly willing to arbitrate labor disputes with its own workers. Congress encourages mediation through the Community Relations Service and, in labor relations, through the Federal Mediation and Conciliation Service.

Federal courts are experimenting with court-annexed arbitration and with mediation by court masters. In all of these developments, one perceives a recognition that alternative, dispute-resolution methods such as arbitration can play a greater role in resolving public controversies.

Adherence to arbitration is inspired by a vision of international disputes being determined in accordance with concepts of international justice, rather than under the threat of force. The mechanics of the process are no problem: arbitration agreements can be made a part of multinational conventions or of bilateral agreements between any two nations. In order to achieve that goal, our leading citizens must be prepared to set aside national prejudices and learn to look at conflicts as citizens of the world. That commitment is not shared by many politicians, most of whom tend to believe that the United States demands such total loyalty that national security must be the primary concern of government and of every citizen. To them, it may seem disloyal for a United States citizen to serve as an impartial arbitrator in an international matter. It takes great intellectual and moral stamina for an American to say that loyalty to humanity and to justice and to the world community should exceed national allegiance. The broader use of impartial arbitration for disputes between nations may require a more acute understanding of the mutual dependence of all peoples. National sovereignty stands in the way of any meaningful allegiance to legal principles accepted by the world community, enforced by impartial arbitrators.

Some United States nationals may be capable of rising above such a national bias. But whether United States nationals can act as impartial arbitrators in situations where the security interests of the United States are concerned is, at least, questionable. As a populace, we have not been encouraged to think of ourselves as citizens of the world.

In about 600 B.C., a controversy between Athens and Megara over possession of the island of Salamis was submitted to an arbitration tribunal consisting of five Spartans, who assigned the island to Athens. Could we believe that any five Americans would have been invited to decide the Falkland Islands' dispute? Americans have earned a reputation as nationalists. With few exceptions, we probably deserve that label.

The Permanent Court of Arbitration at The Hague was established by international conferences in 1899 and 1907. High hopes were current that the Court would provide machinery for preventing future wars. Periodic wars have disabused the world of that expectation. Likewise, the League of Nations and the United Nations have not insured world peace. On the other hand, in areas where multinational cooperation is essential—communications, air travel, space, etc.—conventions and international compacts have been entered into and include mechanisms for resolving disputes through impartial arbitration. The use of arbitration may spread from these limited applications to become the channel for more dramatic confrontations between nations. The pending Convention on the Law of the Sea, for example, is replete with arbitration provisions, although it seems unlikely that the United States will sign it.

The need for defining and implementing a concept of international justice seems increasingly apparent. Burdened by evergrowing military budgets, fearful in the face of threats of violence, and in some cases incapable of providing for basic human needs, the citizens of the world can no longer cope with the present and can articulate no realistic plan for the future. In the absence of precise, operational principles for conflict resolution—substantive principles of justice and fairness—impartial arbitration has demonstrated its value for deciding business controversies and its potential for resolving the pragmatic problems stemming from interconnecting world technology.

Many of the potential causes for war arise from economic or social differences that could be the subject of mediation or arbitration. Trade issues or controversies over raw materials or the rights of minority groups have frequently been the crux of such disputes. By submitting these kinds of issues to impartial dispute resolution, nations may have one last clear chance to escape the horrors of military control. The rule of law, backed by arbitration, may provide the only visible alternative to world government. The modest experiments in international arbitration that are now operating could be expanded. Arbitration might become an active participant in the dance of nations, calling partners together, forging some rational future arrangements for the world community. It is time to invite arbitration to the party.

## Questions

1. Why does the author say that arbitration has become "an international wallflower"? Can you think of military clashes in recent history which could have been avoided by arbitration?

2. Why is the prevailing American view one that seeks to impose its will by force? How does this compare with the high degree of religious observance in this country?

3. Would it be unpatriotic for an American judge to rule against his country in an international dispute? What is your definition of patriotism?

4. Name a recent case before the Permanent Court of Arbitration (World Court) in which the United States was involved. What happened?

5. The author states that the rule of law, using arbitration, may be the only alternative to world government. Give your critique of this opinion.

# 5
# The Lesser Evil over
# the Greater Evil

## *Jeane Kirkpatrick*

This article originally appeared in *Commentary*, November 1981.

---

*Traditional morality has it that a good end does not justify an evil means and that, in certain cases, one may tolerate a lesser evil in order to avoid a greater evil. Jeane Kirkpatrick, U.S. Ambassador to the United Nations in the first Reagan Administration, looks at another dichotomy— that of human rights and the national interest. She finds no basic conflict here because the public good that defines the United States "is and has always been a commitment to individual freedom and a conviction that government exists, above all, for the purpose of protecting individual rights." She defines the purpose of foreign policy as that of "defending these rights or extending them to other peoples."*

*It is not in the acceptance of this principle, but in its application, that Kirkpatrick parts company with human rights advocates of the Carter Administration. She discerns a difference in the Carter years from the policy of its predecessors in that a "cultural revolution" resulted in the questioning of the morality of many aspects of U.S. foreign policy. In a sweeping statement, she declares: "As long as the United States was perceived as a virtuous society, policies that enhanced its power were also seen as virtuous." Under Carter, however, she declares that "morality now required transforming our deeply flawed society, not enhancing its power." The result of the Carter view "was a conception of human rights so broad, ambiguous and utopian that it could serve as the grounds for condemning almost any society."*

*Kirkpatrick criticizes the previous administration for its reluctance to condemn communist (totalitarian) regimes and a willingness to find fault with "authoritarian" recipients of U.S. aid—e.g., Central and South American countries, Iran under the Shah and South Africa. She accuses the Carter people of condemning government "repression" in these countries "while ignoring guerrilla violence." The result, she says, is a reduction of American influence throughout the world.*

*For her part, Kirkpatrick finds authoritarian (non-communist)*

*regimes limited in the damage they can do to the people while the power
of totalitarian (communist) regimes is unlimited. She sees the possibility
of an evolution toward democracy in the authoritarians, a process she does
not see happening in the totalitarians. For these and other reasons, Kirkpatrick exhibits "a steady preference for the lesser over the greater evil."
While conceding that such policies will not make a perfect world, "at least
they will not make the lives of actual people more difficult or perilous, less
free than they already are."*

Politics is a purposive human activity which involves the use of power
in the name of some collectivity, some "we," and some vision of the collective good. The collective may be a nation, class, tribe, family, or
church. The vision of the public good may be modest or grand, monstrous
or divine, elaborate or simple, explicitly articulated or simply "understood." It may call for the restoration of the glory of France; the establishment of a Jewish homeland; the construction of a racially pure one-
thousand-year Reich; the achievement of a classless society from which
power has been eliminated. The point is that government act with reference to a vision of the public good characteristic of a people. If they are to
command popular assent, important public policies must be congruent
with the core identity of a people. In democracies the need for moral justification of political action is especially compelling—nowhere more so
than in the United States. The fact that Americans do not share a common
history, race, language, religion gives added centrality to American values, beliefs, and goals, making them the key element of our national identity. The American people are defined by the American creed. The vision
of the public good which defines us is and always has been a commitment
to individual freedom and a conviction that government exists, above all,
for the purpose of protecting individual rights. ("To protect these rights,"
says the Declaration of Independence, "governments are instituted among
men.") Government, in the American view, has no purpose greater than
that of protecting and extending the rights of its citizens. For this reason,
the definitive justification of government policy in the U.S. is to protect
the rights—liberty, property, personal security—of citizens. Defending
these rights or extending them to other peoples is the only legitimate purpose of American foreign policy.

From the War of Independence through the final withdrawal from
Vietnam, American Presidents have justified our policies, especially in
time of danger and sacrifice (when greatest justification is required), by
reference to our national commitment to the preservation and/or extension
of freedom—and the democratic institutions through which that freedom
is guaranteed. Obviously, then, there is no conflict between a concern for

human rights and the American national interest as traditionally conceived. Our national interest flows from our identity, and our identity features a commitment to the rights of persons. (Conventional debate about whether foreign policy should be based on "power" or morality is in fact a disagreement about moral ends and political means.)

It is true that the explicit moral emphasis on presidential pronouncements on U.S. foreign policy had declined in the decade preceding Jimmy Carter's candidacy, partly because of the diminishing national consensus about whether protecting human rights required (or even permitted) containing Communism even through war, and partly because of concern that moral appeals would excite popular passions and complicate the task of limiting the war in Vietnam. It is also true that Jimmy Carter shared this reticence and only reluctantly—and in response to pressure from Senator Henry Jackson—incorporated the human-rights theme into his presidential campaign.

Almost immediately, however, it became clear that the human-rights policies expounded and implemented by Jimmy Carter were different in their conception and their consequences from those of his predecessors. The cultural revolution that had swept through American cities, campuses, and news rooms, challenging basic beliefs and transforming institutional practices, had as its principal target the morality of the American experience and the legitimacy of American national interests. It was, after all, a period when the leading columnist of a distinguished newspaper wrote: "The United States is the most dangerous and destructive power in the world." It was a time when the president of a leading university asserted: "In twenty-six years since waging a world war against the forces of tyranny, fascism, and genocide in Europe we have become a nation more tyrannical, more fascistic, and more capable of genocide than was ever conceived or thought possible two decades ago. We conquered Hitler but we have come to embrace Hitlerism." It was the period when a nationally known cleric said: "The reason for the paroxysm in the nation's conscience is simply that Calley is all of us. He is every single citizen in our graceless land."

If the United States is "the most destructive power in the world," if we are "capable of genocide," if we are a "graceless land," then the defense of our national interest could not be integrally linked to the defense of human rights or any other morally worthy cause.

The cultural revolution set the scene for two redefinitions: first, a redefinition of human rights, which now became something very different from the freedoms and protections embodied in U.S. constitutional practices; and second, a redefinition of the national interest which dissociated morality and U.S. power.

As long as the United States was perceived as a virtuous society, policies which enhanced its power were also seen as virtuous. Morality and American power were indissolubly linked in the traditional conception. But with the U.S. defined as an essentially immoral society, pursuit of U.S. power was perceived as immoral and pursuit of morality as indifferent to U.S. power. Morality now required transforming our deeply flawed society, not enhancing its power.

In the human-rights policies of the Carter administration, the effects of the cultural revolution were reinforced, first, by a secular translation of the Christian imperative to cast first the beam from one's own eye, and, second, by a determinist, quasi-Marxist theory of historical development. The result was a conception of human rights so broad, ambiguous, and utopian that it could serve as the grounds for condemning almost any society; a conception of national interest to which U.S. power was, at best, irrelevant; and a tendency to suppose history was on the side of our opponents. (Of course, the Carter administration did not invent these orientations, it simply reflected the views of the new liberalism that was both the carrier and the consequence of the cultural revolution.)

Human rights in the Carter version had no specific content, except a general demand that societies provide all the freedoms associated with constitutional democracy, all the economic security promised by socialism, and all the self-fulfillment featured in Abraham Maslow's psychology. And it assumed that governments were responsible for providing these. Any society which did not feature democracy, "social justice," and self-fulfillment—that is, any society at all—could be measured against these standards and found wanting. And where all are "guilty," no one is especially so.

The judicial protections associated with the rule of law and the political freedoms associated with democracy had no special priority in the Carter doctrine of human rights. To the contrary, the powerful inarticulate predisposition of the new liberalism favored equality over liberty, and economic over political rights; socialism over capitalism, and Communist dictatorship over traditional military regimes. These preferences, foreshadowed in Carter's Notre Dame speech, found forthright expression in the administration's human-rights policy. UN Ambassador Andrew Young asserted, for example: "For most of the world, civil and political rights . . . come as luxuries that are far away in the future," and he called on the U.S. to recognize that there are various equally valid concepts of human rights in the world. The Soviets, he added, "have developed a completely different concept of human rights. For them, human rights are essentially not civil and political but economic. . . . " President Carter, for his part, tried hard to erase the impression that his advocacy of human rights implied an anti-Soviet bias. "I have never had an inclination to single out the Soviet Union as the only place where human rights are being abridged," he told a press conference on February 23, 1977. "I've tried to make sure that the world knows that we're not singling out the Soviet Union for criticism." In Carter's conception of the political universe, strong opposition to Marxist-Leninist totalitarianism would have been inappropriate because of our shared "goals." On April 12, 1978, he informed President Ceausescu of Romania that "our goals are also the same, to have a just system of economics and politics, to let the people of the world share in growth, in peace, in personal freedom."

It should not be supposed that under Carter no distinction was made between totalitarian and authoritarian regimes—for while the Carter administration was reluctant to criticize Communist states for their human-rights violations (incredibly, not until April 21, 1978 did Carter officials denounce Cambodia for its massive human-rights violations), no similar reticence was displayed in criticizing authoritarian recipients of U.S. aid. On the basis of annual reports required by a 1976 law, the Carter administration moved quickly to withhold economic credits and military assistance from Chile, Argentina, Paraguay, Brazil, Nicaragua, and El Salvador, and accompanied these decisions with a policy of deliberate slights and insults that helped delegitimize these governments at the same time it rendered them less open to U.S. influence.

President Carter's 1977 decision to support the mandatory UN arms embargo against South Africa; Secretary Vance's call, before a meeting of the Organization of American States in June 1979, for the departure of Nicaragua's President Somoza; the decision in 1979 to withhold U.S. support from the Shah of Iran; and President Carter's decision, in June 1979, not to lift economic sanctions against the Muzorewa government in Zimbabwe Rhodesia expressed the same predilection for the selective application of an "absolute" commitment to human rights.

Why were South American military regimes judged so much more harshly than African ones? Why were friendly autocrats treated less indulgently than hostile ones? Why were authoritarian regimes treated more harshly than totalitarian ones? Part of the reason was the curious focus on those countries that received some form of U.S. assistance, as though our interest in human rights were limited to the requirements of the 1976 Foreign Assistance Act; and part of the reason was the exclusive concern with violations of human rights by governments. By definition, guerrilla murders did not qualify as violations of human rights, while a government's efforts to eliminate terrorism qualified as repression. This curious focus not only permitted Carter policy-makers to condemn government "repression" while ignoring guerrilla violence, it encouraged consideration of human-rights violations independently of their context.

Universal in its rhetoric, unflagging in its pursuit of perceived violations—"I've worked day and night to make sure that a concern for human rights is woven through everything our government does, both at home and abroad" (Jimmy Carter, December 15, 1977)—the Carter human-rights policy alienated non-democratic but friendly nations, enabled anti-Western opposition groups to come to power in Iran, and totalitarians in Nicaragua, and reduced American influence throughout the world.

The Carter administration made an operational (if inarticulate) distinction between authoritarianism and totalitarianism and preferred the latter. The reason for its preference lay, I believe, not only in the affinity of contemporary liberalism for other secular egalitarian development-oriented ideologies (such as Communism) but also in the progressive disappearance from modern liberalism of the distinction between state and society. The assumption that governments can create good societies, affluent economies, just distributions of wealth, abundant opportunity, and all the other prerequisites of the good life creates the demand that they should do so, and provokes harsh criticism of governments which fail to provide these goods. The fact that primitive technology, widespread poverty, gross discrepancies of wealth, rigid class and caste structures, and low social and economic mobility are characteristic of most societies which also feature authoritarian governments is ground enough for the modern liberal to hold the existing governments morally responsible for having caused these hardships.

The same indifference to the distinction between state and society also renders the new liberals insensitive to the pitfalls and consequences of extending the jurisdiction and the coercive power of government over all institutions and aspects of life in society. It is, of course, precisely this extension of government's plans and power over society, culture, and personality that makes life in totalitarian societies unbearable to so many. Authoritarian governments are frequently corrupt, inefficient, arbitrary, and brutal, but they make limited claims on the lives, property, and loyalties of their citizens. Families, churches, businesses, independent schools and labor unions, fraternal lodges, and other institutions compete with government for loyalties and resources, and so limit its power.

Authoritarian governments—traditional and modern—have many faults and one significant virtue: their power is limited and where the power of government is limited, the damage it can do is limited also. So is its duration in office. Authoritarian systems do not destroy all alternative power bases in a society. The persistence of dispersed economic and social power renders those regimes less repressive than a totalitarian system and provides the bases for their eventual transformation. Totalitarian regimes, to the contrary, in claiming a monopoly of power over all institutions, eliminate competitive, alternative elites. This is the reason history provides not one but numerous examples of the evolution of authoritarian regimes into democracies (not only Spain and Portugal, but Venezuela, Peru, Ecuador, Bangladesh, among others) and no example of the democratic transformation of totalitarian regimes.

Authoritarian governments have significant moral and political faults, all the worst of which spring from the possession of arbitrary power. But compared to totalitarian governments, their arbitrary power is limited. Only democracies do a reliable job of protecting the rights of all their citizens. That is why their survival must be the first priority of those committed to the protection of human rights.

The restoration of the subjective conviction that American power is a necessary precondition for the survival of liberal democracy in the modern world is the most important development in U.S. foreign policy in the past decade. During the Vietnam epoch that subjective link between American power and the survival of liberal democratic societies was lost. Its restoration marks the beginning of a new era.

The first implication of that fact is that human-rights policies should be and, one trusts, will be, scrutinized not only for their effect on the total strategic position of the United States and its democratic allies—not because power is taking precedence over morality, but because the power of the U.S. and its allies is a necessary condition for the national independence, self-determination, self-government, and freedom of other nations. The human-rights policy of the Reagan administration has not been fully articulated, but the myriad concrete decisions made so far suggest that it will manifest the following characteristics:

First, clarity about our own commitment to due process, rule of law, democratic government and all its associated freedoms.

Second, aggressive statements in information programs and official pronouncements of the case for constitutional democracy. As the party of freedom we should make the case for freedom by precept as well as by example.

Third, careful assessment of all relevant aspects of any situation in another country in which we may be tempted to intervene, symbolically, economically, or otherwise. In Poland as in El Salvador we should be careful neither to overestimate our power to shape events according to our own preference, nor to underestimate the potential negative consequences of our acts.

Finally, a steady preference for the lesser over the greater evil.

Such policies will not make a perfect world, but at least they will not make the lives of actual people more difficult or perilous, less free than they already are. Conceivably, they might leave some people in some places more secure and less oppressed than they are today.

*Questions*

1. Do you agree with the author that "extending human rights to other peoples" is a necessary consequence of the public good? How would you relate your answer to your conception of the "national interest"?
2. Do you accept Kirkpatrick's statement that "as long as the U.S. was perceived as a virtuous society, policies that enhanced its power were also seen as virtuous"? If not, what qualifications would you make?
3. The author quotes several wholesale condemnations of the United States. Does the use of these quotations strengthen her case against President Carter's policies? Explain.
4. Is it your understanding that "human rights in the Carter version had no specific content"? Explain.
5. Does the author's quotations of President Carter give a complete picture of his attitude toward the Soviet Union? Cite examples.

# 6
# America's Liberal Tradition

## Charles William Maynes

This article originally appeared in *Commentary*, November 1981.

*Taking issue with Jeane Kirkpatrick (see preceding article), Charles William Maynes, editor of* Foreign Policy *magazine, argues for a liberal American tradition that guides its foreign policy even when conservatives are in power. Without claiming that the U.S. has always conducted policy in a liberal way, he asserts that "a foreign policy that is in flagrant conflict with that policy is in trouble." Even conservatives, he says, acknowledge the liberal tradition by contending that, if we do not press too hard on authoritarian regimes, they will "evolve in a democratic direction."*

*In the short run, the author admits that emphasis on human rights can hurt U.S. national interests, as occurred in Turkey and Argentina. But he doubts that the American people, with its free press, would indefinitely tolerate a Realpolitik that respects only power and ignores basic morality. Whereas Kirkpatrick keeps power and morality at arm's length (as representing different categories of reality) Maynes sees them deeply interrelated at every stage of the process. "Foreign policy," as he conceives it, "is basically the effort to manage the resulting tension between short-run policy needs (pragmatism) and long-run policy preferences (American values)."*

*Maynes refuses to draw a sharp distinction between authoritarian and totalitarian governments in terms of their evolutionary possibilities, the severity of their repression and the differences between regimes under each label. "(M)ust (we) place Yugoslavia and North Korea in the same pigeonhole?" he asks.*

*The author also asks whether right-wing dictatorships always serve U.S. interests better than left-wing dictatorships. He gives the Somoza government as a case in point. In wartime, he remarks that countries cannot be overly choosy about their allies, but he denies that the U.S. is at war with the U.S.S.R., as we were with Nazi Germany. Maynes acknowledges the "severe challenge to American interests" presented by the Soviet Union. But he is hopeful that "through logic, diplomacy and appeals to common interest catastrophe could be avoided." Supporters of the*

*Reagan Administration who concentrate exclusively on "the present danger" would have the U.S. court South Africa and embrace reaction in Central America, he says. This, in his opinion, will not be accepted by the American people in the long run because they "remain adherents to the liberal tradition."*

Much of the angry debate over U.S. human-rights policy overlooks one obdurate fact: America is a liberal country. It is not liberal in the sense that conservatives always lose elections. Numerous elections, including those in 1980, have shown that to be false. America is liberal in the sense that even conservative administrations are under pressure to pursue liberal political values.

America's behavior throughout the 20th century demonstrates just how strong the American liberal tradition is. Repeatedly, the country has been willing to sacrifice quite concrete commercial or security interests in order to respond to its liberal tradition. In 1911, when big business dominated American political life in a way it has seldom done since, the United States nonetheless abrogated its commercial treaty with Czarist Russia because of American outrage over the regime's treatment of its Jewish population. In the early 1920's, the vehemently anti-Communist Harding administration undertook a massive food program to feed the starving Russian people even though that move helped to save the new and hated Bolshevik regime. Under President Carter, although the U.S. relationship with Vietnam was one of intense hostility, the United States provided food to millions of starving Cambodians, a step that meant propping up the Vietnamese-supported puppet regime in Phnom Penh.

The existence of the liberal tradition does not mean that the U.S. always has liberal policies. It does mean that a foreign policy that is in flagrant conflict with that tradition is in trouble. The Reagan administration has recognized this point by shifting its stance on human rights. Although it earlier attempted to draw a distinction between human-rights abuses committed by authoritarian regimes and those committed by totalitarian regimes, it now contends it will have a single standard for all countries.

In short, the American liberal tradition of interest in the human rights of others is deeply rooted in the American body politic. It has manifested itself repeatedly throughout our history in both Republican and Democratic administrations. It is in this regard that Americans—whether conservative or radical—are in the end liberal.

Even the heated debates over the U.S. human-rights policy that have taken place in *Commentary* are a tribute to the strength of the U.S. liberal tradition. Many of *Commentary*'s authors want policy results different from those suggested by that tradition. But they are reluctant to call openly for a departure from that tradition. To defend unpopular recommendations, they are forced to argue counter-intuitively that in the Third World the best way to pursue democratic liberties is not to strike out for them directly but to support authoritarian regimes that allegedly will evolve in a democratic direction. Even if the immediate policy recommended violates the American liberal tradition, in other words, the underlying message is that the final result will conform to that liberal tradition.

The traditional American attitude toward human rights has acquired a new contemporary potency, however. The reason is modern-day ethnic politics. Today there is scarcely a nation on earth without some of its citizens or their descendants living in the United States. And in our system of government, with its checks and balances and with the unique power our Congress enjoys in the field of foreign policy, the more significant groups have had and will continue to have a major voice in the development of American foreign policy. In particular, they will be very concerned about the degree of political and economic welfare of their former countrymen or co-religionists. Inevitably, they will seize on the emotive power of the American liberal tradition and its support for democracy and the human rights that flow from that system of government to buttress their concern. Convincing other Americans that the issue is not simply a form of tribal loyalty to Israel or Cyprus or black South Africans but a form of liberal concern for democracy, self-determination, or common decency can only broaden the base of national support.

Can this approach lead to a conflict with U.S. national interest? The answer depends on the time-frame through which one is viewing the national interest. Certainly in the short run the conflict can be severe. The U.S. concern with human rights in the Soviet Union has troubled sensitive negotiations with that country in recent years. When non-Jewish Americans have based their support for Israel on the issue of self-determination and democracy, U.S. relations with oil-producing Arab states have been affected. Relations with South Africa have become increasingly strained because of U.S. attitudes toward the inhumane treatment of blacks in that country. Our bases in Turkey were closed down temporarily because we opposed Turkish suppression of self-determination in democratic Cyprus. Our influence with Argentina has fallen because of opposition to government-sanctioned slaughter of dissidents, real and imagined, in that country.

But those who shake their heads at this price in the American approach to foreign policy should ask themselves: what kind of foreign policy would we end up with over the long run if we were to follow the approach of clear-headed *Realpolitik* they advocate? Isn't our aim a policy that serves our interests and that commands popular support? And in that regard can one imagine the American people over the long run ever supporting a policy toward the Soviet Union that overlooks completely the fate of communities inside the Soviet Union that have so many ties to communities inside the United States? As long as we have a free press, could a policy of *Realpolitik* toward South Africa or Guatemala long survive the continued shocks of the expose of one human-rights outrage after another? Could any relationship with the Arab world be healthy that did not reflect the strong American support for a Jewish people expressing its democratic right of self-determination?

The reality for American foreign-policy "realists" is that their fellow citizens will not support a foreign policy over the long run that offends too frontally the American liberal tradition. Indeed, this is why the Begin government's attitude toward the Palestinians is so critical. For it is not clear that the traditionally warm relationship between the United States and Israel can survive the incorporation into Israel proper of the West Bank, with permanent political repression or expulsion of the Arab majority living there.

Given the American attitude, how should the U.S. handle the hard realities of international politics? In the short run the U.S. should deal on a pragmatic basis with both totalitarian and authoritarian regimes to protect U.S. security and welfare. It should buy key minerals from authoritarian South Africa. It should assist totalitarian China, at least with economic aid, to stand up to the Soviet Union. But over the long run it must be opposed to the political system of both authoritarian and totalitarian regimes, and it should not hesitate to say so. Our people will reject any short-run policy that ignores this long-run American preference. Foreign policy is basically the effort to manage the resulting tension between short-run policy needs and long-run policy preferences.

This observation about tension in any foreign policy is relevant to the contention that somehow authoritarian governments are better than totalitarian governments. Viewed closely, some of the distinctions drawn between the two seem weak at best. For example, it is not at all clear that one is more likely than the other to evolve in directions that we would like to see. There have been repeated efforts to gain political freedom in totalitarian Eastern Europe. Is it not likely that one day they will succeed? Would they not have succeeded already except for the intervention of the Soviet army, which may not be able to move so easily into non-contiguous areas?

Nor are all totalitarian states always more bloody than all authoritarian states. Few places have been more bloody than Guatemala in recent years.

Another major problem with the asserted distinction between

authoritarianism and totalitarianism is that both labels cover too vast a spectrum of countries to be meaningful. Is Mexico, authoritarian but relatively benign, to be placed in the same category as authoritarian El Salvador, in which political opponents are hunted down like some tagged member of the animal kingdom? If we accept, as many who draw this distinction do but I would not, that Communist states cannot change and remain forever totalitarian, then are we comfortable with the fact that we must place Yugoslavia and North Korea in the same pigeonhole? If we are forced to group such wildly different countries under the two labels, is the distinction not useless for policy purposes?

Nor is it always true—certainly in the longer run—that right-wing dictatorships serve U.S. interests better than left-wing dictatorships. Did Somoza of Nicaragua serve U.S. interests? As a right-wing foreign minister from a major Latin American country once explained to the Carter administration, Somoza's main achievement was to develop a plantation and to lose a country.

There is, however, one condition under which the distinction between authoritarianism and totalitarianism might acquire new significance, or at least be viewed in a new light. Suppose that the United States were now effectively at war with the Soviet Union. In wartime a country cannot always be overly selective in its choice of allies. Survival becomes the key issue and at virtually any price. Finland, after the Soviet attack in 1939, later accepted the support of Nazi Germany in an attempt to regain its territory. The Western allies did not hesitate to join hands with Stalin, a dictator of comparable moral degradation, in their effort to crush Hitler.

Are we at war? Some, including the editor of *Commentary*, Norman Podhoretz, in effect argue that we are. The Soviet Union is seen as "exactly" like Nazi Germany. It is seen as posing precisely the same kind of threat to American security and welfare. Whether intended or not, the equation of the Soviet Union with Nazi Germany is incendiary in its policy implications. Given our collective memory of World War II and the lessons we all believe we learned from the history of the 1930's, the evocation of Nazi Germany can only suggest inevitable and fairly immediate conflict. Negotiations begin to seem foolish. Even preemptive war might be in order. We would not want to make the mistake we made in the 1930's of letting the aggressor power choose the time and place of the inevitable attack. In any event, we should join with any allies we can find in combating this new menace, whose appetite, like that of Nazi Germany, cannot be sated. Against such a threat, some would also take action at home. The new chairman of the Senate Judiciary Committee has stated that Senator Joseph McCarthy was doing the right thing, only in the wrong way.

Few would deny that the Soviet Union poses a severe challenge to

American interests worldwide. Indeed, were the Soviet Union to invade Poland, the international situation would begin to resemble the summer of 1914 in its tensions and dangers. Vigorous military and diplomatic measures would become even more pressing than they are now. But even viewing the Soviet Union today in the way the rest of Europe viewed Imperial Germany in the summer of 1914 is very different from viewing the Soviet Union as the modern-day equivalent of Nazi Germany. In the former case, there could still remain some hope that through logic, diplomacy, and appeals to common interest catastrophe could be avoided. The margin of maneuver would be small but it would still allow some room for attention to be given to longer-run considerations. In the latter case, the margin for maneuver disappears altogether. The only value is survival, and the sole test of a foreign-policy relationship is whether it contributes to the pressing goal of survival.

Among the prominent supporters of the Reagan administration there are some who do see American options in the single blinding light of "the present danger" that now transfixes many of the contributors to *Commentary* in its high beam. These supporters would drive the administration to court South Africa, to embrace reaction in Central America, and to condone human-rights abuses so long as they are committed by our friends. They might even nod their heads approvingly when *New York Times* columnist William Safire writes: "What is 'winning' [in El Salvador]? Is it a military junta that kills the opposition but by its repressive nature produces more opposition that it becomes necessary to kill? If need be, yes—considering the aggressive totalitarian alternative. . . . "

The problem for those who espouse such a policy is that their fellow citizens will not accept it. The American people remain adherents to the liberal tradition. They fear the Soviet Union but they are not so terrified that they are willing to abandon long-standing American values. For that reason they have already rejected decisively the administration's initial hard-line and callous policy toward El Salvador. They will reject similar policies elsewhere. The Reagan administration would save itself much political gain if it acknowledged that there are some things that it cannot change and one of them is the basic liberal character of the country it governs.

*Questions*

1. How has the emergence of "modern-day ethnic politics" influenced American foreign policy? Is this good or bad for the national interest? Make any necessary distinctions in your answer.

2. Do you feel with the author that, in the long term, the American people

will not tolerate support for repressive regimes? Explain, giving examples.

3. Are the differences between totalitarian regimes so great as to rule out any consistent U.S. policy toward them? Give examples. Do the same in regard to authoritarian regimes.

4. Should the West view the Soviet Union today as comparable to Germany in 1939 or Germany in 1914? What are the differences, and what policy choices exist between the two situations?

5. The author appeals to the American people as the ultimate arbitrators of political morality. Is there another way to view the source of morality? Explain.

# 7
# Can Peace Be Imagined?

## Elise Boulding

This article originally appeared in *Peace: Meanings, Politics, Strategies.* ed. Linda
Rennie Forcey, Praeger, 1989.

---

*Elise Boulding is one of the founders of peace studies in the United
States. As far back as the 1960s, she combined her peace education and
activism with a serious look at "utopian imagery." This is based on her
conviction that peace cannot be achieved unless people can conceive of
what a world without war would—or should—be like.*

*Boulding, Professor Emerita of Dartmouth College, recalls her
optimistic imaging of the future some thirty years ago. Her viewpoint
is more sober today. In contrast with the past, she found that even
peace activists are doing their work more out of obligation than conviction that a warless world would ever come about. This weakening
of the imagination she attributes to a pervasive technological outlook.*

*Technology, which was designed to free people of burdensome
tasks so that they could think, has resulted in depriving many students
of the capacity to imagine new things—among them, a different
world. Fear, she believes, "produces behavioral rigidity and freezes
the imagination."*

*Instead of computer literacy, she advocates something more vital
—image literacy. Through workshops with Warren Ziegler, a futurist, Boulding assists participants to suspend disbelief and see "with
the inward eye." The result has been a growth in conviction that
peace is possible. By pooling their images of the future with others,
people can gain a collective sense of what is possible.*

*To enhance her "peaceful futurism," Boulding draws on the in-
sights of "The South," countries outside the orbit of Europe and
North America. Optimist that she is, Boulding finds that imagination
has not been destroyed in her contemporaries, only weakened. She
cites the growth of mediation efforts in recent years as proof that
non-violent solutions can be found.*

It was over thirty years ago that Fred Polak wrote his *Image of the
Future*[1] to lament the decline in the ability of the western world to

377

picture a peaceful and better future after the crushing experiences of World War II. It was his contrasting of the immobilizing pessimism of this postwar era with the extraordinarily creative futures-imaging that had been going on from the Renaissance to the Enlightenment, and which had in fact produced the industrial society and the welfare state, which led me to the study of futurism and its relationship to peace in our times.

## THE SIGNIFICANCE OF UTOPIAN IMAGERY

In my first survey of futurism in the 1960s, I divided futurists into (1) social planners/systems designers, brainstormers, and technocratic futurists on the one hand and (2) humanist, participatory, evolutionist, ecological/revolutionary futurists on the other.[2] I dismissed the technocratic futurists as operating within too narrow a frame, both temporally and spatially; the technocrats were projecting western-style development step by step into the global future with no account taken of other civilizational traditions. By contrast I saw signs of thinking in a wider planetary frame of reference among the evolutionary/ecological/revolutionary futurists, with hints of transcendance and societal transformation here and there. Optimism, I noted, rode high in both camps.

Now we are on the verge of the 1990s, on a militarized planet with a life-destroying nuclear holocaust on everyone's mind. The social terrain is strewn with failed liberation movements, domestically and internationally, and the gap between the rich and the poor is wider than ever. The facile optimism of both the technocratic and the evolutionary futurists rings a bit hollow. As my own work has come to focus more and more on possible alternative social orders, I find that the *act* of generating imagery about alternatives, which I took for granted in the 1960s, is now in itself problematic. Why, with all the energy that has gone into peace and social change movements over the past few decades, do we edge steadily closer to the nuclear abyss? I am not exactly sure when it began to dawn on me that most of the peace movement activists I knew, from arms controllers to out-and-out disarmers, did not in their hearts believe that a world without armies was possible. They were working for goals they did not believe were achievable, but they were working for them anyway, because the situation was too dangerous for inaction. Something had to be *done*, but that something was unaccompanied by any mental images of what a successful outcome might be like. Having, in the meantime, satisfied myself through a brief investigation of utopian imagery in other civilizational traditions that an inclination to visualize one's own society in a future peaceable state was testified to in the literary and oral traditions of every major culture,[3] I had to ask why that kind of mental picturing was not going on in our own time. I discovered through intergenerational interviewing,[4] that people born in the first two decades of this century were still doing that kind of picturing, but that it became progressively rarer for more recent generations.

There is of course no simple causal explanation for this state of affairs. Many different strands of culture, science, and technology have helped weaken the social imagination. I have become increasingly convinced, however, that we suffer from an experience deprivation which leads to image deprivation. We who live in the priviledged sectors of the industrialized world, both East and West, inhabit a technological shell that intervenes between us and the actual experience of the physico-social environment in which we live. We interpret the social order in terms of Comtean[5] and Spencerian[6] concepts of successive stages in human development, from tribal to military to industrial, in the largely unquestioned conviction that our particular industrial developmental sequence represents the leading edge, in the Teilhardian sense, of the next development in the species.[7] A fascination with technological mastery of the environment has led many to equate technological mastery with human development. This has produced ways of life insulated from the cycles, ebbs, and flows of the organic surround and the organism within. It is because all social problems are seen as having technological solutions, that industrial societies, East and West, have come to depend on high-tech weapons systems to protect them from having to interact in problem-solving ways with adversaries.

## THE CENTRALIZATION OF DECISION-MAKING

Nowhere has the effect of the technological-fix approach been felt more pervasively than in the educational systems of industrial societies. The same numeracy, letter, and design literacy which provided the tools for the development of the industrial revolution have gradually been harnessed to a kind of product-oriented mental activity, which has left little room for the mental playfulness that has characterized all great civilizational flowerings. Children don't even have to be scolded for daydreaming any more. They move between the two worlds of ready-made imagery-the TV at home, and the computer at school. All reality is on the screens. In front of the TV, one simply absorbs it. In front of the computer, one *makes* it, omnipotently, by manipulating figures and numbers. War games assure us that this kind of training for young children will ensure rational thinking (presumably the kind of rational thinking of which the wargamers themselves are masters). Very little information is stored in the mind, to be played within a process well known to oral tradition societies. Why bother, when it can be so easily accessed on the computer?

As decision making becomes increasingly centralized for efficiency, we are moving toward more and more decision making based on highly schematic computer-screen representations of reality, more and more divorced from the on-the-ground reality of human life in specific local environments. Thus, what began as a movement to free the human mind from the negative constraints of hunger and excessive physical labor has ended by equipping the mind with ever more abstracted representations of reality, and emptying it of concrete local experience outside the office and the laboratory. In short, young people grow up with fewer and fewer opportunities to *exercise* their imaginations on their own. The situation is compounded by a pervasive social fear of the threat of violence, which affects the behavior of adults and children alike. There is violence not only in urban areas, but also in small communities and within households. Behind all other fears lurks the fear of nuclear winter and an end to all life. One indisputable finding of behavioral science is that fear produces behavioral rigidity and freezes the imagination.

To talk of cultivating the social imagination in a society which relies on technological solutions, and is cramped by fear, may sound wildly unrealistic. Nevertheless, Polak's formulation boiled down to its simplest version, that people are empowered to action by their own sense of the possible and desired other, carries even more weight today than when he first proposed it in the early 1950s. It has been empirically demonstrated in all sorts of experiments that people with the same capacities, but with different aspiration levels, perform according to their aspiration levels, not according to their capacities. While there are plenty of successful individual achievers in the "me" generation, the absence of aspiration for the society as a whole, for the planet as a whole, condemns humanity to a sorry performance in terms of human welfare. Polak assumed that if people were told of the importance of imaging the social future, they would do it. He correctly predicted that technological futurists would not be much help because they were not able to make the mental leaps necessary to make what he called a breach in time, into a sense of the other, so powerful that it could act on the present. Why have not the evolutionary futurists (the contemporaries he was really addressing) been able to generate the kind of vibrant, liberating imagery that makes for sustained society-wide action in a new direction over time?

Of course, we are looking at a very short time span, from the 1960s to the 1980s, and social change needs time. However, it is also true that many major social changes have taken place within twenty-year spans. The twenty-year period from 1945 to 1965 saw the addition of about fifty new independent nations to the international system, forever changing its character. The almost fifty additional nations added over the next twenty years has only increased the momentum of international change begun in 1945. I will return to this subject again, because embedded in that phenomenon lie many of the raw materials for futures imaging neglected by the countries of the North. For the moment, it is enough to point out that during this change-rich period, the United States has moved away from the early twentieth-century American Dream of economic and social well-being for all, to fears of armageddon. One of the most determined efforts to avert armageddon, the nuclear freeze movement, is characterized by an absence of imagery about what a post-freeze world could be like.

Who could now turn the tide? Not the aquarians, because they counted on a kind of inevitable social transformationism, sparked by key individual transformers networking with one another. Not the revolutionaries either, because they counted on an equally inevitable political kind of transformationism. The environmentalists have probably provided the strongest impulse for turnaround and social change, because they have the kind of on-the-ground knowledge of the world as it is, and mental pictures of how it could be, that can fire social action. The fact that environmentalists have now joined forces with the peace movement based on a common reaction against the threat of nuclear winter is one of hope to the futurist field. The social evolutionists continue to be front-line imagers, keeping the concept of the future alive. While they cheer up people with their macrohistorical views (no small thing in bleak times) it is hard to translate evolutionary concepts into action-inspiring, concrete social imagery for the public at large.

Surveying the present scene, I see futurists facing a primary challenge of cultivating the social imagination of the post-World War II generations, so individuals can experience hitherto longed-for but not-believed-in possibilities in their own minds, and, thus, be empowered to actions on behalf of those imaged possibilities. Because our own social and educational environment works against this kind of imagery, it has to be taught as a kind of literacy-image literacy.

## IMAGE LITERACY

The person who invented the concept of image literacy is Warren Ziegler,[8] of Futures Invention Associates. Ziegler and I got together several years ago to try to apply his workshop technique of community problem-solving to the macroproblem of the global arms race through imagining what things would be like if a given problem were solved. Since the problem was so much larger in scale than the local problems Ziegler usually dealt with, and visualizing a weapon-free world within the short time span (two decades) required for an appropriate sense of immediacy seemed to require such an overwhelming suspension of disbelief, we were not sure the process could work for imaging within whole social order. While there has been no lack of problems connected with effective workshop development, we were both taken by surprise by the powerful emotional reactions of the majority of people who went through the workshop experience. Even though their imagery of a world without weapons was fragmentary at best, what they saw "with the inward eye" was so compellingly real to them, that they developed convictions about the viability of successful arms reduction that changed their attitudes toward their activity in the present. Some saw new activity directions they had not thought of before, others saw increasing relevance to what they were already doing. With very few exceptions, participants were galvanized by a new sense of the possible in a venture that earlier had looked hopeless.

What is the imaging process that can galvanize people in this way? For many people, it is very difficult to begin imagining in a fantasy mode that is at the same time guided by a certain level of intentionality within the imager. They can daydream and they can use their intellects to make rational scenarios, but they can't easily step into a future world and *see* something. That is precisely what image literacy is about. It is *not* precognition or prediction, and it is *not* simple personal wish-fulfillment. The individual draws on the entire coded store of what has been heard, read, seen, felt, smelled, tasted, and thought, from the womb to the present, in a relaxed free-floating manner, on the other side of a breach in time, to discover what a world would look like with no weapons in it. Getting through the breach in time, liberating the store of impressions in the subconscious, so imagery can form, and letting the *intention* to see that world act as monitor over the imagery, is not easy.[9] For a few, despair prevents the liberation of imagery, or will let only demonic imagery through. These workshops are not for them. However, workshops designed precisely to deal with despair, such as Joanna Macy's Despair and Empowerment workshops,[10] can bring the despairing to the point where they can recover their own capacity to image the good. Most people can find a way through the breach in time to a world, but they need a little help to get started. Every time I conduct a workshop, I learn something new about how to help people into the process. I have also learned humility through the helping role, because, often, would-be imagers can help each other better than a workshop leader can help them.

Of course, the images are of special settings, people doing specific things. The social order, as such, cannot be visualized because it is an abstraction. The important thing is that participants experience in their imaginations some fragments of social life unrelated to anything they now know (though, of course, all imagery is a mosaic of their own store of past impressions), and perceive clues as to how things might be. These image fragments, developed in the fantasy mode, are the raw materials for the more intellectual task of constructing a coherent social order into which the fragments can fit. Since any one individual's image fragments may be too few for the entire construction process, the pooling of individual imagery is very important. Image fragments from different people may contradict each other, so the pooling process is a complex one. I always point out that contradictions and conflicts are at the core of human experience in society, and that a world without weapons would continue to contain contradictions and conflicts. Over time (a serious workshop needs several days to work this out properly), a group is able to work out the implications of their image fragments by constructing a social order that appears to be viable, sustainable, and weapon-free. The most important thing is that it is a world they would like to work toward, and one they would like to live in.

The point of imaging the future is, of course, action in the present. So an important part of these workshops involves returning to the fantasy mode, going back through the breach in time, and remembering from that future world "how it all happened." This is accomplished in five year periods, working from the future back to the present. In the course of these "rememberings," categories of events and actors emerge that one would not necessarily think of while working forward in a planning mode. The final part of the workshop is an analysis of one's own life spaces in the present, in order to determine options for actions in those spaces in the light of the recently visualized future. Obviously, very few people are ever going to participate in imaging workshops. What is interesting is that the very concept of the process of imaging a world without weapons seems to empower people. They may go ahead and do it on their own, which is precisely the way imaging the future has worked over the millennia. What people need today is encouragement for this type of activity, and a removal of opprobrium from the word *utopian*.

So far we have been considering the imaging capacity of the West. If I had written the 1960s assessment in today's language, it would have been entitled the imaging capacity of the North. Although East-West confrontation in the North is so serious that the threat of nuclear winter comes almost entirely from it, both parties to that confrontation are northern industrial societies. Marx and Keynes are both thinkers from the North. In fact, within the working structures of the United Nations, an East-West division does not exist. The ECE (Economic Commission for Europe), established in 1946, includes *all* of Europe and North America in one administrative structure. Both superpower blocs are heirs to the same Greek-Roman-Byzantine traditions. Except for China's role, the major ideological struggles in this century have been among the sister-nations of the North.

All the oldest civilizational traditions on the planet come from the South. All the newly independent nations, from 1946 to the present, are in the South. Most of the new thinking about a new international order, in its many dimensions of economic order, information, culture and security, has been initiated from the South, from ancient cultures progressively impoverished by the "old economic order"— the industrial order created in the North. The first public articulation of the new order came in 1974, when the "Group of 77" (now comprising 118 nations) gained adoption in the United Nations General Assembly under the Program of Action on the Establishment of a New International Economic Order. Since that time there has been a series of international commissions consisting of scholars and leaders from the North (both Eastern and Western blocs), and from the South, to spell out the meaning of each dimension of the new order, to set goals, and to propose mechanisms.[11] Instead of welcoming this opportunity for dialogue with the South to draw on fresh sources of insight and new cultural resources to deal with increasingly pressing world problems, the North has retreated into an aggressive, hostile posture towards anything that hints of new orders. Most of my colleagues in the

United States do not understand, for example, what the new information order is all about. They are convinced that it has to do with a plot to curtail freedom of the press. They have not read the United Nations documents, and writings from the South, about this order.[12] If they had, they would have learned that is has to do with a free information flow concept, applied to the South as well as to the North. It provides for many different source points for information around the globe to replace an information order controlled by the superior communication resources of the North (with source points chiefly in the North).

It is no longer appropriate to treat the imaging capacity of the North (read old West) as a separate resource for human development on the planet, any more than it is appropriate to treat the interests of the North as a set of interests worthy of priority attention in the world. It is true that futurists of the North use the language of globalism a lot more frequently, but it is globalism with a strong northern accent. The emergence of a viable concept of world interest to replace the national or regional interest of Northern countries can come about only through dialogue with the South. Futurists who romanticize the wisdom of the East are not contributing to this dialogue because they are responding to stereotypes, instead of listening to what is being said by the "Group of 77," or by the growing group of nonaligned nations (100 now), who cry to the North, "a plague on both your houses."[13] The images of the future now being generated in the South need to be studied, discussed, and worked over, in a situation of equal dialogue rather than one of condescending interest. Bioregionalism, one of the most promising concepts to come out of ecological futurism, draws heavily on the so-called traditional knowledge of the South in its approach to interdependent self-sufficiency.[14] Because bioregionalism (though not by that name) emerged so often in the imagery of middle-class Americans visualizing a demilitarized world in imaging workshops, it would seem to be a particularly useful bridging concept for North-South dialogue.

When I think back to the 1960s and its can-do optimism, I realize that I vastly underestimated the power of the warrior culture over the human mind, and how this would affect our capacity to image peace in the twentieth century. It is true that every traditional civilization had images of peace in the background, while nations fought their wars. The vision of Zion, where the lion lay down with the lamb and a little child could walk unafraid between them, coexisted with the concept of the holy war, fought with the deity at one's side. In eras of hand-to-hand combat, neither image destroyed the other. In an era when battles are fought on computer screens, Zion fades, because it depends on the experience of *relationship*. War thrives because it depends on non-relationship. In the media, battle imagery has replaced the imagery of peace. Battle imagery is used to make and sell children's toys, to sell clothes (look at a Sears Roebuck catalogue), to sell lifestyles, and to make points in debates. We use battle imagery frequently in ordinary conversations. The man on horseback, who down through the centuries has brandished his sword to defend his people, is now deep in the minds of every man, woman and child, even though we have developed social know-how which should have made him obsolete.

Reconstructing the imagery of societies at peace, at a time when that imagery is disappearing from our culture, will be a very difficult thing to do. Polak thought in the 1950s that it was only necessary to remind people for them to begin to image again. It is now clear that we have some serious work to do with the archetypes within, with the deep structures of the mind that give insidious permission for domination and conquest, if we are to be able to produce imagery that corresponds to our own conscious intentionality, and our wishes for a continued flowering of the human species. I am not proposing a primary focus on an inward journey. Within and without are one. The inward potential, and the outward act, are the two faces of humanity, and they both come to fruition in relationship with other humans, and in relationship with the state of being. I take great comfort from the fact that "mediation" is presently the fastest growing profession in the United States. Mediation is a highly intentional, listening form of relationship that enhances the well-being of all who participate in it, and it thrives on imagery of the "other," the new solution, that which did not exist before. It may seem like an odd source for the reconstruction of imaging capacity, but it is in odd places that we must look. We will not find it on TV screens.

It is clear to me that the human capacity for imaging the good society is not lost, only weakened. It can be nurtured back to vigorousness, liveliness. Vigor in imagery leads to vigor in social action. All human beings have known times of individual despair, times during which they have had to "walk through to the other side" to begin life again. This is a time in human society when we must all help each other walk through the social despair. Retrieving and reiterating messages about the more humane social order we see on the other side is one of the most important things any of us can do.

## IMAGING A WORLD WITHOUT WEAPONS: WORKSHOP PROCEDURES[15]

### *The Goal Statement*

Because the individual's hopes, wishes, and intentions for the future are so important in directing the imaging, the first task in the workshop is to write out a goal statement about what you would like to see achieved in the social order three decades from now—not goals for your personal life, but for society. The goal statement should, by workshop definition, be compatible with an arms-free world. Note that the future moment chosen is 30 years hence. This is far enough into the future for substantial changes to have taken place. Yet it is close enough to the present that many of you will still be alive and, thus, can feel a personal stake in this future.

Giving yourself permission to state what you would like to see achieved in the future rather than what can realistically be expected is generally very difficult. We have all been taught to set a high premium on being realistic. This exercise requires a deliberate setting aside of ordinary notions of the possible, and focusing primarily on hopes and wishes. The effort can be treated as a conscious act of disciplining the mind to ignore what it "knows" about reality constraints in the social order.

### *Childhood Memories*

This exercise is intended to free up your imaging capacity by having you step into remembered images of the past, in order to experience the type of imaging you will be doing when you move into the future.

### *Moving into the Future*

It is the responsibility of the workshop leader to help participants move through the barrier separating the present—present from the future—present. Some can do it easily, for others, it takes longer. An exploratory trip then a brief return to the present to discuss how it is working is provided for, followed by a twenty-minute to half-hour stay in the future, observing and recording.

### *Clarification*

The experienced imagery becomes clarified through explaining it to others. At this point, more can be added to the imagery as each of you checks forward mentally to the future, in response to questions from within the small group in which the clarification takes place.

## Consequence Mapping and World Construction

Given what you have seen in your explorations of the future-present moment, what kind of world is it? How is it ordered, what institutions function and how? Particularly, how is conflict managed? What has been seen in the imaged visit to the future must now be treated as a set of indicators of the condition of that world. These indicators must now be treated analytically to construct the social order they point toward. This is first an individual exercise, although carried out in 2- or 3-person groups. Once each group has *their* individual images clear, then larger groups are formed based on common themes. Contrasting or conflicting imagery among participants is a problem that must be dealt with just as it is in the real world of conflicting perceptions—by negotiation. This world construction is transferred to newsprint, using pictures and/or diagrams, and schematic representations, to indicate how the social order functions. Since the whole social order can not realistically be accounted for in the time available, each group will choose themes based on its own initial input of image fragments, and develop them more fully on the newsprint.

## Futures History

Standing in the future—present moment and looking into the past, you will individually remember how the world got to its future—present state. You will work back from the future to the past of 30 years ago in five-year periods. For some of you, watershed events will appear, others will remember a gradual change. This exercise should also be repeated within the "World Construction" teams, going through the process of negotiating conflicting historical "memories."

## Action Planning in the Present

The pictured future and the remembered events leading up to it now become the basis for short-term action planning in the present, and long-term strategizing about the future. The difference between the planning and strategizing we normally do, and the same activities in this context, is that we now have in a certain sense experienced the future reality of what is being planned. This gives the wished-for future a quality of thereness, of authenticity in relation to the human possibility, which adds new dimensions to practical reality-testing in the present.

## Notes

1. Fred Polak, *Image of the Future,* vols. trans. by Elise Boulding (New York: Oceana Press, 1961); Trans. from *Toekomst is Verleden Tyd* (Utrecht, 1955); also one-vol. abr. by Elise Boulding (San Francisco: Jossey-Bass, Elsevier, 1972).

2. Elise Boulding, "Futuristics and the Imaging Capacity of the West," in *Human Futuristis,* ed. by Magorah Maruyama and James A. Dator (Honolulu: University of Hawaii, Social Science Research Institute, 1971); Repr. in *World Futures Society. Bulletin,* v. 3, no. 12 (December, 1970); also in *Cultures of the Future,* ed. by Majorah Maruyama (Germany: Mouton, 1978).

3. Elise Boulding, "A Disarmed World: Problems in Imaging the Future," *Journal of Sociology and Social Welfare,* v. 4, no. 3/4 (1977): 656–658.

4. Elise Boulding, Evolutionary Visions, Sociology and the Human Life Span," in *The Evolutionary Vision,* ed. by Erich Jantsch (Boulder, Colo.: Westview Press, 1981).

5. Auguste Comte, *Cours de philosophie positive,* tome VI (Paris: Schlacher, 1908).

6. Herbert Spencer, *Principles of Sociology* (New York: Appleton, 1986).

7. Pierre Teilhard de Chardin, *The Future of Man,* tr. by Norman Deumy (New York: Harper & Row, 1964).

8. Warren Ziegler, "Planning as Action: Techniques of Inventive Planning Workshops," in *Participatory Planning in Education* (Paris: OECD, 1974).

9. It should be pointed out that imaging itself is a neutral process and can be used to image the "bad" as well as the "good." That is why intentionality is stressed.

10. Joanna Macy, *Despair and Personal Power in the Nuclear Age* (Philadelphia: New Society Publishers, 1983).

11. The following are examples: *North-South: A Programme for Survival,* Willy Brandt, Commission Chair (London: Pan Books, 1980); *Common Crises North-South: Cooperation for World Recovery,* Willy Brandt, Commission Chair (London: Pan Books, 1983); *Many Voices, One World,* Sean McBridge, Commission Chair (Paris: UNESCO, 1980); *Common Security: A Blueprint for Survival,* Olof Palme, Commission Chair (New York: Simon and Schuster, 1982); and Herbert Shore, *Cultural Policy: UNESCO's First Cultural Development Decade* (Washington, D.C.: U.S. National Commission for UNESCO, 1981). Also note the national *Cultural Policies Studies* (Paris: UNESCO, 1975).

12. See, for example, the Development Dialogue issue on *Towards a*

*New World Information and Communication Order* (Paris: UNESCO, 1981:2).

13. Rikhi Jaipal, *Non-Alignment: Origins, Growth and Potential for Peace* (New Delhi: Allied Publishers, n.d.).

14. *Coevolution Quarterly*, special issue on "Bioregions," no. 32 (Winter, 1981).

15. This workshop draws on procedures developed by Warren Ziegler, *Mindbook for Imaging a World Without Weapons* (Denver, Colo.: Ziegler's Futures Invention Associates, 1982), address at 2260 Fairfax, Denver, Colorado, 80207. For information about future workshops and workshop leadership training opportunities, contact Mary Link, Coordinator, World Without Weapons Project, 4722 Baltimore Ave., Philadelphia, PA, 19143. A full version of the workbook will be found in Elise Boulding, *Building a Global Civic Culture: Education for an Interdependent World* (New York: Columbia University, Teachers College Press, 1988).

## Questions

1. Why does the author dismiss the findings of technocratic futurists? Do you agree or disagree? Why?

2. What evidence can you cite of the "technological-fix approach" in your education? In what ways has it helped or impeded your growth in knowledge?

3. Give some reasons for the growing alliance between environmentalists and peace activists.

4. Describe in your own words what the author means by image literacy. Do you think it is important for you as a person to gain this facility? Give your reasons pro or con.

5. Do you find it hard to state the sort of world you want to see in the next thirty to fifty years? Why or why not? How can the educational system help students become more image-literate?

# 8
# Toward a Paradigm of Peace

## Betty A. Reardon

This article originally appeared in *Peace, Meanings, Politics, Strategies*, Praeger, 1989.

*In our present way of thinking, when the lion lies down with the lamb, it is the lamb that gets devoured. Using this biblical metaphor in its original and idealistic sense, the author, who is director of the Peace Education Program at Teachers College, Columbia University, calls for a new way of looking at the world. This she calls a "paradigm of peace."*

*Drawing on feminist studies, Reardon points out how our thinking, our language and our actions reflect a warrior mentality. She says terms such as "fighting for peace" need to be replaced by less violent alternatives such as "struggle," which implies no harm.*

*The author sets forth a vision of peace as one which elicits inquiry, respects diversity, sees the whole and not just the parts, does no harm and affirms the richness of life. To this she opposes the current mode of thinking, which looks for predetermined answers, tends to be reductionist, separates areas of learning, involves conquest and often stresses the negative.*

*As metaphors for peace, Reardon offers the notion of conception, labor, birth and parenting. This way of thinking, she insists, could move us "from a warring society to a parenting or caring society, in which all adults parent the young and care for the vulnerable."*

*By uniting the personal and the political, making means as important as goals and stressing the whole picture instead of concentrating on the parts, Reardon thinks the voyage to the "new world" of peace can be made more easily. Thus, "the lion can lie down with the lamb in a nurturing rather than devouring relationship."*

### PREFACE

There may be no more significant responsibility and challenge to peace studies than the engagement of learners in the search for a new paradigm of peace to replace the present paradigm of war, which delimits all thinking and determines our culture. That search is the

391

great intellectual adventure of our time. This chapter is intended as an initial inquiry into that search.

Three convictions are central to the assertions and arguments to be made. First, there is the fundamental feminist conviction that there is no essential separation between the personal and the political. Nor is there a legitimate basis to separate means from ends. Second, there is the conviction that processes and methods are equally as important as, sometimes more important than, goals. The educational implications of the second conviction produce the third conviction that learning modes must be organically, systematically, intentionally, and ethically related to instructional goals. Both peace studies and peace education will be used in this discussion of paradigm change. The former is used to focus on the substance or subject matter of the field; the latter on the learning and the educational methods.

## TAMING THE LION WITHIN

The perspectives and parameters of my argument are totally congenial to these convictions. Paradigms are perhaps the most important conceptual tools we have and they not only constrain and influence the way we think but also the way we behave, the way we organize our societies, and conduct virtually all human affairs. As a feminist peace educator, I argue that the present paradigm is at once the source and the product of a war system that, for generations, has been transferred from our minds into our experience and from our experience back into our minds. We engage in war and violence because we think violently in images and metaphors of war. If we are to experience an authentic, fulsome peace, we must think peace. If we are to think peace, we need a paradigm of peace. We need not only a vision of peace but also the concepts, the language, the images, and the metaphors that will comprise a functioning and equally vigorous paradigm *of* peace, so that from it we can construct paradigms *for* peace, those explicit conceptual and political models around which we can organize a peaceful society in which we can conduct human affairs in a more humane manner. Searching for and speculating on such language, images, and metaphors is the stuff of which peace studies should be made. These concepts should be about transcending the war paradigm to enable us to think in terms of a peace system. Peace, then, of necessity, must be conceived in dynamic, active, challenging terms. It must provide for us all of that which we have sought in and through war. It must become the means by which human beings strive for the highest achievements, their most transcendent goals.

"Toward," the word with which I began the title, is most important for the purposes of this chapter, for it is a word which connotes process and action as well as thought. It is the notion "toward" which helps to inform these reflections with the sense of dynamism that is so essential to bringing forth a vigorous peace paradigm that can instill vibrant peace images, images of new forms of power and accommodation that contrast sharply with the present concepts of peace and how it might be achieved.

The shapes and tones of such images are vividly expressed in a story by a naval chaplain and fellow peace educator about a Biblical zoo in Israel, in which the various animals mentioned in the Bible were arranged in tableaux, or Biblical images. The most problematic image was the lion lying down with the lamb. The zookeeper was working on this particular tableau during the time when Henry Kissinger was pursuing shuttle diplomacy for peace in the Middle East. "If anyone could give me the secret how this might be done," thought the zookeeper, "it will be Henry Kissinger." Sure enough, the very day after he had the good fortune to encounter Dr. Kissinger, the lion and lamb were lying down together. The next day, they were lying down together, and the next day and the next. One frequenter of the zoo was determined to discover the secret, and when pressed, the zookeeper did confess that the way to accomplish this was to put in a new lamb every morning. The zookeeper had considered a number of alternative structural arrangements to make this possible, but in the end, because the tableau depended on the behavior both of the lion and the lamb, he took a pragmatic political solution. The sacrificial lamb is very much a part of our politics and our paradigm, an image and symbol of peace through propitiation. It is suggested that the only way the lion and lamb image could be realized without continuing to incur a very high cost on the part of the lambs, would be a profound personal change and major paradigm shift, mainly on the part of the lion. In some respects, that is what we must be about in our attempts to construct a peace paradigm. We are about taming the lion in all of us.

Among the changes that have to be made for the achievement of such a shift, the most significant ones are within ourselves. The way in which we move toward these inner changes, the way in which we envision and struggle for peace and try to construct that new paradigm, is the most essential means through which we will be enabled to make the larger structural changes required for a peace system. Thus the journey is really more personally meaningful to us than the destination. What we are about, on a day-to-day basis, is actually how we change paradigms. We must change ourselves and our immediate realities and relationships if we are to change our social structures and our patterns of thought. We've known this for a long time. Shakespeare told us that the fault is not "in our stars, but in ourselves." St. Augustine reflecting on his own journey wrote, "I have sought thee outside and thou were within." His was a long and tortuous route to a new paradigm. A few decades ago, the Cunard Line tried to convince us that in traveling to Europe "getting there was half the fun." However, there are very few passenger ships that cross the Atlantic these days. We prefer to take the rapid route, by plane, to get to our destination, incurring jet lag and many other negative consequences. Paradigm changing is not only a difficult inner struggle, but also a time-consuming journey, so we had better be ready for a long voyage on turbulent waters.

Long voyages on turbulent waters require patience, steadiness, and strong stomachs. The journey toward a new peace paradigm is not likely to be undertaken by the faint of heart. Those who still fear sea monsters, and tremble at the possibility of sailing over the edge of the present paradigm, will certainly not board the good ship "Peace Studies" on its exploratory ventures. We know full well that few came to wave us off and wish us well in those early years when we first hoisted anchor with but a few courses, and only two programs; when we still purposed to know our destination. Indeed, the queen did not pawn her jewelry, nor did foundations offer portions of their coffers to finance the earlier voyages to peacemaking knowledge. Yet, as the statistics indicate, the fleet has grown and we have the feeling that more are now following our route as we traverse the familiar waters of academe in search of a truly new world. If we are to entice even more educators and students into this search for new horizons of thought, the exploration of the terra incognita of a peace paradigm, we will need the equivalents of the maps of the Indies, the products of the imaginations of early global explorers who captured the minds of seamen and monarchs. For those we would have join us on the journey, we need to evoke images of what the new world might be like, and in which directions we should sail to reach it. World order scholars would say we need models of peace systems and transition strategies for the change from a war system to a peace system. We need an image which may well be as Utopian as the lamb lying with the lion, but we also need specific and particular approaches to the learnings, political movements, and personal behaviors which will take us toward our vision.

## CHANGING LANGUAGE, TRANSFORMING IMAGES

Personal and political changes are very much interrelated and both will be the product of learning processes. It is for this reason that peace studies is central to the task, not only of paradigm change, but also in the achievement of structural and systems change in the global order. Peace studies must take on the task of nurturing new modes of thought. We cannot achieve a change unless we can think it. And we cannot rally others to support the changes if we cannot communicate our visions of change to them. Thus we need not only images and maps but also effective and appropriate language. If both the lion and the lamb are to undergo the personal changes that would make a new relationship possible, first they must be able to communicate the changes to each other.

Reflect for a moment on the language we tend to use most, on the shades of violence and combat which color so much of our discourse. Such language even creeps into the literature and discussions of peace studies and the peace movement. We speak of "fighting for peace" and "ammunition for peace makers." Feminist peace research is no exception. I received an interview questionnaire which included the following questions, "What has sustained you so long on the frontlines of the feminist battle?" We need only to monitor ourselves and others for less than a day to see how such language pervades so many of our exchanges, and includes not only the substance of the subject at hand, but also the standards of the war system which we salute constantly in our choice of words and metaphors. Our language and our metaphors reveal just how we think more clearly than our arguments and proposals.

Our thinking, thus, is frighteningly combative and antagonistic, a fact which has been at the core of much feminist criticism of our culture and scholarship. If we do wish to journey toward the peace paradigm, would it not at least be worth the attempt to change our language as a step toward changing our thinking? Many have conceded the significance of language as the reinforcement of racism and sexism. Can we not admit the same of militarism and the peace system? Would it not be more productive to try consciously to substitute alternatives for combative and militaristic terms? We might at least become more aware of the concepts that influence our thinking. For example, could we use "struggle" instead of "fight"? "Struggle" does not necessarily require an enemy or adversary, or even an opponent, as does "fight." It connotes vigorous effort to transcend an obstacle, resolve a problem, or bring forth a desired end, none of which calls for harm of others. Indeed, we need to think more in terms of avoidance of harm as a primary criterion for behaviors and policies. To do so is hardly a full commitment to nonviolence, but it can help us become aware of how violence evolves and how it might be limited, if not eliminated. In lieu of "ammunition," we can substitute "nourishment" or "food" or "fuel," something than can convey a source of energy for struggle without carrying along the concept of injury and death. I prefer to think of my involvement in the women's movement as tilling the fields of feminism, attempting to cultivate more humane attitudes and social structures. Can we not think in terms of tools and tasks instead of weapons and battles, nourishment and cultivation in lieu of artillery and victory? As we change our words, we will also begin to change our images, and our metaphors may be transformed as we move from the language of war and death toward one of peace and life. If we speak differently, we can become more intentional about changing how we think and teach.

Using images of cultivation in lieu of those of battle to connote energy concentrated toward the fulfillment of a purpose comes very close to common images of peace often articulated in drawings by children, or the pastoral paintings and poetry of some of the great artists of all cultures and languages. Serious peace people, educators, researchers, and activists, especially the "hard heads" among us, have often cited this type of imagery as evidence of our inability to think in as complex and concrete terms about peace, as about war. This assessment is questionable, although the fundamental assertion of this volume is that our education does not prepare us in any systematic way to think about peace. It is precisely for this reason that these types of images are so significant, for they do demonstrate our capacity to image peace. The thinking which rejects the pastoral as a practical or useful image of peace is the same kind of thinking which permits us, in a manifestation of the peace system, to abuse the environment, which is even more threatening to life on this planet than nuclear weapons and war. That is the same kind of thinking which has, in fact, produced weapons of mass destruction and reinforced the war system. This argument, too, has been a major assertion of feminist critiques of peace research and peace education.[1]

## PEACE AS A DYNAMIC, ORGANIC PROCESS

There are several assumptions and assertions that point to peace as a dynamic, organized process. These assertions pertain to notions of peace, concepts of what peace education is and should do, and concerns about the way the present paradigm impedes the purposes of peace education, and is a virtually insurmountable barrier to peace. So long as this paradigm prevails there will be no authentic peace. We may cease to experience as much organized hostility and armed conflict as we presently do but at best, any peace we experience will be truly negative, for it will be nothing more than the kind of peace which oppresses not only women, as Christine Sylvester points out, but any who are vulnerable, less powerful, or "lamblike." Such is indeed the case in areas of the world where there is no serious armed conflict, but structural violence is most evident. We might cite Brazil or Korea as examples of such peace.

There are perhaps as many reasonable and useful definitions of peace as there are approaches to peace studies. My own definitions have become more open, wider in scope-an organic concept of peace. As Warren Wagar asserts, "peace is life." If we define peace in its fullest, most varied sense, it reflects pastoral images. If we need to think of peace in structural or political terms, then we may say that peace results from social and economic structures, and public policies which sustain and enhance life; hence, the notion of harm and injury as primary policy making criteria. Admittedly, these are feminine notions, and to some degree "feminist." While such notions are, of course, repressed by patriarchy, they are in no way exclusively female. We need only look to some of the great religious and ethical traditions which were articulated to the world by such male prophets as Gautama Buddha, Jesus Christ, and Mohandas Gandhi to see that these notions are in fact human universals, only now beginning to be seen as new sources of actual as well as spiritual power, power in the positive life enhancing sense of the capacity to realize values and achieve goals. This is in essence the energy source which "inspires" (i.e., breathes life into nonviolence as social action and political mode, demonstrating quite clear that authentic or "organic" peace is an active, dynamic state).

Organic peace is a source of energy for development, the breath of life which impels action. It does not exclude conflict, as is well argued by Dean Pruitt, but it governs and guides it to become a source of growth and change rather than harm and destruction. Organic peace is, above all else complex, as are life processes in general. It is not so easily modeled in static structural terms. While clearly we need the new structures, institutions, and systems emphasized by Warran Wagar, the structural is but one, quite limited dimension of organic peace, which comprises all those social processes and personal behaviors which facilitate change, growth, and fulfillment. Should we achieve peace by the twenty-first century, it will not be the same peace that prevails in the twenty-second century, else it will not be peace. As Tacitus instructed us, peace does not bloom in a desert. Deserts have limited forms of life, fewer varieties of flora and fauna than other natural environments, the richest being the rain forest which, literally, "is crawling with life." The most complex environments are the richest in diversity and are full of life. Yet we have confronted these natural phenomena as we have the questions of human social order. We reduce everything to its simplest, most manageable form. We seek to control and manage life rather than to live it. We have, in fact, not developed that far emotionally from our forebears who cowered in caves in fear of natural phenomena and other life forms. While the sophistication of our means of subjection has become greater with the evolution of modern science, human attempts to subdue, control, and simplify as a means to security may be as old as the species. It is no coincidence that in the process of seeking security through control, we have destroyed many life forms and are to the point of cutting off the very air we breathe through the destruction of the rain forest.

Critics of the present paradigm, such as Douglas Sloan and Jeremy Rifkin, attribute much of the reductionist character of contemporary thought to the initial intellectual separation of philosophy from the sciences.[2] Other critics, particularly of the sciences, see the drive for control of nature as patriarchal, and a primary cause of the evolution of a dehumanized technology which produces nuclear weapons and isolates genetic material.[3] However, this drive would seem to be far more deeply rooted in our history and our psyches than in Cartesian science or even patriarchy. It may be as much a cause as a consequence of patriarchy, other forms of repression, militarism and war itself.

The linear thinking which has been the dominant mode of thinking not only in the sciences but also in all of academe, is the most serious impediment to us who seek peace through education. Clearly, within the present paradigm, the primacy of a negative peace notion cannot be replaced with that of a positive one, much less one of organic peace. So long as this and the present forms of empiricism are our dominant intellectual values, we will not be effective learners about, or partners with, the complexity that is life. While some physicists and biologists are revealing startling notions about apparent randomness reflecting a beautifully choreographed pattern of interrelationships and repetitions from the smallest to the largest bits of creation,[4] and proposing through the Gaia hypothesis that the Earth itself is a living system, such concepts are by and large subjected to the rational, positivist version of the Galilean syndrome. If it is not revealed in our present scientific scriptures, nor pontificated by the highest authority, it is not true. This circumstance reflects the notion of fixed and limited truth, which cries for the kind of questioning advocated here, in order to open the windows of the frequently stifling ivory towers of academe to the air of new possibilities. The inquiry of peace studies should be based on queries mutually derived by instructor and student, each posing problems calling for various alternative responses, rather than predefined questions by the instructor, calling for predetermined answers from students.

## PEACE EDUCATION AS LIFE ENHANCEMENT

What more comprehensive definition of peace education could we offer than learning to learn about, and functioning in and with complexity, so as to enhance the richness and diversity of life? Such a definition would apply to, and provide deeper purpose for cross-cultural education, conflict studies, world order modeling, human rights education, environmental studies, and most of the themes and subjects which comprise the broad and varied field of peace studies. Profound changes in present educational systems and methods are essential if we are to move toward a new paradigm. For starters, it would help us to comprehend more fully the significance of pastoral images of peace. We should see them as pictures of life in process, of cultivation, of intentional enhancement of life, and, hopefully, of diversity. The reductionist thinking which permits us to dismiss the importance of the loss of some species because they are, but rare insects for which we have no apparent use, is the same mode of thought that prevents us from seeing descriptions of peace in the drawings of children, whose imaginations have not yet been imprisoned by "fixed, demonstrable truth." With such a start, we might open and develop our capacities for imaging, which Elise Boulding sees as necessary to inspire us with viable concepts of peace. Imaging is a skill which can and should be developed through peace education.[5] To develop skill, however, is but a means of directing and giving communicable form to a fundamental capacity of the human imagination. These imaging capacities must be freed by a liberating form of education based on authentic inquiry, rather than the probe for predetermined answers. Only through such open authentic inquiry with students and teachers exploring the terra incognita of peace together, can education make a significant contribution to the formulation of a new paradigm.

Thus, a primary method of peace education should be authentic inquiry. Such a method would be derived from the posing of queries, which would perform three functions: Reveal apparent obstacles to peace, open avenues for exploring the causes of and alternative approaches to transcending the obstacles, and assess the alternatives according to criteria which would result in the most life-enhancing choice. The exploration would be conducted to maximize the possibilities for reflection, creativity, and full participation of all engaged in the study. It would reward rather than impede speculation, the most open form of inquiry, and the most encouraging form of creativity. It would preclude the premature narrowing of the broad creative process of speculation into the limitations of too few scientifically testable hypotheses. It would provide space for, and honor the need for, reticence and silence as a sometimes necessary environment for reflection—that deeper inner questioning that is essential to personal change and evolution on which the political and social changes of a new paradigm will depend. Without such reflection, learning cannot be fully integrated into the thinking and world views that condition our personal interpretations and assessments, from which we make the choices that lead us to action. An emphasis on integration reflects the notion of education and learning as part of the seeking of a wholeness that is the authentic meaning of integrity, and the essence of what has been most trampled upon by the reductionist nature of the present paradigm. Peace education, if not all education, should be intentionally designed to contribute to the search for integrity by individual learners and the whole society.

Integration of diversity in a mutually enhancing relationship is a fundamental process for maintaining life and for achieving peace. Our present emphasis on analysis has encouraged separation at the cost of integration. The reluctance to see things wholistically also may well contribute to the current alienation of individuals and to the disintegration of society. Rather than try to heal and reintegrate it, we have attempted to simplify it to better manage and control the conditions of separation and alienation, conditions largely responsible for the high degree of personal and social insecurity from which we suffer. This insecurity has, in fact, alienated us from life. We shun and fear difference, diversity, and complexity because we have not learned to live with them, and in the process we have shunned life itself. Peace requires the embracing of life in all its problematic fullness.

## METAPHORS OF BIRTH AND LIFE

We need also to devise a life-affirming metaphor to replace the death-prone, war metaphor of destructive struggle that so conditions our language, our thought, and our learning. Since we want a set of images for positive struggle, the most likely new metaphor of life would be one centered on the origins, development, and maturation of living things—one based on conception, labor, birth, and parenting.

Were we to think in terms as all encompassing as conception, gestation, labor, birth, nurturing, parenting, education, and *caring*, we would have a whole new way of thinking about the human experience and social organization. We might think of the desired paradigm shift as one which moves us from a warring society to a parenting or caring society, in which all adults parent the young and care for the vulnerable. Care of the vulnerable, like avoidance of harm, is characteristic of both good parenting and a peaceful society. Our thinking would tend to focus on the long-range health and welfare of living beings, and on the enhancement of life. We might begin to organize intentionally planned learning toward development of the capacity to care, thus embracing one of the most fundamental purposes of peace education—an overarching concept for a comprehensive education for justice and peace, and for humane and fulfilling human relationships.

The concept and value of care as a core notion of peace education illuminates the inextricable interweaving of the personal and the political. As a primary learning goal, care brings into focus the essential significance of diversity and complexity. It makes it possible to sustain the struggle for integrity in the apparent chaos in which the emerging patterns and intricate order of actual relationships give us a glimpse of the multiple possibilities for a transformed reality and a paradigm of peace. In such a paradigm, peace and life would be perceived as the products of a diverse, dynamic, continuous set of processes of change in a magnitude of aesthetic quality we have only begun to grasp. If we can learn to become creative participants rather than destructive controllers of these life processes, we may yet reach a truly new world.

## LEARNING: MERGER OF PERSONAL AND POLITICAL, MEANS AND ENDS

Learning is primarily personal, inward, and interactive. We learn as we use our paradigms (our world views, assumptions, and values) to assess and integrate our experiences. We learn in relationship to experience, to systems, and to persons. Mostly, we learn from and with each other. Authentic learning is a complex and sometimes chaotic process. Our notion of cognitive dissonance as a primary instigator of learning, is evidence to support the argument of authentic learning as far more varied than the linear processes on which most present instruction is based. Learning, like life, is an interrelational and wholistic process. Thus, methodology cannot be separated from purpose. If we seek truly new and transformed realities, we need to construct courses and learning experiences on genuine wholistic inquiry and speculation. Social and political processes, if they are to be viable and effective, must also be wholistic and integrative, recognizing that society, comprised of persons and politics is an aggregate of personal choices. If politics are to be altered to change the society, then people must also change. Personal change, if it is to be sustained over time, and not subject to repeated manipulation of outside forces, must be autonomously and intentionally embraced and integrated into the self. Just as a value consensus within a society is a necessary prerequisite to viable political and structural change, only change in people can change the culture which "cultivates" the values of the society.

Clearly, peace studies must begin to pursue wholism as the framework, process as the primary method, and peace in its widest sense as the goal, if it is to energize the intellectual transformation necessary to a paradigm of peace. The lion can lie down with the lamb in a nurturing rather than devouring relationship, only if each is able to transform its reality by transforming itself. These transformations are what peace studies should be about.

*Notes*

1. Birgit Brock Utne, *A Feminist Perspective on Peace Education* (New York: Praeger, 1986).

2. Douglas Sloan, *Insight-Imagination: The Emancipation of Thought and the Modern World* (Westport, Conn.: Greenwood Press, 1983); Jeremy Rifkin, *Declaration of a Heretic* (Boston: Routledge & Kegan Paul, 1985).

3. Brian Easlea, *Fathering the Unthinkable: Masculinity, Scientists and the Nuclear Arms Race* (London: Pluto Press, 1983).

4. James Gleick, *Chaos: Making a New Science* (New York: Viking, 1987).

5. Betty A. Reardon, *Comprehensive Peace Education* (New York: Teachers College Press, 1988).

*Questions*

1. Give several examples of how our way of thinking and speaking affects the way we act.

2. What effects have reductionist thinking had on the spirit of free inquiry? Give instances.

3. What basic attitudes can you attribute to governments, industries and individuals who despoil the environment in the name of profit? What difference would an attitude—or paradigm—change make in the livability of our world?

4. What does the author have to say about personal responsibility toward changing the values by which our culture operates? Besides issues of peace and war, name other areas in which the individual can make a difference.

5. Do you find the author's views to be too utopian for serious consideration? Give your reasons, pro or con.

# 9
# The Scandal of "Peace Education"

## André Ryerson

This article originally appeared in *Commentary*, June 1986.

*What part, if any, does advocacy play in public education? When one moves from principles (cf. Reardon, Boulding) to curricula, this question assumes great importance.*

*Ryerson, a contributor to Commentary, takes a critical look at three curricular guides currently used in the public school system.*

*He first takes aim at Choices, written for the National Education Association by a member of the Union of Concerned Scientists. In it he finds an appeal to fear, based on studies he finds dubious, and lacking what he considers to be pertinent background. Throughout this junior high school guide, the author detects an anti-U.S. bias, which seems to attribute cold war tensions to American xenophobia, militarism and economic exploitation. He compares the curriculum guide's effort to elicit student response to the witch-hunting craze that swept seventeenth century Salem, Massachusetts. In addition to fear, Ryerson deplores similar appeals to student guilt, horror and anger.*

*Dialogue: A Teaching Guide to Nuclear Issues, and Perspectives: A Teaching Guide to Concepts of Peace come under the author's hostile gaze. Developed by Educators for Social Responsibility (ESR) and used in Boston area elementary schools, Dialogue is found to be even more objectionable than Choices, inasmuch as it makes explicit what the other guide only hinted at. By its use of stories (cf. Reardon's paradigms), Dialogue takes issue with adults' resort to violence, the arms race and the specter of nuclear war. What disturbs the author most is that the Soviets' peaceful intentions are taken at face value without an examination of their belligerent behavior at home and abroad. He is equally critical of recommended student activities, which have a distinctly political tinge.*

*Ryerson names prominent persons (perceived as "left-wingers") who comprise the National Advisory Board of ESR. He concludes with the question of whether, in taxpayer-supported and compulsory*

404

*public educational institutions, such a perspective is appropriate. He asserts that "public schools should remain politically neutral." Asserting that "peace education," as it now exists, is one-sided, he calls upon taxpayers to make their views felt.*

In the fall of 1982 the leaders of the nuclear-freeze movement, still buoyed by what they considered a popular tide, introduced to America's schools the subject of nuclear war, and what they judged fit to prevent it. Assisted by grants from foundations large and small, obscure and famous, educators for the freeze wrote curriculum guides inviting teachers to make this new subject formally a part of their schedule. Some public grumbling was heard when the National Education Association (NEA) in 1983 published *Choices: A Unit on Conflict and Nuclear War,* but then the matter sank from sight as other issues displaced the brief attention provoked by the advent of a new school subject.

Although the nuclear-freeze campaign has faded, it should not be imagined that the schools have abandoned "peace education," "peace studies," or "nuclear war education." Some fifty teaching guides now exist, all managing to fit into a very thin slice of the political spectrum. The two organizations with clear ascendancy in the field are the 1.7 million-member NEA, the largest labor union in America, and Educators for Social Responsibility (ESR). Not content to let the spread of the new curriculum depend on teacher initiative alone, these groups have succeeded in convincing states such as Oregon, and municipalities from New York and Milwaukee to Pittsburgh and Los Angeles, to require legally that "peace" or "nuclear war" education be made part of the short list of subjects which all children must study.

A closer look at the three most widely used curricular guides, *Choices, Dialogue,* and *Perspectives,* is therefore in order.

I

A teaching unit for junior-high-school students written for the NEA by the Union of Concerned Scientists (UCS), *Choices* opens with a justification by John Mack, a professor of psychiatry at Harvard who has made no secret of his desire to change America's defense policy. This desire he readily combines with his professional interest in children:

> Young, and even very young, children are telling their parents and teachers that they are afraid of dying in a nuclear war. In the past,

we have been poorly informed and ill-equipped to respond to these fears and have offered little to young people outside of unconvincing reassurances. This history of silence and ignorance in too many American classrooms is now being overcome, as pioneering curricula on the subject of nuclear war are being introduced in high schools and junior high schools throughout the country.

Dr. Mack goes on to say that "recent studies demonstrate that the nuclear arms race and the experience of living with the threat of nuclear annihilation have had a significantly adverse impact on the emotional lives of young people." In fact, however, as Joseph Adelson and Chester E. Finn, Jr. have shown, such studies for the most part have been produced by amateurs in the field of survey work, and, even when not, they have combined methodological shoddiness with overt political purpose.

As any parent knows, fear is an emotion communicated very readily from adult to child. One would therefore expect evidence far better than that hastily adduced by politically active psychiatrists claiming that children are in a state of terror about nuclear weapons, lest the treatment prove iatrogenic and the fears to be allayed become the effect of the therapy that is applied. Yet teachers sensitive to this consideration, or who might in any case question the propriety of using the classroom to communicate their private fears about the world to children, are told by the authors of *Choices:* "It is also important for you to admit your fears about nuclear war. This may help students more freely admit their own fears."

Lesson 1 of *Choices* begins by distributing to students a picture of a mushroom cloud. The children are asked what it means to them. This is followed by "The First Atomic Bomb," where the teacher is to "read one factual and one personal account of the dropping of the atomic bomb on Hiroshima." The "factual" account gives no background to World War II, and does not even mention who started it. The "personal account" includes a child's description of the Hiroshima devastation. Then, lest the horror of it all be too hastily absorbed, the next steps are these:

2. Divide the class into groups of four to five students.

3. Ask students to discuss their feelings about the Hiroshima accounts.

4. Have the groups list three or four things they felt after hearing these accounts.

5. Ask a spokesperson from each group to present the group's list to the class.

6. Allow students time to discuss their thoughts and feelings about Hiroshima and the atomic bomb.

Further optional exercises, with the class still divided into intimate groups, include distributing "pictures drawn by atomic-bomb survivors 30 years after the event," from the book *Unforgettable Fire*, with the same extended ritual as above, and again concluding, "Allow students time to discuss their thoughts and feelings about Hiroshima and the atomic bomb."

Whatever else their state of ignorance these days, it can scarcely be argued that junior-high-school students do not know that atomic bombs kill people. Given the absence of any context to explain the extremely limited choices imposed by conditions of war in general, and the war waged against the Japanese in particular, these class exercises devised by the Union of Concerned Scientists, which single out from the great lexicon of the war's documented horrors but one sort committed by one side, can only produce in thirteen-year-olds the reactions that UCS surely intends: pity for the Japanese, disgust for America.

The same theme is resumed in Lesson 4 under "Effects of Nuclear Explosions," this time with radiation sickness added to the catalogue of human and material destruction. First, teachers are told to "Ask students to review from Lesson 1 the effects of the bomb dropped on Hiroshima. This discussion gives an introduction to the nature and effects of nuclear weapons." The review completed, the students are to read about radiation sickness "and then discuss the long-term effects on those who are not immediately killed by the explosion." Teachers who might hesitate, at this point, have their resolve strengthened by the UCS: "This part of the lesson may be one of the most disturbing portions of the unit. The students have been given many unpleasant facts, but it is crucial to realize the destructive nature of nuclear weapons." The next message gets repeated at intervals: "Though the first atomic bomb was much smaller than today's nuclear weapons, and therefore does not give a true picture of the extent of destructive capacity, we will use the memories of atomic-bomb survivors to educate ourselves and students about an event we hope to prevent from ever happening again." Students are encouraged to start a private journal in which they may record and elaborate their new-found fears, sense of national guilt, and convictions of how the world in consequence must be changed.

To ensure that sorrow and guilt not distract from the primary emotion of fear, the Union of Concerned Scientists recommends

"Ground Zero," an exercise that permits the children to "detail the effects of a one-megaton bomb at different distances" from "the point on the earth's surface on or above which a nuclear weapon explodes," with concentric circles to distinguish varying effects on humans and property. "Provide students with copies of a map or show an over-head projection of their city. . . . You may choose to have students draw the concentric circles on the maps. If so, they will need compasses." Etc. The authors of *Choices*, as one can see, cannot be faulted for a lack of thoroughness.

The designers of this manual are aware, however, that to construct a whole philosophy of disarmament, more than raw fear and guilt are needed. Broader issues of human relations—economics, the nature of conflict, a general picture of the world—must also be introduced and taught. Thus, among possible explanations of why the West has an adversary relationship with the Soviet Union, there are two that enjoy prominence in *Choices*, as in all the "peace" curricula. The first is that we Americans have a primitive tendency to imagine people who are different from ourselves as our "enemies." Our problem, in a word, is psychological. The second, more hardheaded explanation is that nations, like individuals, are unduly selfish, and refuse to share equally with others their goods and resources; war, in this view, is but the end product of "competitiveness," resulting from the institution of private property.

The UCS offers exercises by which to drive these lessons home. The start of Lesson 2 ("Personal Conflict") presents the psychological thesis: "Whether our opponent is perceived as a friend, enemy, or stranger may produce very different resolutions to the conflict." This prepares students for the assertion that our difficulty with the Soviets is essentially a problem in our heads. And the analogies students are asked to entertain are sufficiently trivial to support this claim.

For instance, in selecting personal conflicts to illustrate the harsher realities of the world, the authors of *Choices* might have examined the situation created, say, by a bully demanding another child's lunch money under threat of violence (a not uncommon occurrence these days). Instead, the situations favored by *Choices* run from borrowing another's bike without asking permission, to stepping ahead in line; the exercise is then to imagine how events would evolve if you "assume that the other person is your friend," or "your enemy," or, finally, "a stranger." *Choices* guides the teacher: "Does assuming the other person is an enemy produce the same result as assuming your opponent is a friend? Does eliminating a 'me vs. you' attitude help resolve conflicts?"

The idea that nothing very serious (other than American cultural prejudice) separates the United States and the Soviet Union is the basis of the "U.S.-USSR Fact Sheet," which informs students that the USSR has 270 million people, a harsh climate in the east, important reserves of minerals, and "some unfriendly countries" on its frontiers, due—among other provocations—to the presence along one border of "as many as 1 million Chinese troops." By contrast, through some circumstance of good luck, "The United States is bordered on the north by Canada and on the south by Mexico, both friendly countries." The U.S. also has not suffered nearly so much from war, having lost only about a million men in battle since its birth, whereas "the Soviet Union lost about 20 million people in World War II in addition to about 11 million in World War I and the Civil War of 1918."

Oddly enough, in this summary of Soviet suffering, the UCS seems to have overlooked one of the most sensational statistics of the century—the number of Soviet citizens done to death by their own rulers. Admittedly, such a statistic of social genocide—even the mere mention of the Gulag—might interfere with the purpose of Lesson 2, which is to show that our dislike of the Soviet system and leadership is merely mental and that it proceeds from a lack of familiarity, an ingrained cultural parochialism, of which Americans should work harder to cure themselves. Of the Soviet habit since 1917 of invading and assimilating neighbors, not a word is said.

In addition to the delusion that the Soviets are our enemies, there is the danger of the world struggle for resources. "What happens when an increasing number of people want scarce resources?" The UCS answer to this problem comes in the form of a game, in which an odd number of candies is given out to groups with an even number of students. The subsequent discussion by the class as to how it overcame this obstacle to perfect sharing constitutes the lesson.

Other exercises of sharing and "cooperation" are suggested, among them "The Dollar Game." Here the class is divided in two, and each side bids how many cents it will pay for a dollar bill offered by the teacher, but with the catch that both sides must pay the teacher the sums they bid, win or lose. The aim is to get the students to set aside competition, and "cooperate": "After one side goes over 50 cents, it may become apparent that *you* will gain at the next bid, since the sum of the two bids will be more than $1. One side may even begin to negotiate with the other at an earlier point." Of course, the idea that eliminating competition among bidders is a virtue would only occur to academics displeased with the workings of a free economy. If companies bidding for a highway contract were to follow the

ethics recommended by the UCS and the NEA, they would be subject
to criminal indictment by the state prosecutor for colluding to fix
prices.

   With the only grounds for tension between the United States and
the Soviet Union being an "us vs. them" mentality (from which we
alone appear to be suffering) and an ill-controlled craving for scarce
resources, the expenditure of U.S. public funds on arms becomes
irrational, not to say immoral. To dramatize this lesson *Choices* has a
game called "The United States National Budget." Again the class
divides into groups, with each group receiving twenty tokens and a
sheet listing the various categories into which the tokens may go. The
students (with no background information whatsoever) are invited to
allocate the tokens as they think right, and are explicitly told: "Your
twenty tokens represent all of the money in the national budget." The
various groups are afterward asked to compare their answers. *Choices*
then instructs the teacher: "Pass out the proposed 1987 National
Budget (Worksheet 603). Tell students this represents the average
figures of the proposed 1987 United States budget."
   Here is how the twenty tokens are distributed in the "National
Budget":

| CATEGORY | NUMBER OF TOKENS |
|---|---|
| 1. Social Needs: <br>     Education <br>     Food and nutrition <br>     Job training <br>     Social services | 1 |
| 2. Social Security, Retirement, <br>     and Unemployment | 6 |
| 3. National Defense | 9 |
| 4. Physical Needs: <br>     Natural resources and <br>       environment <br>     Transportation <br>     Housing <br>     Community development | 1 |
| 5. Health: <br>     Medical research | 2 |

     Medical programs for the
        elderly, handicapped,
        and poor
 6.  Science and Politics:                                          1
        Energy
        Science
        Agriculture
        International affairs

   The purpose of the exercise is to "shock" children about "the truth" of U.S. defense spending, and to demonstrate how miserly and inhumane we are by comparison in allocating funds for "social needs." But either the Union of Concerned Scientists is ignorant of known facts, or it has difficulty performing a task of simple arithmetic: to allot nine out of twenty tokens—or 45 percent—to National Defense, when the actual defense budget in recent years has run consistently between 26 and 29 percent, is a piece of major misinformation for teachers to be telling students.

   Beyond the plain falsehood concerning the proportion of our defense budget, there are, as so often in *Choices*, crucial omissions here, whose purpose can only be to create a false picture of reality. To use the term "national budget" instead of *federal* budget, and then to list "education," "food and nutrition," "retirement," "physical needs," "transportation," "housing," "community development," "health," "medical research," "energy," "science," "agriculture," and so on, is seriously to mislead the young, who may not know that such things are funded overwhelmingly by state or local governments, or are sustained by private enterprise. It might, in addition, interest our children, if not educators inhospitable to defense budgets, that in constant dollars public spending for defense has risen only 1.2 percent in the last twenty years, whereas the increase in America's spending on "social needs" has risen a breathtaking 214 percent. As a consequence, the share of total public spending consumed by defense since 1965 has *declined*, from 37 to about 15 percent. But facts like these have the inconvenience of not conforming to the image of America that the UCS entertains.


                               II


   The programmed feelings that *Choices* is designed to arouse in students—war, horror, shame, and finally righteous indignation-

must, in keeping with the therapy promised from the first page by Dr. Mack, resolve themselves in action. But there is a problem here. Despite what they have been told by the youth culture and by "progressives," children, even as old as thirteen, still tend to believe that adults by and large know more than they. And since adults for the most part have not yet joined the crusade to get rid of the weapons constructed for our defense, children may hesitate to throw themselves into the "peace" movement with quite the alacrity that the UCS and the NEA would like. To overcome this diffidence, *Choices* (along with other "peace" curricula) has come up with an ingenious device—a fable to inspire the young—called "The Hundredth Monkey." So useful is this tale to its purposes that *Choices* makes sure to set it forth as early as Lesson 1, referring back to it reverently in subsequent lessons as though to the founding myth of a religion.

"The Hundredth Monkey" is, among other things, a fascinating instance of the deliberate misuse of scientific knowledge for political ends. The original facts on which it is based are these: in 1952 some Japanese scientists observing the behavior of macaque monkeys on the island of Koshima decided, as an experiment, to leave yams (a food unfamiliar to the monkeys) scattered upon the beach. One of the monkeys, a young female, soon found that the edibility of the yams was much improved by washing them in the nearby water, to remove the sand. Soon other monkeys, beginning with the younger ones, imitated the first, until the washing of yams had become, as it were, an acquired cultural habit.

Those are the facts. In the version given in *Choices*, however, there are significant modifications. The young female, "named Imo," discovers that seawater removes sand from yams. "She taught this trick to her mother. Her playmates also learned this new way and they taught their mothers, too." This mild distortion continues: "Only the adults who imitated their children learned this social improvement. Other adults kept eating the dirty sweet potatoes."

At this point the story acquires wings and takes flight into myth:

> In the autumn of 1958 something startling took place. Though the exact number is not known, let us suppose that when the sun rose one morning there were 99 monkeys on Koshima Island who had learned to wash their potatoes. Let's further suppose that later that morning, the hundredth monkey learned to wash potatoes. THEN IT HAPPENED!
>
> By that evening almost everyone in the tribe was washing sweet potatoes before eating them. The added energy of the hundredth monkey created a breakthrough! Thus, when a critical num-

ber achieves an awareness, this new awareness may be communicated from mind to mind.

Although the exact number may vary, the Hundredth Monkey Phenomenon means that when only a limited number of people know of a new way, it may remain in the minds of only these people. But there is a point at which if only one more person tunes in to the new awareness, the idea is strengthened so that it reaches almost everyone!

Your awareness is needed in preventing nuclear war.

You may be the "Hundredth Monkey."

The idea that a "new awareness" will be accepted by all remaining skeptics "if only one more person tunes in" is a piece of social fantasy. And to apply this fantasy to the monkeys of Koshima, as a scientifically observed event, is complete and utter nonsense. Yet *Choices* with a straight face tells both teacher and students: "The experiment illustrates the concept of 'critical number' whereby the attainment of a certain level of concentration causes some quality, property, or phenomenon to undergo a definite change." And lest the moral be lost on any inattentive student, the teacher is instructed to ask the class: "How are people who learn about nuclear war like the monkeys who learned to wash the sweet potatoes?" And: "Can adults learn about nuclear war from young people?"

Although indifference to American values and to vital facts of world history is apparent in *Choices* from the first lesson to the last, the particular use of the Hundredth Monkey myth adds another dimension to the misuse of public education. Unlike what happened at Koshima, where a young member of the monkey colony did indeed make an autonomous discovery, these junior-high-school students are doing no such thing. They are being coached by adults. And yet they are being made to believe that this is not so, that *Choices* is merely opening a door upon their own privileged perceptions, which possess a superior moral status to those of their parents and other adults.

Now it happens that something very similar occurred in American history once before. In 17th-century Salem a group of children, their status as "innocents" enabling them to command authority over adult society with quite astonishing effect, began denouncing adult members of the community as agents of the devil. We now know more fully what happened: the children were not hearing "divine commands," but had absorbed adult emotions from two unhealthy sources, an atmosphere of bitterness existing between their own village clan and a rival group of families, and the superstitious tales of horror told the children by a kitchen maid. Turned hysterical, the children began identifying members of the rival clan as "witches," and were believed on faith in their natural innocence. This circular pattern of influence, from adults to children and then from children back to adults, but now amplified by the presumption of some moral or divine privilege in children, might appropriately be called the Salem Syndrome. The contemporary usefulness of the concept is that it conforms, in all essentials, to what we observe operating between "peace educators" and children in the public schools.

The emotions induced by *Choices*—fear (of imminent nuclear holocaust, owing to our means of defense), shame (at having invented atomic bombs and made use of them to end World War II), horror (from tireless study of Hiroshima), and above all anger (at adult America for persisting in maintaining its nuclear deterrent, owing to false suspicions of the Soviet Union)—run the risk of simply depressing students and discouraging them from taking any action at all. To counter this danger, Lesson 9 encourages them to imagine, as the title puts it, "A Better World."

On this theme students are asked to compose poems, skits, and songs, to construct collages and paint posters, with the year "2080 A.D." offered as a possible target date for the emergence of a more loving, less hostile America. Lesson 9 also urges teachers to "Have students listen to some music that encourages creativity," listing such options as "There's a Place for Us" from *West Side Story*, "Ain't Gonna Study War No More" by Pete Seeger, and "Imagine" by John Lennon. The first of these is a soulful duet for lovers separated by the ethnic prejudices of a pair of warring gangs; the second preaches the pacifist credo that to stop wars we should get rid of our military; and the last attributes war and the world's other ills to the persistence of religion and the continued existence of national boundaries.

The tenth and concluding lesson of *Choices* opens gravely:

> The final day of the unit will give students time to reflect on the unit and consider ideas for action. At the beginning, you should remind students of the story of "The Hundredth Monkey" and the power of the individual to make a difference, especially when joined with others in a group action. Imagining what a better world could look like (Lesson 9) can also be productive in encouraging students to act on their beliefs.

A list of suggested activities follows, aimed first at the school community itself ("Do a videotape on the unit and play for the school"; "teach younger children within the school topics learned in the unit"; "form student groups on issues of nuclear war and its prevention") and then at the larger adult community, the school now transformed into a center for "peace" activism, provided free of charge by the taxpayers. "Contact the PTA and make the class's concerns known." "Contact the local radio and TV news and ask to present a one-minute summary of class opinions on nuclear weapons or nuclear war." "Set up a literature table at a community event such as a flea market or block party."

That done, the students can begin lobbying regional politicians: "Call or write your state legislators. Find out their positions on arms limitation and peace through strength. Write back expressing your views." Nor should the children's crusade shirk from advancing to the federal level: "Write the White House and tell the President of your concerns." "Write your Representatives and Senators, and ask their views on nuclear war, national defense, and potential arms agreements such as SALT, START, freeze, and No First Use. After you receive their letters, write back explaining how you agree or disagree with their views."

But the most provocative if elliptical suggestion, stopping just short of inciting to civil disruption, is the following: "Find out the role the military plays in the community. Are weapons produced at a local plant (see the map which follows)? Is research and development in progress at a local university? Are weapons stored at a nearby base?" The map on the facing page is the final image the children are shown, and it nicely ties in with the mushroom cloud that opens the manual. It is titled, "Nuclear Weapons Locations in the United States," and is the handiwork of the innocent-sounding Center for Defense Information (CDI), which might more aptly be named the Anti-Defense Center. The map pinpoints every U.S. Air Force base, Navy base, Army base, ICBM missile field, and every research or industrial site suspected of making or housing nuclear weapons. No equivalent map of the USSR is offered. At the foot of the page appears the title of the article in which the map originally appeared: "Preparing for Nuclear War: President Reagan's Program."

## III

When the nuclear-freeze movement was at its apogee, a group calling itself Educators for Social Responsibility (ESR) formed in the Boston-Cambridge area to carry the cause into the public schools. It has been highly successful in its task, assisted by an allied group of youthful recruits (with NEA support as well) called "Student/ Teacher Organization to Prevent Nuclear War" (STOP). Launching its campaign in hundreds of schools across the country with a "Day of Dialogue" in the fall of 1982, ESR subsequently turned out three huge curriculum guides: *Dialogue: A Teaching Guide to Nuclear Issues; Decision Making in a Nuclear Age;* and *Perspectives: A Teaching Guide to Concepts of Peace.* Several of the authors of *Choices* also helped write the teaching guides for ESR, but with a revealing difference. Where *Choices* is content to suggest, the guides produced by ESR assert; where the former allows but a glimpse of occasional intimacy with the Left, in the latter this cautionary veil has become completely transparent.

A specialty of Educators for Social Responsibility is its readiness to begin working on young minds from the earliest school age. While *Choices* is prepared to wait until the young have reached junior high, ESR starts in kindergarten. Accordingly, it is not surprising to find in both *Dialogue* and *Perspectives* a heavy emphasis on children's stories, ideal instruments in the task of teaching the very young the attitudes necessary for changing the world.

To demonstrate to children that Western fears of the Soviet Union are merely based on mistaken perceptions, *Perspectives* recommends "The Stranger: A Modern Fable," which "tells the story about how people, in their fear of a giant stranger, bring out their cannon against him. When they finally get to talk to him, they like him a lot and he is invited to stay in their country." In another story, "The Tears of the Dragon," the misperception idea is neatly fused with another, that of the-child-as-saintly-leader-of-adults: "A little boy refusing to believe a village rumor that a dragon is evil, decides to invite the dragon to his birthday party, thereby overcoming prejudice and misinformation." Then there is "Jonathan and the Dragon," wherein a child once again shows adults the folly of their ways: "After the mayor and townspeople have tried violent means to no avail, a little boy gets the invading dragon out of town simply by whispering a polite request to him." (ESR might consider shipping a few cartons of this invaluable story to assist the mujaheen in Afghanistan.)

Other stories follow, each making its simple and unmistakable point. "The Tomato Patch" demonstrates that it is not real conflict but rather the making of weapons which is the cause of war. "The Pig War" presents two groups claiming the same piece of territory, and has as its moral that "deciding to share avoids conflicts." "Potatoes,

Potatoes" is a "right-to-the-point story about two countries at war, a mother's attempt to shield her two sons from it," and teaches its lesson in the form of a question: "If people spend all their time fighting, building, and polishing weapons, who will have time to grow food to sustain the people?" (A continuous theme of these stories suggests to small children the frightening notion that their food will disappear if we persist in maintaining our defenses.)

Two final stories make the case that enlisting in the military services of one's country adds violence and stupidity to one's character. In "Two Admirals," "Two competitive and egotistical admirals turn the village to a shambles as they try to outdo each other; the innkeeper offers a prize to the one who can keep the peace longer." In "The Generals," a pair of generals "would rather go to the beach and play than fight a war," but their cultural rigidity makes them invent excuses to avoid the effort of changing their routine, so that the story "ends with their destruction."

Nowhere in these teaching guides are children reminded that in America we enjoy a system of government that places the military under the control of elected civilians, voted into office by the people, and that there is not a single case of our military having so much as attempted to break off from this authority to start a war.

If stories are one way to guide children to foreordained conclusions, classroom discussion completes the task. Here is the sort of questioning judged appropriate for a teacher addressing children in the 2nd and 3rd grades (ages 7–8) on the existence of atomic bombs: "Do you really think there is such a thing? Do you think a war could end the world? Does that scare you?" ESR cites one response to such questions in order to justify its own adult activism: "Sam's reaction supports one of our strongly held views: *That adults' peacemaking efforts are a source of reassurance for children*" (emphasis in original). This is one of the favorite devices in the movement's tireless manipulation of children: not only does inducing fear open the way to fresh conversions in the young, but worry about the psychological damage inflicted on children is then used to enlist the support of parents.

While ESR has no qualms about encouraging fears of nuclear holocaust, it is prompt to quell fears related to Soviet aggression. Such fears are "based on misinterpretation and misinformation," and should be gently corrected by the teacher of small children along the following lines: "Judy, you said something interesting about the Russians. But actually the leaders of the Soviet Union have said they want to work on peace, and we know that a lot of people there feel the way we do and are working hard to prevent war."

For slightly older children, in grades 4 to 6, *Dialogue* recommends a more detailed inquiry into nuclear war, with the teacher ready to answer such questions as, "What happens to people when a nuclear bomb explodes near them?" Should a child respond with the anxious complaint that "it's just not fair that other people have made the world like this," the teacher can vigorously nod: "We agree. Lots of grownups all over the world are trying to find ways to make the world better and get rid of things like bombs. Maybe you could help by writing letters."

## IV

One might be tempted to dismiss Educators for Social Responsibility as a marginal left-wing element in the larger scheme of American education. This would be a serious mistake. The National Advisory Board of ESR includes such persons of power and prestige as George Rathjens of MIT; Ernest Boyer, president of the Carnegie Foundation for the Advancement of Teaching; David Fraser, president of Swarthmore College; H. Michael Hartoonian, supervisor of social studies education for the state of Wisconsin; Mary Futrell, president of the NEA; Terry Herndon, former executive director of the NEA; Matthew Prophet, superintendent of schools of Portland, Oregon; Charles Slater, superintendent of schools of Brookline, Massachusetts; Floretta McKenzie, superintendent of schools for the District of Columbia; Harold Raynolds, superintendent of education for the state of Alaska; Reverend J. Bryan Hehir, associate director of International Justice and Peace, U.S. Catholic Conference; Adele Simmons, president of Hampshire College (which serves a consortium of five colleges with a college version of "Peace Studies"); Reverend Theodore M. Hesburgh, president of Notre Dame; and, not least, the omnipresent Carl Sagan.

It is thanks to influential people and institutions like these that state and city governments have been talked into making "peace education" mandatory in their public schools. But now that they have done so, it is appropriate for the rest of us to bethink ourselves what should be done.

The advent of "peace education" raises fundamental questions about the proper function of public education in a democracy. Never in the history of the United States have the public schools been conceived as a licit vehicle for one political segment of the population to convert the children of another. So obvious has this long seemed that there are few (if any) formal laws prohibiting so outrageous an abuse of the public trust as what "peace" educators have ventured.

The assumption that underlies publicly-funded education in a pluralist society where school attendance is compulsory is that the schools exist to teach basic skills, basic knowledge, and uncontested values needed for democratic citizenship. On matters where the people divide, notably in religion and politics, the schools are to maintain a position of strict neutrality. To do otherwise invites the transformation of the schoolhouse into a battleground for community civil wars. This well-established principle in no way prohibits the creation of private schools, in which persons who want their children taught in the particular mores of Christian fundamentalism, Jewish orthodoxy, or Quaker pacifism are at full liberty to do so. What is not permissible is the suborning of public institutions that are the property of all into tools for the specialized beliefs of a zealous few out to convert the children of others.

The large degree of local control which American communities still enjoy over their schools permits relief from the current disorder by those who would wish to correct it. We—taxpayers and parents— have long assumed that public schools should remain politically neutral. We have assumed that teachers' politics are their private business, not the public's, and so have demanded no political tests for the job; but the other half of the implicit contract has been that teachers, in turn, are not to use their authority over children for indoctrinating them in their own political enthusiasms. Teachers who push "peace education" in the classroom are manifestly violating the terms of this trust. The public is entitled to say that they should either cease the indoctrination, or find another form of employment.

*Questions*

1. Examine one of the stories or examples in *Dialogue* and give your opinion as to whether you consider it to be biased. If you feel this is so, can you suggest a way in which a balance might be struck?

2. Do you think it is fair to cite the shortcomings of the United States in promoting cold war tensions without giving equal weight to Soviet violations of the peace? Give examples from the text or from your own experience.

3. Public schools have been asked or required to insert courses on a variety of subjects in recent years—nuclear war, AIDS, drugs, alcohol, etc. What effect, if any, does the inclusion of additional

subjects have on the core curriculum of "reading, writing and 'rithmetic"?

4. Do you think it is legitimate for a public school teacher to give his or her political opinions in elementary school or high school? If you think not, does this mean that no grappling with current issues is possible? Why, and how?

5. Advocates of "peace education" would argue that the traditional curriculum is biased in favor of a conservative political agenda. Do you think the curricula outlined in this article redress the balance? Give reasons for your answer.

# 10
# Scientists and the Peace Movement: Some Notes on the Relationship

## Johan Galtung

This article originally appeared in *Bulletin of Peace Proposals*, #1, 1986.

*As the founder of the International Peace Research Institute in Oslo, Johan Galtung has spent much of his professional life exploring the relation between peace activists and the scientific community. He notes the increasing tendency of scientists to ally themselves with political advocates of nuclear disarmament and other initiatives.*

*Will the scientists be "on top" of such popular-based movements or "on tap" to answer specific questions? he asks. Galtung comes out in favor of the democratic concept that "people should have the final say, not the experts." He calls for a partnership between the two groups. The role of scientific experts in popular movements, in his view, are: (1) data (the facts, within one's field of competence); (2) values (the consequences of actions in such areas as health and rational thought); (3) theories (the contribution of fresh ideas and policies).*

*Galtung asserts that the peace movement is in special need of the third form of assistance, observing that it "is good in criticism, not bad on empiricism, but very poor on constructivism, on designing desirable and viable alternatives." He warns against excessive optimism on the role of scientists because their rational arguments do not always lead to change and their statements tend to be ignored by authorities. He stresses the need for more than negative statements by peace activists: "Most people want vision, hope—not to be told that they are doomed."*

*Galtung thinks that scientists have much to learn from the peace movement: (1) they are exposed to new data; (2) they are exposed to an intense level of value commitment, which may force them to "do their homework"; (3) they are forced to be constructive and perhaps humbled in the process. He does not go so far as to predict that the joining of scientists to peace movements will result in a "happy marriage." But, despite all the pitfalls, he regards such a wedding as "a unique training in the values of democracy—and isn't that also what the peace movement is about?"*

## 1. THE DEMOCRATIC INJUNCTION

We have recently witnessed a considerable increase in the size and the impact of the peace movement, even if the peace movement as an anti-missile movement in Western Europe has suffered a certain defeat, certainly to be expected when the deployment of the missiles nevertheless took place in fall 1983. We have for a long time had a rate of increase in the production of scientists (of all kinds, natural science, social sciences, humanities) possibly sooner or later approaching a saturation point. Naturally, there has been a spill-over from one to the other: scientists as such, physicians, physicists and engineers, social scientists of all kinds, historians, lawyers, theologians are making statements and aligning themselves in various ways with the broad popular movement to avert nuclear war. The interesting point is that they no longer do so as committed individuals only, accepting some very general principles, but try to bring their scientific expertise to bear on their position in favor of the peace movement and its causes. This is my point of departure.

I think there is a basic problem here that needs some exploration: What does it mean to the democratic character of a political process when scientists in great numbers join a popular movement, presumably as experts? Will they try to be in command of the movement, legitimizing a leadership position by reference to superior knowledge? Will they be experts on top, in other words, or be satisfied to remain experts 'on tap', counting one vote only if elections and votes are on the agenda, but at the same time making their knowledge-based insights available?

In a sense the answer is easy: in a democracy, as opposed to an expertocracy, people should have the final say, not the experts. It is pressure from the people rather than from the experts that should lead to course corrections, whether these corrections are carried out by the executive power directly or mediated through the pressures exercised by a popular assembly, parliament. Experts may err, and so may people. In war-peace issues the parliaments and governments of aligned member countries certainly err, if the experience from the past century is a valid guide. Offensive weaponry leads to arms races in offensive weapons; arms races tend to lead to wars. And the consequences of all these errors in the course charted for society as a whole are visited upon the people and not only on the military experts, parliamentarians and governmental bureaucrats. Hence the responsibility should also rest with the people. Societies are not constructed in such a way that only people high up pay the consequences; usually they get off more easily than the people in general. Nor should people abdicate from responsibility. Democracy is based on the principle of and by the people, simply because what happens may not only be for, but also against the people.

The peace movement is an expression of this sentiment. It is the obvious outcome of a situation where it is possible, like in the Federal Republic of Germany, to make a decision with extremely serious potential consequences, such as the deployment of the Euromissiles November 1983, with only a 55% majority in the parliament and probably with not more than 5% of the population at that time really supporting the decision. The peace movement not only stands for, or rather against, a certain course of action; it is also an expression of the democratic urge in large sections of the population to step in where they feel that experts, parliamentarians and bureaucrats fail. In other fields there may be discontent, but nevertheless a feeling that by and large the self-correcting mechanisms of the establishment are sufficient. In the field of security politics this is no longer the case, and the peace movement is one answer to the gap in credibility, even legitimacy.

From this it should follow that it would be very unwise for the peace movement to abdicate to its own experts, the scientists who join. The peace movement should not become an exercise in liberation from one set of experts, only to end up in the arms of another set, certainly with a position closer to that of the peace movement at some place, at some time, but otherwise not differing much from experts in general. The peace movement should keep its distance, listen to all experts carefully (including those from the Establishment), sift the chaff from the wheat, use the experts, and really squeeze them. But there should be no abdication; any leadership should be democratically elected, not selected because of some status in the knowledge hierarchy. It should be remembered that democracy is based on the faith that the insights of everybody concerned can be added up in some meaningful manner, particularly provided a dialogue has taken place, and that the expert's deep insight at some points in the spectrum of knowledge is compensated by the non-expert's intuitions over a wider range. Partnership is the way to democracy, which is neither 'parliamentocracy', nor 'expertocracy', nor 'populocracy'.

## 2. WHAT THE SCIENTISTS CAN CONTRIBUTE TO THE PEACE MOVEMENT

It seems to me that in a popular movement like the peace movement the scientists have three quite clear tasks, based on data, values and theories respectively.[1]

(1) Empirically, to give the data, the facts, in connection with policies

chosen or recommended. This, however, they should above all do within their range of competence, not trying to step outside that range, which is often quite narrow.

It is equally painful listening to a social scientist trying to behave like a nuclear scientist as it is listening to a nuclear scientist who believes that he is a social scientist, pontificating on peace and war. As a regular peace movement member he is, of course, free to do so—but then it should not necessarily be assumed automatically that his insights are particularly deep or valid. They may be, but that will have to be tested. The Pugwash movement, at some time dominated by the superpowers and the nuclear scientists, and particularly by superpower nuclear scientists, had some of this faith built into it, particularly in the first twenty years.

To this it may be objected that scientists are surrounded by an aura anyhow, and this can be utilized and capitalized upon by the peace movement. I doubt it. I think physicians are particularly effective when they pronounce themselves in their capacity as physicians and end up with conclusions underpinning positions taken by the peace movement; not when they pronounce themselves on any and all matters outside their field of competence. On the contrary, others would not fail to pay attention to such mannerisms, and may also make use of such pronouncements in order to illegitimize the specialists, even when they are clearly within their field of competence. Of course, that kind of debating trick will probably be made use of anyhow, and should not be taken too seriously. But the difficulty remains that when the scientists are inside their field of competence the novelty of what they say may not be acknowledged in any case, because people are so used to their positions, which are usually of a pessimistic kind, even apocalyptic. 'Nuclear winter' may be an example here.

(2) Critically, being explicit in their evaluation of courses of action, again within their field of competence. But at this point a new element enters: the scientists not only say what the consequences will be but also deplore them, speak out against them, utter clear warnings. To do so there has to be an element of value commitment, not only good data or reasonable predictions about the empirical consequences of a course of action. Some scientists are better trained in combining empirical projections with a value commitment than others; physicians bring in the supreme value of health, engineers the supreme value of (scientific and economic) rationality. Both commitments are much heralded in our civilization and bring in their wake no particular difficulties to the members of these professions. The same could be the case for peace, particularly when coupled with such other honor words as 'security' and

'freedom'—but we are not yet quite at that stage. However, some scientists have reached that point more than others and do criticize; they do engage in criticism.

It should be pointed out that when they do so they are not outside their realm of competence as scientists, provided they make the value-orientation they use reasonably explicit. The value to which they are committed is trivial, at least as long as we stay within the examples quoted above. What they do is simply to read off the consequences, on which they are presumably experts, on a screen with a value dimension on it. Actually, it is not even required of them that they believe in health, rationality or peace—all they do is spell out the consequences in these terms. If they want to make this very clear, all that is needed is to preface their statements with an 'if': 'If peace is what you want, then this course of action will probably rather bring you the opposite for the following reasons . . . ' Very simple, and doing so in no way interferes with their qualities as scientists. It is only unusual in the sense that many of them are trained in the university to believe that values and facts do not mix at all, in which case medical science and engineering would be impossible. Staying within their empirical field of competence, there should be no problem in this connection, explicitness being compatible with competence.

(3) Constructively, contributing new ideas, suggesting new policies. Here a new element is brought in as there is no longer any solid empirical base. The new courses of action would be located in the interface between theory and value, the values indicating the ends and the theories the means (of course a simplification since the two are rather interrelated). But physicians and engineers, like architects and medical people, are doing this every day, as an obvious part of their professional activities. Lawyers are doing so, often more with a view to preventing wrong courses of action than encouraging the right ones. Hence, this is not so revolutionary either and could safely be engaged in by many more people. Whether one does it well or badly is another matter.

In the three points just mentioned, there is a clear past-present-future dimension. The empirical approach would obviously have to be based on data from the past, since only the past yields data—although projections into the future may be entertained. A critical approach will usually be about current politics, and the scientist will become an actor in the political field. The constructive activity would be with a view to preparing blue-prints for tomorrow, inspiring the peace movement to new vistas.[2]

It goes without saying that some scientists are better at documentation, others at criticism, and still others at proposal-making. It is also obvious that the three activities do not exclude each other. They can be found in the same person, at least two of them if not all three (all three would demand much expertise in one scientist, and for that reason better obtained through dialogue processes in groups, collectively). The peace movement is in need of all three types of activities, singly and combined, which is just another way of saying that scientists are indispensable to the peace movement. Usually the peace movement is good in criticism, not bad on empiricism, but very poor on constructivism, on designing desirable and viable alternatives.

However, from this it does not follow that the peace movement will necessarily make more headway the more scientists there are. In fact, this might be an occasion to warn against two sources of excessive optimism:
—that in an open society rational arguments, and people's movements, will eventually lead to course corrections;
—that strong, warning statements by scientists will eventually lead to course corrections, or at least be heeded.

As to the first assumption we have reasonably open societies in Western Europe; there has been no scarcity of warning voices, nor any absence of movements and demonstrations. It has even been clearly brought to the attention of everybody that the majority of the population in the five Euromissile countries is against deployment. Yet deployment has happened, for the simple reason that however important peace issues are to many people, the peace movement has not yet succeeded in making peace the number one priority issue for the majority of the population. The moment that such is the case, people would vote in favor of a peace party even if that means choosing a party that does not favor the economic policy they themselves would like to see implemented. But that kind of voting hardly takes place to any significant extent today. On the contrary, I think Eastern European countries in general, and the Soviet Union in particular, could learn from the West that they have nothing to fear from the open society: just let people organize, write petitions and thick books, walk any number of kilometers in a straight line or in a circle, with or without torches. All one has to do is not to pay too much attention unless such demonstrations show up in parliament. And there, as the last resort, there is always the possibility of exercising strong idea power, exchange power, or threat power—convincing, buying, cajoling recalcitrant 'dissidents'. Very last resort: a military coup.

As to the second assumption, I am not convinced that science-based stern warnings, and pessimistic predictions, will really bring about change. Rather, I think there are reasons to believe that political establishments accept criticism the moment they see a constructive alternative that is acceptable to them for other reasons. In other words, criticism alone, however well it is backed up by empirical data, will not change the course of action, only marginally modify that course, as I can easily imagine in connection with the 'nuclear winter'. If the prediction is that a certain megatonnage will whirl so much dust into the atmosphere that sunshine will be blocked out with disastrous consequences, then one alternative would not be to ban nuclear war, but to go in for smaller bombs with lower yields, more dispersed, and precise enough to hit targets that do not generate too much dust in the atmosphere. But that was hardly what those emitting those warnings had in mind, nor the peace movement.

It is, therefore, the constructive alternative, coupled to a critical assessment of the current course of action, asserted forcefully and with a tinge of optimism, that probably will win out—if not in the shorter, at least in the longer run. And this also has something to do with the way in which policies are criticized and proposed. That negativism, criticism and pessimism do not necessarily attract more votes than a positive attitude, constructivism and optimism, can be clearly seen from some recent elections: Mondale vs. Reagan in the United States, November 1984 (and November 1980 against Carter also, for that matter); or Kohl vs. Vogel in the Federal Republic of Germany in March 1983 (another example would be the elections for the office of mayor of West Berlin, May 1985). What holds for such elections probably holds for politics in general, and may be one very important reason why the peace movement does not make a more significant breakthrough. When proposals are put forward these are usually in terms of limitation, cuts, 'freeze', disarmament and control—not about something new and expansive, even if it also has to be expensive. Which is just another way of saying that criticism, at least in change and progress-oriented societies like ours, has to be combined with constructivism, with new horizons—not only stopping action, back to status quo ante. Most people want vision, hope—not to be told that they are doomed.

What has just been said are some reasons why the fault may not necessarily be with society if the peace movement is not sufficiently listened to and its proposals are not accepted. There may also be something wrong with the whole style of the peace movement. Similarly, if the peace experts find that the peace movement does not accept their way of thinking in general, and their specific advice in particular, it may not necessarily be the fault of the peace movement. In a democracy scientists should never be arrogant relative to a popular movement, but they should not be submissive either. We have more than enough of submissive intelligentsia who for a salary/honorarium offer the 'advice' the weighty institutions in society want to hear anyhow. Similarly, nobody is served by 'scientists' who give up their precious capacity always to continue asking 'But is that really so?', and instead become the call girls of the tiny peace movement commissariat—differing from those kept by the establishment mainly in not even being paid. But, since the scientist can never predict where unceasing questioning will lead him, there may be conflicts of loyalty—part of the social dialectic.

### 3. WHAT THE SCIENTISTS CAN LEARN FROM THE PEACE MOVEMENT

The other side of the coin of the scientist/peace movement relationship is often forgotten: what the scientists get out of that relationship. I would like to mention three particular points, all of them from my own experience.

First, a scientist is exposed through the peace movement to new data, to combinations of events in the past, the present, and possibly also the future that he would hardly have come up against had he just been engaged in conventional library research. Of course, this is the case whenever a scientist enters some kind of consultancy relationship; the 'client' presents him with situations that are new, if not to the 'client', at least to the scientist. I can only mention the example that gave rise to my own book *There Are Alternatives:* I was questioned by one particular peace-moved person (my own son), 'Where in Europe is it safest to live in case an atomic war should break out?' In all academic settings, such general but basic questions are overshadowed by a plethora of specialised, less basic problems.

Second, the scientist is exposed to a more intense level of value commitment than he usually has himself. Also, he may be exposed to conflicting value commitments, at least if the movement is diverse enough. These values are held with an intensity that makes the problems much more pressing, particularly as there are demands for answers, rewards for good answers and some punishment for the scientist who hedges, who never comes out with anything like a clear answer. Suddenly the scientist realises not only that an answer is requested of him, and if he cannot come up with one, it is not necessarily because he is 'scientific' in the sense of not jumping to conclusions, but simply because he has not done his homework, so that he becomes able to jump to valid conclusions, if jump he must!

Third, the scientist is exposed to the need to be constructive, to propose some alternative and not only to use his knowledge to present and project data, possibly in a critical manner. Only parts of the peace movement will demand this constructive activity of him; most of the movement will be more than satisfied if he can help the movement buttress their essentially critical argumentation against establishment policies engaged in or proposed. The scientist can solve the problem by keeping away from such movements or parts of movements, or demand of them in advance that such pressures should not be exercised. But he will also find himself rejuvenated as a scientist by accepting the pressures, and perhaps become more humble, facing his inability to supply the goods demanded, trying to do something about it. What a challenge to face people who ask difficult, precisely because not 'academic', questions where knowledge of literature and quotations will get you nowhere!

These are high rewards for the scientist, although they are not in monetary terms. Of course they are only rewards for a scientist who feels some kind of basic alignment with the peace movement, its ideas and ideals. He cannot do as the establishment scientist who may be even repelled, or feel aversion in connection with establishment goals but comforts himself that at least he is well paid, his family well fed and clothed and sheltered, and that 'such is life' and 'if I don't do it, somebody else will' and 'I have a mortgage to pay'.

The peace movement might do well to understand that they can keep their scientists particularly happy, and also filter out the scientists less valuable to the movement, by maintaining a certain pressure on them to deliver intellectual goods and services. It is not a bad idea to have a scientist introduce a working group, but only if the questions have been relatively precise and well-formulated, and sufficiently difficult. If a general talk is needed, then a generalist rather than a specialist might be asked to deliver it; in fact, the opposite would be not only abuse but also bad utilization of the specific talents of a scientist.

## 4. CONCLUSION: A HAPPY MARRIAGE?

Not necessarily. To assume this is to be far too optimistic. There are plenty of scientists who feel hurt, even insulted, when 'common people' fail to accept their advice; there are very many 'common people' who much too easily accept what is said by a 'famous' expert. Much of this comes from a lack of inner faith in democratic ideas and ideals, a search for authority and the authority's search for somebody who accepts them in a more unquestioning manner than their colleagues are likely to do.

Further, scientists used to performing brilliantly when relating data to theories and vice versa may become very inadequate when asked just to present the data, relate the data to values critically, or relate the values to theories constructively. They are simply not trained in these activities and often do not even realize that something new is going on. They stick to their old ways, insensitive to the signals of apathy, incomprehension or protestations of irrelevance.

When, even in an open society, the critical prophesies pronounced by scientists and carried into every nook and cranny of society, on the backs of a broad-shouldered popular movement, are not sufficiently paid attention to, scientists might be inclined to blame the peace movement. The movement was not quantitatively big or qualitatively deep enough, or something like that. It may not occur to the scientists that their message was only half of what people want to hear and that the constructive half was missing. Moreover, however brilliant the scientists, they may not be very good at the game of politics and power play. The political establishment will pick those scientists, and take whatever they can use from any scientist which is consistent with their policies. Whatever is incompatible will not even be listened to, or if listened to not understood, or if understood not paid attention to, or if paid attention to used in the wrong way. Except for the very, very rare occasion.

Finally, the scientist, more likely than not, will view the relationship as a one-way relationship where the scientist is 'giving' something to the movement, for instance his valuable time—and he may be reflecting on the opportunity costs, articles not written, books not produced, lectures not given (honoraria not received). It may not occur to him that he perhaps receives more from the thousands or even millions in the movement than he is able or even willing to give, because he has been trained only to perceive experts as real people, and the rest as 'masses'. Listening too much to colleagues may have made him deaf to what others have to say. Hence, a unique training in basic values of democracy—and isn't that also what the peace movement is about?

## Notes

1. See my *Methodology and Ideology*, Ejlers, Copenhagen 1977, Ch. 3 for an exploration of this theme.

2. My own book *There Are Alternatives!* (German, English, Dutch, Spanish editions 1984; Norwegian, Swedish, Italian, Japanese editions 1985) is actually a mix of all three—how successful is another issue.

## Questions

1. How might scientists abuse their authority when they take public positions on political issues?
2. Why must scientists be willing to learn as well as teach?
3. Why is the peace movement long on criticism of governments and short on constructive proposals?
4. The author thinks that the "nuclear winter" issue (Jonathan Schell in *The Fate of Earth*) has been overblown. Do you think he is right? Why?
5. What are some of the responsibilities of the scientist as a citizen?

# SECTION SIX

# Imagination and Hope

# 1
# September 1, 1939

## W. H. Auden

This poem is reprinted from *The Pocket Book of Modern Verse*, Pocket Books, 1954.

I sit in one of the dives
On Fifty-second Street
Uncertain and afraid
As the clever hopes expire
Of a low dishonest decade:
Waves of anger and fear
Circulate over the bright
And darkened lands of the earth,
Obsessing our private lives;
The unmentionable odour of death
Offends the September night.

Accurate scholarship can
Unearth the whole offence
From Luther until now
That has driven a culture mad,
Find what occurred at Linz,
What huge imago made
A psychopathic god:
I and the public know
What all schoolchildren learn,
Those to whom evil is done
Do evil in return.

Exiled Thucydides knew
All that a speech can say
About Democracy,
And what dictators do,
The elderly rubbish they talk
To an apathetic grave;
Analysed all in his book,

The enlightenment driven away,
The habit-forming pain,
Mismanagement and grief;
We must suffer them all again.

Into this neutral air
Where blind skyscrapers use
Their full height to proclaim
The strength of Collective Man,
Each language pours its vain
Competitive excuse;
But who can live for long
In an euphoric dream;
Out of the mirror they stare,
Imperialism's face
And the international wrong.

Faces along the bar
Cling to their average day:
The lights must never go out,
The music must always play,
All the conventions conspire
To make this fort assume
The furniture of home;
Lest we should see where we are,
Lost in a haunted wood,
Children of the night
Who have never been happy or good.

The windiest militant trash
Important Persons shout
Is not so crude as our wish:
What mad Nijinsky wrote
About Diaghilev
Is true of the normal heart;
For the error bred in the bone
Of each woman and each man
Craves what it cannot have,
Not universal love
But to be loved alone.

From the conservative dark
Into the ethical life

The dense commuters come,
Repeating their morning vow;
'I *will* be true to the wife,
I'll concentrate more on my work,'
And helpless governors wake
To resume their compulsory game:
Who can release them now,
Who can reach the deaf,
Who can speak for the dumb?

All I have is a voice
To undo the folded lie,
The romantic lie in the brain
Of the sensual man-in-the-street
And the lie of Authority
Whose buildings grope the sky:
There is no such thing as the State
And no one exists alone;
Hunger allows no choice
To the citizen or the police;
We must love one another or die.

Defenceless under the night
Our world in stupor lies;
Yet, dotted everywhere,
Ironic points of light
Flash out wherever the Just
Exchange their messages:
May I, composed like them
Of Eros and of dust,
Beleaguered by the same
Negation and despair,
Show an affirming flame.

2
# Dover Beach

## Matthew Arnold

This poem is reprinted from *The Pocket Book of Modern Verse*, Pocket Books, 1954.

The sea is calm to-night.
The tide is full, the moon lies fair
Upon the straits; on the French coast the light
Gleams and is gone; the cliffs of England stand,
Glimmering and vast, out in the tranquil bay.

Come to the window, sweet is the night-air!
Only, from the long line of spray
Where the sea meets the moon-blanch'd land,
Listen! you hear the grating roar
Of pebbles which the waves draw back, and fling,
At their return, up the high strand.
Begin, and cease, and then again begin,
With tremulous cadence slow, and bring
The eternal note of sadness in.

Sophocles long ago
Heard it on the Aegean, and it brought
Into his mind the turbid ebb and flow
Of human misery; we
Find also in the sound a thought,
Hearing it by this distant northern shore.

The Sea of Faith
Was once, too, at the full, and round earth's shore
Lay like the folds of a bright girdle furl'd.
But now I only hear
Its melancholy, long, withdrawing roar,
Retreating, to the breath
Of the night-wind, down the vast edges drear
And naked shingles of the world.

Ah, love, let us be true
To one another! for the world, which seems
To lie before us like a land of dreams,
So various, so beautiful, so new,
Hath really neither joy, nor love, nor light,
Nor certitude, nor peace, nor help for pain;
And we are here as on a darkling plain
Swept with confused alarms of struggle and flight,
Where ignorant armies clash by night.

3
# The Soldier

## Rupert Brooke

This poem is reprinted from *The Pocket Book of Modern Verse*, Pocket Books, 1954.

If I should die, think only this of me:
That there's some corner of a foreign field
That is for ever England. There shall be
In that rich earth a richer dust concealed;
A dust whom England bore, shaped, made aware,
Gave, once, her flowers to love, her ways to roam,
A body of England's breathing English air,
Washed by the rivers, blest by suns of home.

And think, this heart, all evil shed away,
A pulse in the eternal mind, no less
Gives somewhere back the thoughts by England given;
Her sights and sounds; dreams happy as her day;
And laughter, learnt of friends; and gentleness,
In hearts at peace, under an English heaven.

# 4
# The Coward

## Eve Merriam

This poem is reprinted from *Poems of War Resistance*, Grossman, 1969.

---

You, weeping wide at war, weep with me now.
Cheating a little at peace, come near
And let us cheat together here.

Look at my guilt, mirror of my shame.
Deserter, I will not turn you in;
I am your trembling twin!

Afraid, our double knees lock in knocking fear;
Running from the guns we stumble upon each other.
Hide in my lap of terror: I am your mother.

—Only we two, and yet our howling can
Encircle the world's end.
Frightened, you are my only friend.

And frightened, we are everyone.
Someone must make a stand.
Coward, take my coward's hand.

5

# Conscientious Objector

## *Edna St. Vincent Millay*

This poem is reprinted from *Poems of War Resistance*, Grossman 1969.

I shall die, but that is all that I shall do for Death.
I hear him leading his horse out of the stall; I hear the clatter on the
    barn floor.
He is in haste; he has business in Cuba, business in the Balkans,
    many calls to make this morning.
But I will not hold the bridle while he cinches the girth.
And he may mount by himself: I will not give him a leg up.

Though he flick my shoulders with his whip, I will not tell him
    which way the fox ran.
With his hoof on my breast, I will not tell him where the black boy
    hides in the swamp.
I shall die, but that is all I shall do for Death; I am not on his payroll.

I will not tell him the whereabouts of my friends nor of my enemies
    either.
Though he promise me much, I will not map him the route to any
    man's door.
Am I a spy in the land of the living, that I should deliver men
    to Death?
Brother, the password and the plans of our city are safe with me;
    never through me
Shall you be overcome.

6

# The March into Virginia
# (July 1861)

*Herman Melville*

This poem is reprinted from *The Pocket Book of Modern Verse*, Pocket Books, 1954.

---

Did all the lets and bars appear
   To every just or larger end,
Whence should come the trust and cheer?
   Youth must its ignorant impulse lend—
Age finds place in the rear.
   All wars are boyish, and are fought by boys,
The champions and enthusiasts of the state;
   Turbid ardours and vain joys
     Not barrenly abate—
   Stimulants to the power mature,
     Preparatives of fate.

Who here forecasteth the event?
What heart but spurns at precedent
And warnings of the wise,
Contemned foreclosures of surprise?
The banners play, the bugles call,
The air is blue and prodigal,
   No berrying party, pleasure-wooed,
No picnic party in the May
Ever went less loth than they
   Into that leafy neighborhood,
In Bacchic glee they file toward Fate,
Moloch's uninitiate;
Expectancy, and glad surmise
Of battle's unknown mysteries.
All they feel is this: 'tis glory,
A rapture sharp, though transitory,
Yet lasting in belaurelled story.
So they gaily go to fight,

Chatting left and laughing right,
But some who this blithe mood present,

   As on it lightsome files they fare,
Shall die experienced ere three days are spent—
   Perish, enlightened by the volleyed glare;
Or shame survive, and like to adamant,
   The throe of Second Manassas share.

# 7
# Independence

## *Henry David Thoreau*

This poem is reprinted from *Poems of War Resistance*, Grossman 1969.

My life more civil is and free
Than any civil polity.

Ye princes, keep your realms
And circumscribed power,
Not wide as are my dreams,
Nor rich as is this hour.

What can ye give which I have not?
What can ye take which I have got?
Can ye defend the dangerless?
Can ye inherit nakedness?

To all true wants Time's ear is deaf,
Penurious States lend no relief
Out of their pelf:
But a free soul—thank God—
Can help itself.

Be sure your fate
Doth keep apart its state—
Not linked with any band—
Even the nobles of the land;

In tented fields with cloth of gold
No place doth hold,
But is more chivalrous than they are,
And sigheth for a nobler war;

A finer strain its trumpet rings—
A brighter gleam its armor flings.

The life that I aspire to live
No man proposeth me—
No trade upon the street
Wears its emblazonry.

8
# War Is Kind

## *Stephen Crane*

This poem is reprinted from *Poems of War Resistance*, Grossman 1969.

Do not weep, maiden, for war is kind.
Because your lover threw wild hands toward the sky
And the affrighted steed ran on alone.
Do not weep
War is kind.

Hoarse, booming drums of the regiment,
Little souls who thirst for fight,
These men were born to drill and die.
The unexplained glory flies above them,
Great is the Battle-God, great, and his Kingdom—
A field where a thousand corpses lie.

Do not weep, babe, for war is kind.
Because your father tumbled in the yellow trenches,
Raged at his breast, gulped and died,
Do not weep.
War is kind.

Swift blazing flag of the regiment,
Eagle with crest and red and gold,
These men were born to drill and die.
Point for them the virtue of slaughter,
Make plain to them the excellence of killing
And a field where a thousand corpses lie.

Mother, whose heart hung humble as a button
On the bright splendid shroud of your son,
Do not weep.
War is kind.

# 9
# Counter-Attack

## *Siegfried Sassoon*

This poem is reprinted from *Poems of War Resistance*, Grossman, 1969.

We'd gained our first objective hours before
While dawn broke like a face with blinking eyes,
Pallid, unshaved and thirsty, blind with smoke,
Things seemed all right at first. We held their line,
With bombers posted, Lewis guns well placed,
And clink of shovels deepening the shallow trench.
The place was rotten with dead; green clumsy legs
High-booted, sprawled and groveled along the saps;
Wallowed like trodden sand-bags, loosely filled;
And naked, sodden buttocks, mats of hair,
Bulged, clotted heads, slept in the plastering slime.
And then the rain began—the jolly old rain!

A yawning soldier knelt against the bank,
Staring across the morning blear with fog;
He wondered when the Allemands would get busy;
And then, of course, they started with five-nines
Traversing, sure as fate, and never a dud.
Mute in the clamor of shells he watched them burst
Spouting dark earth and wire with gusts from hell,
While posturing giants dissolved in drifts of smoke.
He crouched and flinched, dizzy with galloping fear,
Sick for escape—loathing the strangled horror
And butchered, frantic gestures of the dead.

An officer came blundering down the trench:
"Stand-to and man the fire step!" On he went. . . .
Gasping and bawling. "Fire-step . . . counter-attack!"
Then the haze lifted. Bombing on the right
Down the old sap: machine guns on the left;
And stumbling figures looming out in front.

"O Christ, they're coming at us!" Bullets spat,
And he remembered his rifle . . . then a bang
Crumpled and spun him sideways, knocked him out
To grunt and wriggle: none heeded him; he choked
And fought the flapping veils of smothering gloom,
Lost in a blurred confusion of yells and groans. . . .
Down, and down, and down, he sank and drowned,
Bleeding to death. The counter-attack had failed.

# 10
# Strange Meeting

## *Wilfred Owen*

This poem is reprinted from *Poems of War Resistance*, Grossman, 1969.

It seemed that out of battle I escaped
Down some profound dull tunnel, long since scooped
Through granites which titanic wars had ground.
Yet also there encumbered sleepers groaned,
Too fast in thought or death to be bestirred.
Then, as I probed them, one sprang up, and stared
With piteous recognition in fixed eyes,
Lifting distressful hands as if to bless.
And by his smile, I knew that sullen hall,
By his dead smile I knew we stood in Hell.
With a thousand pains that vision's face was grained;
Yet no blood reached there from the upper ground,
And no guns thumped, or down the flues made moan.
"Strange friend," I said, "here is no cause to mourn."
"None," said the other, "save the undone years,
The hopelessness. Whatever hope is yours,
Was my life also; I went hunting wild
After the wildest beauty in the world,
Which lies not calm in eyes, or braided hair,
But mocks the steady running of the hour,
And if it grieves, grieves richlier than here.
For by my glee might many men have laughed,
And of my weeping something had been left,
Which must die now. I mean the truth untold.
The pity of war, the pity war distilled.
Now men will go content with what we spoiled,
Or, discontent, boil bloody, and be spilled.
They will be swift with swiftness of the tigress,
None will break ranks, though nations trek from progress.
Courage was mine, and I had mystery,
Wisdom was mine, and I had mastery;

448

To miss the march of this retreating world
Into vain citadels that are not walled.
Then, when much blood had clogged their chariot-wheels
I would go up and wash them from sweet wells,
Even with truths that lie too deep for taint.
I would have poured my spirit without stint.
But not through wounds; not on the cess of war.
Foreheads of men have bled where no wounds were.
I am the enemy you killed, my friend.
I knew you in the dark; for so you frowned
Yesterday through me as you jabbed and killed.
I parried; but my hands were loath and cold.
Let us sleep now . . ."

11
# The Battle of Blenheim
# (August 13, 1704)

*Robert Southey*

---

It was a summer evening;
  Old Kaspar's work was done,
And he before his cottage-door
  Was sitting in the sun;
And by him sported on the green
His little grandchild, Wilhelmine.

She saw her brother Peterkin
  Roll something large and round,
That he beside the rivulet,
  In playing there, had found:
She ran to ask what he had found,
That was so large and smooth and round.

Old Kaspar took it from the boy,
  Who stood expectant by;
And then the old man shook his head,
  And with a natural sigh,
" 'Tis some poor fellow's skull," said he,
"Who fell in the great victory."

"I find them in my garden,
  For there's many here about;
And often, when I go to plough,
  The ploughshare turns them out;
For many thousand men," said he,
"Were slain in that great victory."

"Now tell us what 'twas all about,"
  Young Peterkin, he cries;
And little Wilhelmine looks up

With wonder-waiting eyes;
"Now tell us all about the war,
And what they fought each other for."

"It was the English," Kaspar cried,
    "Who put the French to rout;
But what they fought each other for
    I could not well make out;
But everybody said," quoth he,
"That 'twas a famous victory.

"My father lived at Blenheim then,
    Yon little stream hard by;
They burned his dwelling to the ground,
    And he was forced to fly;
So with his wife and child he fled,
Nor had he where to rest his head.

"With fire and sword the country round
    Was wasted far and wide,
And many a childing mother then,
    And new-born baby, died;
But things like that, you know, must be
At every famous victory.

"They say it was a shocking sight
    After the field was won;
For many thousand bodies here
    Lay rotting in the sun:
But things like that, you know, must be
After a famous victory.

"Great praise the Duke of Marlborough won
    And our good Prince Eugene."
"Why, 'twas a very wicked thing!"
    Said little Wilhelmine.
"Nay, nay, my little girl," quoth he,
"It was a famous victory."

"And everybody praised the Duke,
    Who this great fight did win."
"But what good came of it at last?"
    Quoth little Peterkin.
"Why, that I cannot tell," said he;
"But 'twas a famous victory."

12

# The Canticle of Brother Sun

## *St. Francis of Assisi*

Most High, omnipotent, good Lord
To you alone belong praise and glory,
Honor, and blessing.
No man is worthy to breathe thy name.

Be praised, my Lord, for all your creatures.

In the first place for the blessed Brother Sun,
who gives us the day and enlightens us through you,
He is beautiful and radiant with his great splendor,
Giving witness of thee, Most Omnipotent One.

Be praised, my Lord, for Sister Water,
So necessary yet so humble, precious, and chaste.

Be praised, my Lord, for Brother Fire,
Who lights up the night.
He is beautiful and carefree, robust, and fierce.

Be praised, my Lord, for our sister, Mother Earth,
Who nourishes and watches us
While bringing forth abundance of fruits with colored flowers
And herbs.

Be praised, my Lord, for those who pardon through your love
And bear weakness and trial.
Blessed are those who endure in peace,
For they will be crowned by you, Most High.

Be praised, my Lord, for our sister, Bodily Death,
Whom no living man can escape.
Woe to those who die in sin.

Blessed are those who discover the holy will.
The second death will do them no harm.

Praise and bless my Lord.
Render thanks.
Serve him with great humility.

## 13
## from *The War Prayer*

## *Mark Twain*

This prayer is reprinted from *Poems of War Resistance*, Grossman 1969.

O Lord our God, help us to tear their soldiers to bloody shreds with our shells; help us to cover their smiling fields with the pale forms of their patriot dead; help us to drown the thunder of the guns with the shrieks of their wounded, writhing in pain; help us to lay waste their humble homes with a hurricane of fire; help us to wring the hearts of their unoffending widows with unavailing grief; help us to turn them out roofless with their little children to wander unfriended the wastes of their desolated land in rags and hunger and thirst, sports of the sun, flames of summer and the icy winds of winter, broken in spirit, worn with travail, imploring Thee for the refuge of the grave and denied it—for our sakes who adore Thee, Lord, blast their hopes, blight their lives, protract their bitter pilgrimage, make heavy their steps, water their way with tears, stain the white snow with the blood of their wounded feet! We ask it, in the spirit of love, of Him Who is the Source of Love, and Who is the ever-faithful refuge and friend of all that are sore beset and seek his aid with humble and contrite hearts. Amen.

# 14
# "A Theft from Those Who Hunger . . ."

*Dwight D. Eisenhower*

---

Every gun that is made, every warship launched, every rocket fired signifies, in the final sense, a theft from those who hunger and are not fed, those who are cold and are not clothed. This world in arms is not spending money alone. It is spending the sweat of its laborers, the genius of its scientists, the hope of its children.

# 15
# Hero—Zero

## *Anonymous G.I.*

This poem is reprinted from *Poems of War Resistance*, Grossman 1969.

---

Soldiers who wish to be a hero
Are practically zero,
But those who wish to be civilians,
Jesus, they run into the millions

*G.I. scribbling on latrine wall in England, World War II.*

# 16
## "A Debt of Generosity . . ."

*Thucydides*

---

If great enmities are ever to be really settled, we think it will be, not by the system of revenge and military success, and by forcing an opponent to swear to a treaty to his disadvantage, but when the more fortunate combatant waives his privileges, to be guided by gentler feelings, conquers his rival in generosity, and accords peace on more moderate conditions than he expected. From that moment, instead of the debt of revenge which violence must entail, his adversary owes a debt of generosity to be paid in kind, and is inclined by honour to stand to his agreement. And people oftener act in this manner towards their greatest enemies than where the quarrel is of less importance; they are also by nature as glad to give way to whose who first yield to them, as they are apt to be provoked by arrogance to risks condemned by their own judgment.

*History of the Peloponnesian War*

# 17
# Incident at Damascus, Arkansas

## *John Fandel*

John Fandel is Professor Emeritus of English and World Literature at Manhattan College.

Silos used to be for wheat for bread.
Now they store warheads to make more wardead dead.

18
# "The Hairy Man from the East . . ."

*Chief Luther Standing Bear
of the Ogala band of Sioux*

This excerpt originally appeared in *Touch the Earth,* Simon and Schuster 1971.

We did not think of the great open plains, the beautiful rolling hills, and winding streams with tangled growth as "wild." Only to the white man was nature a "wilderness" and only to him was the land "infested" with "wild" animals and "savage" people. To us it was tame. Earth was bountiful and we were surrounded with the blessings of the Great Mystery. Not until the hairy man from the east came and with brutal frenzy heaped injustices upon us and the families we loved was it "wild" for us. When the very animals of the forest began fleeing from his approach, then it was the "Wild West" began."

19
# from *My Religion*

## *Leo Tolstoy*

This poem is reprinted from *Poems of War Resistance*, Grossman 1969.

I believe in God, who is for me spirit, love, the principle of all things.

I believe that God is in me, as I am in Him.

I believe that the true welfare of man consists in fulfilling the will of God.

I believe that from the fulfillment of the will of God there can follow nothing but that which is good for me and for all men.

I believe that the will of God is that every man should love his fellowmen, and should act toward others as he desires that they should act toward him.

I believe that the reason of life is for each of us simply to grow in love.

I believe that this growth in love will contribute more than any other force to establish the Kingdom of God on earth—

To replace a social life in which division, falsehood and violence are all-powerful, with a new order in which humanity, truth and brotherhood will reign.

20
# from *The Dhammapada*
# Chapter XXVI. The Brahmin Buddha

*This poem is reprinted from Poems of War Resistance*, Grossman 1969.

. . . Him I call indeed a Brahmin who without hurting any creatures, whether feeble or strong, does not kill or cause slaughter.

Him I call indeed a Brahmin who is tolerant with the intolerant, mild with the violent, and free from greed among the greedy.

Him I call indeed a Brahmin from whom anger and hatred, pride and hypocrisy have dropped like a mustard seed from the point of a needle.

Him I call indeed a Brahmin who utters true speech, instructive and free from harshness, so that he offend no one.

Him I call indeed a Brahmin who takes nothing in the world that is not given him, be it long or short, small or large, good or bad.

# 21
# from *The Way of Life* (The Book of Tao)

## *Laotse*

This poem is reprinted from *Poems of War Resistance*, Grossman 1969.

### LXVIII

The best captain does not plunge headlong
Nor is the best soldier a fellow hot to fight.
The greatest victor wins without a battle:
He who overcomes men understands them.
There is a quality of quietness
Which quickens people by no stress:
"Fellowship with heaven," as of old,
Is fellowship with men and keeps its hold.

### LXXVIII

What is more fluid, more yielding than water?
Yet back it comes again, wearing down the rigid strength
Which cannot yield to withstand it.
So it is that the strong are overcome by the weak,
The haughty by the humble.
This we know
But never learn,
So that when wise men tell us,
"He who bites the dust
Is owner of the earth,
He who is scapegoat
Is King."
They seem to twist the truth.

### LXXIX

If terms to end a quarrel leave bad feeling,
What good are they?
So a sensible man takes the poor end of the bargain

Without quibbling.
It is sensible to make terms,
Foolish to be a stickler:
Though heaven prefer no man,
A sensible man prefers heaven.

# 22
## "Break Up Your Fallow Ground . . ."

*Hosea 10:12–15*

---

Sow for yourselves righteousness,
  reap the fruit of steadfast love;
  break up your fallow ground,
for it is the time to seek the Lord,
  that he may come and rain
    salvation upon you.

You have plowed iniquity,
  you have reaped injustice,
  you have eaten the fruit of lies.
Because you have trusted in your chariots
  and in the multitude of your warriors,
therefore the tumult of war shall arise
  among your people,
  and all your fortresses shall be destroyed,
as Shalman destroyed Betharbel on the day of battle;
  mothers were dashed to pieces with their children.
Thus it shall be done to you, O house of Israel,
  because of your great wickedness.
In the storm the king of Israel
  shall be utterly cut off.

# 23
## "Hear This . . ."

*Micah 3:9–12*

---

Hear this, you heads of the house of Jacob
  and rulers of the house of Israel,
who abhor justice
  and pervert all equity,
who build Zion with blood
  and Jerusalem with wrong.
Its heads give judgment for a bribe,
  its priests teach for hire,
  its prophets divine for money;
yet they lean upon the Lord and say,
  "Is not the Lord in the midst of us."
Therefore because of you
  Zion shall be plowed as a field;
Jerusalem shall become a heap of ruins,
  and the mountain of the house a wooded height.

# 24
# "Swords into Plowshares . . ."

## *Micah 4:1-4*

---

It shall come to pass in the latter days
that the mountain of the house of the Lord
shall be established as the highest of the mountains,
    and shall be raised up above the hills;
and peoples shall flow to it,
    and many nations shall come, and say:
"Come, let us go up to the mountain of the Lord,
    to the house of the God of Jacob;
that he may teach us his ways
    and we may walk in his paths."
For out of Zion shall go forth the law,
    and the word of the Lord from Jerusalem.
He shall judge between many peoples,
    and shall decide for strong nations afar off;
and they shall beat their swords into plowshares,
    and their spears into pruning hooks;
nation shall not lift up sword against nation,
    neither shall they learn war any more;
but they shall sit every man under
    his vine and under his fig tree,
    and none shall make them afraid;
    for the mouth of the Lord of
        hosts has spoken.

# 25
## "Seek Good and not Evil . . ."

*Amos 5:11–15*

Therefore because you trample
    upon the poor
  and take from him exactions of wheat,
you have built houses of hewn stone,
    but have not dwelt in them;
you have planted pleasant
    vineyards,
    but you shall not drink their wine.
For I know how many are your transgressions,
    and how great are your sins—
you who afflict the righteous, who
    take a bribe,
  and turn aside the needy in the gate.
Therefore he who is prudent will
    keep silent in such a time;
  for it is an evil time.

Seek good, and not evil,
    that you may live;
and so the Lord, the God of hosts,
    will be with you,
    as you have said.
Hate evil, and love good,
    and establish justice in the gate;
it may be that the Lord, the God of hosts,
    will be gracious to the remnant of Joseph.

# 26
## "Let Justice Roll . . ."

*Amos 5:21–24*

---

"I hate, I despise your feasts,
   and I take no delight in your
     solemn assemblies.
Even though you offer me your
     burnt offerings and cereal offerings,
   I will not accept them,
and the peace offerings of your fatted beasts
   I will not look upon.
Take away from me the noise of your songs;
   to the melody of your harps I will not listen.
But let justice roll down like waters,
   and righteousness like an
     ever-flowing stream."

# 27
# "He Has Put Down the Mighty . . ."

## *Luke 1:46–53*

---

"My soul magnifies the Lord,
   and my spirit rejoices in God my Savior,
for he has regarded the low estate of his handmaiden.
For behold, henceforth all generations will call me blessed;
for he who is mighty has done great things for me,
and holy is his name.
And his mercy is on those who fear him
from generation to generation.
He has shown strength with his arm,
he has scattered the proud in the imagination of their hearts,
he has put down the mighty from their thrones,
and exalted those of low degree;
he has filled the hungry with good things,
and the rich he has sent empty away.
He has helped his servant Israel,
in the remembrance of his mercy,
as he spoke to our father,
to Abraham and to his posterity for ever."

# 28
## "The Spirit of the Lord . . ."

*Luke 4:23–25*

---

And he came to Nazareth, where he had been brought up; and he went to the synagogue, as his custom was, on the sabbath day. And he stood up to read; and there was given to him the book of the prophet Isaiah. He opened the book and found the place where it was written,
"The Spirit of the Lord is upon me,
because he has anointed me to preach good news to the poor.
He has sent me to proclaim release to the captives
and recovering of sight to the blind,
to set at liberty those who are oppressed,
to proclaim the acceptable year of the Lord."

# 29
## "Blessed are the Poor . . ."

*Matthew 4:23—5:10*

---

And he went about all Galilee, teaching in their synagogues and preaching the gospel of the kingdom and healing every disease and every infirmity among the people. So his fame spread throughout all Syria, and they brought him all the sick, those afflicted with various diseases and pains, demoniacs, epileptics, and paralytics, and he healed them. And great crowds followed him from Galilee and the Decapolis and Jerusalem and Judea and from beyond the Jordan.

Seeing the crowds, he went up on the mountain, and when he sat down his disciples came to him. And he opened his mouth and taught them, saying:
"Blessed are the poor in spirit, for theirs is the kingdom of heaven.
"Blessed are those who mourn, for they shall be comforted.
"Blessed are the meek, for they shall inherit the earth.
"Blessed are those who hunger and thirst for righteousness, for they shall be satisfied.
"Blessed are the merciful, for they shall obtain mercy.
"Blessed are the pure in heart, for they shall see God.
"Blessed are the peacemakers, for they shall be called children of God.
"Blessed are those who are persecuted for righteousness' sake, for theirs is the kingdom of heaven."

# 30
## "Put on the Armor that God Gives . . ."

*Ephesians 6:10–20*

---

Finally, let the mighty strength of the Lord make you strong. Put on all the armor that God gives, so you can defend yourself against the devil's tricks. We are not fighting against humans. We are fighting against forces and authorities and against rulers of darkness and spiritual powers in the heavens above. So put on all the armor that God gives. Then when that evil day comes, you will be able to defend yourself. And when the battle is over, you will be standing firm.

Be ready! Let the truth be like a belt around your waist, and let God's justice protect you like armor. Your desire to tell the good news about peace should be like shoes on your feet. Let your faith be like a shield, and you will be able to stop all the flaming arrows of the evil one. Let God's saving power be like a helmet, and for a sword use God's message that comes from the spirit.

Never stop praying, especially for others. Always pray by the power of the Spirit. Stay alert and keep praying for God's people. Pray that I will be given the message to speak and that I may fearlessly explain the mystery about the good news. I was sent to do this work, and that is the reason I am in jail. So pray that I will be brave and will speak as I should.

# 31
# 198 Methods of Nonviolent Action

## Gene Sharp

Source: Gene Sharp, *The Politics of Nonviolent Action* (3 Vols.). Boston: Porter Sargent, 1973, 11 Beacon St., Boston, MA. 02108.

*Practitioners of nonviolent struggle have an entire arsenal of "nonviolent weapons" at their disposal. Listed below are 198 of them, classified into three broad categories: nonviolent protest and persuasion, noncooperation (social, economic, and political), and nonviolent intervention. A description and historical examples of each can be found in volume two of* The Politics of Nonviolent Action, *by Gene Sharp.*

### THE METHODS OF NONVIOLENT PROTEST AND PERSUASION

*Formal Statements*
1. Public Speeches
2. Letters of opposition or support
3. Declarations by organizations and institutions
4. Signed public statements
5. Declarations of indictment and intention
6. Group or mass petitions

*Communications with a Wider Audience*
7. Slogans, caricatures, and symbols
8. Banners, posters, and displayed communications
9. Leaflets, pamphlets, and books
10. Newspapers and journals
11. Records, radio, and television
12. Skywriting and earthwriting

*Group Representations*
13. Deputations
14. Mock awards
15. Group lobbying
16. Picketing
17. Mock elections

473

*Symbolic Public Acts*
18. Displays of flags and symbolic colors
19. Wearing of symbols
20. Prayer and worship
21. Delivering symbolic objects
22. Protest disrobings
23. Destruction of own property
24. Symbolic lights
25. Displays of portraits
26. Paint as protest
27. New signs and names
28. Symbolic sounds
29. Symbolic reclamations
30. Rude gestures

*Pressures on Individuals*
31. "Haunting" officials
32. Taunting officials
33. Fraternization
34. Vigils

*Drama and Music*
35. Humorous skits and pranks
36. Performances of plays and music
37. Singing

*Processions*
38. Marches
39. Parades
40. Religious processions
41. Pilgrimages
42. Motorcades

*Honoring the Dead*
43. Political mourning
44. Mock funerals
45. Demonstrative funerals
46. Homage at burial places

*Public Assemblies*
47. Assemblies of protest or support
48. Protest meetings
49. Camouflaged meetings of protest
50. Teach-ins

*Withdrawal and Renunciation*
51. Walk-outs
52. Silence

53. Renouncing honors
54. Turning one's back


## THE METHODS OF SOCIAL NONCOOPERATION

*Ostracism of Persons*
55. Social boycott
56. Selective social boycott
57. Lysistratic nonaction
58. Excommunication
59. Interdict

*Noncooperation with Social Events, Customs, and Institutions*
60. Suspension of social and sports activities
61. Boycott of social affairs
62. Student strike
63. Social disobedience
64. Withdrawal from social insitituions

*Withdrawal from the Social System*
65. Stay-at-home
66. Total personal noncooperation
67. "Flight" of workers
68. Sanctuary
69. Collective disappearance
70. Protest emigration (*hijrat*)


## THE METHODS OF ECONOMIC NONCOOPERATION:
### *ECONOMIC BOYCOTTS*

*Actions by Consumers*
71. Consumers' boycott
72. Nonconsumption of boycotted goods
73. Policy of austerity
74. Rent withholding
75. Refusal to rent
76. National consumers' boycott
77. International consumers' boycott

*Action by Workers and Producers*
78. Workmen's boycott
79. Producers' boycott

*Action by Middlemen*
80. Suppliers' and handlers' boycott

*Action by Owners and Management*
  81. Traders' boycott
  82. Refusal to let or sell property
  83. Lockout
  84. Refusal of industrial assistance
  85. Merchants' "general strike"
*Action by Holders of Financial Resources*
  86. Withdrawal of bank deposits
  87. Refusal to pay fees, dues, and assessments
  88. Refusal to pay debts or interest
  89. Severance of funds and credit
  90. Revenue refusal
  91. Refusal of a government's money
*Action by Governments*
  92. Domestic embargo
  93. Blacklisting of traders
  94. International sellers' embargo
  95. International buyers' embargo
  96. International trade embargo

## THE METHODS OF ECONOMIC NONCOOPERATION: *THE STRIKE*

*Symbolic Strikes*
  97. Protest strike
  98. Quickie walkout (lightning strike)
*Agricultural Strikes*
  99. Peasant strike
 100. Farm Workers' strike
*Strikes by Special Groups*
 101. Refusal of impressed labor
 102. Prisoners' strike
 103. Craft strike
 104. Professional strike
*Ordinary Industrial Strikes*
 105. Establishment strike
 106. Industry strike
 107. Sympathetic strike
*Restricted Strikes*
 108. Detailed strike
 109. Bumper strike
 110. Slowdown strike

111. Working-to-rule strike
112. Reporting "sick" (sick-in)
113. Strike by resignation
114. Limited strike
115. Selective strike
*Multi-Industry Strikes*
116. Generalized strike
117. General strike
*Combination of Strikes and Economic Closures*
118. Hartal
119. Economic shutdown


## THE METHODS OF POLITICAL NONCOOPERATION

*Rejection of Authority*
120. Withholding or withdrawal of allegiance
121. Refusal of public support
122. Literature and speeches advocating resistance
*Citizen's Noncooperation with Government*
123. Boycott of legislative bodies
124. Boycott of elections
125. Boycott of government employment and positions
126. Boycott of government depts., agencies, and other bodies
127. Withdrawal from government educational institutions
128. Boycott of government-supported organizations
129. Refusal of assistance to enforcement agents
130. Removal of own signs and placemarks
131. Refusal to accept appointed officials
132. Refusal to dissolve existing institutions
*Citizens' Alternatives to Obedience*
133. Reluctant and slow compliance
134. Nonobedience in absence of direct supervision
135. Popular nonobedience
136. Disguised disobedience
137. Refusal of an assemblage or meeting to disperse
138. Sitdown
139. Noncooperation with conscription and deportation
140. Hiding, escape, and false identities
141. Civil disobedience of "illegitimate" laws
*Action by Government Personnel*
142. Selective refusal of assistance by government aides
143. Blocking of lines of command and information

144. Stalling and obstruction
145. General administrative noncooperation
146. Judicial noncooperation
147. Deliberate inefficiency and selective noncooperation by enforcement agents
148. Mutiny

*Domestic Governmental Action*
149. Quasi-legal evasions and delays
150. Noncooperation by constituent governmental units

*International Governmental Action*
151. Changes in diplomatic and other representations
152. Delay and cancellation of diplomatic events
153. Withholding of diplomatic recognition
154. Severance of diplomatic relations
155. Withdrawal from international organizations
156. Refusal of membership in international bodies
157. Expulsion from international organizations

## THE METHODS OF NONVIOLENT INTERVENTION

*Psychological Intervention*
158. Self-exposure to the elements
159. The fast
    a) Fast of moral pressure
    b) Hunger strike
    c) Satyagraphic fast
160. Reverse trial
161. Nonviolent harassment

*Physical Intervention*
162. Sit-in
163. Stand-in
164. Ride-in
165. Wade-in
166. Mill-in
167. Pray-in
168. Nonviolent raids
169. Nonviolent air raids
170. Nonviolent invasion
171. Nonviolent interjection
172. Nonviolent obstruction
173. Nonviolent occupation

*Social Intervention*
174. Establishing new social patterns
175. Overloading of facilities
176. Stall-in
177. Speak-in
178. Guerrilla theater
179. Alternative social institutions
180. Alternative communication system

*Economic Intervention*
181. Reverse strike
182. Stay-in strike
183. Nonviolent land seizure
184. Defiance of blockades
185. Politically motivated counterfeiting
186. Preclusive purchasing
187. Seizure of assets
188. Dumping
189. Selective patronage
190. Alternative markets
191. Alternative transportation systems
192. Alternative economic institutions

*Political Intervention*
193. Overloading of administrative systems
194. Disclosing identities of secret agents
195. Seeking imprisonment
196. Civil disobedience of "neutral" laws
197. Work-on without collaboration
198. Dual sovereignty and parallel government

32
# Peace Upon Earth

## *Thomas Hardy*

This poem is reprinted from the volume *Winter Words*, 1928.

---

"Peace upon earth!" was said.
We sing it, and pay a million
priests to bring it.
After two thousands years of Mass
    We've got as far as poison gas.

*Christmas, 1924.*

# 33
# "Neither Blame Nor Praise"

## *Dante Alighieri*

---

Here sighs and cries and wails coiled and recoiled
on the starless air, spilling my soul to tears.
A confusion of tongues and monstrous accents toiled
in pain and anger. Voices hoarse and shrill
and sounds of blows, all intermingled raised
tumult and pandemonium that still
whirls on the air forever dirty with it,
as if a whirlwind sucked at sand. And I,
holding my head in horror, cried: "Sweet spirit,
what souls are these who run through this black haze?"
And he to me: "These are the nearly soulless
whose lives concluded neither blame nor praise.
They are mixed here with that despicable corps
of angels who were neither for God nor Satan,
but only for themselves. The High Creator
scourged them from Heaven for its perfect beauty,
and Hell will not receive them since the wicked
might feel some glory over them." And I:
"Master, what gnaws at them so hideously
Their lamentation stuns the very air?"
"They have no hope of death," he answered me,
"and in their blind and unattaining state
their miserable lives have sunk so low
that they must envy every other fate.
No word of them survives their living season.
Mercy and Justice deny them even a name.
Let us not speak of them; look, and pass on."

*The Divine Comedy*
*Inferno, Canto 3*

# 34
# Easy Essay

## *Peter Maurin*

Peter Maurin is co-founder with Dorothy Day of *The Catholic Worker.*

---

Monsignor Fulton Sheen says:
"Modern society is based on greed."
Father McGowan says:
"Modern society
is based on systematic selfishness."
Professor John Dewey says:
"Modern society
is based on rugged individualism."
When conservatives
try to conserve a society
based on greed,
systematic selfishness
and rugged individualism,
they try to conserve something
that is radically wrong,
for it is built
on a wrong basis.
And when conservatives
try to conserve
what is radically wrong.
they are also
radically wrong.

**A New Society**
To be radically right
is to go to the roots
by fostering a society
based on creed
instead of greed,
on systematic unselfishness

instead of systematic selfishness.
on gentle personalism
instead of rugged individualism
to create a new society
within the shell of the old.